Dr Goldstein

6900 Montgomery / Georgia St

Mae - Gray
4770 Pan American

RESPONSE TO DISASTER

I - 25 S Pan

I 40 E To Wyoming Blvd NE. Ex 164

Lomos Blvd NE

Lomas West

Right Wyoming

Left on to I-40 W

Right 3 Lanes Exit 159B-159C mus I-25 N Santa FE

THE SERIES IN CLINICAL AND COMMUNITY PSYCHOLOGY

CONSULTING EDITORS
Charles D. Spielberger and Irwin G. Sarason

Bedell Psychological Assessment and Treatment of Persons with Severe Mental Disorders
Burchfield Stress: Psychological and Physiological Interactions
Burstein and Loucks Rorschach's Test: Scoring and Interpretation
Diamant Homosexual Issues in the Workplace
Diamant Male and Female Homosexuality: Psychological Approaches
Erchul Consultation in Community, School, and Organizational Practice: Gerald Caplan's
  Contributions to Professional Psychology
Fisher The Science of Psychotherapy
Gist and Lubin Response to Disasters: Psychosocial, Community, and Ecological
Approaches
Hobfoll Stress, Social Support, and Women
Kassinove Anger Disorders: Definition, Diagnosis, and Treatment
Krohne and Laux Achievement, Stress, and Anxiety
London The Modes and Morals of Psychotherapy, Second Edition
Muñoz Depression Prevention: Research Directions
Reisman A History of Clinical Psychology, Second Edition
Reitan and Davison Clinical Neuropsychology: Current Status and Applications
Rickel, Gerrard, and Iscoe Social and Psychological Problems of Women: Prevention and
  Crisis Intervention
Rofé Repression and Fear: A New Approach to the Crisis in Psychotherapy
Russ Affect, Creative Experience, and Psychological Adjustment
Savin-Williams Gay and Lesbian Youth: Expressions of Identity
Spielberger and Diaz-Guerrero Cross-Cultural Anxiety, Volume 3
Spielberger and Vagg Test Anxiety: Theory, Assessment, and Treatment
Spielberger, Diaz-Guerrero, and Strelau Cross-Cultural Anxiety, Volume 4
Suedfeld Psychology and Torture
Veiel and Baumann The Meaning and Measurement of Social Support
Williams and Westermeyer Refugee Mental Health and Resettlement Countries

RESPONSE TO DISASTER:
Psychosocial, Community, and Ecological Approaches

Richard Gist, Ph.D.
*Kansas City, Missouri Fire Department Headquarters
and University of Missouri at Kansas City*

Bernard Lubin, Ph.D.
University of Missouri at Kansas City

Routledge
Taylor & Francis Group

LONDON AND NEW YORK

USA	Publishing Office:	BRUNNER/MAZEL *A member of the Taylor & Francis Group* 325 Chestnut Street Philadelphia, PA 19106 Tel: (215) 625-8900 Fax: (215) 625-2940
	Distribution Center:	BRUNNER/MAZEL *A member of the Taylor & Francis Group* 47 Runway Road, Suite G Levittown, PA 19057 Tel: (215) 269-0400 Fax: (215) 269-0363
UK		BRUNNER/MAZEL *A member of the Taylor & Francis Group* 1 Gunpowder Square London EC4A 3DE Tel: +44 171 583 0490 Fax: +44 171 583 0581

RESPONSE TO DISASTER: Psychosocial, Community, and Ecological Approaches

Cover design by Joe Dieter.
Copyedited by Mary Ellen Lanham.
Production Editor, Kerry J. Stanley.

Library of Congress Cataloging-in-Publication Data
Response to disaster: psychosocial, community, and ecological
    approaches / [edited by] Richard Gist, Bernard Lubin.
        p.   cm. -- (Series in clinical and community psychology, ISSN
0146-0846)
    Includes bibliographical references.
    ISBN 0-87630-998-8 (alk. paper). -- ISBN 0-87630-999-6 (pbk. :
alk. paper)
    1. Disaster relief--Psychological aspects.   2. Disasters-
-Psychological aspects.   3. Post-traumatic stress disorder.
4. Community mental health services.   I. Gist, Richard.   II. Lubin,
Bernard, 1923-   .   III. Series.
HV553.R393   1999   99-28627
363.34'8--dc21   CIP

ISBN 0-87630-998-8 (case)
ISBN 0-87630-999-6 (pbk)
ISSN 0146-0846

First published by Brunner / Mazel

This edition published 2012 by Routledge

2 Park Square, Milton Park, Abingdon, Oxfordshire OX14 4RN

711 Third Avenue, New York, NY 10017

Contents

PART 1: THEORETICAL FOUNDATIONS

PART 2: COMMUNITY STRATEGIES FOR INTERVENTION

PART 3: CONTEMPORARY ISSUES IN COMMUNITY SYSTEMS RESEARCH AND PRACTICE

Contributors

DEBO AKANDE
University of the Western Cape
Cape Town, South Africa

DANNY K. AXSOM
Virginia Polytechnic Institute and
    State University
Blacksburg, VA, USA

LEONARD BICKMAN
Vanderbilt University
Nashville, TN, USA

LENNIS G. ECHTERLING
James Madison University
Harrisonburg, VA, USA

CAROL S. FULLERTON
Uniformed Services University of
    the Health Sciences
Bethesda, MD, USA

RICHARD GIST
Kansas City, Missouri Fire Department
    Headquarters and Univeristy of
    Missouri at Kansas City
Kansas City, MO, USA

KRZYSZTOF KANIASTY
Indiana University of Pennsylvania
Indiana, PA, USA

SCOTT O. LILIENFELD
Emory University
Atlanta, GA, USA

JEFFREY M. LOHR
University of Arkansas
Fayetteville, AR, USA

BERNARD LUBIN
University of Missouri at Kansas City
Kansas City, MO, USA

LYNN K. MAGENHEIMER
Deputy Sheriff
Johnson County, KS, USA

ROBERT W. MONTGOMERY
Independent Practice
Roswell, GA, USA

FRAN H. NORRIS
Georgia State University
Atlanta, GA, USA

PATRICK O'NEILL
Acadia University
Wofville, NS, Canada

DOUGLAS PATON
Massey University
Palmerston North, New Zealand

ROBERT RAMSAY
Survey Research Group
Quarry Bay, Hong Kong

BRADLEY G. REDBURN
Johnson County Community College
Overland Park, KS, USA

MARK S. SALZER
University of Pennsylvania
Philadelphia, PA, USA

LEIGH M. SMITH
Curtin University
Western Australia

JEFFREY P. STAAB
University of Pennsylvania School
    of Medicine
Philadelphia, PA, USA

KARYN TIEDEMAN
Virginia Department of Mental Health,
Mental Retardation, and Substance
    Abuse Services
Richmond, VA, USA

DAVID F. TOLIN
Medical College of Pennsylvania/
    Hahnemann University
Philadelphia, PA, USA

ROBERT J. URSANO
Uniformed Services University of
    the Health Sciences
Bethesda, MD, USA

JULIE VAN DEN EYNDE
Monash University
Melbourne, Australia

ARTHUR E. VENO
Monash University
Melbourne, Australia

ERIC M. VERNBERG
University of Kansas
Lawrence, KS, USA

S. JOSEPH WOODALL
Grand Canyon University
Phoenix, AZ, USA

MARY LOU WYLIE
James Madison University
Harrisonburg, VA, USA

SUZANNE YATES
Lehman College - CUNY
Bronx, NY, USA

Foreword

Someone once described the field of traumatic stress studies as a "growth industry." The phrase is apt. Prompted by the ratification of posttraumatic stress disorder as a formal nosological entity in *DSM-III*, researchers have published hundreds of studies on the psychological consequences of combat, sexual assault, and disaster during the past two decades. Professional associations dedicated to the study and treatment of trauma have appeared, as have dozens of books, conferences, and a journal devoted solely to the topic. The concept of trauma itself has broadened so that people who merely learn about someone else's misfortunes now qualify as "trauma-exposed."

Implicit in much of this work is the assumption that certain types of events possess properties likely to induce serious disturbance in anyone and that these psychological consequences call for professional intervention. Vulnerability, not resilience, is emphasized. In response to this perceived need, a vast number of mental health professionals have re-tooled themselves as "traumatologists." The field is thus an "industry" in the literal sense of having spawned proprietary "miracle cures" whose hyperbolic commercial promotion threaten to render it the laughingstock of the behavioral sciences, despite much other outstanding science, scholarship, and clinical work.

Gist and Lubin's edited volume, *Response to Disaster*, provides an important corrective to widespread misconceptions about psychosocial sequelae of events of impact. Several main themes emerge from this book. First, people and communities are remarkably resilient in the face of disaster. Most individuals exposed to disaster do not become mentally ill, and those that do are often characterized by pre-existing vulnerabilities. Hence, the assumption that emergency psychological first aid is widely needed is false. Second, psychologists should foster indigenous support networks, not attempt to supplant them. Toxic events have always been a part of human existence, and cultures and communities have evolved in ways to cope with them long before the traumatology movement appeared on the scene. Psychologists should be invisible facilitators of existing support services following disasters, quietly working behind the scenes. Third, the marketing of proprietary trauma treatments, often in the face of data showing they do not work, is an ominous trend that must be resisted. Indeed, some research suggests that certain of these packaged interventions *impair* post-disaster adjustment.

Gist and Lubin have recruited leading scholars to contribute chapters on every aspect of the field. The result is a comprehensive, in-depth picture of the state of disaster research at century's end. This book is the best single source of the topic.

Richard J. McNally, Ph.D.
Harvard University
Cambridge, Massachusetts
June 1999

Preface

A lot can happen across a decade and a half. The evening of July 17, 1996, was not a seemingly momentous one; it was just another summer evening spent with friends, lounging on the deck and watching fireflies arise from the prairie grasses. Shortly after 7:30 p.m. central time, the wife of our host hastily called the group inside to see what was transpiring on the television. A jumbo jet bound from New York to Paris had exploded shortly following departure, raining fire and debris into the waters off Long Island. It was a chilling moment for several of us present, mostly fire and emergency medical personnel, who had gathered that evening to celebrate a colleague's birthday.

Precisely 15 years earlier—almost to the hour—a number of us had been called, as young persons new to our various trades, into the midst of a similar nightmare. Just after 7:00 p.m. on July 17, 1981, two suspended aerial walkways spanning the lobby of Kansas City's Hyatt Regency Hotel had collapsed in the midst of a crowded promotional affair. The death toll would pass 100 before the sun rose the next morning, and more than 200 injured would be distributed to hospitals throughout the community. Countless others—maybe as many as 2,000 or more—were present as the tragedy unfolded; more than twice that number would somehow be directly involved with or directly affected by the event. An entire community would ultimately struggle to absorb its multifaceted impact.

We knew precious little about "disaster mental health" the night the skywalks fell. There were no Disaster Mental Health Services (DMHS) teams rushing to invade our quiet Midwestern city; there were no Critical Incident Stress Debriefing (CISD) teams swarming in to debrief our personnel or Community Response Team (CRT) squads amassing to console our community. We tried a few primitive overtures toward clinical intervention, but these quickly collapsed under the weight of their own well-meaning but still somewhat misguided assumptions. We were left to regroup our thoughts and redirect our energies toward approaches that would, in the end, return us to the solid foundations that had long defined Midwestern resilience and set the stage for two decades of ongoing research and practice in community response to crisis and calamity.

Much of that early work, as luck would have it, fell to a group of C & E (consultation and education) folk from area community mental health centers (CMHCs). One of the core functions mandated under both the original CMHC enabling legislation and its later extension and expansion, the C & E enterprise was designed to deal with those elements of community interaction that might benefit from behavioral science input but did not deal of necessity with the clinical or the pathologic—things such as prevention, health promotion, and school and law enforcement assistance. Our response to this disaster, we quickly realized, would represent C & E at its most critical and its most rewarding, presenting us the challenge and the opportunity to touch a community at its core to restore its capacity to embrace and support its own.

That group had been meeting regularly for some time before the tragedy of that Friday evening in July; a number of issues related to public education and public information campaigns had been under development as cooperative efforts between several centers and advocacy groups. This made for quick study and a relatively creative capacity to develop and explore a range of novel approaches designed to enhance those elements of the community's social support systems that could empower those affected to more effectively help one another. Much was done with media-centered dissemination of anticipatory guidance and self-help information; forums and opportunities were created for those who had shared elements of this experience to share also their coping strategies and their mutual support. Particular groups of "natural helpers" were specifically targeted for special assistance to prepare them for the roles they would be required to face in the aftermath of a major tragedy. The impact, it certainly seemed, was both broad and positive (Gist & Stolz, 1982).

Although a number of vehicles were also opened for any who might identify themselves as in need of more traditionally defined clinical services, remarkably few elected to enter those systems. That we logged as a triumph. The early pragmatics of the community mental health movement were those of public health and prevention; they centered on elusive, if idealistic, notions like empowerment and resilience, self-efficacy and social support. We assumed that distress and disequilibrium among those exposed to disaster would be, in the overwhelming majority of cases, far more appropriately construed as signs of the uncomfortable but unavoidable processes of normal adjustment than as presumptive symptoms of anything to be labeled "disorder"; we specifically and deliberately avoided even inadvertent suggestion that those reactions might be harbingers linked by either necessity or sufficiency to some Aristotelian causal chain culminating in decompensation into clinical "caseness." We believed then, and we believe just as strongly today, that our best efforts ultimately prove to be those in which we take nearly invisible roles, promoting self-efficacy and resilience from both individuals and their communities as the foundation for recovery and growth.

The responses that followed the first news of TWA Flight 800's disappearance from radar 15 years later were radically different, indeed. There was no shortage of mental health assistance as counselors, therapists, and paraprofessionals of many descriptions mobilized themselves to offer aid and comfort. The Red Cross, the Salvation Army, state psychological association representatives, county mental health authorities, airline management and labor unions, and uncounted other groups and organizations all sponsored contingents of mental health support workers—so many that their numbers quickly exceeded the number of passengers on the airliner by several fold. Although such a massive influx of aid certainly helps ensure that no one is left without opportunity to interact with a mental health worker, those provisos and precautions prescribed to guard against the potentially iatogenic impacts of "pathologizing" the process of adaptation, so carefully crafted and so vigilantly applied in our first forays into community response, seem many times to have been seriously, if inadvertently, diluted in the well-meaning swell of interventions and interventionists. We must now pose some very searching, cautiously skeptical, but imminently empirical questions regarding how so astoundingly wide a swing of the pendulum may have affected the actual outcomes of our endeavors, and ask whether what we have achieved over 15 years represents, when all the king's horses and all king's men have gone home, the kinds of solutions we had envisioned in the days and months that followed the Hyatt collapse.

Help, after all, is a statement of an outcome; it is not simply a description of a process, motive, or intent. It must be demonstrated by analysis, not by accolade; it must be defended through rigor rather than rhetoric. Good intentions and grand designs may be well and good, but both our grandmothers and our grad school mentors told us again and again as impressionable youth that good intentions are never, of themselves, good enough. The essence of our endeavors must always, according to the very first assertions of our ethical principles (American Psychological Association, 1992), be grounded firmly and soundly in the bedrock of science; even the most elaborate structure, if built on sand, will shift and sway and eventually fall.

Nearly two decades after our first experiences with major community cataclysm and a full decade following our first edited volume on the topic (Gist & Lubin, 1989), we have returned to compile again what we believe to represent the best and most critical empirical thought on community response to disaster at this juncture in its evolution. We have asked contributors to challenge our thinking, to question current assumptions and paradigms, and to push us sternly and vigorously toward those questions that remain to be addressed. What they have provided is a credit to their creativity, their skill, and their commitment; how it is packaged and presented here is a credit to a patient but persistent editorial staff at Taylor & Francis who prodded and poked until we, in fact, performed. Whatever limitations are inherent in any edited text are the editors' to bear—a burden we assume with undeserved ease, only because the work of our colleagues has made our task an honor rather than an onus.

Special thanks are due to many who made extraordinary efforts to see this project and its editors through the taxing journey from prospectus to product. Thaisa Tiglao of Taylor & Francis endured frustration, delay, and repeated intrusion from the reality of the senior editor's decidedly nonacademic daily life as she struggled to keep the project on track; she earned in that process our respect and our lasting gratitude. The daily influence and assistance of Lucy McGee, the gentle, kindly, but steadfastly persistent personal assistant to the senior editor, is also found on every page. Alice Lubin and Shannon LaBelle Gist, the endlessly patient partners of hopelessly driven men, deserve more praise than we can ever articulate—not just for their roles in this project, but even more for those contributions that we could never, even at the most eloquent moments of our lives, begin to express in any adequate fashion.

The most important thanks, however, goes to those who have taught us again the lessons in humility that define community psychology in action. Firefighters and police officers, medics and ministers—the silent heroes of every community who have dedicated their lives to ensuring that those who must face the worst moments of their lives will not do so without the comfort of commonwealth and community somewhere at their side—have shown us time and again the true meaning of support. We are much more their students than their teachers; we are the narrators of their stories rather than characters within them. We hope that we have done justice to the lessons we've been taught.

REFERENCES

American Psychological Association. (1992). *Ethical principles of psychologists and code of conduct*. Washington, DC: Author.

Gist, R., & Lubin, B. (Eds.). (1989). *Psychosocial aspects of disaster*. New York: John Wiley & Sons.

Gist, R., & Stolz, S. B. (1982). Mental health promotion and the media: Community response to the Kansas City hotel disaster. *American Psychologist, 37*, 1136–1139.

Chapter 1

Psychosocial, Ecological, and Community Perspectives on Disaster Response

Richard Gist, Bernard Lubin, and Bradley G. Redburn

INTRODUCTION

Mary Shelley (1818/1823) gained a certain measure of immortality through a short novel penned, in effect, to meet a spontaneous if somewhat idle challenge. Her entry in a four-way "ghost story" competition captured the essence of a tragic fault that lurks in even the noblest of our breed: A propensity—often unwitting—to let our own needs and notions supersede the true needs of those we would seek to serve (Glut, 1973).

Frankenstein, the name she lent her fictional protagonist, became a cultural synonym for a creation out of control, but the more profound metaphor was to be found in the failure of its creator to consider the impact of his glorious triumph from the perspective of the creation itself (cf. Levine, 1974). The angst of the creation that turned to bedevil its creator was fed not from raw, uncontrollable aggression somehow left unbridled, but rather from the frustration bred of its inherently human needs for acceptance, affinity, and affection—rendered unattainable by

This chapter first appeared in *Journal of Personal and Interpersonal Loss*, 3(1), as an invited contribution to a special issue on disaster theory and research (Copyright Taylor & Francis, 1998; used by agreement).

the rejection its grotesque form invariably evoked. The creation's quarrel with its creator, then, turned on the question of how one could give life to a creature filled with such splendid needs without regard for the impact its form would engender.

"The road to Hell," Irish grandmothers have long said, "is paved with good intentions." Disaster generally brings, along with its many negative consequences, an upsurge in actions and expressions that would seem to display soundly altruistic goals and intent (Kaniasty & Norris, 1997); these include both service and role expansion for current community agents and agencies to accommodate greater demand for existing services, and the extension of their concepts of mission and charge to include needs seen as emergent from disaster impact (Tierney, 1989). The desire to assist is without question laudable, but not all forms of help, of course, prove equally helpful.

Our own interest in disaster response issues arose from just such a compulsion to assist in the wake of a truly monumental community catastrophe—the 1981 collapse of a pair of suspended walkways transversing the lobby of Kansas City's Hyatt Regency Hotel in the midst of a crowded promotional affair. The death toll that night reached 111 as the number of treated injuries passed 200; the numbers of "walking wounded" were never accurately recorded. It became clear rather quickly, though, that the major impact would be psychological, and that it would envelope not just those in the lobby as the bridges fell, but also the more than 500 rescuers who came to their aid, the employees of the hotel and its associated enterprises, and the many others brought into the event as it progressed. Perhaps more significantly, it was also quickly evident that the impact would spread beyond the families and associates of the dead and injured to encompass the entire community, and that it would ultimately challenge essential elements that lend a community identity, affinity, and purpose.

An initial impulse to open clinical services for those affected rallied many staff but virtually no clients. Attention quickly shifted from clinical interventions toward community-based approaches to information, empowerment, and peer support models (Gist & Stolz, 1982); the principal vehicles for achieving these goals quite specifically eschewed clinical settings or trappings in favor of an array of enterprises geared toward mobilizing, enhancing, and maintaining those natural avenues of social support that typically sustain persons through life crises.

INTERVENTIONISM VERSUS EMPOWERMENT

The vision carried from those early excursions suggested that psychologists could, in times of catastrophe, step back from interventionist mindsets and roles, and reach into their basic knowledge of human behavior and social response to help communities reclaim autonomy and self-efficacy in the face of social disruption. Those first experiences seemed to belie a convincing argument that fundamental determinants of individual reactions arose at least as much from social context, social comparison, and social construction as from any particular configuration of individual impingements; they bred much more a profound respect for the resilience of the human spirit than any fascination with its limits. Work across the intervening period has taken at various times the form of researcher, practitioner, or participant–observer, but those early impressions have continued to stay their course.

The involvement of the mental health industry in disaster response, however, has grown far beyond what that early vision or experience embraced, and has taken directions quite different from—indeed, in some cases seemingly antithetical to—those elegantly understated approaches that ecological and community constructions would typically endorse. Recent large-scale disasters have found communities literally besieged by counselors and would-be counselors clamoring to serve anyone even tangentially connected to the circumstance or event[1]—so much so that analogies to opportunistic lawyers soliciting clients under the ruse of offering uniquely relevant assistance in righting wrongs and resolving grief have become difficult to dispel.

Programs have sprouted in all kinds of arenas for all kinds of purposes (e.g., consult Allen, 1993, for a diverse but reasonably representative collection of recent examples): There are critical incident stress debriefing (CISD) teams that claim their intervention necessary to prevent post-traumatic stress disorder (PTSD) in rescue workers; there are networks of Red Cross "disaster mental health" volunteers; there are internet amalgams such as Figley's "Green Cross" project (Green Cross, 1996) soliciting volunteers and cash contributions for an array of "trauma tourism" junkets, and any number of ad hoc response programs specific to particular locations or events (e.g., the Green Cross "Operation Healing Oklahoma" or "My Heart's in Bosnia" enterprises). Most, on structural reflection, seem hauntingly reminiscent of the suicide prevention/crisis intervention movement of the 1970s (see Echterling & Wylie, 1981, for assessment of those programs as a social movement, or Gist & Woodall, 1995, for discussion of the parallels). Meanwhile, disasters large and small now engender such responses, which in turn become fodder for a burgeoning "show and tell" circuit of conferences, trade shows, and trade publications.

Partly as consequence and partly as cause, PTSD has become an increasingly pervasive diagnosis as case-exclusionary criteria regarding the nature of stressors, duration of symptoms, and pre-extant or comorbid conditions have been progressively diluted or abandoned (Gist & Woodall,

---

[1]News reports, for example, indicated that within 24 hours of the TWA Flight 800 crash off Long Island, numbers of counselors at and around the scene exceeded the number of victims on a multiplicative (rather than simply an additive) order.

1995). Epidemiologic studies using the earlier, more restrictive criteria (Helzer, Robins, & McEvoy, 1987) found the fully diagnosable condition relatively rare outside the combat veterans whose postwar difficulties it was developed to describe; subsequent meta-analysis of a broad range of studies reporting estimates of disaster impact on psychiatric morbidity determined the actual impact to be much smaller than often claimed, and noted that the more specific the design and objective the criteria applied, the smaller the effect reported (Rubonis & Bickman, 1991). The progressive redefinition of the diagnostic rubric, however, has weakened the specificity of the diagnosis in application (cf. Schwarz & Kowalski, 1991), while clinically oriented researchers and practitioners have continued to argue when confronted by "caseness" conclusions below anticipation that these criteria should be broadened further still (cf. Solomon & Canino, 1990).

It should be no surprise, then, that techniques claiming to prevent, ameliorate, or even "cure" the condition have proliferated wildly with the expansiveness of the diagnosis, the endemic (even universal) nature of its purported precipitators, and the presumed pervasiveness of the "disorder" the angst associated with these inescapable life disruptions is said to portray. Moreover, because even the most intense subjective discomfort concomitant to such disruptions will, for most persons, tend to resolve over time (cf. Cook & Bickman, 1990), most any sort of "early intervention" should be expected to correlate with self-reports of improvement. Such an intersection set provides more than an "attractive nuisance" for well-meaning if unsophisticated intervenors; it is also very fecund for the entrepreneurial marketing of patent remedies and treatment schemes, yielding at best the psychosocial analogue of the placebo while generating at worst a contemporary sequitur to snake oil. Add to the equation rapidly swelling legions of potential "providers"—many less credentialed and less trained in the critical tradition of academic skepticism, claiming their principal status through certifications and monikers generated by the intervention marketers to peddle and promote their products—and the result can appear much like a postmodern incarnation of the Roman circus, resplendent with self-help gurus hawking fads and formulas while syndicated talk shows compete for ratings by offering anyone with a story of misfortune or maladjustment an all-expenses-paid trip to Andy Warhol's 15 minutes of fame.

In some senses, then, Mary Shelley's tale strikes chillingly close to our own as we prepare to report again on the nature and efficacy of these outgrowths of early invectives to ply our skills at the community level in the wake of disaster. We have commented elsewhere (Gist & Woodall, 1996) as have others (e.g., Brom, 1996; Lohr, 1996; Rosen, 1996) regarding how the rampant growth of such modalities as CISD, EMDR, TFT, TIR,

TAT, and their ilk[2]—called by their proponents the "power therapies" and by their detractors the "alphabet interventions"—seems to belie a tragic failure to critically and empirically assess efficacy and grounding before vesting credence in radical claims of unique effect. We have also reviewed in a number of places (e.g., Gist et al., 1997) the substantial and growing body of empirical evidence that strongly questions whether these treatment modalities hold any unique impact at all, and which raises the specific question for some (most specifically, CISD) of iatrogenic effects from faithful application of the specific modalities prescribed.

LESSONS IN HUMILITY

Two elements of our earliest work in this arena set the tone for independent if intertwined threads of research and action. The most successful aspects of psychosocial response to the Hyatt hotel disaster centered about the early, somewhat serendipitous decision to turn away from approaches directed toward clinical redress of presumably pathognomonic reactions of individuals in favor of a focus on mobilizing the support of a community and its natural systems to bolster the transitions of those most affected by the event. Vehicles were created through which people whose only real connection to one another was often the accident of propinquity at one particularly propitious moment could exchange that particular genre of support that none but the similarly situated can truly provide. A range of carefully designed and disseminated, principally media-driven approaches to self-help education and information was also implemented across the weeks and months to follow (Gist & Stolz, 1982). These were well-used and seemingly effective, at least at subjective levels.

We have had in ensuing years many opportunities to replicate and refine various aspects of these endeavors, grounded in theoretical positions that quite specifically eschew clinical approaches to treatment and intervention in favor of empowerment models and social support (Gist & Lubin, 1989a, 1989b; see also chapters 2 and 7) in contexts ranging from community impact assessment and systems interventions following the Exxon Valdez oil spill (Gist, 1989) to support of employees affected by

---

[2]These acronyms represent, respectively, Mitchell's *Critical Incident Stress Debriefing*, Shapiro's *Eye Movement Desensitization and Reprocessing*, Callahan's *Thought Field Therapy* (also advertised as *The Five-Minute Cure* and the *Callahan Techniques*), Gerbode's *Traumatic Incident Reduction*, and Fleming's *Tapas Acupressure Technique*; each can be explored through websites of organizations connected to its marketing and promotion (the exception being TAT, referenced principally by its originator, a Redondo Beach acupuncturist, through e-mail lists; a reprinting of her e-mail description of the technique and its origins can be found at http://www.ozemail.com.au/ ~ jsjp/mpt.htm).

various airline bankruptcies or displaced when Hurricane Andrew destroyed both workplace and home.[3] It seems almost paradoxical in retrospect that greatest efficacy has been achieved with those persons without established pre- and post-tragedy connections. Beginning with Hyatt responders, those with relatively constant and even insular connections—specifically, law enforcement, fire service, rescue, and medical personnel who responded to extricate the injured and recover the dead—proved most resistant to intercession. Work begun at that time to apply psychological intervention techniques in that population, however, led instead to serious and surprising findings that continue to compel us to reframe our thinking and our practice.

THE DEBRIEFING DEBATES

Anecdotal accounts of lasting distress as a consequence of rescue work at the Hyatt hotel collapse became a prominent feature of "disaster lore"—the reiterative, often reconstructionist stories that emanate from any catastrophe or trauma, serving a variety of social and therapeutic functions (cf. Tal, 1996). Such accounts played a central role in the final settlement negotiated on behalf of those injured or otherwise affected by that event. Though police officers and firefighters were not permitted to recover damages for any alleged psychological consequences of their work that night, the court agreed to allow residual funds in the settlement account to be directed toward establishment of programs to prepare personnel for and assist them in addressing stressful aspects of their work. The direction elected focused on CISD; the final settlement was but hours old when another major catastrophe opened the rubric to profound practical testing.

A 1988 nuisance fire, started by petty thieves at a Kansas City construction site during the predawn hours of a November morning, sparked an explosion that killed six firefighters, making it one of the worst structural firefighting tragedies of the contemporary era. Attempts to invoke the CISD rubric, though employing its originators and staunchest proponents, were objectively less than remarkable in their impact. Subsequent experiences across a range of settings and circumstances continued to raise quiet questions regarding the actual efficacy of the intervention. A serendipitous happenstance several months later, however, led to a remarkable opportunity for its direct empirical examination.

A wide-body aircraft en route from Denver to Philadelphia experienced catastrophic engine failure leading to total loss of all hydraulic

---

[3] These endeavors were designed and executed as projects on behalf of specific clients who retain proprietary rights respecting the programs and materials employed; detailed descriptions of those projects and their implementation remain in the control of the clients served.

systems in midflight. Its pilots managed to bring it to rest at the Sioux Gateway Airport in Sioux City, Iowa, where emergency crews were assembled awaiting its arrival. The plane cartwheeled and broke apart on impact, killing 112 of the 296 persons aboard. While rescue operations per se were executed with precision and were widely viewed as remarkably successful in all objective senses, the mass casualty aspect alone rendered it a "critical incident" of a very significant magnitude.

The senior author was dispatched to assist with inflight personnel and certain passengers with airline ties on behalf of their labor organization's employee assistance program; while there, a number of observations were made regarding the convergence of CISD teams and the absence of apparent organization and direction in much of that enterprise (Gist, 1990). Nonetheless, one of the principal promoters of this rubric, although never near the scene nor in any way involved in the incident, was heard a few months later in a public forum describing this element of the event as if a highly effective, well-orchestrated response system for which he held direct credit.

This contrasted sharply with both our own assessments and those of a range of personnel with whom we had come into contact. That picture had begun to crystallize 2 weeks after the incident when the airport fire chief requested our assistance for his personnel during a visit to the National Fire Academy. He noted that a CISD team from a neighboring state had presented itself within hours of the crash and had conducted intervention exercises, but he also noted that those personnel held no familiarity with aircraft incidents nor held they any even remotely similar experience of any type on which to draw. He asked if his firefighters could meet with a few selected Hyatt responders—an event, he aptly noted, that mirrored with uncanny precision the numbers and natures of deaths and injuries found in the aircraft incident and the tasks required of responders there.

That session served a number of significant purposes. The palliative effect for recipients was noteworthy, though certainly not phenomenal. It generated, however, a number of very salient hypotheses regarding the nature, sources, and resolution of post-incident distress. First, the principal matters of concern appeared more related to issues of *appraisal* (Taylor, 1983) than to emotional impacts per se, and were specifically related to informational and instrumental exchanges couched in the operational terms of the rescue professions. Second, differences in the organization and execution of rescue operations between the Hyatt response and the airfield event appeared more salient to the efficacy of resolution than did any aspects of post-operational intervention; this was strikingly consistent with the findings of Alexander and Wells (1991) that, compared against their own baselines rather than against general population norms, police officers who conducted an undeniably grizzly but quite well orchestrated body recovery and identification operation actually stood relatively improved on measures of anxiety, hostility, and depression—despite the total absence of typical approaches to psychological intervention.

Third, quite contrary to axioms of the debriefing movement contending that rescue professions are uncommonly insular with respect to social support, both Hyatt responders and airfield crews placed most emphasis on sources of social support *outside* the profession—specifically spouses, family, and close friends—when discussing their most helpful resources. Finally, the principal value of the encounter between Hyatt responders and rescuers from the aircraft incident appeared to take the form described by Taylor and Lobel (1989) as *upward contacts*—opportunities for interaction and modeling with others seen as having successfully addressed challenges equivalent in nature and demand. This became especially salient as it grew apparent that those who had initially presented themselves to assist, though dubbed "peers" in the vernacular of CISD, were perceived more in the context of Taylor and Lobel's *downward evaluation*—persons whose adjustment was clearly below that already achieved by the recipient of aid, and whose lesser adaptation served as reassurance that things could always be worse.

The Redburn study

The scientist-practitioner heritage of our discipline prescribes but one course when seeking definitive resolution of empirical questions: *Grab a handful of rats!* It also offers but one inviolate law: *The rat is always right!* Redburn (1992) was able to capitalize on similarities and differences, both between the two events and within the latter, to address these questions as directly as serendipity will ever allow to direct experimental partitioning.

While sensory impacts and objective demands were remarkably similar across the two events, both anticipatory and organizational factors were radically different. The hotel collapse, like most such events, occurred without warning and was intercepted by rescue personnel as it was evolving. The aircraft accident, however, was preceded by nearly a half-hour of preparation as the plane approached the field, and the incident was quite literally brought to the waiting personnel. Moreover, fire and rescue personnel at the airfield held a specific and well-rehearsed plan for approaching such an occurrence; there was no such plan for the hotel collapse, and even the most rudimentary resources and information were often not readily available.

Perhaps most salient, however, was the use in the airfield event of a generalized approach to incident management, now routinely used to guide organization of any response large or small, exceptional or ordinary. The Incident Command System (ICS) evolved as a synthesis of several systematic strategies for fireground operations, fueled in part by emphatic endorsement from those responsible for command at the Hyatt incident. ICS was designed to provide a flexible template for effective partitioning and handling of the escalating demands of developing incidents, and particularly to bring order and direction in the first critical moments and decisions of a fire or rescue operation. While not a factor in the 1981 hotel collapse, the system was in place, rehearsed, and effectively implemented in the aircraft incident 8 years later.

Proponents of the CISD rubric have offered, as if definitive evidence of efficacy, basically anecdotal contrasts of perceived psychiatric sequelae from two California air collisions: one involving a Pacific Southwest Airlines plane over San Diego in 1978 and the other involving an AeroMexico craft over Cerritos (suburban Los Angeles) in 1986 (see, e.g., Emergency Management Institute, 1992). They have argued that differences in perceived sequelae specifically represent the impact of mandatory debriefing in the latter case. Such assertions blatantly ignore a range of very clear threats to both internal and external validity (Cook & Campbell, 1979); clearest among them in the instant context were *maturation effects* from the development and implementation of ICS in the intervening period. Because debriefing was widely available at the Sioux City event but participation was not mandatory, both treated and untreated groups were present among the rescuers and the contribution of the intervention could be directly assessed.

Three critical hypotheses were therefore subject to direct examination:

1 If it were exposure to sensory impingements (e.g., sights, sounds, smells) that produced stress and sequelae, responses consistent with those widely reported, though never well measured in Hyatt responders (Miles, Demi, & Mostyn-Aker, 1984; Wilkinson, 1983), would be expected from such nearly identical exposure; if, however, organizational elements were more determinative, substantially reduced impact would be anticipated.

2 If debriefing were the major factor in reducing impact, those who participated in such exercises would be expected to show superior resolution when compared with those who deferred.

3 If insularity within the profession (i.e., "keeping it in the firehouse") was in fact a normative coping practice, the most frequent and most helpful exchanges would be expected to involve reliance on coworkers and peers, with contact outside the occupation truncated.

Participants

All field personnel of the Sioux City Fire Department were invited to participate in the study; instruments were administered by the research team at each fire station on each shift to ensure full access and opportunity. Only two refusals were encountered, netting a 97% compliance rate. Those surveys that specifically indicated assignment to duties at the crash

scene were segregated for further study; there were, however, no significant differences identified between those assigned to disaster duties and
those whose duties did not take them to the scene. Fifty-nine respondents
satisfied all criteria for inclusion in the subsequent analyses.

Method

Four instruments were included in the assessments: the Brief Symptom
Inventory (BSI), an abbreviated version of the SCL-90 (Derogatis, 1975,
1977) assessing psychological symptoms along nine dimensions; the Health
Perception Questionnaire (HPQ), Form II (Ware & Karmos, 1976), assessing perceptions of physical health; the Perceived Support Systems Scale
(PSSS) assessing perceptions of social support received in crisis (Procidano
& Heller, 1983), and a variant of the Social Support Access Questionnaire
(SSAQ) used by Quevillon, Yutrzenka, and Jacobs (1991) in an earlier
preliminary study of rescuers from this event. Cronbach alpha calculations
for the instruments as used ranged from .88 to .96, indicating more than
adequate reliability in this application.

Results

Results related to the hypotheses noted above are quickly summarized
here; more complete data were presented in Redburn (1992):

   1   BSI scores indicated no notable clinical impacts persisting across
the interval between incident and assessment. Mean scores in this sample
($\bar{x} = .42$) fell somewhat above general population norms but well below
psychiatric outpatients, easily within the range basically expected for these
occupations, regardless of exposure. There were no reports of unexpected
occupational attrition, leave utilization, or other commonly reported presumed sequelae.
   2   There were no clinically significant differences between the 42.2%
who elected to participate in debriefing exercises and those who did not,
nor were there significant differences in indices of social support. Those
who reported attendance, however, showed a slight but statistically significant elevation in reported symptoms on the BSI, $F(1, 53) = 3.993$, $p = .05$.
   3   Attendance at debriefing sessions was strongly and inversely correlated with years of firefighting experience ($r = -.403$, $p < .01$), and
varied directly with use of other formal treatment systems ($r = .334$, $p <
.05$).
   4   Almost three-fourths (73.9%) of the sample reported principal
use of informal support systems outside the profession. Discussion with
family and friends was strongly and inversely correlated with symptom
levels endorsed ($r = -.446$, $p < .01$), as was informal discussion among
coworkers ($r = -.338$, $p < .01$); these two factors, in turn, were strongly
interrelated ($r = .5198$, $p < .01$).

Discussion

Although among the first serious empirical tests of the impact of debriefing, especially with direct examination of its role as contrasted to organizational interventions and informal social support, each aspect had separately received prior attention with similar results. Hytten and Hasle (1989) found that structured sessions showed no benefit greater than that already accorded through informal exchange. Alexander and Wells (1991) had directly demonstrated that, although postexposure symptom levels fell above general population norms but below patient norms (exactly as demonstrated here), those values were in fact *below* preincident baselines for officers involved in body recovery and identification; the deliberate avoidance of intrusive psychological interventions led the authors to attribute the success in resolution to organizational elements inherent in the management of the incident. Fullerton, Wright, Ursano, and McCarroll (1993), in a reasonably contemporaneous study of mass casualty workers, also reported the preeminent role of support from spouses and others outside the occupational envelope, noting as well the impact of providing that support on individuals and relationships. More significantly, though, the essential elements of the findings regarding treatment efficacy have now been replicated in a growing series of studies (Bisson, Jenkins, Alexander, & Bannister, 1997; Deahl, Gillham, Thomas, Dearle, & Strinivasan, 1994; Griffiths & Watts, 1992; Hobbs, Mayou, Harrison, & Worlock, 1996; Kenardy et al., 1996; Lee, Slade, & Lygo, 1996; Stephens, 1997) and the caution prescribed has been reiterated by many observers and analysts (Bisson & Deahl, 1994; Brom, Kleber, & Hoffman, 1993; Deahl & Bisson, 1995; Foa & Meadows, 1997; Gist, 1996a, 1996b; Gist & Woodall, 1995, 1996; Kenardy & Carr, 1996; Raphael, Meldrum, & McFarlane, 1995; Thompson & Solomon, 1991).

Even greater concern arises from the replication of a possibly iatrogenic consequence of this intervention set. While the slight but significant negative relationship to postincident adjustment found in this study was originally written off to probable correlates of self-selection, McFarlane (1988) had found similar impacts in his studies of Australian firefighters. Similar indicators have since been found by other researchers (Bisson et al., 1997; Griffiths & Watts, 1992; Hobbs et al., 1996) across a range of situations and circumstances. Given a growing tendency, despite obvious ethical concerns, to invoke policies mandating participation in these interventions for all natures of disaster and emergency workers in a vast array of circumstances, these indicators alone should be more than sufficient to suspend investment in and application of this technique unless and until benefit can be established and negative impacts controlled (Gist, 1996a).

Distressingly, however, the marketers and promoters of these intervention schemes have argued instead that established treatments, regardless of the absence of indicators of benefit and presence of indicators of harm, should stand unfettered unless and until critics can definitively prove their worthlessness (Chemtob, 1996). Such argument attempts not only presumptive shifting of the burden of proof from innovator to evaluator, but demands of the critic the logically impossible chore of proving the null hypothesis (cf. Rosen, 1997).

The principal proponents and peddlers of these techniques have, in fashions seemingly reminiscent of those described by Pratkanis (1995; Pratkanis & Aronson, 1991) respecting the dissemination of pseudoscience, attempted to counter criticism in the refereed academic press through trade magazine articles (e.g., Mitchell & Everly, 1997) that ignore the growing body of published research and weave instead a fog of unpublished information and gratuitous self-citation. Despite rejoinder from established researchers and practitioners (cf. Gist et al., 1997), a chilling and disingenuous effect is generated and is likely to persist, if only from exposure and repetition (Zajonc, 1968).

"THERE'S NOTHING SO PRACTICAL AS GOOD THEORY"

Interventionist approaches suffer more from fragmented foundations than from fallacious, factitious, or simply fictitious formulations. Good theory not only guides formulation of strategies and structures; it provides for their refinement through generation of theory-relevant hypotheses and their testing in most application-relevant of all social laboratories: the field and community (Gottfredson, 1984). Because it is only through *disconfirmation* of hypotheses that either theory or practice can be systematically advanced, such study necessarily entails challenges to the presumed efficacy of paradigms and techniques.

Back to the basics

There are several avenues of theory and research that lend both insight and direction to the emerging practice of organizational and community assistance in disaster, and which help to frame and potentially to resolve the dilemmas raised above. Their effective consideration, however, demands that we first retreat to the bedrock of our explanatory frames and consider disaster as a developmental challenge rather than as a pathogenetic threat (cf. McCrae, 1984).

Although the constructs of PTSD may in fact lead us somewhat astray in dealing with disaster as a social experience (see chapter 5), social comparison under threat may prove a particularly salient consideration in understanding both successful adaptation and paradoxical impacts. Charlton and Thompson (1996) found that persons exposed to trauma attempt a wide range of coping strategies; this unbridled experimentation may be due, at least in part, to the novelty of demand and circumstance essential to the concept of trauma. Gump and Kulik (1997) reported that settings comprised of persons who share traumatic exposure contain demonstrable elements of social contagion, suggesting that blanket application of indiscriminate group process designs may stand particularly prone to stimulation of negative outcomes, especially when invoked before constructive coping strategies have had time to fully evolve in an affected population. Perceived threat lends a unique urgency to the search for affiliation and social comparison (Kulik, Mahler, & Moore, 1996), and these contacts follow particular patterns that underscore the perceived need for specifically appropriate models (see also Taylor, 1983). The models preferred are those seen to be similarly situated, especially those offering clear indications of having evolved and sustained successful adaptation to similar demands (Taylor & Lobel, 1989). The more abrupt, unexpected, novel, or ambiguous the experience, however, the less likely that suitable models will be readily available.

Importation of such upward contacts should, at least in theory, prove beneficial, especially since conventional vehicles of support may be particularly inadequate, unavailable, or ineffective in such circumstances (Norris & Kaniasty, 1996). The elements that determine effectiveness, however, include complex interplays between person, event, type of support, and support system (Kaniasty & Norris, 1992, 1997). Mechanistic protocols harboring arbitrary definitions of "peer" relationships are unlikely to result in effective mapping and, more to the point, the predilections that might attract volunteers to seek these roles in the absence of direct definition of demand and circumstance may well dispose the system toward recruiting players of marginal value as social comparison targets.

Those whose prior exposure to traumata has left them with unresolved issues for which vicarious rumination may be sought, for example, might well relish opportunities to enter settings where such reprocessing can be offered as if a therapeutic contribution to others; this can result in unwitting dispatch of responders who serve as inadvertent "downward evaluation" targets. Given the proliferation of "CISD teams" seeking to intervene with emergency services personnel, this becomes a matter of substantial concern. Charlton and Thompson (1996) found only positive reappraisal and distancing to be coping strategies predictive of successful adaptation, and these factors in particular may demand a very specific type of "upward contact" to provide effective modeling and support—a type unlikely to be found in conjunction with persistent cathexis toward reprocessing those very events that should have been adequately distanced and reframed in the adaptive process.

Taylor (1991) presented an hypothesis regarding this seeming paradox of resolution, consistent in many ways with her earlier arguments regarding the role of "positive illusions" in mental health (Taylor & Brown, 1988). The essential premise would suggest that profoundly negative events require major mobilization of resources and defenses to respond effectively and to weather their impacts, but that successful resolution demands subsequent minimization of those very responses initially commanded. Those best adapted and hence best suited to provide *upward contact* modeling are, of course, most likely to be found among those seasoned through occupational experiences that have demanded prior resolution and accommodation; this is certainly consistent with the recurrent finding that experience is among the most robust protective factors mitigating postexposure symptomatology (McCarroll, Fullerton, Ursano, & Hermsen, 1996; McCarroll, Ursano, Ventis, & Fullerton, 1993; McCarroll, Ursano, & Fullerton, 1993; McCarroll, Ursano, Fullerton, & Lundy, 1993). If, however, the essence of successful accommodation entails minimization and its functional analogues (distancing and positive reappraisal), the most effective models would be expected to specifically avoid (rather than to proactively seek) visible interventionist roles. This would certainly stand consistent with Redburn's (1992; see results summarized above) findings regarding a strong inverse relationship between experience and participation in debriefing exercises, and may suggest at least a plausible hypothesis regarding the paradoxical findings respecting the objective efficacy of the intervention.

The types of reframing associated with successful resolution may be specifically inhibited in early post-impact periods by ambiguous appraisals and provocative but unproductive counterfactual thinking. Although counterfactual thought may generate affective comfort under proper conditions (Roese, 1994), it may prove counterproductive for rescue workers seeking to organize an understanding of a major event from their relatively isolated individual positions within it. Counterfactuals are particularly apt to be generated with respect to ascriptions of preventability (Mandel & Lehman, 1996), and hence to influence the "I could have, I should have, I might have..." type of cognitions that so often follow unexpected and unwelcome life events. It is precisely these that most often seem to linger unresolved among rescuers.

Medvec, Madey, and Gilovich (1995) provided some helpful insights into how this may transpire and the effect that may result. They noted that Olympic medalists appeared to show odd reversals in displays of positive affect when receiving their awards and discussing their performances: Silver medalists, though having delivered objectively better performances than the bronze medalists, often seemed more disappointed than elated, and generally were less positive in affect than were the third-place contestants. They speculated, and to some extent verified, that silver medalists generated counterfactual pictures of having just missed the gold, whereas the counterfactual for bronze medal recipients was no award at all. Post-incident sessions that translate incident review into instrumental measures designed to improve later performance may therefore prove beneficial by promoting reframing and distancing features; whereas focus on revelation, exploration, and discussion of emotional content and painful affect may instead drive coping attempts that prove ineffective or counterproductive (Charlton & Thompson, 1996).

Grandma versus grad school

Perhaps the most salient cause for concern in all the interventionist zeal is captured in Gilbert and Silvera's (1996) concept of *overhelping*. They demonstrated that immediate and highly visible attempts to "help" a target individual with processes that the target would, in fact, have successfully executed without aid served to defeat perceptions of self-efficacy central both to personal and interpersonal assessments of mastery on the part of the target. These assessments of self-efficacy, however, may be crucial to successful adjustment (Major, Cozzarelli, Sciacchitano, Cooper, & Testa, 1990). Accordingly, given the consistent finding that most individuals confronted with disaster resolve its impacts with or without intervention (Cook & Bickman, 1990; Helzer et al., 1987; McFarlane, 1988; Redburn, Gensheimer, & Gist, 1993; Rubonis & Bickman, 1991), the very essence of our current trend toward rapid, highly promoted, highly visible intervention may be, at its most essential foundational level, counterproductive for those we most intend to aid.

It becomes clear in this context where the weak links lie. The "symptoms" that have been collectively defined as indicative of PTSD have, if we are to be objectively truthful, no necessary link to trauma, either generally or specifically, nor does trauma hold any particularly sufficient linkage to the symptoms catalogued. The correlative connections, no matter how heretical to so suggest, may not represent much more than numerical commentary on the variability one's grandma knew so well in the reactions of her peers and acquaintances to the severe schematic disequilibrium wrought of life's most unfortunate experiences.

She knew well that those of "weaker constitutions" were often overwhelmed by events, but that others showed remarkable and truly humbling resilience in the face of even the most ghastly misadventures. She likely knew also that the nature and functioning of support systems, belief structures, and community had profound effects on whether these trials became, when later seen in retrospect, landmarks or land mines. But when she spoke of these experiences, her vernacular likely considered "misfortune" rather than "malady"; when she spoke of accommodation, it was probably couched in concepts more like "growth" and "grace" than like "treatment" or "recovery."

Iatrogenesis through conceptual imperialism is a dangerous and insidious specter that lurks close to the heart of all socially constructed nosologies. The struggles and challenges of the human condition are not in most cases essential maladies, no matter how profound the disequilibrium accompanying them—unless and until we assign them that convention.

Tough questions about progressive weakening of the stressor criterion, contamination through exacerbation of or interaction with premorbid conditions, or other such aspects of the assignment of labels bearing some pretty hefty implications all their own do not equate to denial of individual discomfort, much less to denial of validity, dignity, or individual worth. These are, however, signs of a conservative and probably well-reasoned resistance to pernicious assignation of labels that inch ever so insidiously toward the dangerous and distorted postmodern position that all discomfort is pathognomonic and all disequilibrium symptomatic. It is hard to see that as a healthy or a helpful direction.

Every classical theory of development has held—whether implicitly or explicitly stated, whether intuitively or empirically derived—that challenge and disequilibrium are inescapable harbingers of growth, and that arrested development is the basis for much that we label as dysfunction. But this is not, we would contend, basis for conceiving the impact of life events through any implied model of pathological process instituted by traumatic insult. It is rather cause to consider a wide continuum of adaptations to the essential and inescapable confrontations of life and living, and a challenge to bring the best of our foundations to bear on understanding and enhancing those systems of commonwealth and support that lend us the strength to persevere.

REFERENCES

Alexander, D. A., & Wells, A. (1991). Reactions of police officers to body handling after a major disaster: A before and after comparison. *British Journal of Psychiatry, 159,* 547–555.

Allen, R. D. (Ed.). (1993). Handbook of post-disaster interventions (Special Issue). *Journal of Social Behavior and Personality, 8*(5).

Bisson, J. I., & Deahl, M. P. (1994). Psychological debriefing and prevention of post traumatic stress: More research is needed. *British Journal of Psychiatry, 165,* 717–720.

Bisson, J. I., Jenkins, P. L., Alexander, J., & Bannister, C. (1997). A randomised controlled trial of psychological debriefing for victims of acute harm. *British Journal of Psychiatry, 171,* 8–81.

Brom, D. (1996, November). The societal meaning of post-traumatic symptoms. In D. Brom (Chair), *Treating PTSD: The controversy between pathology and functionality.* Symposium conducted at the 12th annual meeting of the International Society for Traumatic Stress Studies, San Francisco, CA.

Brom, D., Kleber, R. J., & Hoffman, M. C. (1993). Victims of traffic accidents: Incidence and prevention of post traumatic stress disorder. *Journal of Clinical Psychology, 49,* 131–140.

Charlton, P. F. C., & Thompson, J. A. (1996). Ways of coping with psychological distress after trauma. *British Journal of Clinical Psychology, 35,* 517–530.

Chemtob, C. (1996, November). In A. C. McFarlane (Chair), *Is debriefing a good practice for individuals and groups exposed to traumatic stress?* Symposium conducted at the 12th annual meeting of the International Society for Traumatic Stress Studies, San Francisco, CA.

Cook, J. D., & Bickman, L. (1990). Social support and psychological symptomatology following a natural disaster. *Journal of Traumatic Stress, 3,* 541–556.

Cook, T. D., & Campbell, D. T. (1979). *Quasi-experimentation: Design & analysis issues for field settings*. Boston: Houghton Mifflin.

Deahl, M. P., & Bisson, J. I. (1995). Dealing with disasters: Does psychological debriefing work? *Journal of Accident and Emergency Medicine, 12*, 255–258.

Deahl, M. P., Gillham, A. B., Thomas, J., Dearle, M. M., & Strinivasan, M. (1994). Psychological sequelae following the Gulf War: Factors associated with subsequent morbidity and the effectiveness of psychological debriefing. *British Journal of Psychiatry, 165*, 60–65.

Derogatis, L. R. (1975). *Brief Symptom Inventory*. Baltimore: Author.

Derogatis, L. R. (1977). *SCL-90: Administration, scoring, and procedures manual for the revised version and other instruments of the psychopathology rating scale series*. Baltimore: Johns Hopkins University Press.

Echterling, L., & Wylie, M. L. (1981). Crisis centers: A social movement perspective. *Journal of Community Psychology, 9*, 342–346.

Emergency Management Institute. (1992). *Mass fatalities: Incident response course*. Washington, DC: Federal Emergency Management Agency.

Foa, E. B., & Meadows, E. A. (1997). Psychosocial treatments for posttraumatic stress disorder: A critical review. *Annual Review of Psychology, 48*, 935–938.

Fullerton, C. S., Wright, K. M., Ursano, R. J., & McCarroll, J. E. (1993). Social support for disaster workers after a mass-casualty disaster: Effects on the support provider. *Nordic Journal of Psychiatry, 47*, 315–324.

Gilbert, D. T., & Silvera, D. H. (1996). Overhelping. *Journal of Personality and Social Psychology, 70*, 678–690.

Gist, R. (1989). *Report to the State of Alaska: Community impact assessments and recommendations regarding the Exxon Valdez oil spill response and recovery*. Juneau: Alaska Division of Emergency Services/Alaska Department of Health and Social Services (Technical Report).

Gist, R. (1990, August). Debriefing and related activities. In G. A. Jacobs (Chair), *Flight 232: Case study of psychology's response to air disasters*. Symposium conducted at the 98th annual convention of the American Psychological Association, Boston, MA.

Gist, R. (1996a). Dr. Gist responds (Letter to the Editor). *Fire Chief, 40*(11), 19–24.

Gist, R. (1996b). Is CISD built on a foundation of sand? *Fire Chief, 40*(8), 38–42.

Gist, R., Lohr, J. M., Kenardy, J. A., Bergmann, L., Meldrum, L., Redburn, B. G., Paton, D., Bisson, J. I., Woodall, S. J., & Rosen, G. M. (1997). Researchers speak on CISM. *Journal of Emergency Medical Services, 22*(5), 27–28.

Gist, R., & Lubin, B. (1989a). Epilogue: Implications for research and practice. In R. Gist & B. Lubin (Eds.), *Psychosocial aspects of disaster* (pp. 341–344). New York: John Wiley & Sons.

Gist, R., & Lubin, B. (1989b). Introduction: Ecological and community perspectives on disaster intervention. In R. Gist & B. Lubin (Eds.), *Psychosocial aspects of disaster* (pp. 1–8). New York: John Wiley & Sons.

Gist, R., & Stolz, S. B. (1982). Mental heath promotion and the media: Community response to the Kansas City hotel disaster. *American Psychologist, 37*, 1136–1139.

Gist, R., & Woodall, S. J. (1995). Occupational stress in contemporary fire service. *Occupational Medicine: State of the Art Reviews, 10*, 763–787.

Gist, R., & Woodall, S. J. (1996, November). "And then you do the Hokey-Pokey and you turn yourself about . . ." In D. Brom (Chair), *Treating PTSD: The controversy between pathology and functionality*. Symposium conducted at the 12th annual meeting of the International Society for Traumatic Stress Studies; San Francisco, CA.

Glut, D. F. (1973). *The Frankenstein legend*. Metuchen, NJ: Scarecrow Press.

Gottfredson, G. D. (1984). A theory-ridden approach to program evaluation. *American Psychologist, 39*, 1101–1112.

Green Cross. (1996). Information posted at World Wide Web site ⟨http://psy.uq.edu.au/ PTSD/trauma/ogcross.html⟩ *et seq.*

Griffiths, J., & Watts, R. (1992). *The Kempsey and Grafton bus crashes: The aftermath.* East Lismore, Australia: Instructional Design Solutions.

Gump, B. B., & Kulik, J. A. (1997). Stress, affiliation, and emotional contagion. *Journal of Personality and Social Psychology, 72,* 305–319.

Helzer, J. E., Robins, L. N., & McEvoy, L. (1987). Post-traumatic stress disorder in the general population: Findings of the Epidemiologic Catchment Area Survey. *New England Journal of Medicine, 317,* 1630–1634.

Hobbs, M., Mayou, R., Harrison, B., & Worlock, P. (1996). A randomised controlled trial of psychological debriefing for victims of road traffic accidents. *British Medical Journal, 313,* 1438–1439.

Hytten, K., & Hasle, A. (1989). Firefighters: A study of stress and coping. *Acta Psychiatrica Scandinavia, 355* (Supp.), 50–55.

Kaniasty, K., & Norris, F. H. (1992). Social support of victims of crime: Matching event, support, and outcome. *American Journal of Community Psychology, 20,* 211–241.

Kaniasty, K., & Norris, F. H. (1997). Social support dynamics in adjustment to disasters. In S. Duck (Ed.), *Handbook of personal relationships* (2nd ed., pp. 595–619). London: Wiley.

Kenardy, J. A., & Carr, V. (1996). Imbalance in the debriefing debate: What we don't know far outweighs what we do. *Bulletin of the Australian Psychological Society, 18*(2), 4–6.

Kenardy, J. A., Webster, R. A., Lewin, T. J., Carr, V. J., Hazell, P. L., & Carter, G. L. (1996). Stress debriefing and patterns of recovery following a natural disaster. *Journal of Traumatic Stress, 9,* 37–49.

Kulik, J. A., Mahler, H. I., & Moore, P. J. (1996). Social comparison under threat: Effects on recovery from major surgery. *Journal of Personality and Social Psychology, 71,* 967–979.

Lee, C., Slade, P., & Lygo, V. (1996). The influence of psychological debriefing on emotional adaptation in women following early miscarriage: A preliminary study. *British Journal of Medical Psychology, 69,* 47–58.

Levine, G. (1974). The ambiguous heritage of Frankenstein. In G. Levine & U. C. Knoepflmacher (Eds.), *The endurance of Frankenstein* (pp. 3–30). Berkeley: University of California Press.

Lohr, J. M. (1996, November). Empirical justification for "emotional reprocessing" of traumatic memories. In D. Brom (Chair), *Treating PTSD: The controversy between pathology and functionality.* Symposium conducted at the 12th annual meeting of the International Society for Traumatic Stress Studies; San Francisco, CA.

Major, B., Cozzarelli, C., Sciacchitano, A. M., Cooper, L., & Testa, M. (1990). Perceived social support, self-efficacy, and adjustment to abortion. *Journal of Personality and Social Psychology, 59,* 452–463.

Mandel, D. R., & Lehman, D. R. (1996). Counterfactual thinking and ascriptions of cause and preventability. *Journal of Personality and Social Psychology, 71,* 450–463.

McCarroll, J. E., Fullerton, C. S., Ursano, R. J., & Hermsen, J. M. (1996). Posttraumatic stress symptoms following forensic dental identification: Mt. Carmel, Waco, Texas. *American Journal of Psychiatry, 153,* 778–782.

McCarroll, J. E., Ursano, R. J., Ventis, W. L., & Fullerton, C. S. (1993). Anticipation of handling the dead: Effects of gender and experience. *British Journal of Clinical Psychology, 32,* 466–468.

McCarroll, J. E., Ursano, R. J., & Fullerton, C. S. (1993). Symptoms of posttraumatic stress disorder following recovery of war dead. *American Journal of Psychiatry, 150,* 1875–1877.

McCarroll, J. E., Ursano, R. J., & Fullerton, C. S., & Lundy, A. (1993). Traumatic stress of a wartime mortuary: Anticipation of exposure to mass death. *Journal of Nervous and Mental Disease, 181,* 545–551.

McCrae, R. R. (1984). Situational determinants of coping responses: Loss, threat, and challenge. *Journal of Personality and Social Psychology, 46*, 919–928.

McFarlane, A. C. (1988). The longitudinal course of posttraumatic morbidity: The range of outcomes and their predictors. *Journal of Nervous and Mental Disease, 176*, 30–39.

Medvec, V. H., Madey, S. F., & Gilovich, T. (1995). When less is more: Counterfactual thinking among Olympic medalists. *Journal of Personality and Social Psychology, 69*, 603–610.

Miles, M. S., Demi, A. S., & Mostyn-Aker, P. (1984). Rescue workers' reactions following the Hyatt hotel disaster. *Death Education, 8*, 315–331.

Mitchell, J. T., & Everly, G. S. (1997). The scientific evidence for critical incident stress management. *Journal of Emergency Medical Services, 22*, 86–93.

Norris, F. H., & Kaniasty, K. (1996). Received and perceived social support in times of stress: A test of the social support deterioration deterrence model. *Journal of Personality and Social Psychology, 71*, 498–511.

Pratkanis, A. R. (1995, July/August). How to sell a pseudoscience. *Skeptical Inquirer, 19*(4), 19–25.

Pratkanis, A. R., & Aronson, E. (1991). *Age of propaganda: The everyday use and abuse of persuasion.* New York: W. H. Freeman.

Procidano, M. E., & Heller, K. (1983). Measures of perceived social support from friends and family: Three validation studies. *American Journal of Community Psychology, 11*, 1–23.

Quevillon, R. P., Yutrzenka, B. A., & Jacobs, G. A. (1991, August). Stress and coping among disaster responders. In G. A. Jacobs (Chair), *Flight 232: Case study of psychology's response to air disasters.* Symposium conducted at the 98th annual convention of the American Psychological Association, Boston, MA.

Raphael, B., Meldrum, L., & McFarlane, A. C. (1995). Does debriefing after psychological trauma work? Time for randomized controlled trials. *British Medical Journal, 310*, 1479–1480.

Redburn, B. G. (1992). *Disaster and rescue: Worker effects and coping strategies.* Doctoral dissertation, University of Missouri-Kansas City. [University Microfilms No. AAD93-12267; *Dissertation Abstracts International, 54*(01-B), 447.]

Redburn, B. G., Gensheimer, L. K., & Gist, R. (1993, June). Disaster aftermath: Social support among resilient rescue workers. Paper presented at 4th biennial conference on Community Research and Action, Society for Community Research and Action (Division 27, American Psychological Association), Williamsburg, VA.

Roese, N. J. (1994). The functional basis of counterfactual thinking. *Journal of Personality and Social Psychology, 66*, 805–818.

Rosen, G. M. (1996, November). After the trauma: Normal coping or PTSD? In D. Brom (Chair), *Treating PTSD: The controversy between pathology and functionality.* Symposium conducted at the 12th annual meeting of the International Society for Traumatic Stress Studies; San Francisco, CA.

Rosen, G. M. (1997). Dr. Welch's comments on Shapiro's walk in the woods and the origin of Eye Movement Desensitization and Reprocessing. *Journal of Behavior Therapy and Experimental Psychiatry, 28*, 247–249.

Rubonis, A. V., & Bickman, L. (1991). Psychological impairment in the wake of disaster: The disaster-psychopathology relationship. *Psychological Bulletin, 109*, 384–399.

Schwarz, E. D., & Kowalski, J. M. (1991). Posttraumatic stress disorder after a school shooting: Effects of symptom threshold selection and diagnosis by DSM-III, DSM-III-R, or proposed DSM-IV. *American Journal of Psychiatry, 148*, 595–597.

Shelley, M. W. (1818). *Frankenstein; or, the modern Prometheus.* London: Lackington, Hughes, Harding, Manor, & Jones. (Reprinted in 1823.)

Solomon, S. D., & Canino, G. J. (1990). Appropriateness of the DSM-III-R criteria for posttraumatic stress disorder. *Comprehensive Psychiatry, 31*, 227–237.

Stephens, C. (1997). Debriefing, social support, and PTSD in the New Zealand police: Testing a multidimensional model of organizational traumatic stress. *Austalasian Journal of Disaster and Trauma Studies, 1*. Electronic journal located at ⟨http://massey.ac.nz/ ~ trauma/issues/1997-1/cvs.htm⟩

Tal, K. (1996). *Worlds of hurt: Reading the literatures of trauma*. New York: Cambridge University Press.

Taylor, S. E. (1983). Adjustment to threatening events: A theory of cognitive adaptation. *American Psychologist, 38*, 1161–1174.

Taylor, S. E. (1991). Asymmetrical effects of positive and negative events: The mobilization-minimization hypothesis. *Psychological Bulletin, 110*, 67–85.

Taylor, S. E., & Brown, J. D. (1988). Illusion and well-being: A social psychological perspective on mental health. *Psychological Bulletin, 103*, 193–211.

Taylor, S. E., & Lobel, M. (1989). Social comparison activity under threat: Downward evaluation and upward contacts. *Psychological Review, 96*, 569–575.

Thompson, J., & Solomon, M. (1991). Body recovery teams at disasters: Trauma or challenge? *Anxiety Research, 4*, 235–244.

Tierney, K. J. (1989). The social and community contexts of disaster. In R. Gist & B. Lubin (Eds.), *Psychosocial aspects of disaster* (pp. 11–39). New York: Wiley.

Ware, J. E., Jr., & Karmos, A. H. (1976). *Development and validation of scales to measure perceived health and patient role propensity*. Carbondale: Southern Illinois University.

Wilkinson, C. B. (1983). Aftermath of a disaster: The collapse of the Hyatt Regency Hotel skywalks. *American Journal of Psychiatry, 140*, 1134–1139.

Zajonc, R. B. (1968). Attitudinal effects of mere exposure (monograph). *Journal of Personality and Social Psychology, 9*, 1–27.

Part One

Theoretical Foundations

The most difficult questions to address through the meticulous, measured methods of science are often those where strong intuitive constructions based on repetition, presumption, and seemingly reasonable beliefs conceal even the need to raise an issue, much less the manifest content of the empirical questions nested beneath. Notions first proffered simply as metaphors can be easily elevated to conceptual models with little more than repeated and expanded articulation as their catalysts; models constructed principally from metaphor can all too easily become reified as if the mechanisms of nature with little addition of substance beyond the durability of their face validity. One person's speculation, once adopted and shared by several, becomes a collective hypothesis and eventually theory; all too easily and all too often, theory can be embraced and even defended as fact with surprisingly little of the empirical challenge and critical analysis that form the bedrock of science.

Psychology may seem uncommonly vulnerable to these perils, but they are hardly our unique inventions. The history of every scientific discipline includes colorful examples of the very same foibles: Consider such easily forgotten but once pervasive positions as Lamarckian concepts of heritability or the evolution of the ubiquitous phlogiston in process of combustion. The vitality of science as an epistemological viewpoint derives from the self-correcting, incremental processes through which ideas are scrutinized, judiciously tested against the empirical events, and refined progressively to reflect the findings of that scrutiny. It is, for our enterprise, the alpha and the omega—we begin any cycle of inquiry with such scrutiny of what we presently believe ourselves to know; we end any cycle with scrutiny of what we believe ourselves to have learned.

Science is, in essence, the unrelenting pursuit of fleeting answers to enduring questions, and scientifically based practice can never allow itself to be separated far from the processes or the products of that inquiry. The comfort of constructions easily integrated into both beliefs and practices must stand constantly ready to yield to the findings of empirical analysis if applications are to keep pace with information. This can place very significant demands of time, attention, and effort simply to keep pace with the volume of information a growing science produces, much less to fully integrate its sometimes subtle and constantly shifting implications. When those shifts turn to challenge very basic presumptions and constructions, it can be all too easy to simply speak them away and continue with what has always seemed adequate and certainly comfortable.

The foundations for our first forays into community response to disaster were borrowed liberally and without much critique from principles of crisis intervention that had been easily embraced in the zeitgeist of the community mental health movement (see Echterling & Wylie, 1981, for discussion of the social movement features); these had, in turn, borrowed liberally—principally in metaphorical form—from basic tenets and principles of public health (cf. Caplan, 1964). These were rational models adopted from authoritative sources, fully backed by the legitimacy afforded through wide acceptance and frequent repetition; they became, for many, postulates if not axioms.

Two decades of increasingly detailed experience have lent many opportunities for critical exploration of our enterprises; those observations and explorations, as well they should, have caused us to examine ever more critically the construction of the theories and propositions that have guided our efforts. We begin, then, by presenting critical examination of those foundations in light of current information and by offering new constructions for several key concepts that have begun to emerge through the process of inquiry.

Kaniasty and Norris (chapter 2) open this section with an overview of crisis and calamity as a community phenomenon; while not at all discounting of the reactions of individuals, the contexts of the events and the social influences on attribution, coping, and resolution may provide a more refined and more productive framework for guiding both intervention and analysis. Salzer and Bickman (chapter 3) then examine epidemiologic data on psychosocial reactions to disaster, demonstrating that social construction of descriptors strongly influence data reported and interpretations made. Smith, Paton, Ramsay, and Akande (chapter 4) then examine more specifically one of the major instruments used both to determine "case-ness" and to assess impacts of interventions, the Impact of Events Scale (Horowitz, Wilner, & Alvarez, 1979). Staab, Fullerton, and Ursano (chapter 5) complete the section with a fascinating proposal for reconceptualizing posttraumatic stress disorder along lines more consistent with socially influenced and constructed attributions and coping.

REFERENCES

Caplan, G. (1964). *Principles of preventive psychiatry.* New York: Basic Books.
Echterling, L., & Wylie, M. L. (1981). Crisis centers: A social movement perspective. *Journal of Community Psychology, 9,* 342–346.
Horowitz, M., Wilner, M, & Alvarez, W. (1979). Impact of Event Scale: A measure of subjective stress. *Psychosomatic Medicine, 41,* 209–218.

Chapter 2

The Experience of Disaster: Individuals and Communities Sharing Trauma

Krzysztof Kaniasty and Fran Norris

INTRODUCTION

Uncovering the complex reality of a disaster is very difficult. Disasters defy geographical, social, and cultural boundaries. Whether they strike predictably or unexceptedly, emerge slowly or suddenly, surround visibly or invisibly, disasters are processes that have dramatic consequences for individuals, families, neighborhoods, communities, and larger entities. They defy time limits, too, as various facets of a disaster eventually imprint themselves on every aspect of life. Adding to the complexity, disasters are often very different from one another, and each may beget very unique demands and create very specific needs. However, as in observing unending fractals, the closer we look, the more detail surfaces—and the more a reliably repeating pattern emerges as well.

When construed from tenets of social and community psychologies, the crux of disaster experience is the dynamic interplay of individual and

Preparation of this chapter was supported by Grant RO1 MH51278 from the Violence and Traumatic Stress Research Branch of the National Institute of Mental Health, Fran H. Norris, principal investigator. We would like to thank Susan Zimmy for her helpful suggestions on an earlier draft of this chapter.

community experiences. Individual suffering unveils itself within the parameters of other people's suffering. Loss and gain, breakdown and recovery, are individual and collective struggles. The reality of individual victimization cannot be understood without consideration of the collective reality at all levels: environmental, psychological, social, political, and cultural. This interactional character of disaster experience should not be ignored or taken for granted, as coping efforts of individuals and their communities are interwoven. One can dominate at times, yet the other never ceases its presence or its influence. Community reactions better or worsen individual reactions; individual reactions become shared reactions and define the collective identity of a coping community.

This emphasis on describing the stress process as an interdependence of individual and collective experiences is not novel. A number of theorists and researchers within different areas of stress and disaster research have made similar proclamations (e.g., Bolin, 1989; Brown & Perkins, 1992; Eckenrode, 1991; Erickson, 1976a; Freedy & Hobfoll, 1995; Gist & Lubin, 1989; Golec, 1983; Hobfoll & deVries, 1995; Kaplan, 1996; Pearlin, 1989; Quarantalli & Dynes, 1985; Ursano, McCaughey, & Fullerton, 1994). Such an emphasis is never the less present only in a fraction of the work on psychological consequences of disasters. Most psychological studies focus on clinical dissections of disaster's meaning and consequences at the individual level. Research on individual psychological functioning has its merits both theoretically and practically, yet concentration on individual realities of disasters in isolation from their social contexts risks oversimplifying, if not distorting the phenomenon. Trickett (1995) vividly evoked a Gestalt image of figure–ground and observed that in current psychological research on coping with collective stress, individual psychological reactions are the figure, whereas the sociocultural context is treated as ground. Advocating an ecological approach to the study of people and their environments, Trickett charged the field to "make a figure out of ground" by "dignifying the role of context and culture" and adopting "a community as well as person-in-context level of analysis" (p. 21).

A dynamic image of shifting figure and ground is very appealing. The charm of this image is that we can viscerally and intellectually experience the sensation of shifting from one image to another; figure–ground, ground–figure, individual–community, community–individual. The power of this metaphor is that we all know how hard it is to make sense of the background once we choose to focus on the figure. Though we realize that any good metaphor can be stripped of its appeal with a bold, literal and mechanistic scrutiny, we still find our figure-ground analogy troublesome. The problem with the figure-ground analogy is inherent in that fact that perception is not only an active process, it is also a categorical one. Once you focus on the black silhouettes of "two people facing each other," the white space between them takes on meaningless properties of ground.

When you reorganize the sensory input and interpret the white space as a "vase" (or candle holder), the black spaces on each side, which before had been meaningful figures, now become a meaningless ground. Thus what the shifting figure–ground image describes, or makes us experience, is "one *or* the other" not "one *and* the other." This, of course, is not the spirit of ecological perspective.

We propose to improve on the figure-and-ground analogy by resorting to the image of a Necker cube (Necker, 1832; see Feldman, 1981, Figure 1). If you fix on the left-bottom vertex you will see a left-facing cube ("shooting down") with a front panel conveniently labeled INDIVIDUAL. Now, reorganize the sensory input by fixing on the right-top vertex. Hopefully, you will see a right-facing cube ("shooting up") with a front panel labeled COMMUNITY. This is still a categorical process because the two visual interpretations are mutually inhibiting. However, the currently dominating interpretation does not void the other, and the perceived object is always the same cube. To describe the cube comprehensively, to experience its depth, we have to let the visual system shift from one variant to another. In this dynamic process, it is easy to discover that these two distinct interpretations are complementing each other and are parts of the same entity. We hope that the cube, in its simplicity, is a fair match for the most eloquent words of Kai Erikson (1967a), who said that individual and collective traumas of most human disasters "occur simultaneously and are experienced as two halves of a continuous whole" (p. 154).

Our thinking about disaster stress as a collective process has been strongly influenced by the social support literature (e.g., Barrera, 1986; Lin, 1986; Vaux, 1988; Wheaton, 1985). Social support, at its essence, is a multifaced construct (see Sarason, Sarason, & Pierce, 1992) circumscribed by a maze of characteristics of the individuals, their communities, and environmental pressures. Social support research had been initially oriented around stressors confined to lone individuals and small groups (e.g.,

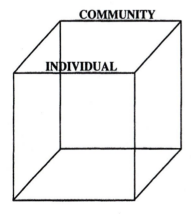

Figure 1   Disaster cube.

bereavement, divorce, illness). We felt it important to examine some basic theoretical approaches to social support in the context of stressful circumstances that affect large groups of individuals. By definition, community-wide stressors, such as natural and technological disasters and catastrophes, affect great numbers of people simultaneously, many of whom are members of one another's support networks and are mutually dependent on one another's coping efforts.

These characteristics of the stress process vividly illustrate the interplay of the individual and communal variants of the "disaster cube." Many forms of interdependence emerge. Connections between individual and collective recovery efforts can take on a synergistic form whereby losses (or gains) in one can be linked to losses (or gains) in the other (see Brown & Perkins, 1992). When losses incurred because of stressor surpass the individual level and cause losses for others in the community as well, the resulting depletion of communal coping resources may easily reduce the community's actual ability to help and protect its members. The individual loss cycles are accelerated (Hobfoll, 1988). These linkages can also take on compensatory form as loss of resources at one level may be compensated by strengths or gains of resources at the other level (see Hobfoll, Dunahoo, & Monnier, 1995b). Loss at the individual level may be counteracted or neutralized by those community resources that are easily mobilized in the face of crisis.

We believe that this focus on "interdependence" helps to organize the mass of information regarding individual and community coping. In the remainder of this chapter, we present a series of vignettes that illustrate the interdependence of individuals and their communities, mobilization and deterioration processes, immediate and delayed consequences, and losses and gains. As implied by the image of the "disaster cube," each facet must temporarily dominate but cannot be understood fully in isolation from the whole.

THE EXPERIENCE OF DISASTER:
SIX FACETS OF THE CUBE

Initial assessments: Self in the context of others

Adverse events evoke strong and rapid physiological, emotional, and social responses (see S. E. Taylor, 1991, for review). Even the most tragic adversities seldom psychologically paralyze people to the extent of rendering them totally powerless. "Disaster victims do not exhibit irrational and self-destructive behavior nor do they become helpless and dependent. While some are killed or injured, most victims are not. They become resources" (Dynes & Drabek, 1994, p. 12). Contrary to common beliefs about mass panic and chaotic disorganization, victims of most disasters quickly tend to regain a collective sense of determination and rapidly immerse themselves in the process of aiding one another. Simply speaking, experience of loss motivates coping behavior (Freedy, Shaw, Jarrell, & Masters, 1992; Hobfoll et al., 1995b).

In their attempt at describing how key elements of the individual stress process translate to the community stress context, Jerusalem, Kaniasty, Lehman, Ritter, and Turnbull (1995) evoked an image of victims "bursting into action." Because many disasters tend to be sudden or inevitably approaching, victims quite frequently find themselves cast in leading roles and must fling themselves into immediate activities. The obvious call for action, even during one's own time of crisis, propels many individuals into extremely high levels of coping. As long as they are physically capable, victims are doers—there is no place for bystanders.

At the level of an individual, for a person who quite possibly just experienced a horrendous psychological and material loss, there may be clear benefits from this "forced" initial coping. The opportunity to act and to help one's self and others could be therapeutic. Rather than focusing on the extent of trauma itself ("Isn't this horrible?"), active copers may focus their attention on "making things better." These instantaneous missions and goals help many victims find meaning in the experienced calamity, and to gain at least some sense of control. Yet the heightened activity also poses risks that might not become apparent until later in the process of recovery. Overinvolvement in collective action may restrain some victims from resolving their own personal problems. Eventually, the potential therapeutical effects of being "forced" to cope may be overshadowed by a lack of personal resolution that might otherwise have been achieved (Jerusalem et al., 1995).

The presence of other victims sharing the same fate and reacting in a similar fashion helps to validate one's own assessments and judgements. For example, Cohn (1978) found that being jobless in times of high unemployment was less psychologically detrimental than being unemployed when unemployment rates were low (see also, Jemmott, Ditto, & Croyle, 1986). Although we do not know of any studies that have assessed this phenomenon in context of disasters, the fact that so many other people are experiencing the stressor may render it somewhat less threatening and severe. In their account of psychological suffering experienced by survivors of air disasters, Butcher and Dunn (1989) suggested that the separation from other victims is an important dimension contributing to the trauma. Reasonably, in the context of centrifugal catastrophes (i.e., survivors do not reside at the site of destruction as contrasted to centripetal disasters where the survivors remain in or near the site; Lindy & Grace, 1986), barriers to building a sense of camaraderie among the victims and lack of opportunities for reciprocal support and comparisons may become prominent features of the individual experience (see also

Tierney, 1989). A conceivable downside of being a part of a larger traumatized collective, however, is that the potential support providers are victims themselves and, as a consequence, the need for support across all those affected frequently exceeds its availability.

Being a part of a collective or larger unit stitched together by the same experience could make this experience less threatening and less confusing, and hence more understandable and tolerable. All victimization experiences have the potential to shatter basic assumptions about justice and fairness in the world, and the loss of these beliefs can be psychologically injurious (see Janoff-Bulman, 1992). Since disasters involve many people who are similarly afflicted, disasters may be less likely to trigger existential doubts about justice and fairness. Accordingly, victims of some disasters may be less likely to experience the collapse of these fundamental assumptions (Jerusalem et al., 1995).

Communal stressors provide victims with abundant comparison targets who may be "worse off" than are they. Such downward comparisons have benefits for victims (Wills, 1981), but they may also increase fears and anxieties about subsequently getting worse. Likewise, upward comparisons (seeing those "better off") may evoke feelings of despair and resentment but can also comfort and inspire if seen as presenting the potential for improvement (see S. E. Taylor & Loeb, 1989). These contrasts underscore the point that, within the ecology of collective stress, every asset has its liabilities and every benefit has its costs, depending on circumstances and context (Trickett, 1995).

Disasters provide people with opportunities for a wide range of social comparisons. Media are omnipresent in the immediate aftermath. Television, radio, and newspapers bombard us with endless stories about victims' heroism, their determination, their servitude in counting remaining blessings ("It could have been worse"), and their courageous sense of hope. It is not clear, however, how these success stories impact on other victims with respect to distress and coping motivations. Media are efficient dispensers of targets for social comparisons (see Wood, Taylor, & Lichtman, 1985), but their influence on disaster victims is yet to be understood. Even more problematic is the fact that these overromanticized stories about a few brave and rugged individuals may create false impressions for the general public about the true meaning of disasters. Heartwarming stories, as much as we like them, should not let us forget that disasters are, first of all, landscapes of countless suffering and destruction. The media could just as easily bend the other way and become insensitive in overdramatizing the experience. McFarlane (1995b) noted that in the Ash Wednesday bushfires disaster, some media greatly exaggerated the extent of the fires, compounding the sense of trauma for many helpless victims as well as the observers.

Individual coping efforts in the context of community stressors are rarely private, and can in fact become very visible and quite open to public scrutiny. On the one hand, the media can be very useful in publicizing the availability of services, describing reactions to disasters, and communicating that victims' reactions are ordinary ways of responding to the tragic and unusual (see Gist & Stolz, 1982). On the other hand, the media may create and fulfill voyeuristic desires without much regard for the victims. Smith and Belgrave (1995) reported that even months after Hurricane Andrew hit South Dade County, Florida, a local radio personality had been encouraging the tourists to take a peek at the devastated areas and the people living there, "just to see for themselves!" A survivor of the 1980 eruption of Mount St. Helens protested in despair: "My parents' bodies have never been found. I don't like the idea of people tramping around up there. It is not a public graveyard" (Murphy, 1986, p. 68). Spectators and news people with their microphones, cameras, production vans, and helicopters continually navigate through victims' lives, beaming them out for those watching in the safety of their own (intact) homes. Victims eventually tire of this curiosity and start resenting these intrusions.

> They were just rubbernecking . . . if I had a bazooka I'd have blown them out of the sky," a victim of Andrew commented angrily. "I felt really invaded. I was so angry at these assholes out there, knowing that if they are out there looking at us, they didn't lose anything." (Smith & Belgrave, 1995, p. 255)

It is rather unlikely that such testimonials will make the 6 o'clock news. While we do not mean to single out and vilify the media and friendly onlookers, it is important to understand that their presence and their actions are often felt as intrusive.

Democracy of common disaster?

Nothing better exemplifies the initial surge of coping activities than the instantaneous postcrisis mobilization of help. For decades now, researchers studying public responses to natural disasters such as hurricanes, floods, or earthquakes have been "taken" by images of high levels of mutual helping engrossing whole communities. This immediate phase has been referred to as the "altruistic or therapeutic community" or "post-disaster Utopia" (see Barton, 1969; Frederick, 1980; Fritz, 1961; Giel, 1990). The most distinguishing features of this collective are heightened internal solidarity, disappearance of community conflicts, Utopian mood, and an overall sense of altruism. In his essay about the 1937 Louisville flood, Kutak (1938) observed that in the postcrisis phase "the inhibitions and the formalities of social life tend to disappear, and the free and easy contacts of the primary group tend to replace the more stereotyped forms of social relationships which exist in an organized urban society" (p. 67). Other researchers have also suggested that the experience of the same faith can cause previous race, ethnic, and social class barriers to crumble, at least temporarily (Bolin, 1989; Drabek, 1986; Enranen & Liebkind, 1993).

> For the moment we were as one, and I was the brother of the toothless Filipino crone who sat besides me and smoked a big black cigar. Near me was a charming Southern woman, the widow of an old friend of mine. She accepted a cigarette from a Negro piano player. A millionaire tourist from Chicago sat on a pile of luggage with one of Shanghai's well-known beachcombers, and the two found a great deal to talk about. Ours was the democracy and brotherhood of common disaster. (Carl Crow's account of the bombing of Shanghai, *Harper's Magazine*, December 1937, cited in Kutak, 1938.)

Whereas mutual helping behavior is clearly abundant in the immediate aftermath of catastrophic events, expressions such as "democracy of common disaster" or "altruistic community" may inadvertently create a false image that all victims are equally involved in these helping collectives. Accounts of a postcrisis sense of unity and fellowship may also create a false expectation that these democracies develop in all disasters. While these images may fulfill our need to romanticize suffering, they must not, no matter how comforting, be uncritically accepted.

Victims of natural disasters report receiving and providing substantial amounts of help (e.g., Bolin, 1982; Drabek & Key, 1984; Haines, Hurlbert, & Beggs, 1996; Kaniasty & Norris, 1995). The altruistic community does not, however, distribute aid randomly or equally. Not surprisingly, priority is given to those victims who experience the most harm and loss. The importance of harm and loss in natural allocation of assistance is consistent with the rule of relative needs. Relative needs, most often operationalized as the severity of experienced stressor, serve as a powerful impetus in mobilizing support from other people in all crisis situations, not only in disasters (e.g., Dunkel-Schetter, Folkman, & Lazarus, 1987; Hobfoll & Lerman, 1989; Kaniasty & Norris, 1992).

Empirical and common observations alike suggest that, irrespective of need, certain people have a relative advantage (or disadvantage) in receiving social support in general. For example, persons who have larger social networks, higher socioeconomic status, or are younger or female usually receive more support (Eckenrode & Wethington, 1990; House, Umberson, & Landis, 1988; Vaux, 1988). This is yet another simple fact of life that gains particular meaning in context of disasters. Research on postdisaster helping behavior suggests that the poor, the elderly, the less educated, and some ethnic minorities may be denied a part in the "democracy of common disaster." In other words, the victimization experience could be a place where, for some victims, their initially disadvantaged status meets their relatively high needs—augmenting preexisting inequalities. This might result in a clear pattern of neglect such that some of the victims could receive less help than other people comparably affected.

Kilijanek and Drabek (1979) coined the term *pattern of neglect* to describe lesser levels of aid allocation to elderly victims of the 1966 Topeka tornado. "Elderly families simply did not participate as fully in the emergent postdisaster therapeutic community as did the younger victims" (Drabek & Key, 1984, p. 100). Elderly victims in our Kentucky floods study (Kaniasty, Norris, & Murrell, 1990) received what appeared to be much less help than they had expected. Apparently, these poor, rural, and older victims were also denied participation in a postdisaster helping collective. Bolin and Bolton (1986) observed following their examination of four natural disasters (tornado, flooding, hurricane, and earthquake) that struck four culturally and ethnically diverse sites (Texas, Utah, Hawaii, and California) that the poor and minorities had the greatest difficulties securing adequate assistance. In his comprehensive review of anthropological research on disasters, Oliver-Smith (1996) noted, too, that factors such as race, age, and economic status are key variables affecting distribution of resources in recovery.

There is a cruel irony in disasters. Socially, politically, morally, and religiously sanctioned patterns of inequality fuel further discrimination and deprivation. Researchers have consistently noted the significance of social stratifications in explaining both the victims' differential exposure to the stressor and their differential access to helping resources.

> The smallest and poorest countries are affected most severely by natural disasters, and the poorest and most disadvantaged members of disaster-affected community are likely to experience the most serious consequences. (Weisæth, 1995, p. 401)
>
> (M)embers who occupy marginal positions experience only a limited sense of 'communality' with the boundaries of particular social clusters. (Golec, 1983, p. 270)
>
> In a sense, the poor in disasters are double victims: there are first of all victims of poverty and that, in turn, adds to the degree of 'victimization' in disasters. (Bolin, 1982, p. 247)

Well-publicized examples of altruism and solidarity in times of crisis should not obscure the fact that the pattern of neglect is equally real.

In our study of helping behavior following Hurricane Hugo (Kaniasty & Norris, 1995), a pattern of neglect emerged such that less educated and Black residents received proportionately less help than equally affected victims who were more educated or White. We uncovered in the same study yet another side of the postcrisis social support allocation: Older respondents who faced threats to their lives and health during the impact of a hurricane experienced a "pattern of concern." Disaster harm reliably mobilized their social networks to provide them with levels of support usually reserved for younger victims. However, older victims were not afforded such a pattern of concern when faced with tangible losses and damages. When blending these results with the findings of other studies (Kaniasty et al., 1990; Kilijanek & Drabek, 1979), an interesting formation of effects emerges: With regard to property damage, older adults may sometimes suffer from a pattern of neglect; with regard to physical illness and injury, however, there may be a pattern of concern that mobilizes support networks to provide more assistance to the elderly. Quite possibly, illness or physical complaints serve as power cues indicating need for attention, concern, guidance, and assistance (see Kaniasty & Norris, 1997). Disasters evoke assortments of norms, motivations, prejudices, and rules; conflicting or paradoxical patterns of functioning may therefore emerge.

Nobody notices and embraces these contradictions more than the victims themselves. Depending on to whom we may listen, the victims may paint their experiences as "the worst of times" or "the best of times." Victims of the 1993 Midwestern floods who participated in Harvey et al.'s, (1995) study gave the following testimonials (pp. 327–330):

> I had no help from my family—10 brothers and sisters (8 of them living close by). I would call for them to help me move our belongings, pets, and vehicles and with kids. No one would help... I blame my family members who could have been supportive and who didn't seem to care.
>
> Friends who you have loved and trusted turn out to be selfish and self-serving.
>
> I sorted my friends about as fast as I had to sort my things in the flooding... Those you thought were friends didn't want to hear about our troubles.
>
> I have gained faith in God, my family, and my friends. Our friends came and helped whenever we needed it. They were wonderful.
>
> Our faith in people was strengthened. Friends, relatives, church friends all pitched in to help. I have so much thankfulness toward so many other people.
>
> The flood renewed my faith in mankind. Despite our losses, we are healthy and happy.

Interestingly, a number of researchers have observed that the high levels of helping emerging within social networks are extensions of precrisis trajectories of personal and community relationships. It might be quite unsettling, but victimization experiences could be the most direct way for people to verify their expectations that help would be available if needed. Another victim from the Harvey et al. (1995) study wrote: "I turned to friends for support, and you definitely found out who was a friend and who wasn't" (p. 329). In their study of a flooded Mormon community, Bolin and Bolton (1986) noted that mutual helping and bonding were an "outgrowth of the local culture," such that therapeutic community was, in essence, already in place prior to the actual emergency. A similar sentiment was voiced in Golec's (1983) study of a Mormon Church ward victimized by a dam collapse. Haines et al. (1996) reported that individuals' membership in community organizations and their trust in local government were strong predictors of how much help they provided to others affected by Hurricane Andrew. All these observations reiterate a simple point that past resources influence acquisition of future resources (cf. Hobfoll, 1988).

Receiving high levels of support and compassion undoubtedly reinforces a sense of community and belongingness, yet it is difficult to determine (for the victims themselves, as well as for us, the researchers) whether the accounts of "bringing the community together" are a reflection of actual gains or a reflection of coping mechanisms at work. Quite possibly, neglect and disappointments may be overlooked or forgotten and, as individuals and communities recover, a sense of gratitude and pride in meeting an arduous and insurmountable challenge will come to dominate. Golec (1983) eloquently captured some of the uncertainties facing the victims when they try to discover if "the flood brought people and families especially closer together or perhaps this is only 'a memory you never forget' rather than a persisting feature of social relations" (p. 264). It has been suggested, however, that these reaffirmations of hope, optimism, and widespread altruism mitigate lasting adverse psychological consequences of disasters. By the same token, negative social and psychological reactions caused by disasters are often attributed to a failure of victimized communities to transcend into a cohesive therapeutic collective (Quarantelli & Dynes, 1985). Quarantelli (1985) evoked an analogy of a "social sponge" to portray the victimized community's ability to withstand the enormous trauma and destruction and still be able to return to its usual state, and has argued further that disasters may actually generate positive social consequences. The heart of the "altruistic community" hypothesis is that cohesion and mutual support become an all powerful shield that protects against longer-term deleterious effects of disasters, a proposition we return to address at the end of this chapter.

These wonderful helpers

> How could you give up? Felt like it—even me—but them volunteers, they just wouldn't let you. (Golec, 1983, p. 262)

The instantaneous influx of unselfish, often heroic, and frequently nameless volunteers and helping professionals strongly contributes to this ethos of common fate and united struggle for survival. These "wonderful helpers" instill hope and serve as a reminder that humanity has not ended, even though it may seem to the momentarily stunned and confused victims that indeed it has. These helpful strangers help the victims "get going" and trust that the nightmare will end.

The pivotal importance of these people in the first moments following the impact of the catastrophe is obvious. In these first minutes and hours of unveiling stress, it is hard to go very wrong when everything else is devastated. Past the initial havoc, however, both the coordination and "philosophy" of providing professional and volunteer assistance requires more than just good will. "The desire to assist is without question laudable, but not all forms of help, of course, prove equally helpful" (Gist, Lubin, & Redburn, 1998). Providing and receiving help in crisis, whether embedded within personal, charitable, or professional relationships, is a complex and difficult process where good intentions and sincere concerns often blend with confusion, skepticism, and psychological threats (Wortman & Lehman, 1985; Yates, Axsom, Bickman, & Howe, 1989).

There are some very informative analyses on the issue of mobilizing and coordinating organized assistance following disasters (e.g., Comfort, 1990; de Vries, 1995; Gist et al., 1998; Golec, 1983; Milgram, Sarason, Schonpflug, Jackson, & Schwarzer, 1995; McFarlane, 1995a; Weisaeth, 1995). We feel the need to offer a few remarks based on that literature because it appears that a significant part of a community's success in postdisaster recovery rides on such coordinated efforts. After all, these "wonderful helpers" are an integral part of a struggling collective; at the same time, however, these helping volunteers and professionals may lack information and understanding of the lives of those individuals they are trying to help.

Helpers' working models of how to help, of what help is needed, or of what is appropriate and when are direct reflections of their own cultural and societal standings and convictions. Hence, at least in this country, middle-class, urban, western, and individualistic worldviews will most likely dominate. Stereotypes about the event, appropriate ways of coping with it, and the victims themselves become rampant. Helping activities may be shaped by those stereotypes, which may compromise their true potential to be supportive (see Wortman, Carnelley, Lehman, Davis, & Exline, 1995). As a result, "disaster victims may be 'touched' by the spontaneous generosity of outsiders but their assistance tends to be valued less than assistance received from locals" (Golec, 1983, p. 270). Of course, it is too much to expect spontaneously recruited professionals and volunteers to share the social status, values, and cultural orientations of the victims, but their sensitivity to preexisting indigenous "ways and morays" is important. Victims are quite aware of these subtleties and, in fact, may insist that their individual experience be gauged based on the "prior understanding of community circumstances" (Golec, 1983, p. 257).

An obvious solution is to involve community representatives and leaders as intermediaries for the outsiders' generosity; these persons can promote local ways of doing things. Involving local people is not just good politics for the sake of respecting indigenous culture. The endorsement of coping efforts by key people in the area validates victims' own appraisals of the experience, builds consensus, and motivates and encourages involvement of the whole community in mutual assistance. The congruence in appraisals of the event as one affecting all people in the community is a very important precursor of collective coping. Clearly, the affected community *does not* need a divisive debate about "what has really happened," and "who is responsible for it," or "who is in charge of taking care of it" (Jerusalem et al., 1995). What the victims *do* need is to hear a sound call: "Roll up your sleeves and get your homes and our communities cleaned up. Don't sit back and wait for the federal government to do it for you. Let's do it ourselves" (Golec, 1983, p. 258).

As much as it is a good idea to involve local people in coordinating relief efforts to provide a perspective on the idiosyncrasies of the community, there is a potential predicament associated with that reasonable approach. Ignorance is bliss, it is said, and the "uncorrected" cultural naivete or ignorance of the outsiders could conceivably bring some benefit. Resorting to tradition and culture often implies continuance of "natural" preferences, divisions, and biases. Golec (1983), in her most insightful analysis of disaster recovery, wrote

> Because outsiders do not have a personal investment in local traditions they may be one of the few resource persons willing to take action to redress perceived injustices which result from established practice... Since [local] patronage follows along the lines of power and privilege the benefits of local programs are likely to be distributed unevenly and in particular, marginal groups are most likely to be disadvantaged" (p. 270–271).

Thus, a first look at organized helping may show a clear need for the involvement of indigenous social and political organizations. A second look, however, may present a risk of surrendering to unjust and discriminating rules for distribution of resources, sanctioned by local traditions and culture. The point we are making is *not* to choose (or believe) one side or the other—the point is to realize that both sides must coexist.

The irony in this conundrum is that customary subdivisions of communities are clear obstacles to all-inclusive intervention efforts (Hobfoll, Briggs, & Wells, 1995), yet resorting to egalitarian distribution patterns, often preferred by outsiders, takes away from the recuperative potential of maintaining traditional social orders (see Oliver-Smith, 1996). Disasters destroy more than a sense of environmental familiarity. They can also destroy cultural familiarity and, with it, the healing potential of traditional and predictable ways of daily living. These losses were a significant part of the collective trauma at Buffalo Creek described by Erikson (1976b). Palinkas and his colleagues (Palinkas, Downs, Petterson, & Russell, 1993; Palinkas, Russell, Downs, & Petterson, 1992) noted that a major dimension of a communal loss in Alaskan communities affected by the Exxon Valdez oil spill was a disruption of fishing activities and, with them, ways of maintaining traditional social structure and order. However, the same "frustrated" culture stood behind strife regarding who should have supervisory roles in the clean-up and other recovery efforts. The authority and leadership allocated by outsiders to the local younger people (as opposed to elders) or women (as opposed to men) met with strong resistance.

Difficulties in providing services to affected communities call for the involvement of the victims and other local residents in the relief efforts. An important role of those coordinating supportive resources "is to identify points at which community residents may make the critical shift from passive victims to active participants in the disaster recovery process" (Comfort, 1990, p. 104). Such recruitment of victims may be very selective and can result in the harmful overreliance on some. We found that, following Hurricane Hugo, some victims were recruited to help more often than others because their resources and skills were in great demand (Kaniasty & Norris, 1995). This, in turn, may create an extra burden for those residents in the community who are, first and foremost, victims themselves—yet are also "drafted" as providers. The influx of additional obligations and responsibilities may disrupt their own coping efforts, making them more vulnerable to postdisaster distress (Solomon, Smith, Robins, & Fischbach, 1987; Thompson, Norris, & Hanacek, 1993). Again, planning and sensitive intertwining of formal and indigenous helping resource seems essential.

When talking about these "wonderful helpers," we must also address the role of mental health workers and mental health interventions. We will do this only briefly (these issues are comprehensively addressed in other chapters of this volume), and again we will pay particular attention to the interplay of individual and social dimensions of the victimization experience. It appears that if the treatment is to produce positive outcomes, it should occur early (McFarlane, 1995a). Possibly this simple and reasonable observation underlies the recent mushrooming of immediate and brief therapeutic interventions. These methods are primarily designed to prevent post-traumatic stress disorder (PTSD). Although exposure to the stressor is a necessary determinant of PTSD, it is not a sufficient cause for development of symptomatology. Many victims of disasters cope quite well with their victimization experience, and only a small subset of the affected persons require mental health services or develop PTSD symptoms or other psychopathologies (Green & Solomon, 1995; McFarlane, 1995b; Norris, 1992; Rubonis & Bickman, 1991; also see chapter 3). Some important questions still await answers: How well do these instantaneous trauma treatments work? Who should be receiving them and when? What are the community implications of focusing on symptomatology at the individual level?

Gist and his colleagues (1998) have leveled a strong indictment of the current emphasis on providing emergency mental health treatment, a trend they unflatteringly labeled *trauma tourism*. Gist et al., as well as other authors (e.g., Foa & Meadows, 1997; McFarlane, 1995b) who have reviewed outcome studies, have reached the unsettling conclusion that not all of these debriefing methods produce benefits. In fact, there is some evidence suggesting that these interventions may worsen the outcomes of at least some participants. Adding to this controversy, it is plausible that the preoccupation of mental health professionals with postcrisis psychopathology itself could produce some unanticipated detrimental side effects for the victimized community. "This raises a series of critical and theoretical issues because attempting to facilitate the psychological process presumed to be associated with [successful] coping may, in fact, have the reverse effect" (McFarlane, 1995b, p. 260). Rumors and fears of becoming "a psychological casualty" could exacerbate the actual victimization experience.

On the other hand, attention to individual psychological suffering may normalize and legitimize the experience. That is, educating the public regarding the fact that many victims' reactions are "normal reactions to abnormal situations" should help the victims externalize their experience, protect them from being stigmatized and marginalized, and counteract their reluctance to seek psychological help when needed. Gist and Stolz's (1982) intervention following the Hyatt Regency disaster in Kansas City was based on such a framework.

Some observers see the role of mental health professionals as providers of vocabulary to affected people to help them describe and normalize their emotional reactions such that "the community will naturally and spontaneously engage in mass group therapy to heal the emotional trauma" (Austin, 1991, p. 524; see Rubonis & Bickman, 1991, for a different view on this issue). Normalization and acceptance of psychological suffering may lead to transformations in the public view of psychopathology and psychic trauma. DeVries (1995) suggested that providing a label for prevalent psychic suffering and placing it in the formal taxonomy of traditional medicine (e.g., including PTSD in DSM-III) not only renders the victims' experiences and emotions meaningful and legitimate, but also mobilizes and justifies societal interventions and resource allocation. Thus, for the individual, the focus on psychopathology and medical taxonomy legitimizes suffering. For the society at large, it serves as a call for action. DeVries referred to this process as "a positive medicalization" but was quick to acknowledge the flip side of it such that labeling "may impede self-help by medicalizing a problem and placing responsibility on experts rather than on friends, family and kin" (p. 381).

Gist et al. (1998) warned that the preoccupation with PTSD may entice professional helpers into conceptualizing disaster as an individual, not social or communal experience, and consequently lead them astray in believing that they are responsible (and most competent) for finding solutions. Overreliance on the medical model of helping (Brickman et al., 1982), or *overhelping*, has been shown to undermine the autonomy of those affected and to beget dependence (see Jerusalem et al., 1995; Oliver-Smith, 1996). Stated simply, professionals cannot act as "surrogate frontal lobes" for communities in crisis, thereby limiting the latter's ability to mobilize their own healing resources.

Another issue, still to be debated, surrounding crisis counseling services is whether these are really the wrong services or rather, the right services provided at the wrong time. The psychological distress for many victims may emerge later than crisis counseling programs allow. Psychological interventions may be needed even more 1 or 2 months after the disaster, when the immediate recovery challenges are met by the victims at the cost of depleting their natural coping reserves and social supports. "Rather than adding to the chaos of the emergency period, mental health workers in disaster-stricken settings might direct their energies toward planning, underwriting, and advertizing later services for distressed, resource-depleted individuals" (Norris & Thompson, 1995, p. 57).

A blow to the tissues of social life

As time passes, the heightened community solidarity, fellowship, and helping must inevitably cease. The initial and short-lived period of intense affiliation, heroic sacrifice, altruism, and hopefulness, a stage somewhat ironically labeled a *honeymoon*—will soon be overtaken by a gradual disillusionment and outright realization of the harsh reality of grief, loss, and destruction (see Frederick, 1980; Raphael & Wilson, 1993). Shortly after most of the professionals, wonderful helpers, generous outsiders, and the media leave for another catastrophe, the victims discover that the struggle to rebuild their physical and social environments has only begun. It is then that the need for support and services is seen to far exceed availability. As a "rise and fall of utopia" (see Giel, 1990), an initial abundance of mutual helping gives way to an often inadvertent longer term depletion of supportive resources.

It appears that the gains based on emerging coping resources in the form of social bonding and mobilization of mutual helping and relief services are doomed to be defeated by an accelerating cycle of losses that sweeps through disaster-stricken communities. According to Hobfoll's (1988) conservation of resources theory, resource loss is difficult to prevent and is more powerful than resource gain. Disasters evoke an array of secondary stressors that continuously challenge victims and their coping at a rate faster than the progress of recovery (see Pearlin, 1989). Our reading of the literature on postdisaster exchanges of support and recovery processes leads us to believe that the initial mobilization of social support is sufficient to conquer neither the immediate nor the delayed deterioration in personal and community relationships.

Disasters break or fracture social networks instantaneously. Simply, some disasters kill people. Those who survive are often forced to abandon whatever remained of their homes and communities and to permanently relocate. Relocation can be very stressful, chaotic, and threatening (Riad & Norris, 1996). Although victims frequently find shelter among people they know, the quality of relationships with hosting families may eventually break down as conflicts emerge. Following large-scale disasters, people in charge of relocation efforts may, out of ignorance or simple expediency, disregard natural groupings traditionally existing within communities, and many victims must rely on temporary housing that seldom reflects predisaster personal relationships and neighborhood patterns (Bolin & Stanford, 1990; Erikson, 1976a; Gleser, Green, & Winget, 1981; Golec, 1983; Riad & Norris, 1996). After their return, many victims will see their neighbors and friends move away and never come back, changing the structure of social relations permanently (Hutchins & Norris, 1989).

> If I'd known that we would have to still be looking at this mess and not having friendly neighbors and having a whole different group of people [neighborhood], I wouldn't rebuilt... Well, we know that we are going to sell this in a year or two anyway and leave. (Smith & Belgrave, 1995, p. 264).

The obvious and unambiguous loss of important attachments is undeniable. At the extreme, disasters are "a blow to the tissues of social life that damages the bonds linking people together and impairs the prevailing sense of communality" (Erikson, 1976b, p. 302).

Although many disasters occur suddenly, the stress inflicted goes beyond the acute.

> I can never/dream this storm away. It was over for maybe minutes/then it was never over. (H. McHugh, *Acts of God*, 1994)

Beyond the most tragic losses distinctively wounding social networks, the progression of declining quantity and quality of personal relationships is more diffused, delayed, and not easily realized.

> The collective trauma works its way slowly and even insidiously into awareness of those who suffer from it, so it does not have the quality of suddenness normally associated with 'trauma.' (Erikson, 1976a, p. 154)

In general terms, Wheaton (1996) noted that the awareness of the aversive potential of a stressor is not a necessary condition for that stressor to have negative consequences. Possibly, the postdisaster erosion in social fabric is a most brilliant illustration of this feature of stress. Drawing on his "engineering stress model," Wheaton cast the following image: "The bridge, in effect, does not feel its rust. And the rust is not a static problem; in Neil Young's wonderful words, 'rust never sleeps.' It grows in scope and virulence, but imperceptibly' (p. 41). Disaster victims and their communities experience many cruel "aftershocks" when they come to realize how much they have lost that they didn't initially see.

Although the instant mobilization of helping behavior is a clear manifestation of received social support, the deterioration processes following disasters are manifested as declines in expectations regarding social support and companionship. Because disasters harm entire communities, the likelihood is high that potential support providers will themselves be victims and, as a result, the need for support across all affected parties frequently surpasses its availability between them. The majority of victims often face the reality of their own interpersonal networks' incapacities as they turn to those systems to fulfill needed supportive roles. To the extent that perceptions of social support are environmentally based, people residing in disaster-stricken areas may have to "revise" their expectations about how much support is currently or realistically available.

We examined (Kaniasty & Norris, 1993; Kaniasty et al., 1990) changes in perceived social support and social embeddedness following a severe and widespread flood in Kentucky. Using a prospective design that controlled for preflood perceptions of social support, we found that the expectations of support from both kin and nonkin sources declined from preflood levels. Similar erosions in perceptions of social support have been documented in other studies. Solomon, Bravo, Rubio-Stipec, and Canino (1993) showed that disaster victims experienced substantial losses in the access to emotional support. Examinations of Hurricane Hugo and Hurricane Andrew have also indicated that those events led to lower perceptions of social support availability (Norris & Kaniasty, 1996) and a general sense of loss of social support (Ironson et al., 1993). These declines in perceived availability of support from personal relationships possibly reflect the victims' "disappointments in the level of support provided by relatives and supposed friends" (Harvey et al., 1995; p. 319). However, the loss of perceived support is not just limited to *primary victims*, that is, those victims who are personally affected by disasters (see Bolin, 1985). In the Kentucky floods study, *secondary victims*—those who lived in the affected area but sustained no personal injuries or damages—reported analogous declines in their perceptions of social support. Accordingly, the decline in perceptions of help availability experienced by both primary and secondary victims could have reflected a veridical assessment of their personal networks, as well as the whole community's inability to provide support at that time. This is, of course, not surprising given the "disaster cube" analogy: Disaster is more than an individual-level event; it is a community-level event with psychological and social consequences—even for those who incur no direct losses.

Communal activities may be thwarted or restricted when physical environments, settings, and places instrumental for maintaining interpersonal contacts are damaged or destroyed. The damage to the physical environment has both symbolic and relational implications. Loss of attachments to places harms individuals and whole communities because certain physical structures with their symbolic, social, and psychological dimensions are foundations of self- and collective- identities. Again, the irony is that most people rarely appreciate beforehand the breadth and magnitude of these connections. "The holistic nature of truly profound [place] attachments means that they are only fully recognized when they have been disrupted" (Brown & Perkins, 1992, p. 283). When these nets of places, rituals, and people are destroyed, they must be grieved in ways analogous to mourning for loved ones (Oliver-Smith, 1996). Losing access to places of cultural and social significance, and the resulting loss of connections to people, undermines the community's ability to turn its "wheels of healing." Quick re-establishment of rituals and symbolic places such as "churches, mosques, trees for gathering, school yards, places for women to talk, and safe evening meeting places, should be a primary goal... This will re-establish previously learned cultural rules and reinstate members of the community in appropriate life cycle role functions" (deVries, 1995, p. 379).

Routine activities such as visiting, shopping, recreation, and attending religious services are frequently curtailed; important day-to-day opportunities to convey and preserve the sense of support and feeling of being reliably attached to valued groups may be curtailed with them. Residents of disaster-stricken areas often report decreased participation in social activities with relatives, friends, neighbors, and community organizations (Bolin, 1993; Hutchins & Norris, 1989; Solomon, 1986). Interpersonal contacts may be disrupted, not only as a direct consequence of disaster but also by the recovery efforts (Palinkas et al., 1993; Palinkas et al., 1992; Trainer & Bolin, 1976). Victims must prioritize the use of their resources and allocate their energies to the physical reconstruction process, often putting "social life" on hold. They feel alone and overwhelmed by their tasks, not daring to expend any time for social and leisure activities (Solomon, 1986). Golec (1983) noted that it took 2 years for the victims to realize that, quite suddenly, "the world got bigger" as they again began considering hobbies, vacations, and world events. Simple, but in a way courageous things such as reinstatement of soccer leagues (see Oliver-Smith, 1992) might do small wonders for traumatized communities. According to Rook (1985), the companionship domain of social support embraces taking part in communal activities, sharing with others the moments of leisure, or just simply enjoying being together. It appears that victimized communities may be denied for a long time this particular aspect of social relationships.

Interpersonal weariness, frictions, fences and toxic communities

In recent years, stress researchers have started paying greater attention to issues of relational interdependence in responding to stressful circumstances (e.g., Coyne & Gotlieb, 1996; Gottlieb & Wagner, 1991; Hobfoll, Dunahoo, Ben-Porath, & Monnier, 1994; Lyons, Mickelson, Sullivan, & Coyne, 1997). Coping with community stressors such as disasters ultimately creates a shared "energy field" wherein reactions and efforts of so many people inadvertently rub off on each other. At times, as possibly in the case of instant mobilization of helping, this field has a synergy force where the efforts of individuals are mutually beneficial and enhance one another's strengths. At other times, and likely more often, this field is a "minefield" where individuals' ways, needs, and wants collide and augment the experience of stress. Victims of stressful events that impact larger groups often subject themselves to "pressure cooker" (Hobfoll & London, 1986) or "stress contagion" phenomena (Riley & Eckenrode, 1986), whereby, paradoxically, social interactions and sharing of feelings and fears may exacerbate their symptoms of distress.

When outcomes are uncertain, rumors often thrive. Unfortunately, these rumors are primarily negative and extreme. "(R)umors that indicate gains [positive] will quickly lose momentum, whereas negative rumors will reverberate on the reactions of those hearing them and be perpetuated with fear and excitement" (Hobfoll et al., 1995, p. 149). Bromet (1995) reported that, after the Chernobyl accident, there were widespread rumors that consumption of vodka and red wine counteracted the effect of radiation. This surely did not help the strained social relations among evacuees who had already faced confusion, hostility, and rejection by their resettlement communities as well as the authorities.

Overexposure to emotional disclosures about trauma can be psychologically threatening and emotionally draining. People become weary of unending exposure to news and testimonials about the experience (e.g., Kaniasty & Norris, 1991). Eventually, the whole community may become saturated with stories of and feelings about the event. Consequently, residents in disaster-stricken communities may begin to downplay or reject the importance of revealed emotions and even escape interacting (see Coyne, Wortman, & Lehman, 1988).

Pennebaker and Harber (1993) proposed a stage model of collective coping that juxtaposes peoples' tendencies to think and talk about the event and their needs to protect the self or escape from "oversharing" of the trauma. They observed that, some time following the Loma Prieta earthquake, people in affected areas greatly reduced their interest in hearing other victims' stories and appeared to be "erecting barriers to prohibit others from bringing up the topic." Four weeks after the disaster, tee-shirts appeared on the streets that read "Thank you for not sharing your earthquake experience" (Pennebaker & Harber, 1993, p. 133).

A paradox looms: Whereas victims want and need to be listened to, they and others may not necessarily wish to be the listeners. Those who need to talk and seek help in validating their subjective realities of trauma risk disapproval. Victims of Hurricane Andrew interviewed by Smith and Belgrave (1995) eloquently described these struggles: "I can't cry in front of my husband because he can't take it. I don't care if people don't want to talk about it at all. That's all I think about" (p. 258). "We were in the bathroom and talking about the hurricane, and this one lady said, 'I can't believe it! Six weeks after the storm, they are still talking about it'" (p. 258).

Research shows that sharing traumatic experiences with respectful and supportive others aids people in discovering the meaning of the experience, gaining control over their emotions, and rebuilding shattered assumptions about the world (see Greenberg, 1995; Janoff-Bulman, 1992; Pennebaker, 1990). Interaction with people who are insensitive and callous impedes that process. A theoretical framework presented by Lepore, Silver, Wortman, and Wayment (1996) captures well the benefits and the costs of disclosing to others one's stress-related thoughts and feelings. According to their social-cognitive-processing model, supportive social responses to victims' disclosures help to blunt the distress associated with victimization cognitions and counteract victims' tendencies to avoid confronting trauma-related thoughts. As a result of these supportive contacts, a cognitive processing of the experience (e.g., contemplation, reappraisal, acceptance) is facilitated. In contrast, unsupportive and negative social responses to victims' disclosures lead to premature inhibition and increased avoidance of trauma-related thoughts and memories. Lepore et al. showed that problematic social interactions interfere with cognitive processing and contribute to increases in psychological distress. Silver and Holman (1999) examined the positive and negative qualities of social interactions following the 1993 Southern California firestorms and again found that unsupported interactions (e.g. conflicts) hindered cognitive processing of trauma experience.

Disasters' influence on personal and communal relationships "ripples outward." Ironically, as time passes from the hour of impact, more and more people become affected. Many alliances and partnerships are discovered to be "blown away by the wind" (Smith & Belgrave, 1995). Families residing in areas affected by disasters are subjected to additional stressors that may include the psychological problems of loved ones and result in interpersonal burdens. Many researchers have observed that, among families victimized by disasters, psychological difficulties experienced by one of the members had a tendency to grate on others, augmenting the adverse effect of the disaster on the whole family (see Green & Solomon, 1995; McFarlane, 1995b).

McFarlane, Policansky, and Irwin (1987), in their study of the Ash Wednesday bushfires, suggested that a mother's response to disaster was a better predictor of symptomatology in children than was a child's direct exposure to the fires. A survivor of the Buffalo Creek flood said: "My kids seem to be doing all right, but when I go to pieces now they go to pieces, too" (Lifton & Olson, 1976, p. 15). Loss of familiarity with physical and social environs, continuous tension, lack of personal resolution, and disagreements about the meaning and consequences of the event may incite family or marital distress and disharmony (Bolin, 1982; Gleser et al., 1981; Haas, Kates, & Bowden, 1977; Harvey et al., 1995; Lifton & Olson, 1976; Palinkas et al., 1993; Solomon, 1986).

Norris and Uhl (1993) showed that Hurricane Hugo led to increases in marital stress, parenting stress, and filial (caretaking) stress. A victim of the 1993 Midwest floods disclosed that the disaster had severely undermined her relationship with her spouse, a consequence that was not altogether unheard of in the community: "We are constantly fighting and thinking of separating. Some of my relatives and friends who were hit hard also have gotten divorces" (Harvey et al., 1995, p. 328). In Buffalo Creek, "wives and husbands discovered that they did not know how to nourish one another, make decisions, or even engage in satisfactory conversations when the community was no longer there to provide a context and set a rhythm" (Erikson, 1976b, p. 304). A few studies of postdisaster social functioning have reported increases in the number of divorces, annulments, alcohol-related disputes, and domestic violence (e.g., Adams & Adams, 1984; Bromet, 1995; Erikson, 1976a; Hall & Landreth, 1975; Palinkas et al., 1993).

Reconstruction efforts themselves can bring about feelings of mistrust, apprehensiveness, and divisiveness. Steinglass and Gerrity (1990) speculated that even swift and effective relief efforts can backfire if directed at assisting a small and clearly identifiable group of victims. They noted that in one tornado site "superbly" performed recovery efforts "may well have inadvertently contributed to a growing estrangement of disaster-impacted families from the rest of the community" (p. 1762). Issues surrounding disaster relief and compensation can also prove extremely contentious. Newly acquired material "wealth" as a result of clean-up business, insurance, or settlement money may raise separating barriers and instill envy and animosities (e.g., Bromet, 1995; Drabek, 1986; Oliver-Smith, 1996; Palinkas et al., 1993). "Sure wish I'd been flooded out: new home, new furniture, new stereo. Must be nice" (Golec, 1983). The "warm glow of benevolence" fades when some of the victims discover that they were left out by compensation programs or that the financial settlements were not sufficient to cover the losses. Others find themselves taken advantage of by the "wonderful helpers." Words like "vultures, profiteer, money-grabber and scavenger were added to the lexicon of disaster terminology" to describe the experience of what Golec labeled "a secondary disaster" (Golec, 1983, p. 264–265).

Some parts of the community may recover sooner than others. More fortunate victims may want to move on with their lives and leave behind those still immersed in the experience. As the majority of victims converge on a smooth and trouble-free recovery, there may be no time or resources left to rescue those entrapped by "secondary victimization." At that point, their trouble may become private issues, private struggles. Thus, ironically, this progression toward recovery removes some of the victims from the collective coping enterprise, leaving them alone, isolated, and defeated. All told, these images are not compatible with the portrayals of omnipotent altruistic communities.

"When the Exxon Valdez ran aground in Prince William Sound, it spilled oil into a social as well as a natural environment" (Palinkas et al., 1993, p. 11). This statement succinctly articulates the gist of empirical observations regarding psychosocial consequences of technological disasters. Although our prior discussion made it clear that disasters in general have pernicious effects on interpersonal dynamics, technological catastrophes warrant additional comments because they do not necessarily elicit an urgent and unequivocal desire for unified communal coping and helping. Where victims of many collective upheavals, and the victims of natural disasters in particular, are afforded (in a paradoxical way) the "privilege" of both the emergence and deterioration of the "cohesive helping collectives," the persons affected by technological and other human-made disasters are more likely to experience *just* deterioration of social support and erosion of their sense of community.

Besides the most salient distinction of origin—nature (God) versus technology (human)—there are many important differences between natural and technological disasters (see Baum, Fleming, & Davidson, 1983; Berren, Santiago, Beigel, & Timmons, 1989; Bolin, 1993). The impact of natural disasters is usually immediate, direct, and clearly visible, whereas the impact of technological disasters is quite frequently slowly evolving, uncertain, and not readily perceptible. Technological emergencies, such as nuclear power plant accidents and chemical or toxic waste spills "contaminate rather than merely damage" (Erikson, 1991, p. 80; see also Edelstein, 1988). Cuthbertson and Nigg (1987) noted that postdisaster altruistic communities are unlikely to develop following technological emergencies because of these hazards' ambiguity, invisibility and the lack of a clearly identifiable low point ("worst is over").

The very first issue faced by the people residing in afflicted areas is "Who are the true victims?" Residents, local authorities, and those considered responsible for the hazard often bitterly debate the severity of the actual threat or the extent of harm. Residents of affected areas divide into antagonistic factions, and those claiming to be victimized or wronged may be rejected, stigmatized, and discriminated against. Most naturally, those who perceive themselves as victimized and those who see no harm or deny it try to empower themselves by forming competing social circles that fuel the process of community polarization and interpersonal conflict.

Bowler, Mergler, Huel, and Cone (1994) observed such dynamics in a study of a community contaminated by a railroad chemical spill of thousands of gallons of toxic substance. The majority of interviewed residents (69%) believed that the community was hurtfully divided between those who felt they suffered from the spill and others who claimed they did not experience any adverse consequences. Moreover, a large number of respondents (36%) reported "having personally suffered from having friends and neighbors who felt that the spill should not create a problem for them" (p. 618). Those respondents who were distraught by the split of the community were more symptomatic, and the entire "spill sample" reported less perceived social support than the control group.

"People who claim to be contaminated are likely to be treated as contagious and routinely placed outside the boundaries of their emotional community" (Kroll-Smith & Couch, 1993, p. 83). A resident of Centralia, Pennsylvania, a small mining community that after a lingering underground mine fire was finally deemed uninhabitable, vividly described such frictions: "The fire has split us up, it has torn us apart, you know—divided us. We're divided this and that way. We're worse than a pie cut into eight pieces" (Kroll-Smith & Couch, 1990, p. 5). Again, the majority of residents of that community reported that interpersonal conflicts caused by the event were more stressful than the fire itself.

"Man-made disasters involve the externalization of evil and responsibility into those to blame" (McFarlane, 1995b). Thus technological disasters are frequently followed by lasting disputes and litigation concerning the allocation of blame for the calamity and issues revolving around restitution mechanisms. On the one hand, such antagonisms further separate, fragment, and politicize the community (Bolin, 1993; Edelstein, 1988). On the other hand, litigation, which is usually regarded as an additional burden and a potential contributor to the "secondary disaster," could also serve as a source of social support (Bowler et al., 1994). In some cases, seeking redress by engaging in legal actions might help victims to form interpersonal units validating their perceptions of reality and providing them with a sense of shared fate. Unfortunately, these collateral benefits are just minuscule particles in the depths of poisonous social disintegration. Numerous studies have documented that victims of technological catastrophes experience high levels of anger, alienation, suspicion and mistrust of others, loneliness, and isolation (see Baum, 1987; Bowler et al., 1994; Bromet, 1989; Cuthbertson & Nigg, 1987; Edelstein, 1988; Green, Lindy, & Grace, 1994; Kroll-Smith & Couch, 1993; Palinkas et al., 1992; Palinkas et al., 1993). The conflicted interpersonal dynamics observed in the aftermath of technological hazards are apparently "toxic" in their own way.

The distinction between technological and natural disasters has been fading. More and more, natural disasters are not perceived as neutral acts of nature or God. Rochford and Blocker (1991) have shown how a natural disaster (a 1986 Tulsa flood) instigated collective protest and conflict because victims appraised the event as *not* solely outside human control. One of the residents in the flooded areas stated in the protest: "It was man-made. God provided the rains but he didn't open the flood gates. Those guys at the Corps [of Engineers] did that" (p. 173). Victimized communities begin to see natural disasters as "unnatural" in origin and, thus, controllable. When inquiries into causal factors move away from *nature* toward *human* agents, community divisions and "cycles of protest" become even more likely to surface (Rochford & Blocker, 1991). Advances in technological control over the forces of nature may eventually change the way people assess and react collectively to so called natural disasters:

> Indeed, the American experience of the past three decades seems to be one wherein God is losing ground very rapidly. Increasingly, disaster victims engage in a blame assignation process. And when a culprit has been identified, their interpretations of the event and its impacts on them and those involved in recovery may reflect processes that do not occur when they view their plight as 'God's doing' (Drabek, 1986, p.201)

Status quo vs. opportunities for social change

Regardless of their origins, disasters vividly expose and augment preexisting social inequalities along the lines of ethnicity, race, and socioeconomic status. Often forceful public emphasis on "getting back to the way things were before" cannot be accepted as a viable option for some of the victims because it would simply mean a "return" to their disadvantaged position. Bolin and Stanford (1990) reported that in some communities damaged by the Loma Prieta earthquake, the process of allocation of temporary housing to victims inspired allegations of racism, political and cultural discrimination, and further marginalization of minorities, elderly, and the poor. This, in turn, led to organized demands for the improvement of political processes and existing social arrangements.

According to Rich, Edelstein, Hallman, and Wandersman (1995), some of the social predicaments of catastrophes and disasters we have described contain, paradoxically, "the seeds for empowerment" because they may provide grounds for an "enabling response" (see also Edelstein, 1988).

> When citizens come together to confront a crisis, their collective efforts may influence institutions and processes in which they had no prior leverage. As a result of their isolation from others in the community and their inability to rely on traditional institutions, they may develop a sense of common purpose among themselves and create new institutions specifically to meet the challenge. (p. 664)

Rich et al. suggested that broad-based community partnership and collaboration could minimize the disempowering impact of stressor, as well as prevent hazards (mainly technological) from developing. Funneling social energies that emerge following the impact of hazards and disasters into constructive activism is an enormous task and needs to be investigated. Literature provides examples of such processes, suggesting that disasters provide venues for the entrance of new groups into the community power structures (see Aronoff & Gunter, 1992; Bolin & Stanford, 1989; Couto, 1989; Gibbs, 1982; Oliver-Smith, 1996; Rich et al., 1995). Although many, if not most, communities stricken by disasters do show terrific resilience, and, in the end, recover, this does not necessarily mean that they were ultimately empowered (e.g., Aronoff & Gunter, 1992). Even if they do reach higher planes of communal beneficence, success in coping cannot blunt the costs incurred in the experience.

At all societal levels, disasters may create opportunities for empowerment and social change, but simultaneous pressures for political consensus and return to the "status quo" may antagonize communities, states, and nations even further (see Stallings, 1988). Disasters may challenge beliefs in the moral order of the society and its ethical standards (see Giel, 1990; Hobfoll et al., 1995; Oliver-Smith, 1996). Disasters may cause radical shifts in fundamental beliefs and philosophical outlooks. Disasters may overthrow aristocracies, dictatorships, and democracies.

ONE WAY TO PIECE THINGS TOGETHER

We hope that the six facets of the "disaster cube" we selectively presented in this chapter told a balanced story about disaster. We aimed at balance because we wanted to show the interdependence of many facets of the experience—interdependence of the individual and the community, inter-dependence of gains and losses. In the final analysis, it is obvious that the experience of disasters is packed with the dynamic mixture of seemingly paradoxical processes of mobilization and deterioration of individual and communal coping resources. But which aspect does dominate? It may even be naive to ask this question, but ultimately what are the end consequences of disaster?

One way to address this issue is to return to the question of whether disaster engendered therapeutic communities can protect individuals from experiencing adverse psychological consequences. Surprisingly, despite general acceptance in the popular and scientific literature of the concept of a "postdisaster altruistic community," not many empirical studies have accepted the challenge to address this question directly. In fact, on the basis of our reading of the available research, we believe that the distress mitigating function of the altruistic community has primarily been inferred from null findings. Disasters have sometimes been found to have no adverse or very modest and time-limited effects on psychological health. Thus it is not at all unusual for the postdisaster phase of altruism to be offered as if *the explanation* for why these disasters caused little or no long-term negative consequences.

Altruistic or therapeutic communities do emerge in the aftermath of many collective catastrophes with their distinguishing characteristics of solidarity, togetherness, and reciprocity. Yet, even in the best of circumstances, they are not able to meet all the community needs. Their patterns of exceptions and limitations must not be ignored. Many victims are excluded from, or overlooked by, helping communities and recovery programs, whereas others have a clear advantage in securing postdisaster relief. Fellowship and consensus are infrequent features of the social milieu following technological hazards and disasters. Most important of all, long before the cycles of losses stop, the intensified levels of mutual support and concern will inescapably be depleted.

On the basis of our studies with victims of floods and hurricanes, we developed a conceptual model that attempts to capture both the complexities of social functioning in the aftermath of community stress and its impact on victims' psychological well-being. Admittedly, this theoretical framework, labeled *social support deterioration deterrence model* (Kaniasty & Norris, 1997; Norris & Kaniasty, 1996), is limited in scope because it deals mainly with interpersonal transactions as manifested by various facets of postdisaster social support. Yet, this model is very relevant to this discussion because it pertains to the question: Can participation in the emergent helping community protect victims against the deleterious impact of disaster stress? The social support deterioration deterrence model directly addresses the issue of whether postdisaster deterioration of social support is inevitable, or if it can be counteracted by the gains of coping resources mobilized via postcrisis mutual helping and social bonding.

In a nutshell, the model speaks to both the instantaneous *mobilization* of received support (i.e., actual receipt of help) and lingering *deterioration* of perceived support and social embeddedness (i.e., the belief that support would be available if needed; quality and type of relationships with other people). The explicit premise of this model (see Figure 2) is that disaster exerts a direct adverse impact on psychological health (*Direct Impact, path A*). The stress that challenges victims of disasters is multifaceted. It often involves immediate trauma arising from exposure to death and injury (horror), extreme physical force (terror), and life-threatening situations. The stress of disasters entails destruction of goods and possessions of substantial monetary value, as well as keepsakes of symbolic and emotional significance. Disasters may diminish victims' sense of self-esteem, feelings of security, and beliefs in justice. Jointly or singularly, all these facets of disaster stress threaten and shatter valued resources needed to sustain physical and psychological health. Not surprisingly then, research has documented reliable increases in physical and psychological symptomatology following disasters (for reviews, see, e.g., Baum, 1987; Freedy, Kilpatrick, & Resnick, 1993; Green & Solomon, 1995; Raphael & Wilson, 1993; Rubonis & Bickman, 1991; see also chapter 3). For most victims, these negative consequences will dissipate within a year or two (e.g., Norris, Phifer, & Kaniasty, 1994; Thompson, Norris, & Hanacek, 1993) but

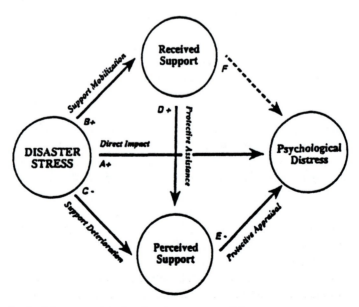

Figure 2 Social support deterioration deterrence model.

for some victims, they may become more lasting (e.g., Green et al., 1990; Green, 1995).

To cope with disaster stress, victims need all the support they can get. Immediately after impact, most victims of disaster are provided with high levels of help. The process of *support mobilization* (path B) is governed, however, by various norms and rules of inclusion and exclusion. Most importantly, the initial rush of spontaneous helping inevitably ceases long before the stress of disaster is over. It is at that time that victims discover that their losses and psychological trauma are accompanied by social disruption, interpersonal conflict, and a depletion of available support. This process of *support deterioration* (path C) is one way through which disasters indirectly exert their detrimental impact on psychological well-being (paths C and E).

We must take both the mobilization and deterioration processes into account to understand psychological adaptation to disasters. However, adequately mobilized received support should be positively associated with perceptions of support availability (Protective Assistance, path D) and could serve to counter or reduce the deterioration in perceived support otherwise seen. Through this process of *deterioration deterrence* (paths B and D), the mobilization of received support indirectly affects mental health (paths B, D, and E) by preserving perceptions of social support. Ultimately, the sense of being reliably connected to others, perceived social support, serves its usual protective role (Protective Appraisal, path E).

Our analyses (Norris & Kaniasty, 1996) of data collected 12 and 24 months following Hurricane Hugo and 6 and 28 months following Hurricane Andrew provided strong evidence for the hypothesized model. Most generally, perceived support mediated the long-term effects on psychological distress of both disaster stress and postdisaster received support. More specifically, although disaster stress led to deterioration of perceived support, the *total* effects of disaster on perceived support were *less severe than they might have been* because the stress of disaster was positively associated with received support. Received support was, in turn, positively associated with ensuing beliefs regarding the perceived availability of support. Clearly, postevent deterioration of social support is not inevitable. When victims receive high levels of help following a disaster, they appear to be protected against a *salient* erosion in their evaluations of support availability.

The language of our conclusions is extremely important. Mobilization of support protected only against "salient" losses in the sense of postdisaster social support and, consequently, the overall effect of disaster was "less severe than it might have been." In other words, we showed that disasters decrease perceived support, but that effect would have been substantially worse if disasters had not also led to a mobilization of received support.

Being protected from "the worst" is a blessing, but it should not obscure the fact that experiencing the "less negative" is not the same as experiencing the positive.

Our findings are consistent with a small set of studies that have shown mobilization of support and postdisaster cohesion in some personal relationships to benefit psychological functioning of the victims. Bolin (1982) and Bolin and Bolton (1986) have observed that primary group aid facilitated emotional recovery from various disasters. Drabek and Key (1984) documented similar effects in their analysis of social functioning 3 years after the Topeka tornado. Controlling for the degree of damage, tornado victims who received help from friends or relatives, compared with those who did not, reported being less alienated, healthier, happier in their marriages, and more involved in activities with friends, churches, or social organizations. More recently, Harvey et al. (1995) presented a series of victim testimonials, and close to half emphasized resilience, optimism, and social bonding. Tobin and Ollenburger (1996) reported that those victims of the 1993 Midwest floods who where able to identify positive outcomes of that experience (e.g., being involved with the community, getting closer to family, making new friends, being helped and helping others) were found to exhibit less severe levels of post-traumatic stress.

However, it is our belief that neither our studies nor (known to us) the research of others have yet provided evidence for the long-term postdisaster interpersonal and communal gains brought about by altruistic communities. Accounts of "good news about disasters" (Taylor, 1977) noting clear enrichments of social and community relations strike us more as vivid exceptions than as rule. At most, the available data suggest only that receiving help and experiencing a unifying sense of collective fate is supportive in the aftermath of disaster, that is, victims who received high levels of support fared better. These "favored," even if many, are not the only victims. (Paradoxically, if the altruistic community was truly all-encompassing, there would not be sufficient variability in received support to show its beneficial effect). And, finally, the same evidence that suggests this resilience also shows clearly that the initial emergence of coping resources is not powerful enough to prevent the rending of the social fabric of victimized communities.

CONCLUSION

We cannot afford to stand on the sidelines and be respectful, encouraging, yet uninvolved observers. The romantic images of genuine unity that societies can drum up in times of crisis must not obliterate the images of lasting deterioration in the quality of victims' lives, relationships, and communities. How can we understand these processes and help those who face them if we let go of these images? The extent of human suffering and the politics of trauma call for professionals to become advocates for the victims (Herman, 1992; McFarlane, 1995a). To advocate means to speak, plead, and argue in favor of. Still, whether as community activists, political organizers, professional helpers, academicians, or researchers, we need to do more than to speak *for* them—we must speak *with* them. If we collaborate, we can empower both the sufferers and the helpers. We should "create a partnership with individuals in crisis, enabling us to take a step together out of this world of trauma" (deVries, 1995, p. 389).

REFERENCES

Adams, P., & Adams, G. (1984). Mount St. Helen ashfall: Evidence for a disaster stress reaction. *American Psychologist, 39*, 252–260.

Aronoff, M., & Gunter, V. (1992). Defining disaster: Local constructions for recovery in the aftermath of chemical contamination. *Social Problems, 39*, 345–365.

Austin, L. (1991). In the wake of Hugo: The role of the psychiatrist. *Psychiatric Annals, 21*, 520–524.

Barrera, M. (1986). Distinctions between social support concepts, measures, and models. *American Journal of Community Psychology, 14*, 413–445.

Barton, A. M. (1969). *Communities in disaster*. Garden City, NJ: Doubleday.

Baum, A. (1987). Toxins, technology, and natural disasters. In G. VandenBos & B. Bryant (Eds.), *Cataclysms, crises, and catastrophes: Psychology in action* (pp. 9–51). Washington, DC: American Psychological Association.

Baum, A., Fleming, R., & Davidson, L. (1983). Natural disasters and technological catastrophe. *Environment and Behavior, 15*, 333–354.

Berren, M. R., Santiago, J. M., Beigel, A., & Timmons S. A. (1989). A classification scheme for disasters. In R. Gist & B. Lubin (Eds.), *Psychological aspects of disaster* (pp. 40–58). New York: Wiley.

Bolin, R. (1982). *Long-term family recovery from disaster*. Boulder: University of Colorado.

Bolin, R. (1985). Disaster characteristics and psychosocial impacts. In B. T. Sowder (Ed.), *Disasters and mental health: Selected contemporary perspectives* (pp. 2–28). Rockville, MD: National Institute of Mental Health.

Bolin, R. (1989). Natural disasters. In R. Gist & B. Lubin (Eds.), *Psychological aspects of disaster* (pp. 61–85). New York: Wiley.

Bolin, R. (1993). Natural and technological disasters: Evidence of psychopathology. In A-M. Ghadirian & H. E. Lehmann (Eds.), *Environment and psychopathology* (pp. 121–140). New York: Springer.

Bolin, R., & Bolton, P. (1986) *Race, religion, and ethnicity in disaster recovery*. Boulder: University of Colorado.

Bolin, R., & Stanford, L. (1990). Shelter and housing issues in Santa Cruz County. In R. Bolin (Ed.), *The Loma Prieta earthquake: Studies of short-term impacts* (pp. 99–108). Boulder: University of Colorado.

Bowler, R. M., Mergler, D., Huel, G., & Cone, J. E. (1994). Psychological, psychosocial and psychophysiological sequelae in a community affected by a railroad chemical disaster. *Journal of Traumatic Stress, 7*, 601–624.

Butcher, J. N., & Dunn, L. A. (1989). Human responses and treatment needs in airline disasters. In R. Gist & B. Lubin (Eds.), *Psychological aspects of disaster* (pp. 86–119). New York: Wiley.

Brickman, P., Rabinowitz, V., Karuza, J., Coates, D., Cohn, E., & Kidder, L. (1982). Models of helping and coping. *American Psychologist, 37*, 368–384.

Bromet, E. J. (1989). The nature and effects of technological failures. In R. Gist & B. Lubin (Eds.), *Psychological aspects of disaster* (pp. 120–139). New York: Wiley.

Bromet, E. J. (1995). Methodological issues in designing research on community-wide disasters with special reference to Chernobyl. In S. E. Hobfoll & M. W. deVries (Eds.), *Extreme stress and communities: Impact and intervention* (pp. 307–324). Dordrecht, The Netherlands: Kluwer.

Brown, B. B., & Perkins, D. D. (1992). Disruptions in place attachment. In I. Altman & S. Low (Eds.), *Place attachment* (pp. 279–304). New York: Plenum Press.

Cohn, R. M. (1978). The effect of employment status change on self-attitudes. *Social Psychology, 41*, 81–93.

Comfort, L. K. (1990). Turning conflict into cooperation: Organizational designs for community response in disasters. *International Journal of Mental Health, 19*, 89–108.

Couto, R. A. (1989). Catastrophe and community empowerment: The group formulation of Aberfan's survivors. *Journal of Community Psychology, 17*, 236–248.

Coyne, J. C., & Gotlieb, B. (1996). The mismeasure of coping by checklist. *Journal of Personality, 64*, 959–991.

Coyne, J. C., Wortman, C. B., & Lehman, D. R. (1988). The other side of support: Emotional overinvolvement and miscarried helping. In B. H. Gottlieb (Ed.), *Social support: Formats, processes, and effects* (pp. 305–330). Newbury Park, CA: Sage.

Cuthbertson, B., & Nigg, J. (1987). Technological disaster and the nontherapeutic community: A question of true victimization. *Environment and Behavior, 19*, 462–483.

deVries, M. W. (1995). Culture, community and catastrophe: Issues in understanding communities under difficult conditions. In S. E. Hobfoll & M. W. deVries (Eds.), *Extreme stress and communities: Impact and intervention* (pp. 375–393). Dordrecht, The Netherlands: Kluwer.

Drabek, T. E. (1986). *Human system responses to disaster*. New York: Springer-Verlag.

Drabek, T. E., & Key, W. M. (1984). *Conquering disaster: Family recovery and long-term consequences*. New York: Irvington Publishers.

Dunkel-Schetter, C., Folkman, S., & Lazarus, R. S. (1987). Correlates of social support receipt. *Journal of Personality and Social Psychology, 52*, 71–80.

Dynes, R. R., & Drabek, T. E. (1994). The structure of disaster research: Its policy and disciplinary implications. *International Journal of Mass Emergencies and Disasters, 12*, 5–23.

Eckenrode, J. (Ed.). (1991). *The social context of coping*. New York: Plenum Press.

Eckenrode, J., & Wethington, E. (1990). The process and outcome of mobilizing social support. In S. Duck and R. Silver (Eds.), *Personal relationships and social support* (pp. 83–103). London: Sage.

Edelstein, M. R. (1988). *Contaminated communities: The social and psychological impacts of residential toxic exposure* Boulder, CO: Westview.

Eranen, L., & Liebkind, K. (1993). Coping with disaster: The helping behavior of communities and individuals. In J. P. Wilson & B. Raphael (Eds.). *International handbook of traumatic stress syndromes* (pp. 957–964). New York: Plenum Press.

Erikson, K. (1976a). *Everything in its path*, New York: Simon & Schuster.

Erikson, K. (1976b). Loss of communality at Buffalo Creek. *American Journal of Psychiatry, 133*, 302–305.

Erikson, K. (1991). A new species of trouble. In S. R. Couch & J. S. Kroll-Smith (Eds.), *Communities at risk: Collective responses to technological hazards* (pp. 11–30). New York: Peter Lang.

Feldman, J. A. (1981). A connectionist model of visual memory. In G. E. Hilton & J. A. Anderson (Eds.), *Parallel models of associative memory* (pp. 49–81). Hillsdale, NJ: Erlbaum.

Foa, E. B., & Meadows, E. A. (1997). Psychological treatments for posttraumatic stress disorder. A critical review. *Annual Reviews of Psychology*, *48*, 449–480.

Frederick, C. (1980). Effects of natural vs. human-induced violence upon victims. *Evaluation and Change*. (Special Issue), 71–75.

Freedy, J. R., & Hobfoll, S. E. (1995). *Traumatic stress: From theory to practice*. New York: Plenum Press.

Freedy, J. R., Kilpatrick, D., & Resnick, H. (1993). Natural disasters and mental health. *Journal of Social Behavior and Personality*, *8(5)*, 49–104.

Freedy, J. R., Shaw, D., Jarrell, M., & Masters, C. (1992). Toward an understanding of the psychological impact of natural disasters: An application of the Conservation of Resources Stress Model. *Journal of Traumatic Stress*, *5*, 441–454.

Fritz, C. E. (1961). Disasters. In R. K. Merton & R. A. Nisbet (Eds.), *Contemporary social problems* (pp. 651–694). New York: Harcourt.

Gibbs, L. (1982). Community response to an emergency situation: Psychological destruction and the Love Canal. *American Journal of Community Psychology*, *11*, 116–125.

Giel, R. (1990). Psychosocial process in disasters. *International Journal of Mental Health*, *19*, 7–20.

Gist, R., & Lubin, B. (Eds.). (1989). *Psychological aspects of disaster*. New York: Wiley.

Gist, R., Lubin, B., & Redburn, B. G. (1998). Psychological, ecological, and community perspective on disaster response. *Journal of Personal and Interpersonal Loss*, *3*, 25–51.

Gist, R., & Stolz, S. B. (1982). Mental health promotion and the media: Community response to the Kansas City hotel disaster. *American Psychologist*, *37*, 1136–1139.

Gleser, G. C., Green, B. L., & Winget, C. N. (1981). *Prolonged psychological effects of disaster: A study of Buffalo Creek*. New York: Academic Press.

Golec, J. A. (1983). A contextual approach to the social psychological study of disaster recovery. *International Journal of Mass Emergencies and Disaster*, 255–276.

Gottlieb, B. H., & Wagner, F. (1991). Stress and support precesses in close relationships. In J. Eckenrode (Ed.), *The social context of coping* (pp. 165–188). New York: Plenum Press

Green, B. L. (1995). Long-term consequences of disasters. In S. E. Hobfoll & M. W. deVries (Eds.), *Extreme stress and communities: Impact and intervention* (pp. 307–324). Dordrecht, The Netherlands: Kluwer.

Green, B. L., Lindy, J., & Grace, M. (1994). Psychological effects of toxic contamination. In R. Ursano, B. McCaughey, & C. Fullerton (Eds.), *Individual and community responses to trauma and disaster: The structure of human chaos* (pp. 154–176). Cambridge, England: Cambridge University Press.

Green, B. L., Lindy, J., Grace, M., Gleser, G., Leonard, A., Korol, M., & Winget, C. (1990). Buffalo Creek survivors in the second decade: Stability of stress symptoms. *American Journal of Orthopsychiatry*, *60*, 43–54.

Green, B. L., & Solomon, S. D. (1995). The mental health impact of natural and technological disasters. In J. R. Freedy and S. E. Hobfoll (Eds.), *Traumatic stress: From theory to practice* (pp. 163–180). New York: Plenum Press.

Greenberg, M. A. (1995). Cognitive processing of trauma: The role of intrusive thoughts and reappraisals. *Journal of Applied Social Psychology*, *14*, 1262–1296.

Haas, J., Kates, R., & Bowden, M. (Eds.). (1977). *Reconstruction following disaster*. Cambridge, MA: MIT Press.

Haines, V. A., Hurlbert, J. S., & Beggs, J. J. (1996). Exploring the determinants of support provision: Provider characteristics, personal networks, community context, and support following life events. *Journal of Health and Social Behavior*, *37*, 252–264.

Hall, P., & Landreth, P. (1975). Assessing some long term consequences of a natural disaster. *Mass Emergencies*, *1*, 55–61.

Harvey, J., Stein, S., Olsen, N., Roberts, R., Lutgendorf, S., & Ho, J. (1995). Narratives of loss and recovery from a natural disaster. *Journal of Social Behavior and Personality*, *10*, 313–330.

Herman, J. (1992). *Trauma and recovery*. New York: Basic Books.

Hobfoll, S. E. (1988). *The ecology of stress*. New York: Hemisphere.

Hobfoll, S. E., Briggs, S., & Wells, J. (1995). Community stress and resources: Actions and reactions. In S. E. Hobfoll & M. W. deVries (Eds.), *Extreme stress and communities: Impact and intervention* (pp. 137–158). Dordrecht, The Netherlands: Kluwer.

Hobfoll, S. E., & deVries, M. W. (Eds.) (1995). *Extreme stress and communities: Impact and intervention*. Dordrecht, The Netherlands: Kluwer.

Hobfoll, S. E., Dunahoo, C., Ben-Porath, Y., & Monnier, J. (1994). Gender and coping : The dual-axis model of coping. *American Journal of Community Psychology, 22*, 49–82.

Hobfoll, S. E., Dunahoo, C., & Monnier, J. (1995b). Conservation of resources and traumatic stress. In J. R. Freedy & S. E. Hobfoll (Eds.), *Traumatic stress: From theory to practice* (pp. 29–48). New York: Plenum Press.

Hobfoll, S. E., & Lerman, M. (1989). Predicting receipt of social support: A longitudinal study of parents' reactions to their child's illness. *Health Psychology, 8*, 61–77.

Hobfoll, S. E., & London, P. (1986). The relationship of self-concept and social support to emotional distress among women during war. *Journal of Social and Clinical Psychology, 12*, 87–100.

House, J., Umberson, D., & Landis, K. (1988). Structures and processes of social support. *Annual Review of Sociology, 14*, 293–318.

Hutchins, G., & Norris, F. H. (1989). Life change in the disaster recovery period. *Environment and Behavior, 21*, 33–56.

Ironson, G., et al. (1993, August). *Social support, neuroendocrine, and immune functioning during Hurricane Andrew*. Paper presented at the 101th annual convention of American Psychological Association, Toronto, Canada.

Janoff-Bulman, R. (1992). *Shattered assumptions: Towards a new psychology of trauma*. New York: Free Press.

Jemmott, J. B., III, Ditto, P. H., & Croyle, R. T. (1986). Judging health status: Effects of perceived prevalence and personal relevance. *Journal of Personality and Social Psychology, 50*, 899–905.

Jerusalem, M., Kaniasty, K., Lehman, D., Ritter, C., & Turnbull, G. (1995). Individual and community stress: Integration of approaches at different levels. In S. E. Hobfoll and M. W. deVries (Eds.). *Extreme stress and communities: Impact and intervention* (pp. 105–129). Dordrecht, The Netherlands: Kluwer.

Kaniasty, K., & Norris, F. (1991). Some psychological consequences of the Persian Gulf War on the American people: An empirical study. *Contemporary Social Psychology, 15*, 121–126.

Kaniasty, K., & Norris, F. (1992). Social support and victims of crime: Matching event, support, and outcome. *American Journal of Community Psychology, 20*, 211–241.

Kaniasty, K., & Norris, F. (1993). A test of the support deterioration model in the context of natural disaster. *Journal of Personality and Social Psychology, 64*, 395–408.

Kaniasty, K., & Norris, F. (1995). In search of altruistic community: Patterns of social support mobilization following Hurricane Hugo. *American Journal of Community Psychology, 23*, 447–477.

Kaniasty, K., & Norris, F. (1997). Social support dynamics in adjustment to disasters. In S. Duck (Ed.), *Handbook of personal relationships* (2nd ed.,), (pp. 595–619). London, England: Wiley.

Kaniasty, K., Norris, F., & Murrell, S. A. (1990). Received and perceived social support following natural disaster. *Journal of Applied Social Psychology, 20*, 85–114.

Kaplan, H. B. (1996). *Psychosocial stress: Perspectives on structure, theory, life-course, and methods*. San Diego, CA: Academic Press.

Kilijanek, T., & Drabek, T. E. (1979). Assessing long-term impacts of a natural disaster: A focus on the elderly. *The Gerontologist, 19*, 555–566.

Kroll-Smith, J. S., & Couch, S. (1990). *The real disaster is above ground: A mine fire and social conflict.* Lexington: University Press of Kentucky.

Kroll-Smith, J. S., & Couch, S. (1993). Technological hazards: Social responses as traumatic stressors. In J. P. Wilson & B. Raphael (Eds.), *International handbook of traumatic stress syndromes* (pp. 79–91). New York: Plenum Press.

Kutak, R. I. (1938). The sociology of crises: The Louisville flood of 1937. *Social Forces, 16,* 66–72.

Lepore, S. J., Silver, R. C., Wortman, C. B., & Wayment, H. (1996). Social constraints, intrusive thoughts, and depressive symptoms among bereaved mothers. *Journal of Personality and Social Psychology, 70,* 271–282.

Lifton, R., & Olson, E. (1976). The human meaning of total disaster: The Buffalo Creek experience. *Psychiatry, 39,* 1–18.

Lin, N. (1986). Modeling the effects of social support. In N. Lin, A. Dean, & W. Ensel (Eds.), *Social support, life events, and depression* (pp. 173–212). San Diego, CA: Academic Press.

Lindy, J., & Grace, M. (1986). The recovery environment: Continuing stressor versus a healing psychosocial space. In B. Sowder & M. Lystad (Eds.), *Disasters and mental health* (pp. 147–160). Washington, DC: American Psychiatric Press.

Lyons, R., Mickelson, K., Sullivan, M. J. L., & Coyne, J. C. (1998). Coping as a communal process. *Journal of Social and Personal Relations, 15,* 579–605.

McFarlane, A. C. (1995a). Helping the victims of disaster. In J. R. Freedy & S. E. Hobfoll (Eds.), *Traumatic stress: From theory to practice* (pp. 263–286). New York: Plenum Press.

McFarlane, A. C. (1995b). Stress and disaster. In S. E. Hobfoll & M. W. deVries (Eds.), *Extreme stress and communities: Impact and intervention* (pp. 247–266). Dordrecht, The Netherlands: Kluwer.

McFarlane, A. C., Policansky, S., & Irwin, C. (1987). A longitudinal study of the psychological morbidity in children due to a natural disaster. *Psychological Medicine, 17,* 727–738.

McHugh, H. (1994). *Hinge and sign.* Hanover, NH: Wesleyan University Press.

Milgram, N., Sarason, B. R., Schonpflug, U., Jackson, A., & Schwarzer, C. (1995). Catalyzing community support. In S. E. Hobfoll & M. W. de Vries (Eds.), *Extreme stress and communities: Impact and intervention* (pp. 473–488). Dordrecht, The Netherlands: Kluwer.

Murphy, S. (1986). Perceptions of stress, coping, and recovery one and three years after a natural disaster. *Issues in Mental Health Nursing, 8,* 63–77.

Necker, L. A. (1832). Observations on some remarkable phenomena seen in Switzerland and on an optical phenomenon which occurs on viewing of a crystal or geometrical solid *Philosophical Magazine, 3(1),* 329–343.

Norris, F. (1992). Epidemiology of trauma: Frequency and impact of different potentially traumatic events on different demographic groups. *Journal of Consulting and Clinical Psychology, 60,* 409–418.

Norris, F., & Kaniasty, K. (1996). Received and perceived social support in times of stress: A test of the social support deterioration deterrence model. *Journal of Personality and Social Psychology, 71,* 498–511.

Norris, F., Phifer, J., & Kaniasty, K. (1994). Individual and community reactions to the Kentucky floods: Findings from a longitudinal study of older adults. In R. Ursano, B. McCaughey, & C. Fullerton (Eds.), *Individual and community responses to trauma and disaster: The structure of human chaos* (pp. 378–400). Cambridge, England: Cambridge University Press.

Norris, F., & Thompson, M. (1995). Applying community psychology to the prevention of trauma and traumatic life events. In J. Freedy & S. Hobfoll (Eds.), *Traumatic stress: From theory to practice* (pp. 49–71). New York: Plenum Press.

Norris, F., & Uhl, G. (1993). Chronic stress as a mediator of acute stress: The case of Hurricane Hugo. *Journal of Applied Social Psychology, 23,* 1263–1284.

Oliver-Smith, A. (1992). *The martyred city: Death and rebirth in the Perusian Andes* (2nd ed.). Prospect Heights, IL: Waveland.

Oliver-Smith, A. (1996). Anthropological research on hazards and disasters. *Annual Reviews of Anthropology, 25,* 303–328.

Palinkas, L. A., Downs, M. A., Petterson, J. S., & Russell, J. (1993). Social, cultural, and psychological impacts of the Exxon Valdez oil spill. *Human Organization, 51,* 1–13.

Palinkas, L. A., Russell, J., Downs, M. A., & Petterson, J. S. (1992). Ethnic differences in stress, coping, and depressive symptoms after the Exxon Valdez oil spill. *The Journal of Nervous and Mental Disease, 180,* 287–295.

Pearlin, L. (1989). The sociological study of stress. *Journal of Health and Social Behavior, 30,* 241–256.

Pennebaker, J. W. (1990). *Opening up: The healing power of confiding in others.* New York: Morrow.

Pennebaker, J. W., & Harber, K. (1993). A social stage model of collective coping: The Loma Prieta Earthquake and the Persian Gulf War. *Journal of Social Issues, 49*(4), 125–145.

Quarantelli, E. L. (1985). An assessment of conflicting views on mental health: The consequences of traumatic events. In C. Figley (Ed.), *Trauma and its wake* (pp. 173–218). New York: Brunner–Mazel.

Quarantelli, E. L., & Dynes, R. A. (1985). Community response to disasters. In B. T. Sowder (Ed.), *Disaster and mental health: Selected contemporary perspectives* (pp. 158–168). Rockville, MD: National Institute of Mental Health.

Raphael, B., & Wilson, J. P. (1993). Theoretical and intervention considerations in working with victims of disasters. In J. P. Wilson & B. Raphael (Eds.), *International handbook of traumatic stress syndromes* (pp. 105–117). New York: Plenum Press.

Riad, J., & Norris, F. (1996). The influence of relocation on the environmental, social, and psychological stress experienced by disaster victims. *Environment and Behavior, 28,* 163–182.

Riley, D., & Eckenrode, J. (1986). Social ties: Subgroup differences in costs and benefits. *Journal of Personality and Social Psychology, 51,* 770–778.

Rich, R. C., Edelstein, M., Hallman, W. K., & Wandersman, A. H. (1995). Citizen participation and empowerment: The case of local environmental hazards. *American Journal of Community Psychology, 23,* 657–676.

Rochford, B., & Blocker, T. (1991). Coping with "natural" hazards as stressors. *Environment and Behavior, 23,* 171–194.

Rook, K. S. (1985). Functions of social bonds: Perspectives from research on social support, loneliness and social isolation. In I. G. Sarason & B. R. Sarason (Eds.), *Social support: Theory, research and application* (pp. 243–267). Dordrecht, The Netherlands: Martinus Nijhoff.

Rubonis, A. V., & Bickman, L. (1991). Psychological impairment in the wake of disaster: The disaster–psychopathology relationship. *Psychological Bulletin, 109,* 384–399.

Sarason, I. G., Sarason, B. R., & Pierce, G. R. (1992). Three contexts of social support. In H. Veiel & U. Baumann (Eds.), *The meaning and measurement of social support* (pp. 143–154), New York: Hemisphere.

Silver, R. C., & Holman, E. A. (1999). The importance of social responses to discussions of traumatic life events. Unpublished manuscript (University of California, Irvine).

Smith, K. J., & Belgrave, L. L. (1995). The reconstruction of everyday life: Experiencing Hurricane Andrew. *Journal of Contemporary Ethnography, 24,* 244–269.

Solomon, S. D. (1986). Mobilizing social support networks in times of disaster. In C. R. Figley (Ed.), *Trauma and its wake: Vol. 2. Traumatic stress theory, research, and intervention* (pp. 232–263). New York: Brunner/Mazel.

Solomon, S. D., Bravo, M., Rubio-Stipec, M., & Canino, G. (1993). Effect of family role on response to disaster. *Journal of Traumatic Stress, 6,* 255–269.

Solomon, S. D., Smith, E., Robins, L., & Fischbach, R. (1987). Social involvement as a mediator of disaster-induced stress. *Applied Journal of Social Psychology, 17*, 1092–1112.

Stallings, R. (1988). Conflict in natural disasters: A codification of consensus and conflict theories. *Social Science Quarterly, 69*, 569–586.

Steinglass, P., & Gerrity, E. (1990). Natural disasters and post-traumatic stress disorder: Short-term versus long-term recovery in two disaster-affected communities. *Journal of Applied Social Psychology, 20*, 1746–1765.

Taylor, S. E. (1991). Asymmetrical effects of positive and negative events: The mobilization-minimization hypothesis. *Psychological Bulletin, 110*, 67–85.

Taylor, S. E., & Loeb, M. (1989). Social comparison activity under threat: Downward evaluation and upward contacts. *Psychological Review, 96*, 569–575.

Taylor, V. A. (1977). Good news about disaster. *Psychology Today, 11*, 93–94, 124–126.

Thompson, M., Norris, F., & Hanacek, B. (1993). Age differences in the psychological consequences of Hurricane Hugo. *Psychology and Aging, 8*, 606–616.

Tierney, K. J. (1989). The social and community contexts of disaster. In R. Gist & B. Lubin (Eds.), *Psychological aspects of disaster* (pp. 11–39). New York: Wiley.

Trainer, P., & Bolin, R. C. (1976). Persistent effects of disasters on daily activities: A cross-cultural comparison. *Mass Emergencies, 1*, 279–290.

Trickett, E. (1995). The community context of disasters and traumatic stress: An ecological perspective from community psychology. In S. E. Hobfoll & M. W. deVries (Eds.), *Extreme stress and communities: Impact and intervention* (pp. 11–26). Dordrecht, The Netherlands: Kluwer.

Tobin, G. A., & Ollenburger, J. C. (1996). Predicting levels of postdisaster stress in adults following the 1993 floods in the Upper Midwest. *Environment and Behavior, 28*, 340–357.

Ursano, R., McCaughey, B., & Fullerton, C. (Eds.). (1994). *Individual and community responses to trauma and disaster: The structure of human chaos*. Cambridge, England: Cambridge University Press.

Vaux, A. (1988). *Social support: Theory, research, and intervention*. New York: Praeger.

Weisæth, L. (1995). Preventive psychosocial interventions after disaster. In S. E. Hobfoll & M. W. deVries (Eds.), *Extreme stress and communities: Impact and intervention* (pp. 401–419). Dordrecht, The Netherlands: Kluwer.

Wheaton, B. (1985). Models for stress-buffering functions of coping resources. *Journal of Health and Social Behavior, 26*, 352–364.

Wheaton, B. (1996). The domains and boundaries of stress concepts. In H. B. Kalpan (Ed.), *Psychosocial stress: Perspectives on structure, theory, life-course, and methods* (pp. 29–70). San Diego, CA: Academic Press.

Wills, T. A. (1981). Downward comparison principles in social psychology. *Psychological Bulletin, 90*, 245–271.

Wood, J. V., Taylor, S. E., & Lichtman, R. R. (1985). Social comparison in adjustment to breast cancer. *Journal of Personality and Social Psychology, 49*, 1169–1183.

Wortman, C. B., Carnelley, K. B., Lehman, D. R., Davis, C. G., & Exline, J. J. (1995). Coping with the loss of a family member: Implications for community-level research and intervention. In S. E. Hobfoll & M. W. deVries (Eds.), *Extreme stress and communities: Impact and intervention* (pp. 83–103). Dordrecht, The Netherlands: Kluwer.

Wortman, C. B., & Lehman, D. R. (1985). Reactions to victims of life crises: Support attempts that fail. In I. G. Sarason & B. R. Sarason (Eds.), *Social support: Theory, research and application* (pp. 463–489). Dordrecht, The Netherlands: Martinus Nijhoff.

Yates, S., Axsom, D., Bickman, L., & Howe, G. (1989). Factors influencing help seeking for mental health problems after disasters. In R. Gist & B. Lubin (Eds.), *Psychological aspects of disaster* (pp. 163–189). New York: Wiley.

Chapter 3

The Short- and Long-Term Psychological Impact of Disasters: Implications for Mental Health Interventions and Policy

Mark S. Salzer and Leonard Bickman

INTRODUCTION

Disaster myths (Wenger, Dykes, Sebok, & Neff, 1975) refer to such commonly held but overgeneralized beliefs as widespread panic among disaster victims, persistent states of shock, or dependence on emergency services for assistance. These misperceptions are perpetuated by stories in the mass media that are often inaccurate or misinformed (Fischer, 1994). Contrary to common beliefs, victims usually organize and react quickly following disasters, with no signs of shock or dependency (e.g., Perry, Lindell, & Greene, 1981; Quartanelli & Dynes, 1972). Disaster myths arise from the reporting of unsubstantiated rumors, rare occurrences of certain behaviors (e.g., looting, panic), or reactions of outliers (e.g., extreme shock or disorientation). These stories capture the attention of news makers and

The writing of this chapter was supported by NIMH training grant #T32MH-19544-02 and grant #RO1-MH41391, both to the second author. The authors would like to thank Virginia Burks Salzer for comments on an earlier draft.

audiences. The frequency and emotional power of these reports potentially produce overestimations of dysfunction that follow in the wake of catastrophic events, including estimates of psychopathology.

Do beliefs about the emotional distress of disaster victims fall within the domain of disaster myths? Emotional distress, shock, and panic are common features of news coverage following a disaster. This information is conveyed in narratives, video footage, and photographs. A contemporary example was the grief evident in the numerous photos on the covers and front pages of magazines and newspapers, and video footage that broadcast the aftermath of the 1995 Oklahoma City bombing.

Mental health organizations also publicize the emergence of psychological distress following disasters (e.g., American Psychological Association, see DeAngelis, 1995; Substance Abuse and Mental Health Services Administration, see Goodman, 1995). Graphic images of the aftermath of disasters have been used by mental health professionals to convey the emotionally devastating consequences of disasters. One well-respected clinician, for example, began a recent presentation on his extensive work with disaster victims by showing numerous magazine covers with images of disaster survivors, many bleeding and in obvious distress (Scott, 1995).

The perceived high levels of distress following disasters has led to concern about the need for psychological interventions. Many groups have responded with organized efforts to address these concerns, including the Disaster Response Network of the American Psychological Association and the Emergency Services and Disaster Relief Branch of the Substance Abuse and Mental Health Services Administration. The American Red Cross is refocusing its efforts on mental health needs following disasters.

Media and professional presentations highlighting the emotional distress of victims likely influence the perceptions of laypersons about the extent of emotional distress following disasters. One study found that laypersons believe disaster victims have significantly disrupted lives, experience moderate to high levels of psychological distress, and need lengthy recovery periods (Yates, 1992). Layperson beliefs about the magnitude of distress, impairment, and the longevity of psychological problems vary by the extent of loss incurred because of the disaster.

The superficial answer to the question posed for this chapter is that a preponderance of research supports media reports, observations of mental health professionals, and the beliefs of laypersons that disasters are, in fact, associated with increased levels of psychological distress. High levels of distress are evident in descriptive reports of disasters, such as Erikson's (1976a) poignant observation of human misery following the Buffalo Creek dam collapse and flood. Moreover, a meta-analysis of quantitative studies found that disasters were associated with an increase in the prevalence rate of psychopathology (Rubonis & Bickman, 1991). The superficial answer, however, fails to address the many important reservations that must be raised when discussing the psychological impact of disasters.

These reservations leave open the possibility for disaster myth-making. While psychological distress is clearly experienced by disaster victims, the level of distress is less clear. The relationship between disasters and the occurrence of new, reliably diagnosable disorders appears tenuous at best. Beliefs that long recovery periods, such as 18–24 months or more (Aptekar & Boore, 1990; Freedy, Saladin, Kilpatrick, Resnick, & Saunders, 1994; Green, Grace, Vary, Kramer, Gleser, & Leonard, 1994), will be needed are not supported by the research. Finally, questions remain about the priorities given various mental health interventions following disasters aimed at facilitating quicker recovery among a community of survivors. The answers to these questions have special significance to policymakers and practitioners responsible for designing services in the aftermath of traumatic events.

PSYCHOLOGICAL DISTRESS FOLLOWING A DISASTER

Disaster victims undoubtedly experience psychological distress following traumatic events. Media reports repeatedly show the pain of men, women, and children, who, for example, watch as their homes and communities are flooded and destroyed. It may also be seen in the tears and halted speech of grieving parents, spouses, and friends who have lost loved ones from some catastrophic incident. Research is not needed to confirm such an obvious conclusion.

Nonetheless, qualitative and quantitative studies have been conducted, and the results are consistent with our expectations. Whereas qualitative studies put a "face" to the disasters and suffering, this review will focus on the results of the quantitative studies. Elevated rates of psychopathology are found among adult and child disaster victims (Rubonis & Bickman, 1991). Specifically, disasters have been associated with an overall increase of approximately 17% in the prevalence of psychopathology compared with predisaster or control-group rates. This number represents the best mean estimate of the effect of a disaster on the prevalence of psychopathology, and suggests that disasters have an impact on the psychological state of victims. The highest rates of impairment were found for anxiety, followed by high rates of alcohol use (Rubonis & Bickman, 1991).

These findings validate the interest drawn to the study of a particular anxiety syndrome, post-traumatic stress disorder (PTSD). PTSD symptoms are common following disasters (Durkin, Khan, Davidson, Zaman, & Stein, 1993; Green, 1991; Green & Lindy, 1994; Lonigan, Shannon, Taylor, Finch, & Sallee, 1994; Shannon, Lonigan, Finch, & Taylor, 1994; Spurrell & McFarlane, 1993; Steinglass & Gerrity, 1990; Ursano, Fullerton, Kao, & Bhartiya, 1995). The emergence of PTSD symptomatology should not be surprising, given that they are viewed as natural reactions to traumatic events and should not be considered aberrant or pathological unless they significantly interfere with normal functioning (Green, Wilson, & Lindy, 1985). PTSD symptoms such as intrusive thoughts and feelings, forgetfulness, trouble concentrating, and sleep disturbances may be especially common; children may also show increases in aggression and enuresis following disasters (Durkin, Khan, Davidson, Zaman, & Stein, 1993).

One must interpret research findings on a disaster–psychopathology relationship with caution, however. In particular, three key issues should be considered: research design, paradigm of the researcher, and definition of "case." The following sections will outline these issues in detail.

Design limitations in disaster research

Methodological rigor should be weighed when interpreting the research on the psychological impact of disasters (Green, 1982, 1991; Rubonis & Bickman, 1991). The factors to consider include sampling strategies, data collection methods (e.g., interviews vs. self-report instruments), and research design (e.g., pre-post, post-only, comparison group). A meta-analytic sub-analysis found that the greater the methodological rigor of a study, the lower the psychopathology effect size (Rubonis & Bickman, 1991). An important factor to consider when interpreting research results is the extent to which a design can be used to rule out threats to validity in the assessment of the disaster–psychopathology relationship. Studies using the more powerful comparison-group and actual pre-post designs had significantly lower effect sizes compared with other designs (i.e., post-disaster, archival pre-post, and post-post designs). Studies using the weaker retrospective pre-post designs where victims are asked to reflect on their emotional distress *before* the disaster at some point *after* the event had significantly higher effect sizes than the others.

The actual pre-post design, where survivors have completed the same measures before and after the traumatic event, is considered one of the more powerful research designs. One strength of the actual pre-post design is that it allows researchers to disentangle premorbid functioning and symptomatology from pathology attributable to the disaster. Although we fully appreciate the difficulty in carrying out these designs (see Reid, 1990, discussed later), only three studies were found that used this type of design (Rubonis & Bickman, 1991).

The importance of obtaining ratings of premorbid functioning in evaluations of the impact of disasters is highlighted in several studies. One study assessing the impact of the Loma Prieta earthquake (Nolen–Hoeksema & Morrow, 1991) found that children with higher predisaster levels of depression and stress and a greater propensity toward a ruminative coping style had higher levels of depression and stress symptoms following the earthquake. In a related study (Elder, Caspi, & van Nguyen, 1985), fathers who experienced economic hardships demonstrated an increase in irritable discipline styles. However, these same fathers used this disciplinary style more often before the economic stress, suggesting that the stress exacerbated a propensity toward irritability.

Another group of researchers was fortunate to obtain predisaster ratings of psychopathology before a series of traumatic events that struck one community (Smith, Robins, Przybeck, Goldring, & Solomon, 1986). Smith et al. compared predisaster and postdisaster assessments for victims with comparison group responses and concluded that disasters "contribute to the persistence or recurrence of previously existing disorders, but are not responsible for the genesis of new psychiatric symptoms or disorders" (p. 75). These findings emphasize the importance of assessing and controlling for predisaster psychopathology and might explain why pre-post studies result in lower effect sizes.

Reid (1990) concluded that pre-event data is crucial to determining the effects of disasters. He suggested that these data could be obtained by incorporating measures concerning disasters and other stressful events into longitudinal research studies. However, he also recognized that base rates for traumatic events are so low that statistical power would be hard to achieve, and that developing measures to assess a broad range of disasters would be challenging.

The use of comparison group designs in disaster research is much more common and easier to obtain than actual pre-post designs. Comparison group designs do not involve random assignment (assigning people to disaster conditions would be highly unethical!), and therefore cannot address selection and mortality threats to validity. Nonetheless, comparison group designs allow researchers to rule out many other threats, including history, maturation, testing, instrumentation, and statistical regression.

An excellent example of the use of comparison groups in disaster research can be found in the study of the impact of the nuclear accident at Three Mile Island conducted by Baum, Gatchel, and Schaeffer (1983). These researchers included two comparison groups to control for living in a potentially stressful environment—one group of individuals living near an undamaged nuclear power plant and another group living near a coal-fired power plant—and a nonexposed-regional community sample. The threats ruled out by using comparison groups may account for the lower effect sizes associated with this design.

Comparison groups must be similar to the experimental group on variables that are likely to affect the dependent measure. Nonexposed regional community samples are commonly used as comparison groups in disaster research. However, while these groups may have similar demographics, there remains a possibility that they differ in other important ways (e.g., community resources and cohesion, social support). Using matched comparison groups (e.g., Bowler, Mergler, Huel, & Cone, 1994) is definitely an improvement over nonmatched samples. Matching on gender, for example, is very important, as research has shown that the proportion of males to females in disaster research samples is significantly associated with psychopathology effect sizes (Rubonis & Bickman, 1991)—the greater the number of female victims, the higher the effect size. However, attempts should be made to match on premorbid functioning, social support, coping style, and other potentially important variables, in addition to matching groups based on demographics alone.

Finally, retrospective pre-post designs involve asking disaster victims to assess their functioning and psychological symptoms *before* the traumatic event at some point *after* the event occurred. These designs were found to result in higher effect sizes than all other designs (Rubonis & Bickman, 1991). One explanation for these results may be that disaster victims are systematically biased to report fewer psychological problems before the disaster than after.

One study found evidence of systematic bias in recall of disaster experiences (Hopwood & Guidotti, 1988). Respondents in this study recalled, after 6 months, having experienced more psychological symptoms immediately following the disaster compared with what they reported immediately following the event. This bias may be consistent with their expectation that disasters are associated with a decrement in psychological health, and may help to maintain a positive self-image (i.e., attribution that poor psychological health must be due to disaster; see Ross & Fletcher, 1985). Although another study found retrospective reports of disaster loss and preparedness to be highly reliable, reports of social support were less reliable (Norris & Kaniasty, 1992). Memory and recall of specific events, behaviors, or items associated with disaster loss and preparedness are likely to be more reliable compared with recall involving complex cognitive processes such as those involved with reports of social support, coping (Ptacek, Smith, Espe, & Raffety, 1994), and psychological distress.

Paradigm of disaster researcher

Differences in paradigm may also contribute to variability in research findings. For example, psychodynamically oriented researchers are thought to be inclined toward finding that disasters produce mental illness, whereas behaviorists come to the opposite conclusion (Perry & Lindell, 1978). The discipline of the researcher has also been proposed as a factor that may be associated with discrepant findings (Green, 1991). Sociologists and social and community psychologists are hypothesized not to assess or expect severe forms of psychopathology following disasters, whereas clinicians examine the most severe responses to develop disaster typologies. Mental health professionals are also considered more likely to interpret behavior as indicative of psychopathology when compared with other researchers and observers (Horwitz, 1982). Therefore, differences in reported effect sizes for the disaster–psychopathology relationship may be partially explained by paradigmatic and disciplinary differences between researchers and reporters.

Definition of case

The vague criteria used to detect the presence or absence of psychopathology in disaster research also inhibits firm conclusions about the extent of the disaster–psychopathology relationship. Widely discrepant approaches to defining a "case" are used in disaster research (Green, 1982). Estimates of the level of psychopathology vary due to the use of different measurement approaches, choice of conservative versus liberal cutoff points on scales, and research goals. It was noted recently (Green, 1991) that even the assessment of PTSD in disaster survivors is at an early stage of development, thereby making conclusions about the incidence of PTSD following disasters tenuous at best. Green (1982) suggested that thinking about "degree" of impairment rather than estimating psychopathology rates might be more productive.

Standardized measures, such as the Symptom Checklist 90–Revised (SCL-90–R; Derogatis, 1983), Brief Symptom Inventory (BSI; Derogatis & Meliseratos, 1983), and Impact of Event Scale (IES; Horowitz, Wilner, & Alvarez, 1979), make this task easier. These instruments include normed scales on various dimensions of psychopathology (e.g., anxiety, depression, somatization), allowing for comparisons between a sample of interest and norms for the general population. The SCL-90–R and BSI also have norms for outpatient and inpatient samples. Scores on these instruments can be compared with norms for non-patient, outpatient, and inpatient samples to obtain a better sense of how much impairment is associated with disasters. More recent research on disasters has used such standardized measures.

Summary

We feel secure in concluding that increased levels of psychological distress occur in the general population following traumatic events despite the limitations of current research. However, the magnitude of this distress is quite small for the vast majority of disaster victims (Drabek, 1986). This is exemplified in the conclusions from one study where authors report statistically significant but "clinically insignificant" levels of psychopathology following a disaster (Bravo, Rubio–Stipec, Canino, Woodbury, & Ribera, 1990). In addition, the prevalence of new diagnostic cases remains obscured as most studies do not use diagnostic interviews or sufficiently distinguished new cases from those persons with poor premorbid functioning. We agree with those who conclude that disasters generally do not produce new diagnostic cases (Breslau & Davis, 1987; Smith et al., 1986). Nonetheless, psychological distress, whatever its degree or caseness, is not to be discounted, particularly if the distress becomes chronic. This leads to the next question: What is the longevity of psychological distress following disasters?

LONGEVITY OF PSYCHOLOGICAL DISTRESS FOLLOWING DISASTERS

Length of time between the disaster event and measurement of psychological distress is proposed as another important factor in examining the disaster–psychopathology relationship (Green, 1982). Rubonis and Bickman (1991) found a significant negative relationship between the length of time elapsed between the disaster and data collection and effect-size estimates. Specifically, the greater the length of time between the event and assessment, the lower the effect size. One reasonable conclusion from this finding is that disaster-induced psychological distress is elevated immediately following disasters but remits over time.

Crude estimates have been made for how long it takes symptoms to remit. Some authors conclude that the mental health consequences associated with natural disasters show substantial decreases after about 18 months (Freedy et al., 1994; Green et al., 1994). The mental health of children is thought to be altered for at least 2 years following a disaster (Aptekar & Boore, 1990). The impact of human-caused disasters, in particular, is theorized to endure for much longer periods (Green et al., 1994), as will be discussed later.

In contrast with these estimates, a growing number of longitudinal studies suggest that psychological problems following disasters may decrease significantly in much less than 18 months. One study assessed PTSD symptoms in adults from two communities impacted by disasters, one a tornado and the other a flood (Steinglass & Gerrity, 1990). Assessments were conducted at 4 and 16 months after the disaster. Significant decreases in PTSD symptoms were found by 16-months postdisaster. Other studies using even shorter follow-up periods suggest that significant decreases in psychological distress occur over much briefer periods.

One study obtained psychopathology data using standardized instruments (e.g., BSI administered 1, 6, 11, 16, and 21 weeks following a flood in Virginia (Cook & Bickman, 1990). BSI scores obtained 1 week after the flood were significantly elevated compared with the nonpatient norms for this instrument. Six weeks after the flood these scores were significantly decreased, and no longer differed from nonpatient norms. In another study, college students reported significantly fewer psychological symptoms

1 week after the Loma Prieta earthquake compared with their reports 48 hours after the earthquake (Manuel & Anderson, 1993). The lessening of symptoms continued through 3 weeks after the earthquake. Persons who had contact with the bodies of those killed in Operation Desert Storm reported significant decreases in PTSD symptoms between 3–5 months and 13–15 months after returning to the United States (McCarroll, Ursano, & Fullerton, 1995). Finally, survivors of residential fires show significant decreases in psychological distress between 3 and 6 months after the fires (Keane, Pickett, Jepson, McCorkle, & Lowery, 1994). Mean distress levels at 3 months were between the norms for outpatient and nonpatient norms and showed continued declines at the 6-month follow-up.

The results for children and adolescents also suggest that psychological distress associated with disasters may not be as long-lasting as hypothesized for the vast majority of child survivors. For example, a significant proportion (40%) of children involved in a school bus accident were found to have moderate to high levels of distress 1 week after the accident (Milgram, Toubiana, Klingman, Raviv, & Goldstein, 1988). However, this proportion decreased to 6% by 9 months. Children's PTSD symptoms were also found to dissipate within 14 months after a sniper attack at their school (Nader, Pynoos, Fairbanks, & Frederick, 1990). Another study assessed psychological symptoms of adolescents 1 year after Hurricane Hugo (Hardin, Weinrich, Weinrich, Hardin, & Garrison, 1994); scores on the depression, anxiety, or global distress scales on the BSI were not significantly higher than national norms. The sample, however, did have elevated scores on a measure of anger.

Long-term impact of natural versus human-made disasters

One possible exception to the general finding of relatively short recovery periods following disasters may be found in the proposed distinctions between the long-term psychological effects expected for natural and human-made disasters (Baum & Davidson, 1985; Baum, Fleming, & Davidson, 1983; Bolin, 1985). Although the immediate psychological impact of natural disasters (e.g., floods, tornadoes, volcanic eruptions) may be more devastating and severe than human-made disasters (e.g., toxic waste exposure, nuclear plant accident, dam collapse; see Baum & Fleming, 1993), a hypothesis supported by a meta-analysis of the research (Rubonis & Bickman, 1991), human-made disasters are thought to be associated with higher levels of long-term psychological distress. It is quite plausible to expect that human-made disasters where there exists a strong, yet unknown probability of future negative health consequences (for example, exposure to radiation or toxic substances) will be associated with some degree of long-term psychological distress. An unclear low point and a greater perceived threat associated with events involving a temporary loss of control over situations normally under human command are other hypothesized attributes of human-made disasters thought to produce long-term distress.

Baum and Fleming (1993) reviewed their research on chronic stress and PTSD symptoms in survivors of the Three Mile Island (TMI) accident and toxic landfills. They reported that survivors of TMI had higher levels of somatic distress, anxiety, and depression symptoms compared with control groups more than one year after the incident. Elevated levels of psychological symptoms continued up to six years post-accident. Continued elevations in biological measures of stress were also found over this time period. Recovery on stress indices was found beginning 7 years after the accident.

Many articles have reported findings on the mental health status of adult and child survivors in "the second decade" after the Buffalo Creek dam collapse and flood of 1972 (Green et al., 1990a; Green et al., 1990b; Green et al., 1994; Honig, Grace, Lindy, Newman, & Titchener, 1993). Despite significant decreases in psychopathology over a 14-year period, the authors estimated that approximately 30% of the Buffalo Creek sample was still determined to have "clinically noteworthy levels of psychopathology" (Green et al., 1990b, p. 51). Significant differences were found for symptoms of anxiety and depression compared with a nonexposed sample (Green et al., 1990a). Bonferroni corrections for multiple univariate tests were apparently not conducted, though, and thus the effects may be overestimated.

The authors noted, however, that the responses of the Buffalo Creek sample were in the normal range for the standardized instruments that were used. Psychopathology data obtained after 17 years from survivors who were children at the time of the dam collapse and flood were also compared with data obtained from a demographically similar sample in a nonexposed community (Green et al., 1994). No differences were found between the groups on the standardized instruments or PTSD rates.

Summary

The psychological distress experienced by most disaster survivors is relatively short-lived. Although some have proposed that decreases in psychological distress are seen 18 months after a disaster (Freedy et al., 1994; Green et al., 1994), significant decreases, well within the normal range on standardized instruments, occur over a few short weeks or months. Survivors of human-made disasters experience significantly longer periods of psychological distress. This may result from the chronic stress associated with the unknown physiological consequences of certain types of human-made disasters and continuing to live in or near a contaminated or threatening (e.g., flood-prone) environment. However, research shows that even those exposed to, for example, high levels of radiation or toxic waste experience significant decreases in psychological symptoms over time.

The use of mental health services following disasters is not a plausible explanation for these decreases. Victims are generally reluctant to use mental health services (Hartsough, 1982; Lindy, Grace, & Green, 1981). What accounts for decreases in psychological distress over time?

DESTRUCTION, DISRUPTION, DISTRESS, AND RECOVERY

Some answers to the above question might be found in the relationship between disasters, loss of resources, disruptions in social support and community cohesion. Recouped losses, the reestablishment of social support networks, and the "return to normalcy" all partially account for psychological recovery following a disaster.

Resource loss and psychological distress

Earthquakes, hurricanes, fires, floods, nuclear accidents, toxic waste spills, and other disasters are all associated with significant losses, sometimes loss of life and injury, but almost always loss of resources. These include loss of shelter, food, water, clothing, household items, and basic services. Financial resources might also be drained from loss of employment. Resource loss resulting from disasters appears to account for a significant amount of variance in psychological distress.

Freedy and colleagues examined the relationship between resource loss, demographic characteristics, coping behavior, and psychological distress among victims of an earthquake (Freedy et al., 1994) and hurricane (Freedy, Shaw, Jarrell, & Masters, 1992). Resource loss was correlated .54 and .64 with psychological distress and was the most important factor in predicting psychological distress in both studies. Although these results are far from proving a causal relationship, it logically follows that the replacement of material losses or compensation for losses would be associated with decreased levels of psychological stress. The following hypothesis was advanced based on the reported relationship between resource loss and psychological distress: "The norm of psychological recovery across time probably occurs in proportion to an individual's capacity to reverse losses created by a natural [we would add human-made] disaster" (Freedy et al., 1994, p. 259).

Thankfully, resource loss, at least in the United States and other industrialized nations, is temporary. The response to disasters in the United States is exceptional, especially in terms of quick access to low interest loans and insurance payments.[1] These funds can be used to obtain new housing and to purchase food, clothing, and other necessities. Of course, the time it takes to replace material losses will take longer, if it occurs at all, for the poor and others without insurance or unable to repay loans. The unemployment experienced by disaster survivors is also temporary as businesses reopen and adults reclaim positions within a few months after a disaster has struck.

Disruptions in social support and psychological distress

Some of the most damaging aspects of a disaster are disruptions in social support networks (Solomon, 1985) and community cohesion. Extreme disasters, such as the Buffalo Creek dam collapse, are viewed as "a blow to the tissues of social life that damages the bonds linking people together and impairs the prevailing sense of communality" with the clinical distress of victims "as much a reaction to the shock of being separated from meaningful community bases as to the actual disaster itself" (Erikson, 1976b, p. 302).

Disruptions in social networks occur through two paths (Bolin, 1985). Death or severe injury of relatives and friends is one obvious path. A second path is through changes in normal patterns of social interactions resulting from social responses to disasters, such as evacuation, temporary housing, breakdown in transportation and communication systems, the relocation of victims to other communities, and destruction of settings conducive to social interactions (e.g., malls, schools, restaurants, recreational activities,). Kin, non-kin (e.g., friends, neighbors, acquaintances), and professional networks are all interrupted by disasters (Solomon, 1985).

Research results validate the notion that disruptions in social support networks are one consequence of disasters (Kaniasty & Norris, 1993, 1995b; Kaniasty, Norris, & Murrell, 1990). One study compared persons living in a community affected by a railroad chemical spill to an unaffected matched sample (Bowler et al., 1994). The impacted group reported significantly lower levels of social support than the non-impacted group 2 to 3 months after the accident. Survivors of Hurricane Andrew also reported significant disruptions of routine activities, loss of recreational opportunities, and less satisfaction with their social lives (Kaniasty & Norris, 1995a).

Disruptions in social support networks can negatively impact psychological distress in two ways (Kaniasty & Norris, 1993). First, social support normally serves as a buffer against developing elevated levels of distress

---

[1]However, we are familiar with the delays in acquiring low interest government loans and cases in which insurance companies held back payments in disputes over amount of losses. These disputes likely add to the distress already felt by the insured victim.

during stressful times. This buffer is reduced if social supports are disturbed. This is an indirect model, in that it presupposes that the connection between social support and psychological health only comes into play when there is a threat during stressful times. Second, social support is directly associated with psychological well-being. Any disruption in social support, regardless of the presence of a stressor, results in reductions in psychological health.

Many studies have found a relationship between social support and psychological distress following disasters (e.g., Baum, Fleming, & Singer, 1983; Hardin et al., 1994; Murphy, 1988). For example, a study of older adults found evidence that decreases in social support were associated with increases in depression following a flood (Kaniasty & Norris, 1993). However, only nonkin support and social embeddedness were significantly related to depression. Kin support did not appear to play a significant role in this process in the population studied. Most studies have examined the relationship between social support and psychological distress at one point in time. The results from one study (Cook & Bickman, 1990) suggest that understanding the relationship across time is important. As mentioned previously, this study of Virginia flood victims found high levels of psychological distress 1 week after the flood but significantly decreased levels, within the normal range, within 6 weeks of the flood that remained stable for the rest of the study (5 months). Social support was not predictive of psychological distress immediately following the disaster when distress levels were at their highest but was predictive of distress levels at 6, 11, and 16 weeks post-flood. Social support was again uncorrelated with psychological distress at 21 weeks post-flood.

Cook and Bickman suggest that disasters produce immediate overwhelming stress that is unmitigated by social support. As the stress of the traumatic event subsides, social support serves as a resource to help survivors cope with the results of the disaster. Those with higher levels of social support recover faster than those with lower levels. However, at some point in time (within 5 months in this study), even those with low levels of social support achieve the same levels of psychological recovery as those with high social support.

This study also found that certain types of support had a greater association with psychological distress. Specifically, perceived availability of tangible support (i.e., financial, transportation, material goods, etc.) and belongingness support (i.e., social embeddedness and availability of friends with whom to engage in social activities) were most predictive of psychological distress. Appraisal support (i.e., provision of advice about a wide range of topics) was only weakly correlated with psychological distress.

Tremendous levels of social support follow in the wake of most disasters. Those experiencing the most loss or who experience the greatest potential for harm are generally the recipients of the most support, though the race and age of the victim appear to play a role in received support

(Kaniasty & Norris, 1995b). The extreme outpouring of support following disasters, usually tangible support, is followed by the re-establishment of normal social support networks as survivors return to their homes, schools, and workplaces. Businesses and public meeting places reopen, and other routine activities are restarted.

Return to normalcy and psychological recovery

Destruction and disruption are two universal features of all disasters, both of which are associated with psychological distress. The "return to normalcy" (Drabek, 1986) in both these areas is another probable universal for the vast majority of those impacted by disasters. Although destruction and disruption likely account for the high levels of distress that immediately follow disasters, the return to normalcy likely accounts for the decay curve (Drabek, 1986) in distress that is found over the course of a few weeks and months after the disaster.

Use of the concept "return to normalcy" is not meant to imply a return to pre-disaster state. We take an ecological-transactional perspective that views individuals, families, and communities as ever-changing entities that are continuously impacted by changes in the systems in which they are embedded. These entities do not revert to previous states; some change is always evident. Changes are particularly obvious for extreme disruptions, such as those resulting from disasters, that produce significant and often permanent alterations (e.g., loss of home after flood or fire, workplace destroyed by a bombing). The significant changes, both material and psychological, that result from disasters can never be wiped away or reversed. However, while individuals, families, and communities are changed by disastrous events, there is eventually a return to a state of equilibrium, balance, and adjustment as resources are recouped and social support networks are reestablished.

IMPLICATIONS FOR INTERVENTIONS AND POLICY

Disaster survivors tend not to use formal psychological services following disasters (Hartsough, 1982; Lindy et al., 1981). Some authors have commented that humans are incredibly resilient following disasters (Bravo et al., 1990; Lyons, 1991) and that most victims do not require extensive mental health services (Summers & Cowan, 1991, as cited in Freedy et al., 1994). The perceived underuse of traditional mental health services may actually reflect a minimal need for increases in such services following a disaster. Instead, victims may choose to receive or seek out alternative types of help that better match their needs.

It has been proposed that the psychological well-being of victims will be maximally benefitted "if the specific demands of the stressor and supportive provisions are congruent with each other" (Kaniasty & Norris, 1995a, p. 95). The destruction and disruptions caused by disasters suggest that tangible support and efforts to rebuild social networks and sense of community should be the primary focus of efforts to enhance the psychological health of disaster victims.

One primary mental health intervention in response to disasters should be to address material resource losses (Farberow & Frederick, 1978; Myers, 1994). This includes assisting victims with problem-solving and decision-making, including identifying needs, setting priorities, exploring alternatives, seeking out resources, developing plans of action, and choosing a plan of action. It also can involve helping victims complete the necessary paperwork for getting aid. Mutual aid processes are also found to occur in communities devastated by catastrophe, including the provision of financial and material support (Kaniasty & Norris, 1995b).

Mental health professionals can help facilitate this natural process by, for example, becoming sources of information to victims by familiarizing themselves with local and national, public and private financial resources, and helping to create formal and informal settings where help can be requested and provided. Special attention can also be paid to ensuring that the needs of those people who might receive less tangible support because of racial or educational level (see Kaniasty & Norris, 1995b) are also addressed.

Finally, one role for mental health professionals is that of a victim advocate who, among other things, facilitates the empowerment of victims in demanding a speedy and substantial return of basic services, financial aid, and insurance reimbursements. The importance of addressing material losses as an important mental health intervention is highlighted in the statement, "The impact of essential goods and services upon positive mental health should not be underestimated" (Freedy et al., 1994, p. 269).

The facilitation of social support networks also will significantly benefit the mental health of disaster victims. This refers to support other than tangible support (e.g., money, food, shelter). Mental health interventions aimed at re-establishing social support networks include bringing families, neighborhoods, and the larger community back together as soon as possible after a disaster. This is particularly important following emergency evacuations and long-term evacuations.

In cases of displacements that last for more than a few days, a computerized system should be put in place to catalogue the whereabouts of family members and friends. Access to this system should be readily available, and information about how to access the system should be disseminated widely through the media. Efforts should also be made to help reopen schools, places of employment, and informal meeting places, such as malls and recreational centers, within reasonable periods of time following the disruptive event.

Alternative settings, such as drop-in centers, could also be used as public meeting places for community members to gather. Victims also might express interest in organizing self-help groups. Self-help groups can be quite beneficial to members in dealing with mental health problems and coping with life crises and transitions (Riessman & Carroll, 1995), beyond serving as a way to decrease isolation following a disaster (Scanlon-Schlipp & Levesque, 1981). Given interest on the part of disaster victims, mental health professionals could play crucial secondary roles as referral agents and offer financial and material resources and a place for the group to meet.

Helping rebuild the sense of community unsettled by disasters is another important role for mental health professionals. This might involve facilitating the telling of stories about the disaster and recovery to help victims incorporate disastrous events into their individual stories and community narratives. Shared narratives about the event might be associated with increased community identification (Mankowski & Rappaport, 1995). Community organizing may also be an important role for mental health professionals to take following a disaster. This role is especially important in response to victim dissatisfaction with local and national government actions following the disaster, concerns about long-term effects associated with technological disasters (e.g., exposure to radiation or toxic waste), and to prevent future incidents from occurring (Rich, Edelstein, Hallman, & Wandersman, 1995).

CONCLUSION

Current research confirms observations that people experience elevated levels of distress following traumatic events. However, the convergent findings from longitudinal studies indicate that the overwhelming majority of disaster victims recover quickly, sometimes within days or weeks of the event. The long-term distress experienced by survivors of technological disasters may be accounted for by fears of the unknown long-term health consequences of these events and potential continued exposure to toxic substances, rather than being a direct result of distress associated with the disastrous event.

These conclusions are not meant to downplay the great emotional distress experienced by a small minority of disaster victims, especially those who have lost loved ones or have suffered severe personal injury. Yet, our concern is that disaster myths have been created by overemphasizing the relatively small increases in psychological distress following disasters across whole populations of survivors, or focusing on the small percentage of survivors whose lives are devastated by these events. These myths are likely associated with the exceptional steps taken to enhance access to traditional mental health interventions (i.e., psychotherapy), although the vast majority of disaster survivors do not require these services. Relatively sparse efforts are taken to set up nontraditional mental health interventions to help all disaster victims "return to normalcy" more quickly and with greater resources, both materially and psychologically, than might be expected without these types of interventions.

Greater research efforts are needed to study the strengths and resiliency of individuals and communities following disasters, as well as the natural recovery processes that occur. Interventions based on this research can be created, if needed, to help facilitate faster recovery. Priority needs to be given to mental health interventions that address loss of resources and disruptions of social networks and sense of community. We concur with one group of researchers (Bravo et al., 1990) who reasoned that it might be more desirable to incorporate community psychologists rather than psychotherapists in an attempt to alter disaster response intervention priorities.

REFERENCES

Aptekar, L., & Boore, J. A. (1990). The emotional effects of disaster on children: A review of the literature. *International Journal of Mental Health, 19(2)*, 77–90.

Baum, A., & Davidson, L. M. (1985). A suggested framework for studying factors that contribute to trauma in disaster. In B. J. Sowder (Ed.), *Disasters and mental health: Selected contemporary perspectives* (pp. 29–40). Rockville, MD: National Institute of Mental Health.

Baum, A., & Fleming, I. (1993). Implications of psychological research on stress and technological accidents. *American Psychologist, 48*, 665–672.

Baum, A., Fleming, R., & Davidson, L. (1983). Natural disaster and technological catastrophe. *Environment and Behavior, 15*, 333–354.

Baum, A., Fleming, R., & Singer, J. E. (1983). Coping with victimization by technological disaster. *Journal of Social Issues, 39*, 117–138.

Baum, A., Gatchel, R. J., & Schaeffer, M. A. (1983). Emotional, behavioral and physiological effects of chronic stress at Three Mile Island. *Journal of Consulting and Clinical Psychology, 51*, 565–572.

Bolin, R. (1985). Disaster characteristics and psychosocial impacts. In B. J. Sowder (Ed.), *Disasters and mental health: Selected contemporary perspectives* (pp. 3–28). Rockville, MD: National Institute of Mental Health.

Bowler, R. M., Mergler, D., Huel, G., & Cone, J. E. (1994). Psychological, psychosocial, and psychophysiological sequelae in a community affected by a railroad chemical disaster. *Journal of Traumatic Stress, 7*, 601–624.

Bravo, M., Rubio–Stipec, M., Canino, G. J., Woodbury, M. A., & Ribera, J. C. (1990). The psychological sequelae of disaster stress prospectively and retrospectively evaluated. *American Journal of Community Psychology, 18*, 661–680.

Breslau, N., & Davis, G. (1987). Posttraumatic stress disorder: The stressor criterion. *Journal of Nervous and Mental Disease, 175*, 255–264.

Cook, J. D., & Bickman, L. (1990). Social support and psychological symptomatology following a natural disaster. *Journal of Traumatic Stress, 3*, 541–556.

DeAngelis, T. (1995, June). Responding to Oklahoma City's need. *APA Monitor, 26*, 22, 26.

Derogatis, L. R. (1983). *SCL-90-R version: Manual I.* Baltimore, MD: Johns Hopkins University.

Derogatis, L. R., & Meliseratos, N. (1983). The Brief Symptom Inventory: An introductory report. *Psychological Medicine, 13*, 595–605.

Drabek, T. E. (1986). *Human system responses to disaster: An inventory of sociological findings.* New York: Springer-Verlag.

Durkin, M. S., Khan, N., Davidson, L. L., Zaman, S. S., & Stein, Z. A. (1993). The effects of a natural disaster on child behavior: Evidence for posttraumatic stress. *American Journal of Public Health, 83*, 1549–1553.

Elder, G. H., Caspi, A., & van Nguyen, T. (1985). Resourceful and vulnerable children: Family influences in stressful times. In R. K. Silbereisen, K. Eyferth, & G. Rudinger (Eds.), *Development as action in context: Problem behavior and normal youth development* (pp. 167–186). Hillsdale, NJ: Erlbaum.

Erikson, K. T. (1976a). *Everything in its path.* New York: Simon and Schuster.

Erikson, K. T. (1976b). Loss of communality at Buffalo Creek. *American Journal of Psychiatry, 133*, 302–305.

Farberow, N. L., & Frederick, C. J. (1978). *Training manual for human service workers in major disasters.* Rockville, MD: National Institute of Mental Health.

Fischer, H. W. (1994). *Response to disaster: Fact versus fiction and its perpetuation: The sociology of disaster.* Lanham, MD: University Press of America.

Freedy, J. R., Saladin, M. E., Kilpatrick, D. G., Resnick, H. S., & Saunders, B. E. (1994). Understanding acute psychological distress following natural disaster. *Journal of Traumatic Distress, 7*, 257–273.

Freedy, J. R., Shaw, D. L., Jarrell, M. P., & Masters, C. R. (1992). Towards an understanding of the psychological impact of natural disasters: An application of the conservation resources stress model. *Journal of Traumatic Stress, 5*, 441–454.

Goodman, D. (1995, Summer). SAMHSA responds to Oklahoma bombing. *Substance Abuse and Mental Health Services Administration News, 3*, 1–4.

Green, B. L. (1982). Assessing levels of psychological impairment following disaster: Consideration of actual and methodological dimensions. *The Journal of Nervous and Mental Disease, 170*, 544–552.

Green, B. L. (1991). Evaluating the effects of disasters. *Psychological Assessment, 3*, 538–546.

Green, B. L., Grace, M. C., Lindy, J. D., Gleser, G. C., Leonard, A. C., & Kramer, T. L. (1990a). Buffalo Creek survivors in the second decade: Comparison with unexposed and nonlitigant groups. *Journal of Applied and Social Psychology, 20*, 1033–1050.

Green, B. L., Grace, M. C., Vary, M. G., Kramer, T. L., Gleser, G. C., & Leonard, A. C. (1994). Children of disaster in the second decade: A 17-year follow-up of Buffalo Creek survivors. *Journal of the American Academy of Child and Adolescent Psychiatry, 33*, 71–79.

Green, B. L., & Lindy, J. D. (1994). Post-traumatic stress disorder in victims of disaster. *Psychiatric Clinics of North America, 17*, 301–309.

Green, B. L., Lindy, J. D., Grace, M. C., Gleser, G. C., Leonard, A. C., Korol, M., & Winget, C. (1990b). Buffalo creek survivors in the second decade: Stability of stress symptoms. *American Journal of Orthopsychiatry, 60*, 43–54.

Green, B. L., Wilson, J. P., & Lindy, J. D. (1985). Conceptualizing post-traumatic stress disorder: A psychosocial framework. In C. R. Figley (Ed.), *Trauma and its wake, Vol. 1: The study of post-traumatic stress disorder.* New York: Brunner/Mazel.

Hardin, S. B., Weinrich, M., Weinrich, S., Hardin, T. L., & Garrison, C. (1994). Psychological distress of adolescents exposed to Hurricane Hugo. *Journal of Traumatic Stress, 7*, 427–440.

Hartsough, D. M. (1982). Planning for disaster: A new community outreach program for mental health centers. *Journal of Community Psychology, 10*, 255–264.

Honig, R. G., Grace, M. C., Lindy, J. D., Newman, C. J., & Titchener, J. L. (1993). Portraits of survival: A twenty-year follow-up of the children of Buffalo Creek. *Psychoanalytic Study of the Child, 48,* 327–355.

Hopwood, D., & Guidotti, T. (1988). Recall bias in exposed subjects following a toxic exposure incident. *Archives of Environmental Health, 43,* 234–237.

Horowitz, M. J., Wilner, N., & Alvarez, W. (1979). Impact of Event Scale: A measure of subjective distress. *Psychosomatic Medicine, 41,* 209–218.

Horwitz, A. (1982). *Social control of mental illness.* Orlando, FL: Academic Press.

Kaniasty, K., & Norris, F. (1993). A test of the social support deterioration model in the context of a natural disaster. *Journal of Personality and Social Psychology, 64,* 395–408.

Kaniasty, K. & Norris, F. H. (1995a). Mobilization and deterioration of social support following natural disasters. *Current Directions in Psychological Science, 4(3),* 94–98.

Kaniasty, K. & Norris, F. H. (1995b). In search of altruistic community: Patterns of social support mobilization following Hurricane Hugo. *American Journal of Community Psychology, 23,* 447–477.

Kaniasty, K., Norris, F., & Murrell, S. (1990). Received and perceived social support following natural disaster. *Journal of Applied Social Psychology, 20,* 85–114.

Keane, A., Pickett, M., Jepson, C., McCorkle, R., & Lowery, B. J. (1994). Psychological distress in survivors of residential fires. *Social Science and Medicine, 38,* 1055–1060.

Lindy, J. L., Grace, M. C., & Green, B. L. (1981). Survivors: Outreach to a reluctant population. *American Journal of Orthopsychiatry, 51,* 468–478.

Lonigan, C. J., Shannon, M. P., Taylor, C. M., Finch, A. J., & Sallee, F. R. (1994). Children exposed to disaster: II. Risk factors for the development of post-traumatic symptomatology. *Journal of the Academy of Child and Adolescent Psychiatry, 33,* 94–105.

Lyons, J. A. (1991). Strategies for assessing the potential for positive adjustment following trauma. *Journal of Traumatic Stress, 4,* 93–111.

Mankowski, E., & Rappaport, J. (1995). Stories, identity and the psychological sense of community. In R. S. Wyer, Jr. (Ed.), *Advances in social cognition* (Vol. 8, pp. 211–226). Hillsdale, NJ: Erlbaum.

Manuel, G., & Anderson, K. M. (1993). Stress and coping: The Loma Prieta earthquake. *Current Psychology: Developmental, Learning, Personality, Social, 12(2),* 130–141.

McCarroll, J. E., Ursano, R. J., & Fullerton, C. S. (1995). Symptoms of PTSD following recovery of war dead: 13–15-month follow-up. *American Journal of Psychiatry, 152,* 939–941.

Milgram, N. A., Toubiana, Y. H., Klingman, A., Raviv, A., & Goldstein, I. (1988). Situational exposure and personal loss in children's acute and chronic stress reactions to a school bus disaster. *Journal of Trauma and Stress, 1,* 339–352.

Murphy, S. A. (1988). Mediating effects of intrapersonal and social support on mental health one and three years after a natural disaster. *Journal of Traumatic Stress, 1,* 155–172.

Myers, D. (1994). *Disaster response and recovery: A handbook for mental health professionals.* Washington, DC: U.S. Department of Health and Human Services.

Nader, K., Pynoos, R., Fairbanks, L., & Frederick, C. (1990). Children's post-traumatic stress disorder reactions one year after a sniper attack at their school. *American Journal of Psychiatry, 147(11),* 1526–1530.

Nolen-Hoeksema, S., & Morrow, J. (1991). A prospective study of depression and posttraumatic stress symptoms after a natural disaster: The 1989 Loma Prieta earthquake. *Journal of Personality and Social Psychology, 61,* 115–121.

Norris, F. H., & Kaniasty, K. (1992). Reliability of delayed self-reports in disaster research. *Journal of Traumatic Distress, 5,* 575–588.

Perry, R. W., & Lindell, M. K. (1978). The psychological consequences of natural disaster: A review of research on American communities. *Mass Emergencies, 3,* 105–115.

Perry, R. W., Lindell, M. K., & Greene, M. R. (1981). *Evacuation planning in emergency management*. Lexington, MA: Lexington Books.

Ptacek, J. T., Smith, R. E., Espe, K., & Raffety, B. (1994). Limited correspondence between daily coping reports and retrospective coping recall. *Psychological Assessment, 6*, 41–49.

Quarantelli, E. I., & Dynes, R. R. (1972). *Images of disaster behavior: Myths and consequences*. Newark: The University of Delaware, Disaster Research Center.

Reid, J. B. (1990). A role for prospective longitudinal investigations in the study of traumatic stress and disasters. *Journal of Applied Social Psychology, 20*, 1695–1703.

Rich, R. C., Edelstein, M., Hallman, W. K., & Wandersman, A. H. (1995). Citizen participation and empowerment: The case of local environmental hazards. *American Journal of Community Psychology, 23*, 657–676.

Riessman, F., & Carroll, D. (1995). *Redefining self-help: Policy and practice*. San Francisco: Jossey-Bass Publishers.

Ross, M., & Fletcher, G. J. O. (1985). Attribution and self-perception. In G. Lindzey & E. Aronson (Eds.), *The handbook of social psychology* (3rd ed., pp. 73–122). Reading, MA: Addison-Wesley.

Rubonis, A. V., & Bickman, L. (1991). Psychological impairment in the wake of disaster: The disaster–psychopathology relationship. *Psychological Bulletin, 109*, 384–399.

Scanlon-Schlipp, A. M., & Levesque, J. (1981). Helping the patient cope with the sequelae of trauma through the self-help group approach. *The Journal of Trauma, 21*, 135–139.

Scott, R. T. (1995, August). *Treatment intervention strategies for children and families following disasters: Integrated, phase-oriented approaches for children*. Presentation at the American Psychological Association Annual Conference, New York, NY.

Shannon, M. P., Lonigan, C. J., Finch, A. J., & Taylor, C. M. (1994). Children exposed to disaster: I. Epidemiology of post-traumatic symptoms and symptom profiles. *Journal of the Academy of Child and Adolescent Psychiatry, 33*, 80–93.

Smith, E., Robins, L., Przybeck, T., Goldring, E., & Solomon, S. (1986). Psychological consequences of a disaster. In J. H. Shore (Ed.), *Disaster stress studies: New methods and findings* (pp. 49–76). Washington, DC: American Psychiatric Press.

Solomon, S. D. (1985). Enhancing social support for disaster victims. In B. J. Sowder (Ed.), *Disasters and mental health: Selected contemporary perspectives* (pp. 107–121). Rockville, MD: National Institute of Mental Health.

Spurrell, M. T., & McFarlane, A. C. (1993). Post-traumatic stress disorder and coping after a natural disaster. *Social Psychiatry and Psychiatric Epidemiology, 28*, 194–200.

Steinglass, P., & Gerrity, E. (1990). Natural disasters and post-traumatic stress disorder: Short-term versus long-term recovery in two disaster-affected communities. *Journal of Applied Social Psychology, 20*, 1746–1765.

Summers, G. M., & Cowan, M. L. (1991). Mental health issues related to the development of a national disaster response system. *Military Medicine, 156*, 30–32.

Ursano, R. J., Fullerton, C. S., Kao, T., & Bhartiya, V. R. (1995). Longitudinal assessment of posttraumatic stress disorder and depression after exposure to traumatic death. *The Journal of Nervous and Mental Disease, 183*, 36–42.

Wenger, D. E., Dykes, J. D., Sebok, T. D., & Neff, J. L. (1975). Its a matter of myths: An empirical examination of individual insight into disaster responses. *Mass Emergencies, 1*, 33–46.

Yates, S. (1992). Lay attributions about distress after a natural disaster. *Personality and Social Psychology Bulletin, 18*, 217–222.

Chapter 4

Assessing the Impact of Trauma in Work-Related Populations: Occupational and Cultural Determinants of Reactivity

Douglas Paton, Leigh M. Smith, Robert Ramsay, and Debo Akande

INTRODUCTION

Several professions, most notably emergency service and law enforcement, anticipate by the very nature of their enterprises exposure to work-related demands that ostensibly increase the likelihood of traumatic stress reactions. These groups can be designated "high risk" for traumatic reactivity because they face the possibility, even the probability, of repeated exposure to traumatic work-related incidents over the course of their working lives. This pattern of repetitive exposure has been reported to be associated with the development of chronic traumatic stress symptoms, behavioral addiction to stress and risk, post-traumatic stress disorder (PTSD), and at an organizational level, increased staff turnover, performance losses, and increased economic cost (Friedman, Framer, & Sheaver, 1988; Miller & Ford, 1996; Stephens, Long, & Miller, 1997).

Although this risk status has been accepted as established, the interventions it has stimulated have focused almost exclusively on support and recovery procedures (e.g., psychological debriefing, peer support, counseling). The basic assumptions underlying these developments, though most often not articulated or examined, reflect the view that observed reactions are a direct result of exposure to some specific traumatic event, with a consequent focus on treating presumed proximal causes and designated symptoms. Although a need for effective support measures—whether formal or informal in nature—appears reasonable on its face, the nature of the phenomena we are attempting to address may be considerably more complex than this view would suggest. Consequently, support efforts may be rendered less effective and, indeed, their conceptual foundation and design may be inappropriate for achieving their desired objectives (Paton, Smith, & Stephens, 1998).

As research in the area of psychological trauma has extended into the workplace, a more prominent role for the organizational environment in the etiology of work-related traumatic stress reactions has been suggested. Control systems, administrative procedures, and prevailing managerial practices have been implicated in this context (Doepal, 1991; Powell, 1991; Stephens et al., 1997). Despite the growing body of evidence to support this interpretation, it has not gone unchallenged. Although a causal role for organizational factors has been generally accepted, the rationale for their implication has been questioned. It has been suggested, for example, that self-reports implicating organizational factors may reflect the operation of denial processes rather than the objective identification of causally significant factors attributable to extrapersonal features of the organizational environment (Graham, 1981; McCammon & Allison, 1995).

Much of the work conducted in this field has involved emergency and law enforcement professionals who operate within an organizational culture that has been portrayed as encouraging of emotional denial and suppression. Graham (1981) argued that the operation of this cultural norm renders it more difficult for those affected to admit emotional vulnerability, and, instead, they transfer blame to the work environment (e.g., management practices, organizational systems), making the latter more a scapegoat than a legitimate causal factor. Clearly, a need to empirically test for the influence of environmental factors remains. It is important, however, to ensure that this work extend beyond the boundaries of any one organization or professional group if its hypotheses are to prove robust, especially across occupational or cultural boundaries.

Exposure to traumatic incidents, as already noted, is an accepted occupational reality within professional groups whose social functions clearly call for their intervention in perilous, poignant, and disruptive life occurrences. The range of such groups, from emergency services through mental health professionals to construction and mineral exploration organizations, reveals that the populations at risk represent a far from uniform group in terms of history, nature, membership, affiliation, proclivities, social pragmatics and norms, or any of a broad spectrum of characteristics that might reasonably be expected to influence reactivity and resolution. This diversity, however, is often ignored, and assessment instruments are used as if there were uniformity between populations studied in research and practice contexts and those populations within which a given scale was derived and standardized.

Separate, though related, is the question of how differences between groups should be represented. A developing theme in the methodological literature on change has been concerned with the form it may take (Golembiewski, Billingsley, & Yeager, 1976; Porras & Singh, 1986; Millsap & Hartog, 1988; Magnusson & Bergman, 1990; Collins & Horn, 1991). Golembiewski et al. proposed three types of change, nominally designated *alpha*, *beta*, and *gamma*. From the perspective of a structural measurement model, an alpha change occurs when an increase or a decrease in the score from a multi-item scale directly reflects a corresponding change in the latent construct. A beta change occurs where an increase or decrease in the score signals a recalibration of the scale in terms of item responses within the target population. When the structural relations of the items to the latent construct(s) alter, a gamma change is said to have occurred. It would seem appropriate to extend this typology of change to differences between groups, on the basis of occupation, culture, or experience, in their reactivity to traumatic stress as measured by psychometric instruments. Groups may differ quantitatively along consistent constructs (an alpha difference), in their anchoring of the scale components (a beta difference), or qualitatively respecting the relationships between items and their anchoring (a gamma difference). It follows from this conception of the response patterns of groups to multi-item scales that not only differences in magnitude of responses are important, but also the manner in which groups structure the item set in relation to the latent constructs (Byrne, 1991; Paton & Smith, 1996; Viet & Ware, 1983). This becomes particularly salient where, in the final analysis, subjective ordinal ratings of subjective perspectives regarding subjective elements of a highly subjective experience are inherent in the response set to be measured.

THE DEVELOPMENT AND USE OF ASSESSMENT INSTRUMENTS

Any comprehensive understanding of the relationship between occupational (or any other) experiences and traumatic stress reactions is, at its most essential level, dependent on the availability of assessment instruments capable of valid and reliable measurement of key constructs (Paton & Smith, 1996). Sound assessment instruments play a prominent role in several activities: identifying individuals affected or at risk, defining the nature and intensity of impact, monitoring recovery processes, and intervention planning and evaluation. Paton and Smith argued that the development of work-related traumatic stress research requires that the processes and mechanisms underlying the development of traumatic stress be understood and be capable of measurement using instruments of known structure and reliability. The quality of interventions, like the data produced by the research instrument, can be best interpreted when the nature and behavior of the research instrument itself is known and studied. Although this issue is especially relevant to the development of new instruments, it also has implications for assumptions of validity made with respect to existing instruments.

Effective use of scales requires knowledge of both the structure of a measurement device and the factors that influence its items. Structural equation modeling provides a formal basis for analyses relevant to understanding the behavior of multi-item measures in this manner (Bollen, 1989). Item sets that are indicators for a specific latent construct should converge, while simultaneously diverging from item sets that are indicators for other latent constructs (Brooke, Russel, & Price, 1988); it may also prove prudent to identify causally ambiguous items that can be eliminated from the instrument without compromising its psychometric utility (Byrne, 1991). Confirmatory factor analysis is the appropriate tool for this task.

Too many measures, it would certainly seem, are developed instead on an ad hoc basis. Such measures tend to contain a plethora of items whose selection was driven by loose theory or apparent face validity; the construct validity of such item sets generally remains unestablished and, hence, questionable at best. The standard practice of reporting Cronbach's alpha as an index of reliability is then conflated with the question of validity. Without knowing the structural characteristics of the item set that forms the "scale," Cronbach's alpha is uninterpretable—in fact, quite "respectable" values can occur for large item sets where subgroups of items are totally unrelated (Cortina, 1993).

The practice of using an aggregate score from a set of items with an "acceptable" reliability coefficient that allegedly measures a psychological construct is fraught with dangers when the set of items is not known to be congeneric. Although it is possible for conglomerate measures of unknown and heterogeneous structure to have some predictive utility, it must be acknowledged that this observation is, at best, of only actuarial value and may reflect little more than a methodological artifact in any given case (Paton & Smith, 1996).

If scale items are indeed representative of latent constructs suggested by a specified theoretical model, consistent structural relationships should emerge irrespective of the population or event being researched. In other words, the effectiveness of a scale requires knowledge of both the structure of a measurement device and the causes that influence variation within its items (Bollen, 1989). This requires that structural integrity be examined across different populations and events. Only when this has been done is it feasible to comment on its validity regarding latent constructs with any degree of certainty. Moreover, such structural reanalysis can raise interesting methodological and theoretical questions.

This was illustrated by Viet and Ware's (1983) analysis of the Mental Health Inventory and by Byrne's (1991) analysis of the Maslach Burnout Inventory. Byrne compared groups of intermediate, secondary, and tertiary educators and found that, while some structural features of the item set were appropriate across all groups, each group had structural features peculiar to itself. The conclusions reached in these studies highlight the need for vigilance with respect to assumptions made about and applications endorsed for psychometric instruments; they also post a warning against any assumptions of structural invariance. Constructs may be more accurately viewed as contingent phenomena, leading to questions regarding what aspects of personal experience or environment could influence the nature of the underlying construct.

Several facets of organizational experience might influence response to traumatic events. Differences in training, job expectations, task and role performance, operational and organizational "culture,"and demographic differences between members could readily yield diversity between and within designated risk groups. Instruments used to measure reactivity consequently require well-documented reliability and validity, and must be rigorously evaluated for applicability across a wide range of populations and events before meaningful conclusions can be drawn regarding the impact of occupational events or the efficacy of occupational or organizational interventions.

Even where structural qualities are adequately articulated in the course of development, it remains open to question whether the assumptions and parameters of standardization hold true when a scale is administered to different populations or following exposure to a range of differing events and demands. Scales are generally administered with the assumption that dispositional and environmental factors do not impinge on the manner in which participants respond; this contention, however, is rarely put to the test. The development and the evaluation of the scales used to support research in a particular area of study thus represents an important activity. In general, there has been a seeming imbalance between development and evaluation, with the majority of effort being expended on the former. In the absence of evaluation, the quality of instruments used, irrespective of their quality when first developed, should be viewed with caution. This chapter will pursue this issue in relation to the use of the Impact of Event Scale (IES; Horowitz, Wilner, & Alvarez, 1979; Horowitz, Wilner, Kaltreider, & Alvarez, 1980).

There are several ways that reaction to traumatic stress can be studied in relation to various population groupings. Existing groups such as occupational categories (police, fire fighters, nurses), groups defined by the nature of the traumatic event (road accidents, refugee), treatment groups, and national or cultural groups can be compared and contrasted. These groups represent appropriate foci both for determining norms and, by contrasting patterns of symptoms and reactions, for isolating factors that affect reactions. This chapter will focus on intergroup comparisons.

METHOD

The IES is used extensively to assess intrusion and avoidance in populations exposed to traumatic events. In the light of the foregoing discussion, questions can be asked of the IES on the grounds that its use has transcended the population and purposes for which it was developed. Differences between populations, their backgrounds, and the nature and frequency of the traumatic events to which subsequent populations have been exposed provide good opportunities to test the structural consistency of the scale. Preliminary analyses of data obtained from distinct occupational groups in several different countries were conducted to examine structural properties of the IES and to explore the stability of these characteristics over time and across occupational groups and cultures. The common denominator between all groups was high risk status with respect to likelihood of exposure to traumatic incidents.

Data were obtained from fire-fighter, nursing and social service groups (see Table 1). These data provided an opportunity to explore the structural integrity of the IES by enabling comparisons to be drawn within and between professions and, by collecting data from different countries, to examine structural integrity within a cross-cultural framework. English versions of the questionnaire were administered to the Australian, Scottish, and Nigerian samples; for the Japanese group, the questionnaire was translated into Japanese and then translated back into English. The

Table 1 The occupation, national origin, and sample size of the populations used in the analyses.

Population	Country	N
Fire-fighters	Scotland (Sco)	69
	Nigeria (Nig)	224
	W. Australia (Aus)	137
	Japan (Jap)	670
Theater nurses	W. Australia (Nur)	76
Social Service	W. Australia (AIH 1 — 1993)	231
Social Service	W. Australia (AIH 2 — 1995)	262

consistency between the original and the retranslated version was sufficient to assume that all groups were responding to comparable questions.
Data were collected from the social service population (AIH 1 [Authority
for Intellectually Handicapped persons] and AIH 2) on two occasions, with
data collection points separated by a period of 2 years.

Given the differences between these groups with regard to professional status, the nature of their work, and the kinds of incidents to which
they might be exposed, it was not feasible to use a common checklist of
traumatic experiences to define precipitating incidents. This problem was
surmounted by asking respondents to complete the IES with respect to the
most recent work-related experience (within a 6-month period) that resulted in unpleasant or disturbing feelings unlike those normally experienced in their work, and which led to feelings of inability to perform to
levels they would otherwise have expected.

RESULTS

Items comprising the IES are reproduced in Table 2; letters refer to
designations of items in the subsequent analyses. Analyses revealed several

Table 2   The Impact of Event Scale.

Designations of items in subsequent analyses	Item
A.	I thought about it when I didn't mean to [I]
B.	I avoided letting myself get upset when I thought about it or was reminded of it [A]
C.	I tried to move it from my memory [A]
D.	I had trouble falling asleep or staying asleep, because of pictures or thoughts about it that came into my mind [I]
E.	I had waves of strong feelings about it [I]
F.	I had dreams about it [I]
G.	I stayed away from reminders of it [A]
H.	I felt as if it hadn't happened or it wasn't real [A]
I.	I tried not to talk about it [A]
J.	Pictures about it popped into my mind [I]
K.	Other things kept making me think about it [I]
L.	I was aware that I still had a lot of feelings about it, but I didn't deal with them [A]
M.	I tried not to think about it [A]
N.	Any reminder brought back feelings about it [I]
O.	My feelings about it were kind of numb [A]

Note. The items forming the Intrusion and Avoidance subscales are marked with a super-
script I and A, respectively.

inconsistencies, with respect to both scale content and the structural relations between items.

Psychometric analysis

No coherent structure emerged when aggregate data from all groups were analyzed collectively. Separate exploratory factor analyses (principal axis with varimax rotation—SPSS; Norusis, 1992) indicated that for each group except the Japanese, some "avoidance" items clustered together as did some "intrusion" items. In all analyses, items with a face validity claim to these two categories had ambiguous or idiosyncratic loadings. All analyses delivered qualitatively different patterns of loading, with the degree of commonality differing for comparisons between groups. No recognizable pattern emerged for any item that could not be categorized as an "avoidance" or an "intrusion" item. These analyses suggested that a more detailed analysis of the structure of the responses to the IES would be required for each group.

To determine whether the lack of coherence in the data was endemic, or was rather a reflection of quantitatively or qualitatively different structures among the groups, the data were subjected to cluster analysis. The K-means method of cluster analysis (SPSS; Norusis, 1992) based on the full item set of the IES was used. As six sets of data representing samples that differed culturally and occupationally were available (see Table 1), a target of six clusters was set on the rationale that this would allow for unique assignment of groups to clusters. The centroids of the clusters are of no consequence for the purpose to be argued here, hence only the percentage of cases within groups for each group is presented in Table 3. As the bold italicized percentages show, there was a tendency for cases to cluster by occupation and by culture; this evidence suggested that structural analyses at the group level would be warranted. Further analyses were undertaken using confirmatory factor analysis (LISREL − 8.2; Jöreskog & Sörbom,

Table 3   Percentage of each sample in each of the six cluster analysis groups.

Group	AIH	JAP	SCO	NIG	NUR	AUS
Group 1	0.00	0.20	**86.70**	0.00	0.00	0.00
Group 2	31.20	2.60	0.00	10.80	2.70	11.00
Group 3	**37.20**	27.80	0.00	5.60	**84.90**	**78.00**
Group 4	20.20	2.30	0.00	35.70	1.40	1.60
Group 5	9.20	28.80	10.00	**40.80**	9.60	8.70
Group 6	2.30	**38.50**	3.30	7.00	1.40	0.80

Note. Bolded type indicates the cluster to which each sample was assigned. AIH = Authority for Intellectually Handicapped Persons; JAP = Japan; SCO = Scotland; NIG = Nigeria; NUR = Theater Nurses in Western Australia; AUS = Australia.

Table 4   "Intrusion" item loadings.

	A	D	F	J	K	N	NFI	Rel.
AIH 1	.81	.81[a]	.68[a]	.85	.91	.87	.99	.93
AIH 2	.88	.92	.80	.94	.92	.87	.99	.96
NIG	.61	.66	.76	.76	.60	.67	.96	.84
AUS	.91[a]	.75	####	.82	.81	.97[a]	.99	.93
SCO	.83	−.81	####	.71	.75	−.78	.96	.88

Note. #### = Item omitted from analysis to achieve fit; NFI = Normed fit index; Rel.= Reliability; AIH 1 = Authority for Intellectually Handicapped Persons, 1993 Data; AIH 2 = Authority for Intellectually Handicapped Persons, 1985 Data; NIG = Nigeria; AUS = Australia; SCO = Scotland.
[a]Correlated error variances.

1993). For each group, items initially designated as "avoidance" (B, C, G, I, L, M) and "intrusion" (A, D, F, J, K, N) were tested for fit to a unidimensional congeneric model. Parameter estimates were based on the method of weighted least squares, using polychoric correlations. This method is recommended by Jöreskog and Sörbom (1988) where the data consist of ordered categories. In all instances where there were sufficient cases (except for the Japanese sample with respect to "intrusion" items), a satisfactory fit was achieved for a subset of the items (χ^2 Type I error rate > .05; NFI > .9). For each group, the maximum reliability was calculated for both derived scales using the method described by Werts, Rock, Linn, and Jöreskog (1978). The results of these analyses are summarized in Tables 4 and 5. Table 4 lists the intrusion loadings (weighted least squares estimate) for the individual one-factor solution; Table 5 lists the avoidance loadings (weighted least squares estimate) for the individual one-factor solution.

Confirmatory factor analyses showed that a congeneric subset of the items existed for both sets, except for the "intrusion" items in the Japanese group. Data for the other four groups revealed that the same six "avoidance" items and the same five "intrusion" items formed congeneric sets.

Table 5   "Avoidance" item loadings.

	B	C	G	I	L	M	NFI	Rel.
AIH 1	.55	.86	.78	.72	.79	.89	.97	.89
AIH 2	.69	.87	.83	.80	.83	.88	.97	.92
JAP	.46	####	####	.43	.76	.57	.96	.66
NIG	.43	.69	.79	.73	.56	.56	.95	.80
AUS	.82	.86	.88	.85	.79	.70	.97	.92
SCO	####	.84	−.79	−.89	−.72	.99	.99	.93

Note. #### = Item omitted from analysis to achieve fit; NFI = Normed fit index; Rel.= Reliability; AIH 1 = Authority for Intellectually Handicapped Persons, 1993 Data; AIH 2 = Authority for Intellectually Handicapped Persons, 1985 Data; JAP = Japan; NIG = Nigeria; AUS = Australia; SCO = Scotland.

Inspection of the loadings suggested that the structures differ quantitatively between the groups and, in the case of the Scottish data, qualitatively as well. In short, reliable unidimensional measures of "avoidance"
and "intrusion" can be established for all but one of the groups (Japanese).
There are, however, beta (quantitatively different loadings) and gamma
(different patterns of loadings and/or sign of loadings) differences (Paton
& Smith, 1996) among the remaining groups.

Having established that the item sets for "avoidance" and "intrusion"
differed quantitatively and qualitatively between the groups, a further
analysis was undertaken to determine whether the reduced item set
corresponding to the defined subsets formed a two-dimensional space for
the groups on which they had been verified—namely, both the AIH
samples and the Scottish, Nigerian, and Australian fire-fighters. These data
were analyzed using INDSCAL (SPSS; Norusis, 1992) based on Euclidean
distances. Figure 1 shows the two-dimensional item-plot (stress = .314,
R^2 = .41) and Figure 2 shows the location of the groups in the two-dimensional space by derived subject weights. The two-dimensional item-plot
shows that the items are neatly grouped along a clear "intrusion–avoidance" axis and an axis that we have tentatively called "action–thought."
The derived subject weights show grouping by culture (Australian vs.
other) and occupation fire-fighter vs. AIH).

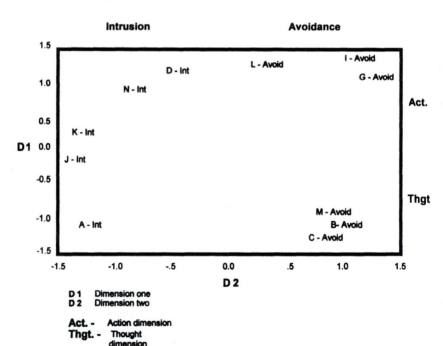

Figure 1   Plot of MDS two-dimensional solution.

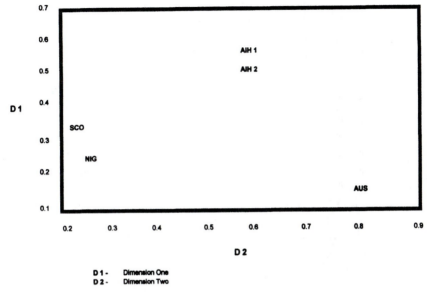

Figure 2 Derived subject weights by dimensions.

While the analyses are not completely commensurable because of differences in variables and groups, they nevertheless support the following conclusions:

1   Responses to the IES in these groups are functions of both occupation and culture.

2   Reliable congeneric subsets of "avoidance" and "intrusion" items can be established for cultural/occupational groups. The status of the remaining IES items remains ambiguous.

3   There is no common structure for the IES; a general classification of the 11 verified items along the dimensions of "avoidance–intrusion" and "action–thought" is, however, warranted.

DISCUSSION

Before proceeding to discuss these findings, some methodological issues need to be considered. Although an attempt was made to control for the nature of the event experienced (by asking respondents to define the event in terms of subjective experience), it was not possible to control for differences in intensity or timing of the traumatic experience reported. Although this represents a significant hurdle when examining symptoms, establishing norms, or making a direct comparison between scores recorded by individuals, it is less problematic when examining structural integrity. If a scale is accessing a latent construct, the structural relations between items should hold irrespective of, for example, the intensity of response or the time between an event and assessment of reactions. Although caution should still be exercised with respect to their interpretation, these data can be considered to represent an appropriate basis for comment on structural consistency and its implications.

Generally, when a scale is administered, interest is focused on scores obtained and their comparison to appropriate norms; interest here was focused instead on structural relationships. In comparison to the original scale, the data presented here revealed several inconsistencies in both item content and the structural relations between items, with both occupational and cultural differences evident. These data suggest that the IES is not tapping into homogeneous constructs, and that what we are observing is instead the interaction between the effects of latent variables and environmental and dispositional contingencies. Traumatic reactivity, as measured by the IES, can thus be more accurately described as a contingent phenomenon.

The removal of causally ambiguous items revealed a solution containing 11 rather than the original 15 items. Examination of the structural relations between these items revealed an interesting picture. Intrusion and Avoidance remained discreet subscales, but their interpretation requires some qualification. Contrary to expectations, intrusion–avoidance emerged as one dimension in the solution derived here; a second dimension, tentatively labeled "action–thought" (see Figure 1) was a particularly interesting finding, and one with both theoretical and practical implications. While the appearance of an intrusion–avoidance dimension in this analysis was consistent with the theoretical model that provided foundation for development of the original scale, the appearance of a second dimension is not easy to accommodate within that model. The implications of the action–thought dimension for theories of traumatic reactivity remain to be articulated, but suggest at the very least a need for further investigation into the theoretical nature of work-related psychological trauma in high-risk occupations.

Structural inconsistencies were also evident in the two-dimensional data (presented in Figure 2). It is possible to discern within these data some similarities between occupations, in that the fire-fighters were more similar to each other on Dimension 1 than they were to the AIH group, but cultural similarities were also evident on Dimension 2 between the Australian groups (AIH and the Australian fire-fighters).

Differences between groups were particularly evident in cluster analysis data (Table 3); this would appear to reveal at least two things. First, it is evident that the analysis revealed a considerable degree of structural heterogeneity, even within the same professional groupings. Although there is some overlap between the Japanese and Australian fire-fighter groups, the overall level of consistency between these groups is low. What is particularly interesting is the similarity between the Australian samples, where the social service, nursing, and fire-fighter samples fall generally into Group 3. According to these data, cultural factors appear to be the more important determinant of observed structural relationships.

The structural consistency between the AIH 1 and AIH 2 samples suggests that the organizational environment exercises a relatively uniform influence on the response to, and expression of, trauma impact; however, a measure of caution should be exercised in the interpretation of this observation. Because it was impossible to distinguish those who responded at both data collection points from those who responded only at the latter, these data represent the combined influence of dispositional, organizational, and, given their position relative to the Australian fire-fighter group, cultural influences. The structural differences evident between cultures, professional populations, and organizations indicates that the scale must be calibrated for each unique population under study. Once this is done, the AIH 1 and AIH 2 data suggest that it can be used reliably within an organization.

Developing a dialectic between theory and measurement can afford opportunities for theory development. Conversely, failure to examine the structural relations outlined here may result in misleading, and certainly incomplete conclusions being drawn regarding traumatic reactivity. The development of such a dialectic can thus make a valuable contribution to debate on the manner in which trauma reactivity is conceptualized and the nature of the factors likely to influence it (Paton et al., 1998).

Structural, training, and managerial factors may all play etiological roles in the development of traumatic stress reactions in organizational contexts. Organizational structure has been implicated as a determinant of work-related traumatic stress reactions. Organizations with a hierarchical, bureaucratic structure have been said to increase risk status (Doepal, 1991; Dunning, 1994; Powell, 1991). Strict adherence to hierarchical reporting and authority systems may increase demands on staff when responding, slow the response, increase time that staff are in contact with the event, or intensify and prolong reactivity. Hierarchical systems are also often motivated more by protecting the organization from blame than by effectiveness in supporting staff and activity. When organizational needs supersede staff needs, or where staff needs are neglected or denied, staff reactivity may be exacerbated. This suggests that, for effective response and the promotion of staff well-being, normal administrative procedures should be relaxed and, in their place, crisis management procedures specifically designed to manage impact and recovery should be implemented. In addition, staff well-being can be promoted by organizational ownership of both the crisis and its implications, rather than seeking to apportion blame.

Training represents another area of organizational intervention that can serve to minimize reactivity and promote quality of life. Reducing the likelihood of traumatic demands being perceived as stressors and facilitating preparation can lessen psychological morbidity and hasten reconciliation of impact (Alexander & Wells, 1991; Grant, 1996; Paton, 1994). Paton (1994, 1996) identified several issues here. One issue is related to the need to identify hazard characteristics faced by high-risk professionals within the training needs analysis process, and to then develop programs that facilitate these characteristics being incorporated into their operational schemata. Areas identified as being important within a training context include, for example, developing understanding and acceptance of the emotional and psychological impact of operating in high-risk situations, developing realistic operational and performance expectations, understanding the nature of disaster environment and its implications for well-being and performance, developing a capability in managers and leaders to work in high-risk environments, developing a team culture and effective support networks, and ensuring that the simulations and exercises used in training are sufficiently comprehensive to facilitate the development of a flexible and adaptable response capability.

Managers have a key role to play in both response and recovery phases, but often lack the capability and/or willingness to realize their potential in this context (Alexander & Wells, 1991; Dunning, 1994; Paton, 1997; Violanti, 1996). Managerial preparation can be facilitated through specially developed training programs that build on existing capabilities. Paton (1997) identified several areas that should be covered in these training programs, including developing a participative and supportive management style; acknowledging staff needs; identifying staff presenting immediate needs for intervention; planning to effectively meet staff needs; developing communication, planning, and implementation skills; delegating; managing uncertainty and ambiguity; and managing recovery and the return to productive functioning.

The data reported here also hold implications for the design and management of support resources intended to prevent the development of traumatic stress reactions. The fact that reactivity is not just a function of exposure to specific (traumatic) characteristics makes it unlikely that short-term, event-focused interventions such as psychological debriefing will be effective in achieving this goal. Indeed, an event-centered focus could exacerbate problems by detracting attention from such things as organizational factors and managerial style. The analysis discussed here highlights the need for interventions designed to prevent traumatic stress reactions to adopt a more holistic approach, and one that involves making more holistic changes in organizational design and management.

CONCLUSION

The data described here provide a tentative basis for arguing against the notion of traumatic reactivity, at least with respect to how it is defined by current applications of the IES, representing a homogenous construct and an invariant aspect of the human response to a particular class of event. In work-related contexts, traumatic stress reactions appear to reflect causal influences emanating from the interaction between a specific traumatic event and organizational, professional, and cultural influences, rather than their emergence as a direct consequence from the experience of any specific traumatic event. At an organizational level, the physical, social, interpersonal, and performance context of work interact with the demands of the traumatic experience to define the manner in which traumatic events are conceptualized and processed, and hence determine the nature and extent of reaction and response. Cultural influences were also discernible and influence the response to, and the expression of, traumatic reactions. It could be inferred that organizational and cultural factors will also influence how people cope with trauma and respond to support interventions. Only by expanding research agendas to incorporate comparative studies will it be possible to develop a comprehensive and accurate understanding of these phenomena.

This approach also holds out the possibility of exploring the manner in which groups are formed on the basis of peoples' reactions to events. Groups defined in this manner would represent an appropriate means of determining whether different patterns of individual reactions are present within pre-existing groups—for example, can police be divided into meaningful subgroups on the basis of their reactions to murder victims? This approach could also be used to determine whether distinctive groupings occur across occupations—for example, do police and fire-fighters form the same range of subgroups following exposure to similar events (e.g., road traffic accidents)? Cluster analysis is an appropriate method for separating individuals into groups based on their scores on a set of measures; this technique, when extended to the effects of trauma, would operate on the assumption that groups could be defined on the basis of disposition and response patterns.

Some preliminary work along these lines (Paton, Cacioppe, & Smith, 1992) indicated that fire-fighters can be classified into a limited number of groups on the basis of their responses to stress and symptom measures. Despite the crudeness of the measures, the results indicated that the method can be useful in planning training programs for fire-fighting personnel. On a broader front, empirical groupings can be useful in determining the degree to which responses and reactions are driven by individual traits in relation to structural factors. Clearly determining this relation can provide valuable input into the development of effective inoculation and treatment programs.

In conclusion, the data presented here suggest that we are observing the interactive effects of latent variables with environmental and dispositional contingencies. These data also suggest that researchers may be making inappropriate assumptions about the latent constructs that these scales purport to assess. Theory development and testing can readily be hindered under such constraints, while productive exploration of broader, more complex and more interactive models of traumatic experience, reactivity, and resolution may be overlooked or even dismissed. Responsible science and responsible practice both demand better.

REFERENCES

Alexander, D. A., & Wells, A. (1991). Reactions of police officers to body handling after a major disaster: A before and after comparison. *British Journal of Psychiatry, 159,* 517–555.

Bollen, K. A. (1989). *Structural equations with latent variables.* New York: Wiley.

Brooke, P., Russel, D., & Price, J. (1988). Discriminant validation of measures of job satisfaction, job involvement, and organizational commitment. *Journal of Applied Psychology, 73,* 139–145.

Byrne, B. M. (1991). The Maslach Burnout Inventory: Validating factorial structure and invariance across intermediate, secondary and university educators. *Multivariate Behavioral Research, 26,* 583–605.

Collins, L. M., & Horn, J. L. (1991). *Best methods for the analysis of change: Recent advances, unanswered questions, future directions.* Washington, DC: American Psychological Association.

Cortina, J. M. (1993). What is coefficient alpha? An examination of theory and applications. *Journal of Applied Psychology, 78,* 98–104.

Doepal, D. (1991). Crisis management: The psychological dimension. *Industrial Crisis Quarterly, 5,* 177–188.

Dunning, C. (1994). Trauma and countertransference in the workplace. In J. P. Wilson & J. D. Lindy (Eds.), *Countertransference in the treatment of PTSD* (pp. 351–367). New York: The Guilford Press.

Friedman, R. J., Framer, M. B., & Shearer, D. R. (1988). Early response to posttraumatic stress. *EAP Digest, 8,* 45–49.

Graham, N. K. (1981, January). Done in, fed up, burned out: Too much attrition in EMS. *Journal of Emergency Medical Services, 5,* 24–29.

Golembiewski, R. T., Billingsly, K., & Yeager, S. (1976). Measuring change and persistence in human affairs: Types of change generated by OD designs. *Journal of Applied Behavioral Science, 12,* 133–157.

Grant, N. K. (1996). Emergency management training and education for public administration. In R. T. Styles & W. L. Waugh (Eds.), *Disaster management in the U.S. and Canada: The politics, policymaking, administration and analysis of emergency management* (2nd ed., pp. 313–327). Springfield, IL: Charles C. Thomas.

Horowitz, M., Wilner, M., & Alvarez, W. (1979). Impact of Event Scale: A measure of subjective stress. *Psychosomatic Medicine, 41,* 209–218.

Horowitz, M. J., Wilner, N., Kaltreider, N., & Alvarez, W. (1980). Signs and symptoms of post-traumatic stress disorder. *Archives of General Psychiatry, 37,* 85–92.

Jöreskog, K. G., & Sörbom, D. (1988). *PRELIS: A program for multivariate data screening and data summarization.* Mooresville, IN: Scientific Software, Incorporated.

Jöreskog, K. G., & Sörbom, D. (1993). *LISREL 8: Structural equation modeling with the SIMPLIS language.* Hillsdale, NJ: Erlbaum.

Magnusson, D., & Bergman, L. R. (1990). *Data quality in longitudinal research.* Cambridge, England: Cambridge University Press.

McCammon, S. L. & Allison, E. J. (1995). Debriefing and treating emergency workers. In C. R. Figley (Ed.), *Compassion fatigue* (pp. 115-130). New York: Brunner/Mazel.

Miller, I., & Ford, G. (1996). *Patterns of exit from the New Zealand Police: A study of disengagements 1985-95.* Unpublished report, New Zealand Police, Wellington.

Millsap, R. E., & Hartog, S. B. (1988). Alpha, beta and gamma change in evaluation research: A structural equation approach. *Journal of Applied Psychology, 73,* 574-584.

Norusis, M. J. (1992). *SPSS for Windows: Professional statistics.* Chicago, IL: SPSS, Inc.

Paton, D. (1994). Disaster relief work: An assessment of training effectiveness. *Journal of Traumatic Stress, 7,* 275-288.

Paton, D. (1996). Training disaster workers: Promoting well-being and operational effectiveness. *Disaster Prevention and Management, 5,* 10-16.

Paton, D. (1997). *Dealing with traumatic incidents in the workplace* (3rd. ed.), Queensland, Australia: Gull Publishing.

Paton, D., Cacioppe, R., & Smith, L. M. (1992). *Critical incidents stress in the West Australian Fire Brigade.* Perth, Australia: West Australian Fire Brigade.

Paton, D., & Smith, L. M. (1996). Assessment of work-related psychological trauma: Methodological issues and implications for organizational strategies. In D. Paton, & J. Violanti (Eds.), *Traumatic stress in critical occupations: Recognition, consequences and treatment.* Springfield, IL: Charles C. Thomas.

Paton, D., Smith, L. M., & Stephens, C. (1998). Developing interventions for managing occupational and traumatic stress: Integrating the recovery and organizational environments. *Australasian Journal of Disaster and Trauma Studies, 2*(1) [Online serial: URL http://www.massey.ac.nz/ ~ trauma/].

Porras, J. I., & Singh, J. V. (1986). Alpha, beta, and gamma change in modeling based organization development. *Journal of Occupational Behavior, 7,* 9-24.

Powell, T. C. (1991). Shaken, but alive: Organizational behavior in the wake of catastrophic events. *Industrial Crisis Quarterly, 5,* 271-291.

Short, P. (1979) Victims and helpers. In R. L. Heathcote & B. G. Tong (Eds.), *Natural hazards in Australia.* Canberra, Australia: Australian Academy of Science.

Stephens, C., Long, N., & Miller, I. (1997). The impact of trauma and social support on posttraumatic stress disorder: A study of New Zealand police officers. *Journal of Criminal Justice, 25,* 303-314.

Viet, C. T., & Ware, J. E. (1983). The structure of psychological distress and well-being in general populations. *Journal of Consulting and Clinical Psychology, 51,* 730-742.

Violanti, J. (1996). Trauma stress and police work. In D. Paton & J. Violanti (Eds.), *Traumatic stress in critical occupations: Recognition, consequences and treatment.* Springfield, IL: Charles C. Thomas.

Werts, C. E., Rock, D. R., Linn, R. L., & Jöreskog, K. G. (1978). A general method of estimating the reliability of a composite. *Education and Psychological Measurement, 38,* 933-938.

Chapter 5

A Critical Look at PTSD: Constructs, Concepts, Epidemiology, and Implications

Jeffrey P. Staab, Carol S. Fullerton, and Robert Ursano

INTRODUCTION

Disasters and traumatic events are an all too common part of everyday life. From earthquakes to hurricanes, war and terrorist events, we are constantly told of the frequency of these frightening events by televisions, radios, and newspapers that have made us a global village. Breslau and colleagues (1991) estimated that the lifetime prevalence of exposure to traumatic events in the United States was 39.1%.

Most individuals exposed to traumatic events will do fine. However, some will experience psychological distress and illness. Although posttraumatic stress disorder is perhaps the best known outcome of trauma, it is not the only, or perhaps even the most important psychological response to trauma (Ursano, Fullerton, & Norwood, 1995). Acute stress disorder, depression, substance abuse, somatization, and personality change as well as resiliency have all been reported. Both acute and chronic symptoms have been the focus, but the relationships between immediate and subsequent psychological morbidity or recovery are uncertain.

Some authors have suggested that acute dissociation may be a particularly good predictor of chronic psychopathology (Classen, Koopman, & Spiegel, 1993). For this reason, the new DSM-IV diagnosis of acute stress disorder (ASD) has a criterion for dissociation that is not found in PTSD (see the Appendix). However, the definition of dissociation is not entirely clear. For example, the symptoms of numbing and derealization are considered dissociative in ASD but avoidant in PTSD. The rationale for adding ASD to the diagnostic nomenclature included identifying those who may benefit from early intervention and the possibility that ASD may be a harbinger of posttraumatic stress disorder (PTSD; Koopman, Classen, Cardeña, & Spiegel, 1995).

A number of studies have investigated acute and chronic symptoms of intrusion, avoidance, arousal, and dissociation following a wide variety of traumatic events (for reviews, see Green, 1993; Koopman et al., 1995). Early studies of traumatic events also included descriptions of dissociative phenomena such as time distortion and numbing (Lindemann, 1941; Terr, 1983). More systematic studies of dissociation have been done recently. Retrospectively, peritraumatic and posttraumatic dissociative symptoms have been reported in Vietnam veterans (Bremner et al., 1992; Hyer, Albrecht, Boudewyns, Woods, & Brandsma, 1993; Marmar et al., 1994), genocide survivors (Carlson & Rosser-Hogan, 1991), and anxiety disorder patients with personal trauma histories (Warshaw et al., 1993). Studies of earthquake (Cardeña & Spiegel, 1993) and firestorm victims (Koopman et al., 1994), and witnesses to an execution (Freinkel et al., 1994) emphasized the importance of dissociative symptoms. These studies indicated that peritraumatic dissociation is related to the severity of the traumatic stressor (Bremner et al., 1992; Marmar et al., 1994; Koopman, Classen, & Spiegel, 1994) and may predict the subsequent development of more severe, posttraumatic psychopathology (Koopman et al., 1994; Solomon, Mikulineer, & Benbenistry, 1989). In a prospective study, Cardeña and Spiegel (1993) found that dissociation in the San Francisco earthquake victims at 1 week predicted later symptoms.

There is, however, no consensus as to which of the acute symptom(s) —intrusion, avoidance, arousal, dissociation—if any, predict later psychopathology. Feinstein and Dolan (1991) found that the severity of acute intrusion and avoidance was a better predictor of subsequent PTSD than was the severity of injury in a series of accident victims. McFarlane (1992a), studying survivors of the 1983 Ash Wednesday bushfires in Australia, found that intrusion predicted avoidance. Shalev (1992) found no consistent pattern in the intrusion and avoidance experienced by victims of a terrorist attack on a bus. He concluded that hyperarousal was the driving force behind his participants' symptoms, though he did not measure arousal explicitly. McFarlane (1992b) expanded this, hypothesizing that hyperarousal is the core deficit in PTSD.

Given the interest in the time course of posttraumatic symptoms and the interrelationship among the various symptoms, the development of models of traumatic stress responses over time is needed. Recently, the important distinction of acute and chronic PTSD and acute stress disorder has highlighted several questions. What is the relationship of early symptoms to later symptoms? What is the course of illness? How does one set of symptoms relate to another? What maintains symptoms in some individuals while others "recover" rapidly? All of these questions require a thoughtful approach to the possible relations between time, symptoms, and sustaining mechanisms. In this chapter, we use a systems approach often seen in engineering to describe the dimensions critical to the modeling of PTSD.

A MODEL OF TRAUMATIC STRESS

A control systems model of traumatic stress (see Figure 1) considers the dynamic interactions between stressors, traumatized individuals, and the environment. The control systems perspective focuses on the time course of stress responses and the biopsychosocial mechanisms that regulate them. Stressors are conceptualized as events that disturb the internal homeostasis of an individual and alter his or her relationships with

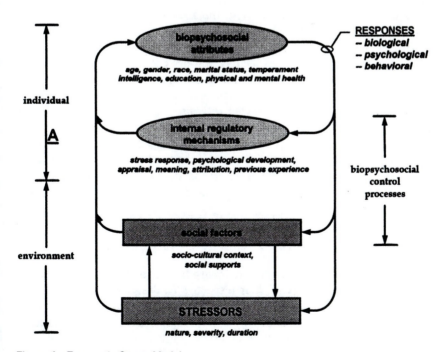

Figure 1   Traumatic Stress Model.

significant others and the community. Stress responses are affected by the circumstances at the time of the trauma, the nature and severity of the stressor, and importantly, by the function of biopsychosocial control processes including the individual's internal regulatory mechanisms and environmental or sociocultural factors regulatory forces.

Several outcomes are, therefore, possible. The impact of a stressor may be counteracted completely, restoring internal homeostasis and eliminating all effects on interpersonal relationships. Conversely, the stressor may change the individual or environment in such a way that pre-event conditions cannot be restored. Instead, a new relationship is established between the individual and the environment, with potentially different dynamics. The long-term outcome of this new relationship depends on its stability and benefits. Psychopathology is expected whenever the trauma reverberates within the individual, generates new and unfavorable dynamics, or creates a condition to which the individual cannot adapt. In physical systems, these situations occur when control mechanisms fail to offset the effects of a disturbance, become dysregulated, or are forced to operate outside their designed range. The impact of these circumstances on traumatic stress responses is examined below.

A control systems model also investigates the time course of traumatic stress responses from the acute, posttraumatic period through long-term outcome. This focuses attention on the dynamics of posttraumatic changes within the individual and between the individual and the environment. Significant relationships among biological, psychological, and social variables, vulnerabilities in the system, and potential predictors of outcome can be identified by this approach. A well-designed control model requires short- and long-term data about important system variables. In the traumatic stress field, there is a wealth of information about long-term, biological, psychological, and social responses to traumatic events. Unfortunately, there are considerably fewer longitudinal studies of the acute posttraumatic period, largely because of the logistical difficulties in reaching recently traumatized individuals. As a result, the control systems model is more speculative about the initial impact of traumatic events but is able to raise several salient hypotheses about acute stress responses and their long-term sequelae.

Control theory

Control processes are familiar to many biological and social scientists, albeit in the terminology of their respective fields. A brief review of three control mechanisms will introduce the concepts of control theory that are most salient for the model of traumatic stress and clarify differences in nomenclature. The simplest, and most familiar, control mechanism is classical feedback control, where the controlled variable influences its own production. The level of the variable is measured and compared with a reference range or set point. A signal related to the difference between these values drives the system (Brogan, 1985). Household thermostats are simple feedback controllers. They measure room temperature, compare the measured value with the thermostat setting, and signal the furnace or air conditioner to produce or remove heat. The reference range for a feedback controller is not always constant. When the reference changes with time, the controller tracks it. An example of this situation is the feedback control of basal cortisol concentrations that have a diurnal rhythm (Berne & Levy, 1983).

Self-tuning control   Self-tuning or adaptive control represents a more sophisticated feedback control mechanism. Self-tuning controllers measure a system's inputs and outputs but do not feed this information back as a control signal. Instead, they use it to track the internal conditions (state variables) of the system that are manipulated to control its performance. This type of control provides greater flexibility because the system can adapt to changing environmental conditions or variations in its own functioning (Brogan, 1985). Some luxury automobiles, for example, have suspension systems that automatically adjust to speed and road conditions. The control mechanism does not directly change the car's orientation with respect to the road. Rather, it manipulates the parameters of the suspension system (stiffness of the struts and/or damping of the shock absorbers) so that the response is best suited to traveling conditions. The suspension stiffens to minimize body sway during high-speed turns and softens to absorb the impact of rough roads. A smooth ride is the result of effectively adjusting the system's internal dynamics to the environment in which it operates.

A biopsychological example of adaptive control is habituation, in which the intensity of psychological or physiological responses varies with the novelty of the stimulus. Receptor upregulation and downregulation illustrates self-tuning at the cellular level. Cells exposed to a chronic overabundance or deficiency of a transmitter substance will decrease (downregulate) or increase (upregulate) their receptors for that substance. This adjustment to cellular dynamics normalizes the cell's function in its new environment. Although self-tuning controllers provide more flexibility than classical feedback controllers, they can generate unexpected and potentially unstable behavior in some circumstances. Receptor downregulation, for instance, is responsible for drug tolerance and withdrawal. The range of adaptability is limited by controller's initial design, just as genetic determinants constrain biopsychological behavior.

Optimal control   In many cases, controlling a system involves trade-offs among internal variables, output, and additional considerations such as economic factors and time demands. Optimal control is a process for achieving the best balance among these sometimes competing influences (Brogan, 1985). The heart of an optimal controller is its "cost function," a weighted sum of the impact of significant variables on system performance. An optimal controller drives the system so that the cost function is minimized. This focus on important parameters and minimal cost is also a useful tool for investigating the behavior of existing systems.

Consider eye movements as an example. Smooth pursuit eye movements track targets of interest. The most important variable is the difference between the path of the eyes and the path of the target. Energy consumption is a secondary consideration to limit muscle fatigue during extended tracking. Saccadic eye movements, on the other hand, focus the eyes rapidly on new targets. Here the most significant variables are the duration of the saccade and the final position of the eyes, which must be on target. Energy consumption cannot be a limiting factor if the eyes are to move as quickly as possible. Therefore, a cost function for smooth pursuit would weigh path differences heavily and energy consumption moderately but would discount time and final position. A cost function for saccades would weigh time and final position heavily but would disregard path and energy consumption. Each cost function can be minimized to provide optimal control for its own type of eye movement, but the two are not compatible with one another. This predicts that a single control mechanism cannot direct smooth pursuit and saccades at an optimal level. Not surprisingly, the brain uses different neural control mechanisms for each one (Robinson, 1981). Behavioral scientists have found that human decision-making is a dynamic process of weighing costs, benefits, and information feedback (Brehmer, 1990; Payne, Bettan, & Johnson, 1990). In other words, at the highest levels of thought, humans use optimal control processes in which the cost functions are adaptively tuned to changes within the individual and ongoing interactions between the individual and the environment.

Hierarchical control structures   Individual control mechanisms are often combined in cascades or hierarchies with the output of higher controllers setting parameters for the lower ones. The controller at the top of the cascade is the "master controller" (Luyben, 1973). In homes with advanced energy-saving features, a central computer lowers the thermostat setting at night and raises it again in the early morning as part of an optimal control algorithm to minimize energy costs. The thermostat operates in its usual manner to control the furnace, but the central computer determines its set point. Hierarchical control is commonplace in biological systems. The hypothalamic-pituitary-adrenal (HPA) axis has several levels of hierarchical control including classical, negative feedback of cortisol to the pituitary and hypothalamus, self-tuning control of receptor sites at all levels, and multiple neural inputs to the hypothalamus (Berne & Levy,

1983). Many psychological models of mental function are organized hierarchically, as are most social organizations.

The major advantage of hierarchical control is that division of labor increases flexibility and efficiency for the system as a whole. However, there are disadvantages. Just as micromanagement or conflicts within a social system degrade the performance of the entire organization and expend large amounts of energy, so too with control systems. The complexity of hierarchical control demands attention to the interrelationships of the various components. When self-tuning controllers are included, a malfunction at one level may lead to a cascade of adjustments at other levels that are less than satisfactory.

Structure of the control systems model of traumatic stress

Individual attributes   Figure 1 shows individual and environmental factors within the control systems model of traumatic stress. The individual is described in terms of the biopsychosocial attributes and internal regulatory mechanisms that define who the person is and how he or she responds to change (i.e., the static and dynamic elements of the individual). Some individual attributes are constant, such as gender and race, whereas others change over the life cycle.

Characteristics that change can be divided into two groups, those that are essentially constant with respect to the time course of a traumatic event (age, intelligence, education, temperament), and those that may be altered by the stressor (marital status, health). This division provides the first level of structure to the model. The constant variables are known to influence traumatic stress responses, but stressors cannot change them. In other words, stress responses are functions of gender and race, but the converse is not true. The essentially constant variables also affect stress responses, but stressors have, at best, an indirect influence on them. For example, a traumatic event could conceivably affect an individual's educational and career choices, but this would be mediated by other factors such as scholastic abilities or the need to return to work following the death of a supporting spouse. Therefore, stress responses are functions of this group of variables, but stressors have only an indirect impact on these characteristics. The last group of individual attributes has a reciprocal relationship with traumatic events. Marital status and health influence stress responses while traumatic events can have immediate and dramatic effects on these parameters. By keeping these relationships in mind, circular arguments about causes and effects of traumatic stress can be reduced.

Regulatory mechanisms   Internal, biological, and psychological regulatory mechanisms control the dynamic responses of the individual at several levels. Peripheral reflexes such as those that maintain skeletal muscle tone, cardiorespiratory rates, and gastrointestinal motility are classical feedback controllers with some adaptability that receive their set points from central mechanisms. Reflexes that involve brainstem nuclei and the pituitary regulate functions such as the sleep-wake cycle and hormone secretion using combinations of classical and self-tuning control as was described above for the HPA axis.

At the top of the hierarchy are neural circuits through the frontal lobes, basal ganglia, thalamus, and limbic structures. These are the brain's optimal controllers that receive information from internal and external sources, effect compromises among the various demands of the human system, and coordinate behavioral output. Other areas of the brain serve this system. The primary sensory and association cortices digest information from the environment and the body while memory systems maintain a database of information that is essential for constructing and fine-tuning cost functions.

Discussion of internal regulatory mechanisms from a psychological perspective depends on the specifics of various theories of mental function. In general terms, the least sophisticated processes are instincts, inborn determinants of behavior and temperament. At the next level are defense mechanisms or conditioned responses that generate behaviors refined by experience (i.e., adaptive control). The master controller carries out executive functions, cognitive processes that are responsible for decision-making (i.e., construction of cost functions), and the conscious direction of human activities (i.e., optimal control). Learning and memory are essential components of adaptive and optimal control.

Social factors   A review of many of the social factors investigated in the context of traumatic events can be found elsewhere in this volume. Social support, social networks, interpersonal debriefing and many of the psychotherapeutic interventions after trauma offer support for the regulatory effects of interpersonal interactions on traumatic stress. A developmental perspective is helpful for appreciating the relationship between social factors and individual regulatory mechanisms in the control systems model of traumatic stress.

The proposed model includes a reciprocal relationship between the individual and society that changes over time. In particular, the balance between internal and societal control mechanisms shifts as the individual matures. At birth, the infant is endowed genetically with its basic control structure. However, this includes only initial settings for the self-tuning controllers and a limited database from which to construct cost functions for high-level, optimal control processes. Most master control functions come from the child's principal caretakers and local community, who provide feedback about his or her behavior.

These experiences provide information to the child's maturing control systems in a culturally sanctioned manner. As the child develops, behavior is controlled to a greater extent by internal regulatory mechanisms. The biopsychological and sociocultural legs provide the control system with a degree of redundancy because both are capable of directing aspects of the individual's behavior. Redundancy can cause conflict, but more importantly for trauma recovery, it provides a level of overlapping control and more than one site for targeting interventions.

Nature and severity of stressors   Table 1 is a summary of the relationship between the nature and severity of stressors and individual traumatic stress responses distilled from many investigations of this topic (Bownes, O'Gorman, & Sayers, 1991; Carlson & Rosser-Hogan, 1991; Cohen & Roth, 1987; Kuch & Cox, 1992; Norris, 1992; Smith & North, 1993; Steinglass & Gerrity, 1990; Weine et al., 1995; Yehuda, Southwick, & Giller, 1992; for review, see Green, 1993). Posttraumatic stress symptoms and rates of PTSD increase along the nature and severity axes as indicated by the arrows. Several general statements can be made about this method of classifying traumas. At the top of the list are genocide and warfare, orchestrated inhumanity on a large scale. These cause the most suffering for the individual, followed by sexual and physical assaults, terrors directed at one person by another (or small number of others). Accidents with physical injury that cause disability and the disruption of one's physical integrity are next in terms of psychological morbidity. At the bottom of the list are technological and natural disasters. Technological disasters generate higher rates of posttraumatic symptoms and PTSD possibly because

Table 1   Summary of research relating the nature and severity of stressors to posttraumatic symptoms and PTSD.

nature of stressor	genocide	death camps
	combat	wartime atrocities
	sexual assault	death threats
	physical assault	use of a weapon
	serious accident	physical injuries
	exposure to death	grotesque, unexpected
	technological disaster	injuries, financial loss
	natural disaster	injuries, financial loss

severity of stressor

Note. This table is a compendium of numerous research studies using different methodologies to examine the relationship between stressors, posttraumatic stress symptoms, and rates of PTSD. Few studies have compared stressors directly.

they are perceived as having preventable (and human) causes (Weisæth, 1994).

Within each type of disaster, certain measures of severity are commonly associated with a poorer outcome. For example, those who suffer personal injuries or significant financial loss in natural disasters are likely to have more symptoms (Green, 1993). Those assaulted with deadly weapons or threatened with death fare worse than other victims of assault (Bownes, et al., 1991; Cohen & Roth, 1987). Holocaust victims who survived death camps had higher rates of PTSD than those in work camps or other circumstances (Kuch & Cox, 1992). However, measures of severity did not correlate with risk of PTSD in survivors of the Khmer Rouge atrocities in Cambodia (Carlson & Rosser-Hogan, 1994).

Dynamic interactions

Individual attributes, regulatory mechanisms, and stressors Table 2 summarizes numerous studies (Breslau, Davis, & Andreski, 1995; Carlson & Rosser-Hogan, 1991; Davidson, Hughes, Blazer, & George, 1991; Green, Grace, Lindy, Gleser, & Leonard, 1990; Green et al., 1991; Hiley-Young, Blaka, Agueg, Rozynka, & Gusman, 1995; Kuch & Cox, 1992; Lee, Valiant, Torrey, & Elder, 1995; Marsella, Friedman, & Spain, 1993; McCranie, Hyer, Boudewyns, & Woods, 1992; McNally & Shin, 1995; Norris, 1992; Penk et al., 1989; Resnick, Kilpatrick, Best, & Kramer, 1992; Roesler & McKenzie, 1994; Schnurr, Friedman, & Rosenberg, 1993; Smith, North, McCool, & Shea, 1990; Ullman, 1995; Weine et al., 1995) that have examined the relationships between individual characteristics and traumatic stress responses. These data are not as strong or as consistent as the findings relating stressors to outcome. Nevertheless, they highlight a num-

Table 2   Summary of research relating individual attributes to traumatic stress susceptibility.

Characteristic	Greater susceptibility
Age	Adolescents, Young adults
Gender	Women
Race/culture	Unclear
Intelligence	Lower ?
Education	Less
Temperament	Introverted
Locus of control	External
Psychological development	Complex interaction
Psychiatric history	Pre-existing disorder
Trauma experience	Dual effect

Note. This table is a compilation of many investigations covering a variety of traumatic events. Individual susceptibility to traumatic stress is a topic of considerable debate. Please refer to the text for additional information.

ber of dynamic interactions that can be understood, or about which hypotheses can be formulated, with the control systems model in Figure 1.

Most studies have found that younger adults are more susceptible to the effects of traumatic events than older adults (Davidson et al., 1991; Norris, 1992; Ullman, 1995), but the impact of trauma at different stages of life is more complex (Green et al., 1991; Roesler & McKenzie, 1994). In a study of the population affected by the collapse of a dam in Buffalo Creek, West Virginia, Green and her colleagues (Green et al., 1991) found that responses of the youngest children (aged 2–7) depended on their parents' reactions and the atmosphere in the home. In other words, they relied heavily on social input received from their parents and immediate surroundings to control their behavior. Older children and adolescents (ages 8–15) had more symptoms and were more affected by their perceptions of life threat than by their parents' or family's reactions. They may have had a greater capacity to comprehend the enormity of the disaster. They also were operating with tenuously independent, psychological regulatory mechanisms and more complex social support structures. In contrast, the relative resilience of older adults may arise from internal control processes and social supports that are forged over time.

The relationship between childhood developmental factors and susceptibility to traumatic stress has been difficult to ascertain, due in part to the paucity of studies with data collected prior to the traumatic event. McCranie et al. (1992) found a relationship between poor fathering and risk of PTSD in combat veterans exposed to lower, but not higher, levels of combat. Two other studies (Green et al., 1990; Hiley-Young et al., 1995) reported no impact of negative childhood factors on PTSD, though the latter authors did find an effect on rates of substance abuse and depressive disorders. This raises the possibility that childhood problems may create defects in the control systems that lead to relatively minor instabilities in traumatic stress responses. Individuals with such instabilities would be noticeable in comparison to others only at low levels of stress, since higher levels could wash out the differences. (A big hammer will break all the glasses in a set, while a small one may break only the glass with a defect.) Racial and cultural factors have not been well studied. (Marsella et al., 1993). Culture may influence the expression of symptoms, particularly dissociation. However, traumatic stress responses are univeral experiences, and rates of PTSD for severe stressors such as genocide are similar across ethnic groups (Carlson & Rosser-Hogan, 1991; Kuch & Cox, 1992; Weine et al., 1995).

Data on individual temperament and locus of control provide some insight into the relationship of traumatic stress responses to the biopsychological and sociocultural components of the control system. Some data (Schnurr et al., 1993) suggest that extraverts are less susceptible to the negative effects of traumatic stress than introverts, even though they have a tendency to expose themselves to more incidents (Breslau et al., 1995; Lee et al., 1995). Other investigations have not found this dimension of temperament to be important.

The possible negative impact of introversion can be understood in terms of how the individual weighs variables in calculating his or her own sense of well-being. Introverts weigh internal states most heavily and rely more on internal than social control mechanisms to counteract negative disturbances to their well-being. When their circumstances are favorable, this provides a degree of insulation from the impact of external events. When faced with traumatic stressors, however, this tendency isolates them from available social supports. Not only do they reach out less often, but they weigh the feedback they receive less heavily than their extraverted counterparts. If the trauma limits the efficacy of their internal regulatory mechanisms (e.g., through physical injury), they are forced to rely on the weaker leg of their control system. For extraverts, their stronger external focus is a double-edged, but apparently more favorable, arrangement. They may be more affected by negative events, but in the aftermath of trauma, the environment can provide powerful forces for recovery.

Locus of control may be one of the more important individual attributes for predicting outcome following trauma (Baum, 1987). Locus of control differs from the dimension of introversion and extraversion. It measures the individual's belief about whether internal or external factors ultimately control one's life, rather than the day-to-day reliance on internal or external regulatory mechanisms. Those with an internal locus of control seem to fare better in the aftermath of traumatic events. They seem better able to marshall available resources, whether internal or external, for all aspects of the recovery process from practical matters (e.g., time to shovel out the basement) to psychological recuperation. It remains to be seen if introversion and external locus of control yield an interactive effect. Such a person would be reliant on internal regulatory mechanisms while believing that ultimate control was outside of his or her reach, a recipe for hopelessness following trauma.

Previous trauma experience has proven to be a double-edged sword. In two Norwegian disasters, firefighters and rescue workers felt that previous experience or disaster training was beneficial to them (Ersland, Weisæth, & Sund, 1989; Hytten & Hasle, 1989). Among Israeli combat veterans of the 1982 Lebanon campaign, the picture was more complicated (Solomon, 1993). Soldiers with combat experience who did not have a combat stress reaction during previous battles were less likely than inexperienced troops to have a combat stress reaction in Lebanon. However, soldiers who developed a combat stress reaction during earlier wars were the most susceptible to combat stress in Lebanon.

Therefore, the impact of experience seems to depend on the individual's response to the previous trauma. Those who weathered the earlier incidents well showed a positive adaptive response by their control systems. They were more capable of counteracting disturbances induced by subsequent events. Individuals with a poor previous outcome demonstrated the limits of their regulatory mechanisms for those circumstances. Unfortunately, their failed attempts at adaptation seem to decrease their system's resilience to later trauma. Biological studies have demonstrated persistent maladaptations in those with chronic PTSD (for review, Southwick, Yehuda, & Charney, in press).

Studies of the HPA axis among combat veterans (Yehuda et al., 1995a) and Holocaust survivors (Yehuda et al., 1995b) give an indication of the effects of trauma history on biological feedback control mechanisms. Both groups had lower free cortisol levels than comparison groups without PTSD. Dexamethasone suppression tests in the combat veterans showed that the HPA axis was more sensitive to glucocorticoid feedback. The study of Holocaust survivors showed that these effects may last many years. Holocaust survivors with PTSD had low levels of cortisol 50 years after their traumatic experiences while those without PTSD did not. Furthermore, cortisol levels correlated significantly with the severity of avoidant symptoms among Holocaust survivors with PTSD.

These findings suggest that the HPA axis has a chronically increased sensitivity to cortisol feedback following trauma, though this effect may occur only in those with significant posttraumatic symptoms. The full dynamics of these changes remain to be elucidated. Research using acoustic startle paradigms in participants with PTSD (Orr, Pitman, Lasko, & Herz, 1993) provide further evidence of chronic maladjustments to control mechanisms in PTSD. Individuals with PTSD do not habituate to a series of tones as measured by psychophysiological responses including heart rate and skin conductance. Habituation is a self-tuning control mechanism in which the strength of responses varies with the novelty of the stimulus.

Social factors and stressors   Another consideration is the reciprocal interaction between stressors and social factors depicted in Figure 1. For example, a stressor such as the death of a spouse due to an accident or violence simultaneously disturbs the individual and weakens the social leg of the control processes. Conversely, social supports can mitigate the negative impact of an ongoing stressor, providing relief from the aftereffects of trauma (e.g., support from friends, disaster relief, etc.).

Table 1 indicates another level of interaction between stressors and social supports. In the hierarchy of trauma types in Table 1 (the nature axis), social disasters are at both ends of the spectrum with individual traumas in the middle. This suggests that belonging to a community of similarly exposed individuals may mitigate the disturbances induced by a stressor, provided that the community is not the source of the trauma. This hypothesis could be tested by measuring the outcomes of individuals exposed to objectively similar levels of threat in three conditions (human-induced social trauma, individually experienced events, and natural or technological disasters).

Initial conditions   The response of a system to a disturbance depends on the circumstances of the system at the time of the event (i.e., the initial conditions). A well-tuned controller may fail to contain a disturbance if the system it is regulating is at its limit of stability when the event occurs. A less capable controller may perform adequately in the face of a similar disturbance if its initial conditions are more favorable. Very little attention has been paid to initial conditions in traumatic stress research. Initial conditions describe the state of an individual at a time just preceding the trauma. They are not the same as individual attributes or internal regulatory mechanisms, which are traits. Initial conditions also differ from the acute posttraumatic states that have been measured in a few recent studies (Cardeña & Spiegel, 1993; Shalev, Peri, Canetti, & Schreiber, 1996).

Data relating pre-existing psychiatric disorders to posttraumatic outcome indicate the possible effects of initial conditions on traumatic stress responses. Individuals with active psychiatric disorders at the time of a trauma, particularly major depression, anxiety disorders, and PTSD (Resnick et al., 1992; Smith et al., 1990; Staab et al., unpublished data), are at higher risk for a poor outcome than their healthy counterparts. Unfortunately, these data cannot distinguish between the pre-existing pathological states and the potentially problematic control systems underlying them. Research on initial conditions would be particularly useful for those who can predict their exposure to trauma (e.g., emergency personnel).

APPLICATIONS OF THE MODEL

Now that the structure and function of the control systems model have been reviewed, it is possible to examine two unanswered questions about PTSD. Is PTSD on a continuum with normal stress responses or is it a separate pathological state? Does the acute stress response predict long-term outcome? A third question follows from the first two and places PTSD back into the context of the community. Can community interventions have an impact on the development of PTSD, and if so, how?

Defining PTSD

Military psychiatrists beginning in World Wars I and II formulated the combat stress reaction as a "normal response to an abnormal event." This de-emphasis of psychopathology served combat units well because it led to short-term interventions that returned large numbers of able-bodied men to the front lines. Combat stress symptoms were treated with short periods of rest and the overtly stated expectation of recovery and return to duty. There is no doubt that this type of intervention reduced acute symptoms and preserved acceptable levels of functioning for most service members. Initial data suggested that it also reduced long-term psychiatric morbidity, though more recent research on combat veterans in Israel (Solomon, 1993) is less clear on this point.

The fundamental concepts of these wartime treatment plans were translated into intervention programs for communities affected by civilian disasters. The focus on the abnormal event also was adopted by victims rights advocates because it emphasized the trauma and its perpetrator as the cause of suffering rather than the character of the victim (Yehuda & McFarlane, 1995). Posttraumatic symptoms were considered to be normally distributed and proportional to the severity of the stressor. From this perspective, PTSD is the most severe and enduring reaction to trauma, at one end of a continuum of stress responses. In other words, PTSD is quantitatively different but qualitatively similar to normal stress reactions.

The enduring nature of PTSD and its significant resistance to biological and psychological therapies are evidence that it is qualitatively different than a normal stress reaction. The two may share some symptoms, but their time course is decidedly different. Yehuda and McFarlane (1995) argued that biological abnormalities, such as blunted cortisol levels and the acoustic startle reflex, distinguish chronic PTSD from other traumatic stress responses. However, there are no data regarding when these chronic abnormalities develop or the specific factors that trigger them. The debate about the definition of PTSD, though, is not a purely academic one. At the heart of the matter lie important distinctions about the etiology of the disorder and implications of these distinctions for community interventions as well as the early identification and treatment of individual trauma survivors.

On a continuum with normal?   The debate about the continuum of traumatic stress responses has included an examination of symptom structure, including the issue of core symptom(s) addressed earlier in this chapter. This focus has not resolved the continuity question in part because normal stress responses and PTSD share symptoms, continuum or not. A potentially more important reason is that the debate usually concerns only one, sometimes two, dimensions of symptomatology at a time. Most studies report intrusion, avoidance, and arousal symptoms separately, even if they all are measured with the same instrument. Other studies report the number of symptoms, also a single dimension of pathology.

One of the most striking aspects of PTSD, however, is the requirement that there are symptoms present simultaneously in three distinct clusters.

The DSM-IV defines PTSD as a three-dimensional disorder. Therefore, a more elegant way of investigating the continuum of symptoms would be to determine if normal stress responses and PTSD lie within the same area of three-dimensional space. Intrusion, avoidance, and arousal are positively correlated with one another in trauma victims, so they will not be distributed randomly in three space. Figure 2 is a hypothetical depiction of this concept. Figure 2.A, region *a*, when taken by itself, represents posttraumatic stress responses on a continuum. (Ignore the other regions until the next section.) The shaded area of region *a* is the normative, posttraumatic stress response. The upper right quadrant is the area of high intrusion, avoidance, and arousal. At point *a*, these three symptoms are at moderate levels. PTSD is located at the outer reaches of this quadrant. The other areas represent non-diagnostic combinations of two or fewer symptoms. It is assumed that individuals who experience lower than normal levels of intrusion and/or avoidance have to exert effort to maintain that state. Therefore, the lower left is depicted as an area of low intrusion and avoidance, but elevated arousal. If future studies map PTSD and non-diagnostic stress responses onto the same region of three space as hypothesized in region *a*, this will be stronger evidence of a continuum than existing data about symptom structure. This construct, however, does not explain the chronic nature of PTSD. In fact, individuals are expected

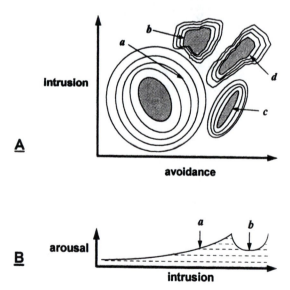

Figure 2 Topographical representation of posttraumatic psychopathology. In Panel *A*, the level of arousal is represented by the contour lines. Shaded areas are local minima (valleys). Panel *B* is a cross-section through points *a* and *b* along the intrusion axis. Point *a* is a symptomatic point within a potentially normal posttraumatic stress response; *b* depicts PTSD; *c* represents posttraumatic major depression; and *d* delineates comorbid PTSD and depression.

to settle back into the low energy, shaded area with time. The maintenance of chronic posttraumatic symptoms cannot be explained by symptom structure alone. Dynamic forces within the biopsychosocial control structure are required.

For PTSD to lie on a continuum with normal reactions to trauma, the principal factor(s) distinguishing PTSD from normal reactions must differ only by degrees. This is not an a priori exclusion of qualitative differences in symptoms or behavior. Rather it requires that mechanisms underlying qualitative differences operate on a continuous spectrum from normal to pathological. This can occur in control systems where continuously adjustable parameters generate qualitatively different system behaviors. In classical feedback control, systems are often stable for a range of feedback sensitivities (i.e., feedback is negative and disturbances eventually die out) but unstable at higher sensitivities (i.e., the feedback becomes positive, magnifying the impact of disturbances). Stability is a dichotomous variable, but its underlying mechanism is continuous. If the system is defined by behavioral stability, it has two distinct states. If defined by feedback sensitivity, however, the stable and unstable behaviors are on a continuum.

A similar situation occurs with adaptive control mechanisms. Adaptive controllers track incoming data from the environment. The sensitivity of controllers to new information is set largely by one parameter, the "forgetting factor" (Brogan, 1985), that determines how much old data are included in a moving average of environmental inputs. When the forgetting factor is too high, the controller retains so much old information that it becomes impervious to new inputs. When the forgetting factor is too low, the controller "forgets" old data, treating new inputs as unique events. As with feedback controllers, a continuous process underlies system behaviors that appear qualitatively different.

Consider this somewhat fanciful example of a driver in an automobile with an adjustable suspension system. The driver is the (hopefully) optimal and master controller, whereas the suspension is a lower level, self-tuning mechanism. The environment consists of typical streets and highways populated by average drivers and potholes. The car hits a large pothole, but the suspension works well and no damage is done. The car stabilizes quickly, and the driver's acute stress reaction subsides. The driver, however, vows never to hit such a hole again. This changes the usual cost function of driving as the weight given to pothole avoidance is adjusted upward. The new cost function demands increased attention to visual inputs about road conditions ahead. The driver decreases the forgetting factor of hand movement control so that the hands will respond instantly to current visual inputs and not factors in historical data. The hands now drive the car around every irregularity in the road without considering recent history about the car's ability to withstand the impact of many potholes. In response to this increased swerving, the suspension stiffens to provide more stability for rapid maneuvers. However, it is now less able to absorb bumps. The greater intrusion of these bumps increases the driver's resolve to avoid potholes, so the cost function is adjusted again.

The driver's interaction with environment changes as other cars give wider berth or speed past. Others on the road make less than friendly gestures. The driver ratchets up the cost function term for avoiding other cars in response to this new environmental challenge. Two-footed driving becomes necessary to ensure a rapid reaction when other cars approach. The suspension stiffens again and erratic brake lights further irritate other drivers. On top of that, the driver is quickly exhausted by hypervigilant, white-knuckled, two-footed trips in a car with a stiff suspension. The driver concludes that the car hasn't been the same since that big pothole.

At the end of this example, none of the individual control mechanisms are defective, but many of them have been adjusted from their original settings in a cascade of events. The system as a whole is behaving in a decidedly abnormal manner, generating intrusion, avoidance, arousal, social isolation, and sore gluteus maxima. Yet each separate control parameter is not far from its original value. Nonetheless, it would be difficult to retune the system. In its final condition, a change in any one element could destabilize it. Lifting the foot off the brake pedal without adjusting pressure on the accelerator or easing the suspension while swerving wildly to avoid potholes could be disasterous. This complex interplay of symptoms and behavioral responses sustains the system in a pathological state despite the fact that the underlying maladaptations are on a continuum with normal.

Recovery would require a multilevel readjustment. In this example, the cascade of maladjustments started at the top and worked down. This is not to imply that cognitive changes are the primary focus of pathology in PTSD. The example could easily have started with a stiffer suspension in response to the first pothole, followed by intrusion of road irregularities and maladjustments upward. This analysis only suggests that it is possible for PTSD to lie on a continuum with normal stress reactions if one considers the function of biopsychosocial regulatory mechanisms. The systems found to be abnormal in chronic PTSD (e.g., blunted cortisol output, lack of habituation to acoustic startle) are intriguing, but their dynamics are not characterized well enough at present to understand whether or not they result from continuous disturbances in underlying control mechanisms.

A separate pathological state?   Return again to Figure 2.A and consider all four regions. This is a hypothetical representation of symptom mapping in three dimensions for the possibility that PTSD is not continuous with normal stress responses. In this case, PTSD and other posttraumatic disorders map onto separate regions of the three symptom dimensions. Here the symptom structure explains the chronic and enduring clinical course of PTSD. Regions *b*, *c*, and *d* are stable, but pathological, states in which the relationships among the three symptom clusters differ from normal stress reactions. In this example, region *a* represents only nonpathological traumatic stress responses. Figure 2.B clarifies the differences in relationships among the symptoms. Note the different levels of intrusion between points *a* and *b* for the same level of arousal.

Evaluating Figure 2 in topographical terms suggests a possible mechanism for the development of posttraumatic psychopathology. A traumatic stressor pushes individuals out of the normal valley of region *a* and over the acute symptom peaks between regions where they settle into one of the chronic pathological valleys. The direction of symptoms determines the pathological outcome. Early and persistent intrusion drives individuals into region *b* (PTSD), while early and persistent avoidance pushes them into region *c* (depression). The pathological valleys are at a higher altitude of symptoms than region *a*. However, they are relative minimal compared with the surrounding, acute pathological peaks, hence their relative stability. Figure 2.B shows that energy has to be applied to the system to push individuals from any of the pathological valleys. The energy has to be applied in the proper direction to send them back to recovery in region *a*.

This topographical illustration of traumatic stress cannot explain the etiology of the chronically abnormal relationships among symptoms in PTSD. This is a dynamic process that can be investigated with the control systems model. Figure 2 proposes that traumatic stressors are overwhelming events that push individuals beyond the boundary of normal stress responses and into a different environment. In control systems terminology, the system is pushed outside its region of stability, beyond the region in which the control mechanisms are capable of effecting recovery and into a state in which the systems dynamics change. Initial conditions and predisposing factors determine whether the trauma is sufficient to push an individual beyond his or her envelope. Because the system's dynamic relationship with the environment is changed, control mechanisms honed by previous experience may be ineffective and have to adapt to new circumstances to restore some form of stability.

Consider again the automotive analogy. This time the driver is forced off of a well maintained highway by a sudden accident ahead. The car slides over an embankment onto icy, unfamiliar roadway. A stable response to this abrupt change and any hope for recovery depend on the adaptability of car and driver to the new environment. Some attributes of the car and driver may increase the chances for recovery (e.g., four-wheel drive, experience), whereas others are likely to have a negative impact (e.g., bald tires). The car, driver, and icy road have a different three-dimensional relationship than the car, driver, and highway. Pre-existing control algorithms such as habits of rapid acceleration and hard braking may exacerbate problems. If the driver does not adapt these control processes to the new circumstances, car and road may have a wintery fling, leaving him or her stuck until spring. Even with the most optimal adaptation, however, the dynamic interactions of the car and driver with the icy road will not be the same as those on the highway. If the driver manages to steer back or is towed back to the main highway (or when spring arrives), readaptation to the normal environment is required. If the driver continues to navigate slowly, make very leisurely starts and stops, and maintain long following distances, he or she will be as much a pariah on the highway as the driver in the first example. Recovery will be incomplete, even though the initial event was managed reasonably well.

Given the present state of knowledge, the control systems model cannot answer the question of whether PTSD lies on a continuum with normal stress responses or not. However, it suggests directions in which to pursue the answer. The first step is to investigate PTSD as a multidimensional entity, not just in terms of its symptom structure as in Figure 2, but across the spectrum of trauma-induced biological dysfunctions, psychological experiences, and strained social interactions. More fundamentally, however, the control systems model defines traumatic stress as a dynamic process. The database of knowledge in the traumatic stress field is filled with snapshots in time that have yielded a wealth of information about the biopsychosocial components of traumatic stress responses. The next step is to examine the dynamic mechanisms that posed these components for their pictures. It is intriguing that acute and chronic posttraumatic cortisol levels differ in individuals with PTSD. It is exciting that this biological change correlates with the psychosocial symptoms of avoidance. It is essential to investigate the control processes behind this change.

Early detection of psychopathology

The second question posed to the control systems model of traumatic stress concerned the prognostic value of acute stress symptoms. Table 3 presents a summary of four studies using demographics, stressors, acute stress symptoms, and ASD to predict PTSD. The data in Table 4 indicate that the diagnosis of ASD may be an important step forward in identifying individuals at risk for developing posttraumatic psychopathology. In the Guam and Pittsburgh studies, the presence of ASD at 1 week was a highly specific indicator of PTSD at 8 months after the disasters. However, its sensitivity in the Guam communities was fairly poor. In the small group of Pittsburgh disaster workers, however, ASD measured by the Stanford Acute Stress Reactions Questionaire (SASARQ; Cardeña & Spiegel, 1993) identified workers who were classified as positive for PTSD. Better results overall were obtained from stepwise (best predictors) logistical regression analyses that considered demographics and stressors in addition to acute

Table 3   Post-traumatic stress disorder (PTSD) case identification in disaster communities

Traumatic event	Sensitivity (%)/ specificity (%)	N	Identified at risk for PTSD	Cases of PTSD in risk group	Cases of PTSD missed
Guam typhoons					
ASD[1]	36.8/94.7	320	23	7	19
Model	63.2/90.7	320	40	12	7
Guam earthquake[2]					
ASD	57.1/91.8	92	11	4	3
Model	80.0/92.4	89	14	8	2
Pittsburgh body recovery[3]					
ASD	100.0/100.0	43	2	2	0
Jerusalem physical injury[4]					
Acute IES	92.3/65.8	51	25	12	1
Model	30.8/94.7	51	6	4	9

Note.   Case prediction (logistical regression) models in Guam typhoons (injury to self, acute dissociation, acute intrusion), Guam earthquake (age, race, typhoon stressors [financial loss, injury to self, separated from family], typhoon-induced PTSD), and Jerusalem (age, gender, education, trauma severity, immediate response [pain, fear, sense of doom], acute symptoms [dissociation, intrusion, avoidance, anxiety, depression]).
[1] Staab et al., 1996, retrospective study of five typhoons that struck Guam in 1992, ASD (acute stress disorder) measured with an instrument developed by the authors.
[2] Staab, J., et. al, unpublished results of effects of an 8.2 earthquake that occurred one year after the typhoons.
[3] Grieger et al., in press, retrospective study of rescue workers at an airline crash site., ASD measured with the Stanford Acute Stress Reactions Questionnaire (SASRQ), Cardeña et al. (1993).
[4] Shalev et al., 1996, prospective study, IES = Impact of Event Scale (Horowitz, et al., 1979), administered 2–6 days after injury.

stress symptoms. However, as shown in the right hand columns of Table 3, these models either missed a number of PTSD cases (sensitivity too low) or identified a large percentage of participants at risk (specificity too low).

The control systems model suggests what data are needed for improved predictions of outcome. From a control systems perspective, the response of a system to any disturbance can be predicted completely if the system's dynamics, initial conditions, and the nature and severity of the stressor are known. As discussed previously, research in the field of traumatic stress has focused on stressors, static attributes of the individual, and a few interactions. This covers little more than one of the three requisites for fully describing a system's response, so it is not surprising that investigators have been stymied in their efforts to predict outcomes from demographics and stressors alone.

A system's acute response to a disturbance, however, is a function of the initial conditions, severity of the disturbance, and the system's ability to absorb the initial impact of the stressor (i.e., early dynamics). The only information missing is the capacity of the control mechanisms to restore order over time (i.e., long-term dynamics). In other words, two and part of the third requirements for predicting outcome manifest themselves in the acute response. The importance of knowing long-term dynamics depends on the nature of the acute response and capabilities of the control processes. If the stressor drives the system clearly outside the stable response range of all control mechanisms, detailed information about controller function over the long-term is not necessary to predict a poor outcome. If the acute response may be within the controllers' envelope, however, control algorithms will determine outcome and predictions are guesswork without a knowledge of the system's regulatory dynamics. This has important implications for ASD. If ASD is a clearly distinct, abnormal stress response, then anyone who manifests ASD following a traumatic event is at enormous risk for subsequent psychopathology. However, if ASD is on a continuum with normal, predictions will be more difficult because of the paucity of data on individual, biopsychosocial control processes. The acute stress response alone may not be able to predict delayed-onset PTSD. This will require knowledge of the relationship between the acute stress state and control processes. Control mechanisms functioning at their limits may keep the acute stress response in check for a time, until they break down, consume their available energy, or face an additional challenge.

Figure 3 is an idealized drawing of four traumatic stress responses over time that illustrates these issues. Lines **1** and **2** have normal, long-term outcomes, whereas **3** and **4** represent long-term psychopathology. The acute stress response identifies line **2**, incorrectly, as a high-risk case, but

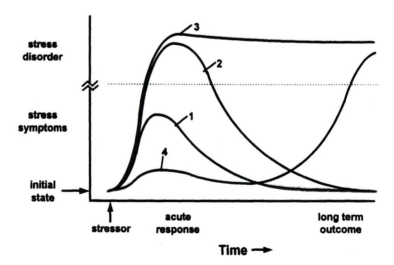

Figure 3 Traumatic stress responses over time. Line **1** represents acute stress symptoms that resolve with time; **2** depicts ASD that also resolves; **3** is ASD that progresses to PTSD; and **4** shows delayed onset PTSD.

misses **4**. If ASD could ever be defined as a pathological entity that inevitably leads to PTSD, line **2** would disappear and the specificity of ASD as a screening tool for PTSD would be 100%. The extent to which this fantasy is realized will determine the ratio of cases **2** to **3** and the prognostic value of ASD, or any other construct of acute stress responses. Early studies (Staab, Grieger, Fullerton, & Ursano, 1995; Staab et al., 1996; see Table 4) show some promise. A multidimensional analysis of acute symptom structure (as in Figure 2) may be helpful. The early identification of delayed onset PTSD, line **4**, is a much more daunting task because the distinguishing characteristics of control processes, whether biological, psychological, or social, will have to be uncovered. Therefore, the answers to the question, "Does the acute stress response predict long-term outcome?" are *maybe*, *sometimes*, and *wait and see*.

Control systems analysis of community interventions

The last question for the control systems model is whether community interventions have an impact on PTSD. In some ways, this is not a fair question because the core concepts of most community intervention programs accent wellness and recovery over illness, just as their wartime progenitors emphasized return to duty over psychopathology. Very limited systematic research in this area is available. For those at high risk for trauma-induced psychiatric illnesses, those whose control structures are completely overwhelmed or destabilized, community interventions may not be potent enough to effect recovery. However, the majority of disaster victims have posttraumatic symptoms, not outright disorders. They experience suffering and functional impairments at the same time that their demands are increased. Community interventions are exactly on target for this population. Well-structured programs aid biological (counseling regarding rest, diet, alcohol), psychological (cognitive emphasis on recovery, perspectives on meaning and attribution), and social (at many levels) control mechanisms in the process of recovery.

In disaster communities with fixed resources, the goal of decreasing morbidity for large numbers of people with symptomatic, but not pathological, stress responses may be at odds with the more labor intensive process of identifying the smaller number of individuals at risk for psychiatric illness. Current investigations of acute stress symptoms and a growing interest in stress response dynamics may offer better screening tools in the near future. This would lead to a more efficient, two-tiered structure for community disaster programs in which high-risk individuals would be identified reliably and routed to intensive treatment, while others would receive services designed to decrease morbidity and promote recovery. This will answer, we hope, the third question.

CONCLUSION

As we learn more about posttraumatic responses, it is very important for us to begin to conceptualize trauma responses using more comprehensive models. Such models aid us in identifying the important questions for study. The control model presented here emphasizes the importance of understanding the mechanisms that affect the time course of the disease—regulators, sustainers, and feedback loops. These may be basic brain and psychological mechanisms and social interactions that operate at all times, or they may be particular to traumatic stress symptoms. Through such modeling and research, we will better understand the issues of illness as well as resiliency in response to trauma.

REFERENCES

Baum, A. (1987). Toxins, technology, and natural disasters. In G. R. VandenBos & B.D. Bryant (Eds.), *Cataclysms, crises, and catastrophes: Psychology in action* (pp. 5–54). Washington, DC: American Psychological Association.

Berne, R. M., & Levy, M. N. (1983). *Physiology.* St. Louis, MO: The C. V. Mosby Co.

Bownes, I. T., O'Gorman, E. C., & Sayers, A. (1991) Assault characteristics and posttraumatic stress disorder in rape victims. *Acta Psychiatric Scandinavica, 83,* 27–30.

Brehmer, B. (1990). Strategies in real time dynamic decision making. In R. M. Hogarth (Ed.), *Insights in decision making: A tribute to Hillel J. Einhorn* (pp. 129–153). Chicago: University of Chicago Press.

Bremner, J. D., Southwick, S., Brett, E., Fontana, A., Rosenheck, R., & Charney, D. S. (1992). Dissociation and posttraumatic stress disorder in Vietnam combat veterans. *American Journal of Psychiatry, 149,* 328–332.

Breslau, N., Davis, G. C., & Andreski, P. (1995). Risk factors for PTSD-related traumatic events: A prospective analysis. *American Journal of Psychiatry, 152,* 529–535.

Brogan, W. L. (1985). *Modern control theory* (2nd ed.). Englewood Cliffs, NJ: Prentice-Hall.

Breslau, N., Davis, G. C., Andreshi, P., Peterson, E. (1991). Traumatic events and post traumatic stress disorder in an urban population of young adults. *Archives of General Psychiatry, 48,* 216–222.

Cardeña, E., & Spiegel, D. (1993) Dissociative reactions to the San Francisco Bay area earthquake of 1989. *American Journal of Psychiatry, 150,* 474–478.

Carlson, E. B., & Rosser-Hogan, R. (1991). Trauma experiences, posttraumatic stress, dissociation, and depression in Cambodian refugees. *American Journal of Psychiatry, 148,* 1548–1551.

Carlson, E. B., & Rosser-Hogan, R. (1994). Cross-cultural response to trauma: A study of traumatic experiences and posttraumatic symptoms in Cambodia refugees. *Journal of Traumatic Stress, 7,* 43–58.

Classen, C., Koopman, C., & Spiegel, D. (1993) Trauma and dissociation. *Bulletin of Menninger Clinic, 57,* 178–194.

Cohen, L. J., & Roth, S. (1987) The psychological aftermath of rape: Long-term effects and individual differences in recovery. *Journal of Social and Clinical Psychology, 5,* 525–534.

Davidson, J. R. T., Hughes, D., Blazer, D. G., & George, L. K. (1991). Post-traumatic stress disorder in the community: An epidemiological study. *Psychological Medicine, 21,* 713–721.

Ersland, S., Weisæth, L., & Sund, A. (1989). The stress upon rescuers involved in an oil rig disaster. "Alexander L. Kielland" 1980. *Acta Psychiatrica Scandinavia 80* (Suppl. 355), 38–49.

Feinstein, A., & Dolan, R. (1991). Predictors of post-traumatic stress disorder following physical trauma: An examination of the stressor criterion. *Psychological Medicine, 21,* 85–91.

Green, B. L. (1993). Identifying survivors at risk. In J. P. Wilson and B. Raphael (Eds.), *International handbook of traumatic stress syndromes* (pp. 135–144). New York: Plenum.

Green, B. L., Grace, M. C., Lindy, J. D., Gleser, G. C., & Leonard, A. (1990). Risk factors for PTSD and other diagnoses in a general sample of Vietnam veterans. *American Journal of Psychiatry, 147,* 729–733.

Green, B. L., Korol, M., Grace, M. C., Vary, M. G., Leonard, A. C., Gleser, G. C., & Smitson-Cohen, S. (1991). Children and disaster: Age, gender, and parental effects on PTSD symptoms. *Journal of the American Academy of Child and Adolescent Psychiatry, 30,* 945–951.

Hiley-Young, B., Blake, D. D., Agueg, F. R., Rozynko, V., & Gusman, F. D. (1995). Warzone violence in Vietnam: An examination of premilitary, military, and postmilitary factors in PTSD in-patients. *Journal of Traumatic Stress, 8,* 125–141.

Horowitz, M., Wilner, N., & Alvarez, W. (1979). Impact of Event Scale: A measure of subjective distress. *Psychosomatic Medicine, 41,* 209–218.

Hyer, L. A., Albrecht, J. W., Boudewyns, P. A., Woods, M. G., & Brandsma, J. (1993). Dissociative experiences of Vietnam veterans with chronic posttraumatic stress disorder. *Psychological Reports, 73,* 519–530.

Hytten, K., & Hasle, A. (1989) Fire fighters: A study of stress and coping. *Acta Psychiatric Scandinavica, 80,* (Suppl 355), 50–55.

Koopman, C., Classen, C., Cardeña, E., & Spiegel, D. (1995). When disaster strikes, acute stress disorder may follow. *Journal of Traumatic Stress, 8,* 29–46.

Koopman, C., Classen, C., & Spiegel, D. (1994). Predictors of posttraumatic stress symptoms among survivors of the Oakland/Berkeley, Calif. firestorms. *American Journal of Psychiatry, 151,* 888–894.

Kuch, K., & Cox, B. J. (1992). Symptoms of PTSD in 124 survivors of the Holocaust. *American Journal of Psychiatry, 149,* 337–340.

Lee, K. A., Vaillant, G. E., Torrey, W. C., & Elder, G. H. (1995). A 50-year prospective study of the psychological sequelae of World War II combat. *American Journal of Psychiatry, 152,* 516–522.

Lindemann, E. (1941). Symtomatology and management of acute grief. *American Journal of Psychiatry, 101,* 141–148.

Luyben, W. L. (1973). *Process modeling, simulation, and control for chemical engineers* (pp. 326–328). New York: McGraw–Hill.

Marmar, C. R., Weiss, D. S., Schlenger, W. E., Fairbank, J. A., Jordan, B. K., Kulka, R. A., & Hough, R. L. (1994). Peritraumatic dissociation and posttraumatic stress in male Vietnam theater veterans. *American Journal of Psychiatry, 151,* 902–907.

Marsella, A. J., Friedman, M. J., & Spain, E. H. (1993). Ethnocultural aspects of posttraumatic stress disorder. In J. M. Oldham, M. B. Riba, & A. Tasman (Eds.), *American Psychiatric Press review of psychiatry,* (Vol. 12, pp. 157–181). Washington, DC: American Psychiatric Press.

McCranie, E. W., Hyer, L. A., Boudewyns, P. A., & Woods, M. G. (1992). Negative parenting behavior, combat, exposure, and PTSD symptom severity: Test of a person-event interaction model. *Journal of Nervous and Mental Disease, 180,* 431–438.

McFarlane, A. C. (1992a). Avoidance and intrusion in posttraumatic stress disorder. *Journal of Nervous and Mental Disease, 180,* 439–445.

McFarlane, A. C. (1992b). Commentary. Posttraumatic stress disorder among injured survivors of a terrorist attack: Predictive value of early intrusion and avoidance symptoms. *Journal of Nervous and Mental Disease, 180,* 599–600.

McNally, R. J., & Shin, L. M. (1995). Association of intelligence with severity of posttraumatic stress disorder symptoms in Vietnam combat veterans. *American Journal of Psychiatry, 152,* 936–938.

Norris, F. H. (1992) Epidemiology of trauma: Frequency and impact of different potentially traumatic events on different demographic groups. *Journal of Consulting and Clinical Psychology, 3,* 409–418.

Orr, S. P., Pitman, R. K., Lasko, N. B., & Herz, L. R. (1993). Psychophysiological assessment of posttraumatic stress disorder imagery in World War II and Korean combat veterans. *Journal of Abnormal Psychology, 102,* 152–159.

Payne, J. W., Bettan, J. R., & Johnson, E. J. (1990). The adaptive decision maker: Effort and accuracy in choice. In R. M. Hogarth (Ed.), *Insights in decision making: A tribute to Hillel J. Einhorn* (pp. 129–153). Chicago: University of Chicago Press.

Penk, W. E., Robinowitz, R., Black, J., Dolan, M., Bell, W., Dorsett, D., Ames, M., & Noriega, L. (1989). Ethnicity: Post-traumatic stress disorder (PTSD) differences among Black, White, and Hispanic veterans who differ in degrees of exposure to combat in Vietnam. *Journal of Clinical Psychology, 45,* 729–735.

Resnick, H. S., Kilpatrick, D. G., Best, C. L., & Kramer, T. L. (1992). Vulnerability-stress factors in development of posttraumatic stress disorder. *Journal of Nervous and Mental Disorder, 180,* 424–430.

Robinson, D. A. (1981). The use of control systems analysis in the neurophysiology of eye movements. *Annual Review of Neuroscience, 4,* 463–503.

Roesler, T. A., & McKenzie, N. (1994). Effects of childhood trauma on psychological functioning in adults sexually abused as children. *Journal of Nervous and Mental Disorder, 182,* 145–150.

Schnurr, P. P., Friedman, M. J., & Rosenberg, S. D. (1993). Premilitary MMPI scores as predictors of combat-related PTSD symptoms. *American Journal of Psychiatry, 150,* 479–483.

Shalev, A. Y. (1992). Posttraumatic stress disorder among injured survivors of a terrorist attack: Predictive value of early intrusion and avoidance symptoms. *Journal of Nervous and Mental Disorder, 180,* 505–509.

Shalev, A. Y., Peri, T., Canetti, L., & Schreiber, S. (1996) Predictors of PTSD in injured trauma survivors: A prospective study. *American Journal of Psychiatry, 153,* 219–225.

Smith, E. M., & North, C. S. (1993) Posttraumatic stress disorder in natural disasters and technological accidents. In J. P. Wilson, & B. Raphael (Eds.), *International handbook of traumatic stress syndromes* (pp. 405–420). New York: Plenum.

Smith, E. M., & North, C. S., McCool, R. E. & Shea, J. M. (1990). Acute postdisaster psychiatric disorders: Identification of persons at risk. *American Journal of Psychiatry, 147,* 202–206.

Solomon, Z. (1993). Immediate and long-term effects of traumatic combat stress among Israeli veterans of the Lebanon war. In J. P. Wilson, & B. Raphael (Eds.), *International handbook of traumatic stress syndromes* (pp. 321–332). New York: Plenum.

Solomon, Z., Mikulincer, M., & Benbenistry, R. (1989) Combat stress reaction: Clinical manifestations and correlates. *Military Psychology, 1,* 35–47.

Southwick, S., Yehuda, R., & Charney, D. S. (in press). Neurobiological alteration in posttraumatic stress disorder: A review of the clinical literature. In C. S. Fullerton & R. J. Ursano (Eds.), *Acute and long term responses to trauma and disaster.* Washington, DC: American Psychiatric Press.

Staab, J. P., Grieger, T. A., Fullerton, C. S., & Ursano, R. J. (1995, May). *Predictors of acute stress disorder and its sequelae in a military community exposed to repeated natural disasters.* Braceland Navy Symposium, 148th Annual Meeting of the American Psychiatric Association, Miami, FL.

Staab, J. P., Grieger, T. A., McCarroll, J. E., Brandt, G. T., Fullerton, C. S., & Ursano R. J. (1996, May). *The relationship between acute stress disorder and subsequent posttraumatic stress disorder in three disaster populations.* New Research. Proceedings of the 149th Annual Meeting of the American Psychiatric Association, New York.

Steinglass, P., & Gerrity, E. (1990). Natural disasters and post-traumatic stress disorder: Short-term versus long-term recovery in two disaster-affected communities. *Journal of Applied Social Psychology, 20,* 1746–1765.

Terr, L. C. (1983). Time sense following psychic trauma: A clinical study of ten adults and twenty children. *American Journal of Orthopsychiatry, 53,* 244–261.

Ursano, R. J., Fullerton, C. S., & Norwood, A. (1995). Psychiatric dimensions of disaster: patient care, community consultation and preventive medicine. *Harvard Record of Psychiatry, 3,* 196–209.

Ullman, S. E. (1995). Adult trauma survivors and post-traumatic stress sequelae: An analysis of reexperiencing, avoidance, and arousal criteria. *Journal of Traumatic Stress, 8,* 179–188.

Warshaw, M. G., Fierman, E., Pratt, L., Hunt, M., Yonkers, K. A., Massion, A. O., & Keller, M. B. (1993). Quality of life and dissociation in anxiety disorder patients with histories of trauma or PTSD. *American Journal of Psychiatry, 150,* 1512–1516.

Weine, S. M., Becker, D. F., McGlashan, T. H., Laub, D., Lazrove, S., Vojvoda, D., & Hyman, L. (1995). Psychiatric consequences of "ethnic cleansing": Clinical assessments and trauma testimonies of newly resettled Bosnian refugees. *American Journal of Psychiatry, 152,* 536–542.

Weisæth, L. (1994). Psychological and psychiatric aspects of technological disasters. In R. J. Ursano, B. G. McCaughey, & C. S. Fullerton (Eds.), *Individual and community responses to trauma and disaster: The structure of human choas* (pp. 72–102). Cambridge, England: Cambridge University Press.

Yehuda, R., Boisoneau, D., Lowry, M. T., & Giller, E. L. (1995a). Dose-response changes in plasma cortisol and lymphocyte glucocorticoid receptors following dexamethasome administration in combat veterans with and without posttraumatic stress disorder. *Archive of General Psychiatry, 52,* 583–593.

Yehuda, R., Khana, B., Binder-Brynes, K., Southwick, S. M., Mason, J. W., & Giller, E. L., (1995b). Low urinary cortisol excrertion in Holocaust survivors with posttraumatic stress disorder, *American Journal of Psychiatry, 152,* 982–986.

Yehuda, R., & McFarlane, A. (1995). Conflict between current knowledge about posttraumatic stress disorder and its original conceptual basis. *American Journal of Psychiatry, 152,* 1705–1713.

Yehuda, R., Southwick, S. M., & Giller, E. L. (1992). Exposure to atrocities and severity of chronic posttraumatic stress disorder in Vietnam combat veterans. *American Journal of Psychiatry, 149,* 333–336.

Appendix

DSM-IV Traumatic Stress Disorders

Acute stress disorder

A. *Exposure*
  1. Experienced or confronted with actual or threatened death or injury to self or others.
  2. Response included intense fear, helplessness, or horror.

B. *Dissociation* (three or more)
  1. numbing, detachment, emotional unresponsiveness
  2. reduced awareness of surroundings
  3. derealization
  4. depersonalization
  5. dissociative amnesia

C. *Reexperiencing* (one or more)
  1. intrusive images or thoughts
  2. recurrent distressing dreams
  3. reliving experiences/flashbacks
  4. distress on exposure to reminders

D. *Avoidance* (marked symptoms)
  1. avoid thoughts, feelings or conversations about the trauma
  2. avoid activities, people, places that arouse recollections

E. *Arousal* (marked symptoms)
  1. insomnia
  2. irritability
  3. poor concentration
  4. hypervigilance
  5. exaggerated startle response
  6. motor restlessness

F. *Functioning*
  Symtoms cause clinically significant distress or fuctional impairment.

G. *Duration* — 2 days to 4 weeks

Posttraumatic stress disorder

A. *Exposure*
  1. Experienced or confronted with actual or threatened death or injury to self or others.
  2. Response included intense fear, helplessness, or horror.

B. *Reexperiencing* (one or more)
  1. intusive images or thoughts
  2. recurrent distressing dreams
  3. reliving experiences/flashbacks
  4. intense psychological distress on exposure to reminders
  5. phsological reactivity on exposure to reminders

C. *Avoidance* (three or more)
  1. avoid thoughts, feelings, or converstions about the trauma
  2. avoid activities, people, places that arouse recollections
  3. amnesia for aspects of trauma
  4. diminished interest or participation in activities
  5. feelings of detachment or estrangement from others
  6. restricted affect
  7. sense of a foreshortened future

D. *Arousal* (two or more)
  1. insomnia
  2. irritability
  3. poor concentration
  4. hypervigilance
  5. exaggerated startle response

E. *Duration* — more than 1 month

F. *Fuctioning*
  Synptoms cause clinically significant distress or functional impairment.

Part Two

Community Strategies
for Intervention

Since its origins at Swampscott, community psychology has struggled with its identity. Many, especially those outside its rather amorphous boundaries, saw it more or less as an egalitarian offshoot of clinical practice, taking the ministrations of mental health practitioners into streets and storefronts to deal with the problems and pathologies of the proletariat. Another prominent faction saw it not so much as a psychological specialty, but more as a training ground for interdisciplinary problem solvers whose "action research" would guide the efforts of politicians, planners, and third sector agencies to ameliorate social problems in our communities. Still others saw it as an applied technology for consultation and education, program evaluation, and similar components of the community mental health movement and related enterprises, whereas others saw it principally as an applied domain of social psychology. A consistent body of knowledge or domain of practice that might functionally define the area remained difficult to establish.

The notion of a scientist-practitioner whose base of skills and information would be broad enough to encompass a wide range of psychological information and to reach beyond it into other areas of social science inquiry, whose research skills would permit investigation of issues defined by community context and interaction as well as by individual attitudes and behavior, and whose practice would be based in consultation and empowerment more than in treatment or intervention has remained an attractive, if elusive, ideal. Such a scientist-practitioner, it was envisioned, would strive to become a jack of all trades and the master of many; he or she was expected to ply that Renaissance synthesis as a catalyst more than a reagent in the workings of people and their communities.

The truly competent practitioner of that synthesis and ethic will almost never be known through any overt visibility of his or her efforts. Though some may see it as paradoxical, the truly competent community psychologist tends to be acutely aware that visibility and efficacy will generally hold a strongly inverse relationship when autonomy, empowerment, and resiliency are the principal outcomes sought. If people triumph over the obstacles before them but never recall our contributions, we have cause, perhaps, to celebrate our success. Accordingly, some of the best examples of community psychology in action often go unreported and, hence, unnoticed.

Although community crises, calamities, cataclysms, and catastrophes are particularly salient to these sorts of facilitated responses—and although a number of sterling efforts have been undertaken in that arena—reports and descriptions of such efforts are dwarfed in both literature and awareness by a rapidly growing mountain of clamors and claims for increasingly pervasive, clinically oriented, interventionist designs. Indeed, where the community psychologist often seeks to minimize his or her visibility in response and recovery, many of these efforts and approaches have intentionally sought the highest possible profiles and have in many cases sought quite deliberately to promote the very sort of visibility so often eschewed by their community psychology colleagues as an intended outcome of their intervention. The distinction is not one of modesty or feigned humility; it is, in fact, a very rudimentary distinction in design and intent that begins at very fundamental levels of axiom and assumption and continues through the definition of outcome and the assessments of success.

The second section of our treatment begins with Yates, Axsom, and Tiedeman (chapter 6) exploring a distinction that may seem subtle on its surface, but represents a profound and truly fundamental distinction in the conceptual foundations of community and ecological approaches: the distinction between efforts to define and enhance the natural *help seeking* patterns of individuals and communities on the one hand, and enterprises that seek to develop, implement, and promote *help delivery* systems on the other. We follow this insightful treatment with a series of case examples.

The first exemplar comes from van den Eynde and Veno (chapter 7), who describe a unique set of strategies—some successful, some less so—that were evolved to help deal with several generations of sexual abuse in an insular Australian community. Interacting challenges of culture, caste, social roles, and a wide array of "turf" issues are all clearly evident in the efforts of these scientist-practitioners and their colleagues to forge workable approaches to solution and healing. Vernburg (chapter 8) next describes family systems issues as observed through field studies of intervention efforts among children affected by Hurricane Hugo and other disasters. Gist and Woodall (chapter 9) finish the section with an examination of a popularized organizational intervention scheme and an exploration of the implications of current research for revisit and revision of a model now reified in its own social movement.

Chapter 6

The Help-Seeking Process for Distress after Disasters

Suzanne Yates, Danny Axsom, and Karyn Tiedman

INTRODUCTION

Nature has a way of periodically reminding us of its awesome power of destruction. From the Johnstown Flood to Hurricane Camille to the recent Red River Flood, disasters have taken a serious toll on the lives of many. Researchers warn that we should expect more major storms and increased property damage as North America moves out of an unusually quiescent weather pattern and as more people have moved to inhabit vulnerable flood plains, hillsides, and coastal flats (Stevens, 1997).

Disasters are not the most common traumatic event we encounter, nor are they generally the most serious in terms of their psychological sequelae (Kessler, Sonnega, Bromet, Hughes, & Nelson, 1995; Norris, 1992). Victims, even those who sustain serious tangible losses, usually rebuild their homes and lives. But the images of families surveying a disaster scene where a loved one died or the faces of victims as they stand amidst the ruins of their homes linger in our minds. And although evidence of widespread or chronic psychopathology following disasters is rare (Rubonis & Bickman, 1991a), shorter term stress reactions are common. At a more existential level, disasters may threaten our most basic assumptions, such

Leonard Bickman and George Howe assisted in formulating the original model and writing the previous chapter. We gratefully acknowledge their contributions.

as that the world is generally a benevolent place where bad outcomes do not occur randomly (Janoff-Bulman, 1992).

Reactions to disasters are in fact highly variable, from post-traumatic stress disorder (PTSD) to heroic resilience. In attempting to understand this variability, one potentially important moderating variable is people's help-seeking behavior in the aftermath of the disaster. To meet the mental health needs of victims, an array of federal, state, and local interventions are typically available. For a host of possible reasons (many of which we detail in this chapter), such services are often underused. People may turn to existing support networks such as family or friends, to other professionals such as physicians or clergy, to multiple sources, or to no one. What influences people's help-seeking decisions? And how can intervention efforts be optimized by being sensitive to major determinants of the help-seeking process?

This chapter represents an update of a previous effort on our part (Yates, Axsom, Bickman, & Howe, 1989) to provide a framework for organizing and specifying the many variables likely to influence help-seeking for mental health problems after disasters. It incorporates more recent research on disasters, as well as additional concepts and findings from beyond the disaster setting that we think are relevant to help-seeking. The updated model itself is substantively similar to our earlier presentation, though there are differences in emphasis (e.g., a greater focus on issues of perceived control). The model is descriptive and heuristic rather than formal and statistical; we hope it will be generative for both researchers and practitioners.

We have continued to draw on theories and findings from beyond the disaster setting, including laboratory-based experiments. Though the content of this research may sometimes have little directly to do with disasters, the processes examined (e.g., attribution) are more general and potentially quite relevant. Consistent with this reasoning, findings from nondisaster settings often parallel what we know about disasters, for example, that people are more reluctant to seek help than we might otherwise assume (see Wills & DePaulo, 1989, for a review).

Fundamentally, though, the chapter is about post-disaster help-seeking. As we noted earlier (Yates et al., 1989), there are two features of disasters that are especially important for understanding disaster-related help-seeking. The first, shared by other more individual-based traumas (e.g., cancer), is that disasters create *heightened uncertainty*. Uncertainty increases attempts to make sense of the situation, as well as social comparisons with others affected by the disaster (Taylor, Wood, & Lichtman, 1983; Wills, 1983; Wortman & Dunkel-Schetter, 1979); it also heightens susceptibility to social influence as people look to others for help in interpreting the situation. The second feature is more unique to disasters, that they typically *affect many people simultaneously*, indeed, entire communities. This may disrupt people's normal social support networks, allow for the emergence of collective definitions of reality (e.g., that distress will only be transient), provide greater opportunities for social comparison with other victims, create frequent opportunities for help-giving (which, as we will detail, may make it easier to receive help), and lead to more frequent offers of help from others (e.g., through outreach mobilization or as one seeks non-psychological assistance).

These combined features of disasters emphasize the role of social influence in affecting help-seeking. Thus, in our model and throughout the chapter we highlight such constructs as attribution, social support, social comparison, and external information (e.g., from friends, media, outreach efforts). We now turn to an overview of the model itself.

CONCEPTUAL OVERVIEW

Like other models of help-seeking, our framework assumes the decision whether to seek help is the product of not one but several prior subprocesses. The first concerns one's awareness of distress. The presence of symptoms does not guarantee that a person will be aware of distress, and a host of factors determine whether a person concludes he or she has a problem. If one does conclude that a problem exists, the next decision is how to interpret it. Again, we detail many factors likely to influence how a problem is defined. Once the problem is defined, the person turns to a consideration of coping alternatives. The solution(s) chosen will depend on a variety of factors we attempt to detail. The actual enactment of a coping option or options will depend crucially on these prior steps.

The model depicts help-seeking as an iterative process. As coping attempts are made, changes in level of distress will be assessed to determine the success of the strategy. If the distress persists, a reassessment of the nature of the problem and/or of possible coping alternatives is likely. Thus, we see the post-disaster coping process as an ongoing cycle of coping attempts, assessments, and revised strategies. The process will end when the person concludes either that the distress is no longer a problem or that the distress has no real solution.

Our discussion of the subprocesses that influence help seeking is organized from the standpoint of a person's schema. Schemas are knowledge structures that guide a person's perception, organization, and recall of information (Bartlett, 1932; Fiske & Taylor, 1991). They help simplify the world around us by abstracting the essential features of events, roles, people, etcetera, and by assisting in the development of expectations and inferences. We posit that people possess three different schemas that will influence the help-seeking process: A distress awareness schema that contains information about emotional and behavioral functioning, a problem schema that contains information about the essential characteristics of distress, and a solution schema that contains information about a range of coping alternatives. The distress awareness schema will determine whether symptoms occurring after a disaster are seen as indicators of distress; the problem schema will determine how the distress is interpreted; and the solution schema will determine the appropriate coping alternative(s). Although these schemata are conceptually distinct, we recognize that in reality they are likely to overlap, or even exist as one general "psychological functioning" schema. We have drawn certain distinctions to parallel the stages of the help-seeking process outlined above. The many specific factors thought to affect help-seeking are included in our model, either as components of a schema or as variables that influence the content of a schema.

Several assumptions about our organizing framework should be made explicit. First, our model is psychological in nature and individual-based. We recognize that other perspectives (e.g., sociological) and other levels of analysis (e.g., family, community) are important. To the extent that variables such as the structure of community outreach efforts and family problem-solving style affect help-seeking, they are represented in our model in terms of their impact on people's *perceptions* of resource alternatives. We believe that what is lost in breadth of constructs is compensated for by a single level of analysis that makes exposition of the help-seeking process more clear.

The second assumption is that the help-seeking process is best understood not in terms of people's static personality but in terms of generally applicable social influence processes that take place in the aftermath of disasters. In our emphasis on social influence constructs (e.g., social support, attribution, social comparison, external information) and on the importance of people's construal of the post-disaster situation (e.g., schemas, attributions) as a major determinant of their behavior, our model is social–psychological in nature. The model makes no explicit mention of demographic or personality variables. This is not because we consider these variables trivial. Quite the contrary, a person's sex, age, socioeconomic standing, or self-esteem, to cite only a few examples, may be highly related to help-seeking. However, we believe demographic and personality variables will be important only to the extent that they influence variables already specified by our model. For example, demographic factors such as age may effect help-seeking because of differences in behavioral response during the disaster, in the perceived stigma attached to acknowledging emotional distress, in the perceived efficacy of coping options, and so forth. As one example, the elderly are less likely to evacuate endangered areas (Friedsam, 1960). In contrast, families with preschool age children are more likely to take protective measures and to respond to evacuation notices (Lechat, 1979). These differences may lead to differences in amount of distress experienced, thereby affecting the help-seeking process. Beyond such indirect effects, demographic and personality variables are hypothesized to have little influence on help-seeking. Our model attempts to explicate the underlying processes that affect help-seeking. As such we are most concerned with why people do or do not seek help. This type of process model can then help us understand individual- and group-level differences in help-seeking.

A third assumption is that people follow no set sequence of coping solutions. Other models of help-seeking usually assume that people will first attempt to solve a problem themselves, then turn to informal sources before seeking professional help. Although this is a generally reasonable assumption, it is not one we make for mental health problems in post-disaster settings for a number of reasons. First, choice of coping alternative depends on people's interpretation of the distress. For certain kinds of distress, people may feel that self-help or aid from family or friends will be ineffective or inappropriate. Second, as noted earlier, because of the widespread impact of disasters, people's social network may be disrupted or severely strained. Those from whom support is normally sought may be in need of aid themselves and unable to meet the person's needs. Third, offers of help from formal sources should be more common after disasters than when a single individual experiences distress. Finally, professional sources may be a last resort in other situations because they cost money. But after disasters, mental health services are frequently provided at little or no charge. This may remove a large barrier so that, in some cases, formal sources are sought before informal ones. Further, although help-seeking has been discussed as though different coping alternatives are mutually exclusive, there is no reason to assume this. Just as people with colds may try several remedies—getting more sleep, taking non-prescription medications, eating chicken soup, seeing a doctor—so might people experiencing emotional distress enlist the help of sources at several levels simultaneously.

Not only do we make no assumptions about where people will turn for help, we make no assumptions about where people *should* turn for help. A plethora of therapies has arisen in recent years to address trauma-related distress. But as Gist, Lubin, and Redburn (1998) have noted, the popularity of these therapies exceeds the empirical evidence for their effectiveness. In the absence of such evidence, and with the knowledge that informal and nonpsychological sources of help that exist within the community can be valuable resources, we are reluctant to be prescriptive about any one form of intervention.

A final assumption we make is that although the subprocesses of help-seeking depicted in Figure 1 are conceptually distinct, in practice help-seeking is more complex. In particular, it may not, as suggested by Figure 1, always be linear or unidirectional. Processes identified as occurring later in the help-seeking sequence may affect processes that, conceptually, occur earlier. For example, the interpretation of distress may be

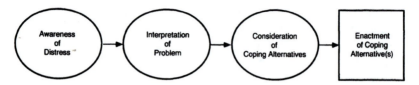

Figure 1   Model overview of the help-seeking process.

influenced on occasion by considerations about coping alternatives (such as their perceived availability).

With these assumptions and the conceptual overview in mind, we now turn to a more detailed consideration of the factors that influence help-seeking.

THE AWARENESS OF DISTRESS

Help-seeking begins with the awareness that one is experiencing distress. As we noted earlier, we do not consider the presence of symptoms necessarily synonymous with the level of distress one is experiencing. Rather, the person's awareness and interpretation of emotional and behavioral disruptions are key. Within the coping literature, Lazarus (1966) was among the first to argue that identical levels of objective impact might produce different reactions depending on people's cognitive appraisal of the event and their capacity to deal with it.

The appraisal process will also influence the person's awareness of dysfunctional behavior or symptoms. A person who has become withdrawn may not be aware that she or he is being unresponsive to the needs of family members. Similarly, a person may report drinking a six-pack of beer or more every night without concluding such behavior indicates any degree of alcohol abuse. If people do not view feelings or behaviors as dysfunctional, they will not interpret them as problematic or consider various coping alternatives.

Recognition of distress will depend largely on what people believe constitutes acceptable behavioral and emotional functioning. As Figure 2 indicates, we have posited that such information is organized into a distress awareness schema. We first address the content of this schema, then the various factors that influence it.

Expectations about behavioral functioning will be influenced in part by one's perceived role obligations (e.g., as a worker, spouse, parent). In general, the more role obligations one has to fulfill, the greater the likelihood that a person will experience stress (Cooke & Rousseau, 1984; Pearlin, Lieberman, Menaghan, & Mullan, 1981). In times of disaster, those whose role obligations are more extensive may find themselves

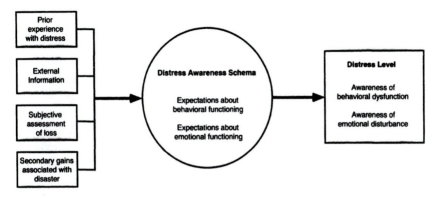

Figure 2 Awareness of distress.

overwhelmed. Women with large social support networks, for example, display increased levels of stress compared with others (Solomon, Smith, Robins, & Fischback, 1987). This is because women are more likely to be the support providers in their networks. During disaster, they must contend not only with their own personal distress but experience increased demands from others for extra support. In a similar vein, a curvilinear relationship between age and stress has been reported (Gleser, Green, & Winget, 1981; Price, 1978; Thompson, Norris, & Hanacek, 1993). Thompson et al. suggested that this relationship is because middle-aged people generally experience greater role strain in the aftermath of a disaster than either younger or retired individuals. If the impact of the disaster may be more keenly felt by people with many social roles, then one line of intervention for outreach workers might be to help victims engage in a form of emotional triage to determine whether any role obligations can be put aside or reduced during the recovery phase.

Simplifying role obligations, however, need not, and should not, come at the expense of reducing a person's sense of self-complexity. Self-complexity (Linville, 1985) refers to the degree to which people have highly differentiated views of themselves. People with a high degree of self-complexity think of their subselves as incorporating a variety of different traits. In contrast, those low in self-complexity describe themselves using similar attributes across their social roles. Linville (1987) proposed that self-complexity acts as a cognitive buffer against depression because a setback will have a more limited impact on one's view of the self. Morgan and Janoff-Bulman (1994) offer a refinement and an extension of this basic notion among trauma victims. They found that only positive self-complexity was associated with better adjustment among trauma victims while negative self-complexity was associated with poorer adjustment for both trauma and non-trauma victims. Positive self-complexity, it would seem, allows the person to recognize that the traumatic event need not be a globally defining event. This suggests that appraising the event as being more limited in its scope has important consequences. As such, therapeutic interventions should underscore and foster positive self-complexity in victims, even as they may encourage a reduction in role obligations.

Expectations about emotional functioning may also be affected by one's social roles, which may include information about emotional responses to role obligations (e.g., that fatigue and distress are normal). Social roles convey not only information about behavioral functioning, but emotional functioning as well. This includes information about emotional responses to role obligations (e.g., that fatigue and distress are normal for heads of households after disasters).

More generally, people possess implicit theories of emotional functioning (e.g., the causes, varieties, and prevalence of distress; how long recovery will take) that may vary in sophistication and accuracy. Wortman and Silver (1987) have proposed that several widely held assumptions about response to irrevocable loss (e.g., the relative absence of positive emotions such as humor) do not match existing empirical evidence. How these implicit theories relate to coping is an interesting topic for future research.

There are many factors that influence the content of a person's distress awareness schema. As noted in Figure 2, the first is a person's prior experience with distress. This is likely to play a large role in determining whether current behavioral or emotional reactions are experienced as distress because prior experience establishes expectations about functioning. These expectations, in turn, help determine whether current symptoms are noticed and how they are interpreted. Perhaps more importantly, chronic stressors and distress reactions indicate that the person's resources are already strained. The addition of acute disaster-induced stress is, therefore, more likely to be appraised as exceeding the person's coping resources (Norris & Uhl, 1993).

In addition to influencing a person's distress awareness schema, prior symptoms are likely to affect post-disaster symptoms in at least two ways. First, there is often continuity of functioning before and after a disaster; in general, individuals and families with prior histories of poor coping skills or who report a history of chronic stressors experience elevated levels of distress during the post-disaster period (Birnbaum, Coplon, & Scharff, 1973; Freedy, Saladin, Kilpatrick, Resnick, & Saunders, 1994; Norris & Uhl, 1993). Second, pre-disaster emotional distress may affect one's preparedness before and behavioral response during the disaster. A person whose functioning is only marginal is not likely to have engaged in many preparedness activities and may be unable to respond in a prompt, flexible, and appropriate manner during the height of a crisis. As a result, both the tangible and intangible losses suffered by such persons may be greater. For example, a study of victims of a factory explosion (Weisæth, 1989) found that the single strongest predictor of optimal response during the event was an individual's level of disaster training/experience. Although 71% of the victims with a lot of disaster training/experience responded optimally during the height of the crisis, not one of those with little or no training did.

Unfortunately, preparedness does not ensure that the psychological impact of a disaster will be lessened. Specifically, Faupel and Styles (1993) report that residents who had attended disaster education workshops and who had engaged in the greatest number of preparedness activities experienced *higher* levels of both physical and psychological stress after Hurricane Hugo than did more unprepared victims. Why might this be? Individuals engage in preparedness activities in an effort to allay threat. This may lead participants to develop (or indicate a propensity toward having a need for) a heightened sense of control. Discovering that being prepared does not totally shield the person, their family, and their belongings from the disaster is apt to cause these individuals to experience a profound loss of control. Thus, although preventive campaigns to encourage preparedness may be critical for optimizing reactions during a disaster, it should be recognized that individuals who do actively prepare but who find their efforts unable to stave off the disaster completely are at heightened risk for the experience of distress. A good illustration of this may be seen in the April 1997 flooding of the Red River. Residents in towns along the river were given early warning and began building sandbag dikes in advance of the arrival of the flood waters. In some communities, the dikes held and helped spare some or all of the town. In many other communities, however, exhausted citizens who labored tirelessly for days saw the water eventually overwhelm the dikes and wreak total devastation on homes and businesses alike. We would predict that these victims, who sustained extensive damage after laboring so intensively to avert disaster will display heightened levels of distress compared with flash flood victims who have no opportunity to attempt preventive actions.

External information (e.g., from family, friends, the media, mental health outreach efforts) may also play a critical role in determining one's distress awareness schema. Awareness that one's emotions or behaviors have changed or become dysfunctional sometimes does not occur until questions or comments from family, friends, or co-workers prompt self-reflection. Of course, external information can serve to decrease as well as increase awareness of distress. Sometimes, a person initiates conversations with others in an attempt to engage in self-evaluation. If listeners dismiss or minimize the described behavior, then the person may deny or minimize internal cues of distress. More generally, the relevance of social comparison processes should be emphasized. The notion that our self-concept is socially constructed is longstanding (Festinger, 1954). We evaluate our distress both by reflected appraisal (others' real or imagined responses to us) and comparative appraisal (comparing our outcomes with those of others). Though we have some control over the composition of these "comparison others" (e.g., by "niche-picking" and what Taylor (1983) calls *selective evaluation*), the environment often plays an active role in forcing comparisons (Wood, 1996). In this regard, the possibly iatrogenic role that some relief workers—armed with pet (and possibly erroneous) theories of adjustment—may play in enhancing distress has been recently noted (Gist et al., 1998).

Another important professional source of external information is the primary care physician who is the first person many turn to for help with psychological as well as physical symptoms. Physicians typically receive little training in recognizing or treating depression and anxiety and often fail to correctly diagnose distress-related symptoms. They are also generally reluctant to discuss psychosocial issues with patients because of the assumed stigma, and believe most psychological problems will resolve themselves given time (Curran, 1988; Ormel & Tiemens, 1995). The tendency for the primary care physician to respond to symptoms of anxiety, depression, or somatization by reassuring people that there is nothing *physically* wrong with them may well foil victims' willingness to seek help with these problems. Bruno Lima (Lima et al., 1990; Lima, Pai, Santacruz, & Lozano, 1991) has argued that health care workers need to be provided for simple screening devices and training focused on the treatment of anxiety and depression. Although his argument is directed at the specific need in developing countries where mental health needs exceed the resources of available mental health professionals, some variant of it is surely applicable to any outreach setting where mental health services tend to be underused.

Awareness of distress is no doubt influenced by the person's subjective assessment of loss due to the disaster. In a straightforward way, the assessment of loss is probably positively related to symptomology. But the assessment of loss may also affect the help-seeking process by influencing the person's distress awareness schema. The disaster may serve as a salient event that sensitizes the person to everyday stressors. Norris and Uhl (1993), for example, found that the degree of life threat experienced during a hurricane was correlated with reported ecological stress. They suggest hypervigilance in the aftermath of the disaster may sensitize victims to formerly ignored stressors such as crowding, noise, and crime.

The sense of loss from the disaster may stem from both tangible and intangible sources. Tangible losses, such as deaths, injuries, property damage, and disaster-related unemployment, serve as the primary basis by which the government calibrates the devastation wreaked by a disaster. Although both injury and material loss contribute to the development of acute stress reactions, the former is associated with more serious and sustained psychological distress (Gleser et al., 1981; Norris & Uhl, 1993).

An appreciation of the full impact of disasters requires attention to intangible losses as well. A person who has sustained extensive tangible losses will probably also report extensive intangible losses, but the tangible and intangible impact of a disaster need not be closely related. Rescue and relief workers not directly harmed by the disaster, for example, may still suffer from survivor guilt, anxiety, and depression (Dunning, 1991; Hodgkinson & Shepard, 1994; Weiss, Marmar, Metzler, & Ronfeldt, 1995). Similarly, when other family members are at risk, fearing for their safety may be more common than fearing for one's own safety (Freedy et al., 1994; Hanson, Kilpatrick, Freedy, & Saunders, 1995). More importantly, these studies found that the threat to family members' safety was more likely to produce PTSD than was fear for one's personal safety. Similarly, people who do not sustain actual injury may have believed their lives were in great jeopardy. Studies examining the etiology of PTSD in both disaster (LaGreca, Silverman, Vernberg, & Prinstein, 1996) and nondisaster (Resnick, Kilpatrick, Best, & Kramer, 1992) settings underscore the importance of the individual's perception of life threat in the development of the disorder.

The sense of loss of control may well be the most fundamental form of intangible loss. Indeed, in their analysis of the social causes of psychological distress across the lifespan, Mirowsky and Ross (1989) state that, "Of all the beliefs about self and society that might increase or reduce distress, one's sense of control over one's own life may be the most important" (p. 131). Perceived lack of control has been shown to be critical to the development of stress following disaster (Fleming, O'Keeffe, & Baum, 1991; Freedy et al., 1994; Solomon, Regier, & Burke, 1989). Perceived lack of control, for example, accounted for 35% of the independent variance in psychological symptoms among a group of residents attending an information session shortly before the restart of Three Mile Island (Prince-Embury, 1992). As speculated earlier, the increased stress reported by those who had made the most efforts to prepare for Hurricane Hugo might have reflected an acute sense of loss of control by those who found preparedness an imperfect talisman, not capable of completely shielding families from disaster impact. Janoff-Bulman's (1992) notion of shattered assumptions is relevant here. She posits that the threat to one's basic assumptions —among them, that the world is benevolent and meaningful—is a defining theme for victims of trauma. Taylor and Brown (1988) also suggest that a mildly exaggerated illusion of control is conducive to mental health. Given the potential impact of this variable, it is unfortunate that it is often left off the list of items actually measured when assessing disaster-related losses.

It is important to note that perceptions of loss of control may vary as a function of the type of disaster experienced. Baum (1987) has argued that victims of technological disasters are at greater risk for developing stress reactions because technological disasters represent a loss of control over systems that were assumed to be controllable. Others caution that the line between technological and natural disasters may be blurred from the victim's perspective (Blocker & Sherkat, 1992; Rochford & Blocker, 1991). Victims of an earthquake may experience additional levels of rage and loss of control if, for example, they believe the collapse of their home was due to faulty engineering (Horowitz, Stinson, & Field, 1991). Also, Erikson (1976) noted that many survivors of the Buffalo Creek disaster attributed its cause not to excess rainfall but to a faulty dam. Thus, it seems critical for outreach workers to explore victim's constructions of their loss experience to appreciate the nature and source of the distress. Outreach efforts designed to explicitly address, legitimize, and treat victims' sense of loss of control, as well as other challenged assumptions, may be particularly fruitful (Horowitz et al., 1991; Parson, 1995).

A final, but typically overlooked, influence on distress awareness is whether there are secondary gains associated with having gone through the disaster. A person may make new friends, be freed from oppressive obligations, have the neighborhood draw closer together, become more spiritual, and so forth. Following a serious maritime accident, for example, most survivors reported positive life changes—mainly in the form of developing a deeper appreciation for life—in addition to the negative consequences (Joseph, Williams, & Yule, 1993). In our own examination of flash flood victims (Axsom, Yates, Howe, & Bickman, 1990), we found widespread evidence of secondary gains ranging from over half of the participants who reported improved personal and interpersonal developments (including finding that someone cared for them, discovering personal strength, and having the family grow closer) to a subset (20%) who said that they had moved to a better area as a result of the flood. Research efforts are needed to explore the extent to which such secondary gains may be able to offset negative consequences in the development of stress. We suspect that outreach efforts that encourage individuals to recognize the possibility of potential gains may help individuals regain a sense of optimism, meaning, and control over their future. As such, these gains may help abate the negative consequences associated with disaster.

THE INTERPRETATION OF THE PROBLEM

Becoming aware that one is distressed begs the question, "What kind of distress?" This is critical because how distress is interpreted determines to a large extent the range of coping options one will consider. Mental health professionals and disaster researchers have long observed that victims tend to underuse available psychological services. The belief that services are underused probably reflects fundamental differences between professionals and lay persons in their willingness to attribute disruptions in functioning to psychological causes. Participants in one study who read case vignettes could readily identify abnormal behavior, but did not label it as psychopathological (Levav, Kohn, Flaherty, Lerner, & Aisenberg, 1990). While the physical loss of home and possessions is likely to be accompanied by psychological suffering, many victims focus on the visible loss and identify post-disaster difficulties as being solely economic in nature (Feld, 1973; Poulshock & Cohen, 1975). In other cases, symptoms generally attributed to psychological concerns by counselors are labeled as physical ailments by victims (Abrahams, Price, Whitlock, & Williams, 1976).

Figure 3 identifies basic elements involved in interpretation of the problem. The problem schema itself will reflect the person's attribution of the cause of the problem, the degree of stigma associated with the problem, and any secondary gains associated with the experience of the distress. Once established, the problem schema will give rise to a problem definition that will include information about the actual label placed on the distress and the person's expectations about associated symptoms, the course, duration, and controllability of the problem.

The first component of a problem schema involves the attributions made about the likely cause(s) of distress. Attribution theory is largely concerned with the rules lay people use to understand the world, especially in terms of causality (Heider, 1958; Kelley, 1973). Important dimensions of causality include locus (internal–external to the person), stability (stable–unstable), and globality (global-specific). In general, victims who perceive the distress as being due to unstable external factors are less likely to seek formal help (Robbins, 1981). Given this, it is hardly surprising that disaster victims tend to underuse services: Because the precipitating cause is a disaster that has come and gone, it is easy for victims to assume the distress is unstable, specific, and external. Seeing distress as being due solely to the temporary impact of the disaster and not related to anything about the person should result in less help-seeking (Yates, 1998).

In addition to the stability of the cause, Kelley's (1973) covariation model specifies that the degree of perceived consensus about a reaction

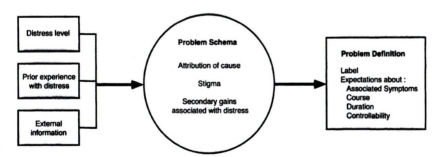

Figure 3 Interpretation of the problem.

will be important. *Consensus* refers to the degree to which the person's experience is thought to be similar to (high consensus) or dissimilar to (low consensus) the experiences of others. High consensus encourages external attributions. Disasters are unique stressors in that, by virtue of affecting large groups of people at the same time, a high degree of consensus can be assumed to exist. When perceived consensus is high, the distress reaction may be seen as normal. It is less likely to be viewed, therefore, as "a problem." For example, Robbins (1981) reported that individuals who judge their unique emotional distress as similar to the everyday suffering of their peers tend to conclude that their own symptoms are not serious. Unfortunately, consensus estimates made in the aftermath of disasters, when the everyday suffering of peers is extreme, may lead individuals to make external attributions about the cause of the distress and to conclude no help is warranted for this "natural" reaction.

Consensus estimates may also discourage help-seeking by a different process that is more related to stigma. Specifically, if victims underestimate the prevalence of certain kinds of distress, they may conclude that their own experience is abnormal and indicative of weakness. We seldom wear our hearts on our sleeves. Sometimes this may lead to a gap between our relatively calm and collected public face and our distressed private experience. Although we may be aware that our self-presentations of calm do not closely reflect our internal states, we often take *others'* calm demeanor at face value. Brief public social interaction, which is usually marked by individuals assuming an upbeat, confident tone, may lead people to underestimate others' distress. This process, labeled pluralistic ignorance (Allport, 1924), was invoked by Latané and Darley (1970) to help account for people's reluctance to provide help in emergencies. Miller and Prentice (1994) pointed out that certain consequences of pluralistic ignorance— feeling one is uniquely troubled, or socially deviate, or uniquely sensitive to social pressures—may all conspire to lower the person's self-esteem, make the person feel more alienated from the group, and/or convince the person to modify their beliefs or actions to become more like the supposed norm.

Pluralistic ignorance may be most likely when distress lingers, surfaces later, or results from intangible losses. In each case the distress may be unexpected, and we may therefore be more likely to accept others' calm demeanor at face value. Yates's (1992) work exploring reactions to the coping strategies used by victims of a natural disaster is relevant here. Observers responded to scenarios of victims coping with the aftermath of a flash flood. Even though all victims were portrayed as experiencing identical levels of depression, observers believed that the depression experienced by the minor property damage victim must actually be less severe. Further, they attributed the source of this victim's depression to internal causes rather than the flood and disapproved when the minor property victim sought professional help for the depression. These reactions were based on an assumption of low consensus for the distress reaction: Observers thought almost no one else without major tangible losses would experience such distress. A general assumption appears to be that severity of response should correspond to severity of the tangible loss. Individuals may be reluctant, therefore, to discuss distress caused by a perceived loss of control or other intangible losses, such as life threat, for fear of being seen as overreacting. One of the goals of outreach efforts, therefore, must be to provide individuals with information and testimonials about stress reactions to intangible loss.

In a study of victim's attributions made in the aftermath of the flood, Rubonis and Bickman (1991b) found evidence that consensus was related to externality for anxiety and depression but not for somatization. The fact that consensus affected attributions about the causes of psychological symptoms but not physical ones may be related to stigma. People are typically more willing to seek expert help for medical problems than they are psychological ones (e.g., Waxman, Larner, & Klein, 1984). In trying to understand this phenomenon among the elderly, Ray, Raciti, and MacLean (1992) asked seniors to read a set of symptoms as part of a vignette labeled either a psychological or a medical problem. While a large percentage of the sample said they would seek help for solving the problem regardless of its label, their selection of help sources differed greatly. In response to the medically labeled vignette, 63% of those who said they would seek help said they would turn to a physician. In contrast, only 16% of those who said they would seek help after reading the psychologically labeled vignette indicated they would turn to a mental health worker. Nearly half said they would rely on their family and friends and a third said they would turn to their physicians for help with a problem that was presumed to be psychological in nature. This suggests that identical symptoms can be labeled quite differently and that the selection of the label has important consequences for help seeking. As suggested above, the stigma attached to certain kinds of distress may influence a person's interpretation of the distress (Archer, 1985; Katz, 1981; Mechanic, 1972). If distress levels are high and the person wishes to seek help, there may be a strong tendency to focus on somatic complaints. The tendency to interpret psychological distress as being a physical problem allows the person to turn to a preferred help source, the medical doctor, for aid. This underscores the point discussed earlier that primary care physicians and settings represent a critical link in the delivery of services. Ensuring that medical doctors are aware of referral sources and/or establishing temporary alliances after a disaster to allow mental health workers to operate out of medical clinics may be key.

The final component of a person's problem schema is whether there are secondary gains associated with the distress. As noted above, secondary gains from the disaster may attenuate the distress one experiences. In a similar vein (but different direction), secondary gains associated with the distress itself (such as increased attention from others) may influence how the distress is interpreted. If the potential gains are high, a person may conclude that a problem exists irrespective of his or her level of distress. This may account in part for why people without diagnosable disabilities sometimes seek and receive professional mental health services. As society grows increasingly litigious, there may also be increased pressures for victims to highlight and dwell on their experiences of "emotional pain and suffering" to qualify for compensation.

To this point, we have been describing the content of a person's problem schema. We now turn briefly to an examination of factors hypothesized to influence this schema (see Figure 3). First, distress level plays an important role in activating the problem schema. In general, the higher a person's distress level, the more likely the person should be to see the distress as a problem that must be diagnosed. Second, a person's experience with distress in the past will likely affect their interpretation of the current situation. Prior experience provides information about the nature and course of distress. It may therefore mean that current distress is interpreted in ways that are consistent with prior distress (e.g., those with previously diagnosed physical ailments may favor somatic explanations for current distress). Third, external information will influence one's problem schema. Such information may come from a variety of sources, including family, friends, co-workers, the media, and relief workers. It can be solicited or unsolicited. In the aftermath of a disaster, the desire for information is high. Nearly three-quarters of the surveyed residents affected by an earthquake, for example, reported using the media more than usual (Mileti & O'Brien, 1992). Further, the authors found that the more damage a community experienced, the more likely it was that residents reported attending to media announcements. The search for information is also expected to increase informal communication within social networks and throughout the community. According to social comparison theory (Festinger, 1954), uncertainty leads people to compare their own situation with that of others. Whereas the theory originally assumed that people strive to develop an accurately calibrated sense of their abilities, recent work points out that individuals make comparisons for a variety of different goals, including self-improvement and self-enhancement (see Diener & Fujita, 1997; Wood, 1989, for reviews of this literature). Taylor and her colleagues, for example, have found that one way people who have encountered misfortunes such as breast cancer cope with their plight is by actively seeking "downward" social comparisons with others whose plight is worse, thereby lessening their own distress (Taylor & Lobel, 1989;

Taylor, Wood, & Lichtman, 1983). Consistent with this, most victims we interviewed 3–4 months post-flood felt they had experienced less distress and recovered more than other victims (Axsom et al., 1990). The net result of choosing social comparison targets that can enhance one's sense of well-being may be that victims conclude that their losses are more manageable and their own coping skills more developed than the average victim's. Although this may serve to elevate self-esteem in the short run, it may also discourage individuals from seeking needed help because victims assume there are many who are in greater need of services than they.

THE CONSIDERATION OF
COPING ALTERNATIVES

Once a problem has been noticed and interpreted, the individual may attempt to alleviate distress through coping alternatives that are vast in number and scope (e.g., help-seeking, social support, selective evaluation, self-blame, positive appraisal, avoidance, distancing). A useful and popular way of organizing these strategies has been proposed by Lazarus & Folkman (1984), who distinguish between emotion-focused and problem-focused coping. Emotion-focused coping is aimed at managing internal distress, whereas problem-focused coping is aimed at changing the external environment creating the distress.

The decision to use a particular strategy will be based on information about various ways of dealing with distress. We propose that this information is organized into a solution schema, the content of which overlaps partially with one's problem schema, and is depicted in Figure 4.

Knowledge of coping alternatives is obviously a prerequisite for their use. Available sources of help will not be sought if individuals are unaware of them (Friedman, Bischoff, Davis, & Person, 1982). Knowledge of coping alternatives includes not only an awareness of their existence, but also of the services they offer. The Veterans Administration (VA), for example, may offer mental health assistance, but if the VA is mainly viewed in terms of medical and financial aid, help will not be sought there for emotional distress. The media is one important avenue for disseminating information regarding available resources (Aguilera & Planchon, 1995; Gist & Stolz, 1982). Thus, it is particularly important that a relationship is immediately established between outreach programs and the media to relay accurate information regarding coping resources to disaster victims.

A factor closely related to knowledge of resources is the perceived availability of different coping alternatives. An individual may be aware of a particular option (such as visiting a mental health professional) but feel the option is not readily available. The literature on barriers to seeking mental health services (McKinlay, 1975; Mechanic, 1982) has identified several variables, such as inconvenience, expense, and lack of insurance,

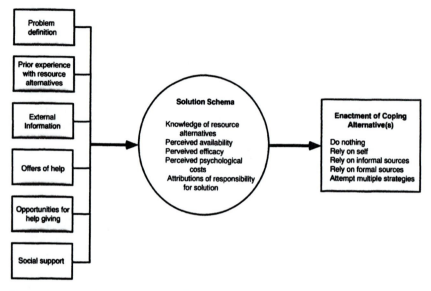

Figure 4 Consideration of coping alternatives.

that may discourage use. People may be more likely to make one visit to a physician because it is perceived as less costly than numerous visits to a mental health counselor. Indeed, one study found that the most common reason for not seeking help from professional sources when there was a high perceived need was the expense (Wells, Robins, Bushnell, Jarosz, & Oakley-Browne, 1994). Recall that mental health services in the aftermath of a disaster may be available at little or no cost. Thus it is perceptions about costs that can create a psychological barrier to help seeking even if they are wrong.

The nature of disasters may also influence the perceived availability of help-seeking sources. A disaster may severely decrease the ability of others to provide support due to the disruption in their own lives (Kaniasty & Norris, 1993; Kaniasty, Norris, & Murrell, 1990; Solomon, 1986). Help from informal sources (e.g., family, friends) within the community may not be perceived as a viable alternative. People who think that help from both formal and informal sources is not readily available may be more likely to select self-reliant coping alternatives.

The perceived efficacy of coping alternatives is another important component of the solution schema. Outcome expectancies refer to the perception that a particular behavior will lead to a desired outcome (Bandura, 1997). Help-seekers are more likely to ask for help from individuals who have specific resources that will meet their needs (De-Paulo, 1982). Indeed, the special skills of a particular helper was the most common reason flood victims reported for seeking help from both informal and formal support sources (Axsom et al., 1990). Because of the tangible losses typically incurred during disasters, we would expect that material aid would be viewed as an effective coping resource, especially during the early stages of recovery. Thus, it is not surprising that disaster victims who have property loss are more likely to seek tangible support compared with victims without such loss (Kaniasty & Norris, 1995; Murphy, 1988). Disaster victims in general are more likely to seek support from relief agencies compared with mental-health practitioners (Solomon et al., 1989). In addition to reflecting differences in problem interpretation, it is possible this difference reflects the belief that therapy does not offer an effective strategy for dealing with disaster-related stress. The common (but increasingly outdated) image of therapy involving a patient laying on a couch and free-associating about childhood experiences, and doing so for years, may need to be vigorously counteracted in outreach efforts.

Relevant to the perceived efficacy of the coping strategy itself is the perception that one will be able to initiate and carry out a particular strategy, a construct Bandura (1997) referred to as self-efficacy. The perception that one has control over reducing distress will increase the likelihood that available resources will be used following a negative life event (Ross & Mirowsky, 1989). Thus, high perceived control should result in an increase in help-seeking behaviors. In support of this hypothesis, individuals with high perceived control were more likely to seek both informal and formal support following a violent crime (Norris, Kaniasty, & Scheer, 1990). In addition, the choice of problem- versus emotion-focused coping may be influenced by perceived control (Lazarus & Folkman, 1984). High perceived control is more likely to lead to problem-focused coping (such as social protest) or preventative behaviors (such as evacuation; Flynn, 1982; Rochford & Blocker, 1991; Sims & Bauman, 1972), whereas low perceived control is more likely to lead to emotion-focused coping (Sims & Bauman, 1972). One danger that mental health outreach programs must be sensitive to is the possibility of undermining victims' sense of self-efficacy and personal control by implying that all victims are unable to cope without formal assistance (see Gist et al., 1998, for a full discussion of this issue). For many victims, mental health interventions that describe, through media announcements, steps individuals can enact without formal intervention might represent an effective form of assistance.

The perceived psychological costs associated with the use of a particular strategy represent another important schema component. Indeed, psychological costs are probably more important than tangible costs in post-disaster settings, where outreach services are frequently available for little or no money. One psychological cost is the extent to which a coping alternative threatens one's self-esteem (Fisher, Nadler, & Whitcher-Alagna, 1982). People are more likely to seek help when their need does not reflect an ego-relevant inadequacy (Tessler & Schwartz, 1972). Some help sources, such as seeing a mental health professional, may have a great deal of stigma associated with them, in spite of the perception that one's distress is valid (Yates, 1992). Stigma associated with the actual problem may also influence help-seeking behavior. One study found that distressed individuals who perceived that they needed help for alcohol-related problems, for example, were less likely to seek help because of embarrassment associated with this problem (Wells et al., 1994). Similarly, when asked their reasons for seeking help from various sources, a number of flood victims said the main reason they sought help from friends was because they could discuss their distress without feeling embarrassed or inhibited (Axsom et al., 1990). Feelings of dependency, inferiority, and inadequacy are all potential psychological costs associated with help-seeking (Fisher, Goff, Nadler, & Chinsky, 1988; Fisher et al., 1982; Fisher, Nadler, & Whitcher-Alagna, 1983). The importance of psychological costs is underlined by the reluctance of individuals to seek help even when help is more efficient than self-reliance (Ames, 1983; Fisher et al., 1988; Nadler, 1991). Victims of a natural disaster may already suffer lowered self-esteem (see Rubonis & Bickman, 1991a). Thus, help-seeking situations that are threatening may be particularly aversive to this population. Consequently, people may select less threatening cognitive strategies, such as minimization, which are also more likely to elicit favorable reactions from potential support providers (Gibbons & Gerrard, 1991; Herbert & Dunkel-Schetter, 1992). Communications aimed at bolstering victims' sense of competence, personal control, and potential for full-recovery may help allay the sense that one is "damaged" or no longer competent to manage one's own affairs.

There are other psychological costs as well. Receiving help may create an onerous sense of indebtedness to the helper, particularly, and ironically, if the source is one where no fee-for-service transaction takes place. Social psychological studies based on equity theory (Clark, Gotay, & Mills, 1974; Greenberg & Shapiro, 1971) have shown that people are sometimes reluctant to accept even necessary aid when they lack the ability to reciprocate. This finding may help explain the reluctance of individuals to seek help from "free" outreach programs. A sense of indebtedness is aversive and only reduced through direct reciprocation to the helper (Greenberg, 1980; Greenberg & Westcott, 1983; Hatfield & Sprecher, 1983). Moreover, when one cannot reciprocate in kind, what is given back to the helper is often acknowledgment of status and power (Blau, 1964). Conceding status and power to a helper gives the helper a degree of control over the help-seeker, a fate that people may be motivated to avoid if they already feel a loss of control from the disaster itself.

Attributions of responsibility for the solution of emotional distress comprise the final component of one's solution schema. Brickman and colleagues have noted that attributions of responsibility for solutions to a problem are conceptually distinct from attributions for the cause of the problem (Brickman et al., 1982). Different coping alternatives are likely to be considered, depending on whether one makes an internal or external attribution of responsibility for the solution. Internal attributions may lead to the perception that the individual is responsible for solving the problem in whatever manner he or she has available, whereas external attributions may lead to passivity. The current literature on this issue supports the notion that internal attributions are more likely to lead to the activation of multiple coping strategies, including self-reliance and help-seeking (Tellen, 1990; Wills & DePaulo, 1989), whereas external attributions are more likely to lead to "null coping" or a passive reliance on others or fate (Dimsdale, 1980). The overlap between the problem schema and the solution schema is underlined in this area. Attributions made as part of the problem schema will work in conjunction with attributions made in the solution schema to influence strategies. It has been suggested that external attributions for the *cause* of the problem and internal attributions for the *solution* of the problem will increase help-seeking (Ames, 1983; Brickman et al., 1982).

As with attributions about distress, attributions about solutions are likely to be influenced by perceived consensus regarding others' selection of coping strategies. If strategies such as self-reliance are thought to be prevalent, the likelihood of an internal attribution of responsibility will be enhanced. Of course, perceived use of coping alternatives may have little relation to actual use. Pluralistic ignorance (described above) is one process that may affect perceptions of others' coping (Miller & McFarland, 1991). Users of professional mental health services, for instance, may, for privacy reasons, not divulge to others that they are seeking help. If the use of such services is not well publicized, people may make erroneous consensus estimates that hinder use. For this reason, outreach efforts such as media campaigns and the use of models are important for heightening public awareness about mental health resources and their use (Freedy & Kilpatrick, 1994; Parson, 1995). Outreach programs using testimonials from community members (who are potential comparison others) may be particularly effective (Gist & Stolz, 1982). First, testimonials should increase the perceived efficacy of an option. Second, knowing that relevant peers have sought help should decrease perceived psychological costs by reducing stigma. Third, such efforts may influence attributions concerning who is responsible for solving the problem in ways that legitimate the search for outside aid when needed.

As depicted in Figure 4, several factors influence the content of one's solution schema. The definition of the problem is especially important because it answers the question, "Coping with what?" The solution schema one holds for economic problems is likely to be different from the one held for emotional distress. The definition of the problem as psychological, spiritual, or physiological will have a major impact on one's solution schema (Wills, 1987). Distress that is defined as physiological will more likely lead to a consideration of solutions aimed at reducing physical symptoms such as visits to a physician or use of over-the-counter drugs. This distinction is particularly important because of the tendency of individuals to attribute psychophysiological symptoms to illness or disease (Tessler & Mechanic, 1978; Van Den Bout, Havenaar, & Meijiler-Iljina, 1995). Distress defined as psychological will more likely lead to a consideration of solutions aimed at reducing emotional distress, such as seeking social support, cognitive reappraisal, etcetera. Distress defined as spiritual may lead to help-seeking from a spiritual advisor or other efforts to seek meaning. Therefore, how the problem is defined will influence from whom, or if, one seeks help (see Wills, 1983, for review). The tendency of victims to seek help from physicians and clergy (Axsom et al., 1990; Van Den Bout et al., 1995), suggests that these individuals may act as important referral sources for mental health professionals. Training programs may be beneficial for physicians and clergy to help them offer short-term intervention for transient problems and to provide them with diagnostic tools so that more serious problems can be identified and referred.

Prior experience should affect one's solution schema in a straightforward way. Past experiences provide the person with a basis for estimating the availability, effectiveness, and costs associated with different solutions. A potential solution may not be considered seriously if past attempts to implement it indicated it was unavailable, costly, or ineffective. For example, an easily accessible help source such as a parent may be avoided because, in the past, the resulting threat to the person's sense of autonomy was too high. An unproductive previous encounter with a mental health professional (Norris et al., 1990) may discourage the person from pursuing this option with another counselor. Coping attempts judged as effective in the past, on the other hand, will receive more serious consideration. As strategies are implemented, new information about their efficacy, psychological costs, and so forth, will feed back into the preexisting schema, either strengthening or otherwise altering it.

External information, especially in the form of media announcements that will affect knowledge of resource alternatives, was discussed above. In addition, the media may provide information regarding effective coping strategies for common reactions to disaster (Parson, 1995). External information may also come from informal sources such as family and friends. As was the case with both the awareness and interpretation of distress, information about "comparison others," or those in the community who have had similar experiences, may have strong effects on choice of coping strategy. Knowing others who have sought help is a strong predictor of both formal and informal help-seeking (Rickwood & Braithwaite, 1994). Community members may relay information regarding others' choice of coping strategies. If comparison others maintain that only the destitute accept financial aid or that well-adjusted people can adapt to any stressful situation, then individuals should be more likely to favor self-reliance than the use of formal helpers. People in the rural town of Buchanan, Virginia, for example, have turned down outside flood assistance so often and so completely in the past few decades that the *Washington Post* was moved to write about "The Buchanan Syndrome" (Allen, 1985). Individuals in one's social network may also act as a referral source for outreach programs and mental health services (Frieze, Hymer, & Greenberg, 1984; Norris et al., 1990; Veroff, Kulka, & Douvan, 1981) and/or encourage particular forms of coping. For instance, following a chemical disaster it appears that support sources may have encouraged victims to become involved in litigation (Bowler, Mergler, Huel, & Cone, 1994).

Informal sources not only provide referral information, they also may provide direct offers of help or requests for assistance as well. Although individuals often rally to the aid of a family member of friend in need, the disaster context itself may influence perceived psychological costs associated with coping alternatives. Disasters are unique in that a large number of others are also affected. Following a disaster, the opportunity for reciprocity is high because of the need of potential support providers (Giel, 1990). Kaniasty and Norris (1995) found that following a natural disaster victims typically provide a similar amount of help as they receive. Thus, individuals may be more likely to seek help, at least from informal sources, because of the opportunity to reciprocate. The opportunity to help may also increase perceptions of control over the solution to a problem, thereby increasing the use of other effective coping strategies (Krause, 1987; Krause, Herzog, & Baker, 1992). In addition, awareness that a large number of others are also in need of help may, by influencing perceived consensus estimates, attenuate the threat to one's own self-esteem. It is also possible, however, that some victims will attempt to avoid taking help because excessive demands for help by others tax already depleted reserves (Solomon, Bravo, Rubio-Stipec, & Canino, 1993; Solomon et al., 1987). In this case, the cost of using valuable resources to help others may override the potential benefits of reciprocity inherent in help-giving (Hobfoll, 1989).

Social support may influence one's solution schema at several levels. Social support is likely to influence knowledge of coping alternatives as well as their perceived availability, efficacy, and psychological costs. It is also important to note that social support is itself a coping strategy (Thoits, 1986). Therefore, the decision to seek help from support sources will be subject to the same processes that influence decisions to use other strategies (e.g., perceived availability, psychological costs, prior experience, etc.). In general, the greater one's perceived social support (i.e., perceived availability), the greater the likelihood those sources will be used to help with distress (Kaniasty et al., 1990; Rickwood & Braithwaite, 1994). Typically, following a negative life event, individuals rely primarily on informal sources of support (McCrae, 1984; Axsom et al., 1990). One explanation is that the perceived psychological costs of seeking help are attenuated when there is a close relationship with the helper (Anderson & Williams, 1996; Wills, 1991). Also, people within highly supportive networks may receive help within the context of everyday interactions, thereby eliminating the need for active solicitation (Fisher et al., 1988; Pearlin & Schooler, 1978). Moreover, the opportunity to reciprocate is greater for individuals with whom one has greater contact (Shapiro, 1980).

Finally, an individual's social network itself is likely to be disrupted in the wake of a disaster. As community destruction increases, perceived social support decreases (Kaniasty & Norris, 1993; Kaniasty et al., 1990). Although it is commonly believed that social support, in general, will increase as one's need increases (Hobfoll & Lerman, 1989; Kaniasty & Norris, 1991, 1995), following a natural disaster perceived support is relatively low (Bowler et al., 1994; Kaniasty & Norris, 1993; Kaniasty et al., 1990). Thus, because of network disruption, disasters may have a unique affect on perceptions of the availability of support. This suggests that efforts aimed at helping people develop or re-establish their social support networks may help victims recover more quickly from the effects of the disaster.

Coping is a dynamic process. One's choice of coping alternatives may change with changes in awareness or interpretation of the problem. If one strategy is ineffective in reducing distress, the individual may search the solution schema for alternative strategies. In one study on women with breast cancer, perceived control over the course of illness significantly declined over time (Newsom, Knapp, & Schulz, 1996). The relationship between perceived control and depression also declined over time. These women may have initially used problem-solving strategies to try and influence the course of their illness. The belief that their behavior could influence the disease may have resulted in decreased distress. However, over time, if the disease continued to progress regardless of their behavior, perceptions of control would be attenuated and emotion-focused strategies may have been more effective in reducing distress. As this example implies, different strategies may be effective at different times throughout the coping process. Immediately following the disaster, coping may focus on "clean up" efforts. Thus, the use of problem-focused strategies such as help-seeking for tangible support may predominate. Subsequently, more emotion-focused coping may dominate as victims attempt to reconcile disaster-induced thoughts—such as that bad things can happen to good people in a somewhat random, uncontrollable universe (Benner, Roskies, & Lazarus, 1980; Lerner, 1980)—with their prior "world assumptions" (Janoff-Bulman, 1992).

ENACTMENT OF THE COPING ALTERNATIVE

On the basis of the consideration of the coping alternatives, the person will select the most desirable option(s). The decision as to which coping alternative(s) to choose will likely be a combined function of the value placed on reducing the distress, the expectancy that a given coping alternative will be successful at reducing the distress, and the expected costs for employing the given alternative. It is possible that people will conclude, after considering their distress and various coping alternatives, that, at least for the moment, nothing can or should be done. Otherwise, people will actively attempt to ease the distress themselves and/or enlist the aid of others. Outside help may come from informal sources such as family and friends or formal sources such as mental health professionals or others (e.g., medical doctors). As we noted earlier, help may be sought from several sources simultaneously. As each coping strategy is enacted, the person will reassess the level of distress. If distress still exists, then people can be expected to reconsider their interpretation of the problem or their assessment of coping alternatives to determine whether the current mode of coping should be continued or changed.

CONCLUSION

We see this chapter as making two primary contributions. The first is a detailing and updating of the many factors relevant to disaster-related mental health help-seeking. We have argued that people's help-seeking decisions result from a series of subprocesses that are each multiply determined. By spelling out these many determinants, we hope we have conveyed the complexity that surrounds help-seeking. The second contribution is more general. We have attempted to provide a perspective or way of thinking about help-seeking that emphasizes underlying social influence processes and sensitivity to context rather than more static variables such as individual or demographic differences. In other words, rather than focusing on who does or doesn't seek help, we have emphasized why help might be sought or avoided.

This perspective suggests many reasons why formal mental health services after disasters might be underused. From lack of awareness of distress (and why this might be so) to failure to interpret the distress as a psychological problem to various barriers associated with formal mental health services (e.g., low knowledge of resources alternatives, stigma), hurdles exist at each step of the help-seeking process. Optimal interventions are likely to be those that take advantage of the many influences on people's help-seeking schemas identified by the model.

The sensitivity to context implied by the model also suggests caution about "one-size-fits-all" interventions. Depending on the particulars of a given disaster and the community it affects, there may be several different kinds of interventions that are effective in reducing distress, from those emphasizing individual-based therapies to those that use or enhance existing community resources (e.g., media to counter misperceptions, social networks).

Finally, we need to understand better people's resilience after disasters, and to think about resilience as something more than simply a personality characteristic. As we noted earlier, though disasters present great challenges to people and communities, evidence for long-term psychopathology is rare, despite the fact that formal mental health services are underused. How does this recovery unfold? To say that "time heals" is a description, not an explanation of how. Blake, Albano, and Keane (1992) have noted that research on the impact of disasters has shown only a modest increase over the last two decades, especially in comparison with work on other forms of trauma. Perhaps one avenue for future research is to devote closer attention to how people use naturally occurring resources (from family and friends to the media and nonpsychological professionals such as physicians and clergy) to cope with trauma. Quarantelli (1985) noted, in reference to the atomic bombing of Hiroshima, that, "The day after the bombing, survivors from the 12 banks got together and resumed banking services, one of the few standing steel companies resumed activities when 20% of the employees reported to work, the trolley lines were completely cleared and some electric services were restored... The tremendous physical destruction was not matched by any comparable social disintegration" (p. 177). Resilience is not just an individual difference, it is also a property of systems. Understanding and nurturing this resilience will enhance the outcomes of everyone in the face of the extreme challenges that disasters represent.

REFERENCES

Abrahams, M. J., Price, J., Whitlock, F. A., & Williams, G. (1976). The Brisbane Floods, January 1974: The impact on health. *The Medical Journal of Australia, 2,* 936–939.

Aguilera, D. M., & Planchon, L. A. (1995). The American Psychological Association–California Psychological Association Disaster Response Project: Lessons from the past, guidelines for the future. *Professional Psychology: Research and Practice, 26,* 550–557.

Allen, H. (1985, December 1). The Buchanan Syndrome. *The Washington Post,* p. C5.

Allport, F. H. (1924). *Social psychology.* Boston: Houghton Mifflin.

Ames, R. (1983). Help-seeking and achievement orientation: Perspectives form attribution theory. In B. M. DePaulo, A. Nadler, & J. D. Fisher (Eds.), *New directions in helping: Vol II. Help-seeking* (pp. 143–163). New York: Academic Press.

Anderson, S. E., & Williams, L. J. (1996). Interpersonal, job, and individual factors related to helping processes at work. *Journal of Applied Psychology, 81,* 282–296.

Archer, D. (1985). Social deviance. In G. Lindzey & E. Aronson (Eds.), *The handbook of social psychology* (Vol. 2, pp. 743–804). New York: Random House.

Axsom, D., Yates, S., Howe, G., & Bickman, L. (1990, July). *Coping with a natural disaster: Help-seeking and mental.* Poster presented at the 22nd International Congress of Applied Psychology, Kyoto, Japan.

Bandura, A. (1997). *Self-efficacy: The exercise of control.* New York: W. H. Freeman and Company.

Bartlett, F. (1932). *A study in experimental and social psychology.* New York: Cambridge University Press.

Baum, A. (1987). Toxins, technology, & natural disasters. In G. R. VandenBos & B. K. Byrant (Eds.), *Cataclysms, crises, and catastrophes: Vol. 6. Psychology in action* (pp. 5–53). Washington, DC: American Psychological Association.

Benner, P., Roskies, E., & Lazarus, R. S. (1980). Stress and coping under extreme conditions. In J. E. Dimsdale (Ed.), *Survivors, victims, and perpetrators: Essays on the Nazi Holocaust* (pp. 219–258). Washington, DC: Hemisphere.

Birnbaum, F., Coplon, J., & Scharff, I. (1973). Crisis intervention after a natural disaster. *Social Casework, 54,* 545–551.

Blake, D. D., Albano, A. M., & Keane, T. M. (1992). Twenty years of trauma: *Psychological Abstracts* 1970 through 1989. *Journal of Traumatic Stress, 5,* 477–485.

Blau, P. M. (1964). *Exchange and power in social life.* New York: Wiley.

Blocker, T. J., & Sherkat, D. E. (1992). In the eyes of the beholder: Technological and naturalistic interpretations of a disaster. *Industrial Crisis Quarterly, 6,* 153–166.

Bowler, R. M., Mergler, D., Huel, G., & Cone, J. E. (1994). Psychological, psychosocial, and psychophysiological sequelae in a community affected by a railroad chemical disaster. *Journal of Traumatic Stress, 7,* 601–624.

Brickman, P., Rabinowitz, V., Karuza, J., Coates, D., Cohn, E., & Kidder, L. (1982). Models of helping and coping. *American Psychologist, 37,* 368–384.

Clark, M. S., Gotay, C., & Mills, J. (1974). Interpersonal attraction in exchange and communal relationships. *Journal of Personality and Social Psychology, 37,* 12–24.

Cooke, R. A., & Rousseau, D. M. (1984). Stress and strain from family roles and work-role expectations. *Journal of Applied Psychology, 69,* 252–260.

Curran, P. S. (1988). Psychiatric aspects of terrorist violence: Northern Ireland 1969–1987. *British Journal of Psychiatry, 153,* 470–475.

DePaulo, B. M. (1982). Social-psychological processes in informal help seeking. In T. A. Wills (Ed.), *Basic processes in helping relationships* (pp. 255–277). New York: Academic Press.

Diener, E., & Fujita, F. (1997). Social comparisons and subjective well-being. In B. Buunk & R. Gibbons (Eds.), *Health, coping, and social comparison.* Hillsdale, NJ: Erlbaum.

Dimsdale, J. E. (1980). The coping behavior of Nazi concentration camp survivors. In J. E. Dimsdale (Ed.), *Survivors, victims, and perpetrators: Essays on the Nazi Holocaust* (pp. 163–174). Washington, DC: Hemisphere.

Dunning, D. (1991). Mental health sequelae in disaster workers: Prevention and intervention. *International Journal of Mental Health, 19,* 91–103.

Erikson, K. T. (1976). *Everything in its path.* New York: Simon & Schuster.

Faupel, C. E., & Styles, S. P. (1993). Disaster education, household preparedness, and stress responses following Hurricane Hugo. *Environment and Behavior, 25,* 228–249.

Feld, A. (1973). Reflections on the Agnes Flood. *Social Work, 18,* 46–51.

Festinger, L. (1954). A theory of social comparison processes. *Human Relations, 7,* 117–140.

Fisher, J., Goff, B. A., Nadler, A., & Chinsky, J. M. (1988). Social psychological influences on help seeking and support from peers. In B. H. Gottlieb (Ed.), *Marshaling social support: Formats, processes, and effects* (pp. 267–304). Newbury Park, CA: Sage.

Fisher, J., Nadler, A., & Whitcher-Alagna, S. (1982). Recipient reactions to aid. *Psychological Bulletin, 91,* 27–54.

Fisher, J., Nadler, A., & Whitcher-Alagna, S. (1983). Four conceptualizations of reaction to aid. In J. D. Fisher, A. Nadler, & B. M. DePaulo (Eds.), *New direction in helping, Vol I: Recipient reactions to aid* (pp. 52–84). New York: Academic Press.

Fiske, S., & Taylor, S. E. (1991). *Social cognition* (2nd Ed.). New York: McGraw-Hill.

Fleming, I., O'Keeffe, M. K., & Baum, A. (1991). Chronic stress and toxic waste: The role of uncertainty and helplessness. *Journal of Applied Social Psychology, 21,* 1889–1907.

Flynn, C. (1982). Reactions of local residents to the accident at Three Mile Island. In D. Sills, C. P. Wolk, & K. Shelanski (Eds.), *Accident at Three Mile Island: The Human Dimension* (pp. 49–61). Boulder, CO: Westview Press.

Freedy, J., & Kilpatrick, D. (1994). Everything you ever wanted to know about disasters and mental health (well, almost!). *National Center for PTSD Quarterly, 4,* 6–8.

Freedy, J. R., Saladin, M. E., Kilpatrick, D. G., Resnick, H. S., & Saunders, B. E. (1994). Understanding acute psychological distress following natural disaster. *Journal of Traumatic Stress, 7,* 257–273.

Friedsam, H. J. (1960). Older persons as disaster casualties. *Journal of Health and Human Behavior, 1,* 269–273.

Friedman, K., Bischoff, H., Davis, R., & Person, A. (1982). *Victims and helpers: Reactions to crime.* Washington, DC: United States Department of Justice, National Institute of Justice.

Frieze, I. H., Hymer, S., & Greenberg, M. S. (1984). Describing the victims of crime and violence. In S. S. Kahn (Ed.), *Victims of crime and violence: Final report of the APA task force on the victims of crime and violence* (pp. 19–78). Washington, DC: American Psychological Association.

Gibbons, F. S., & Gerrard, M. (1991). Downward comparisons and coping with threat. In J. T. Suls & T. Wills (Eds.), *Social comparison: Contemporary theory and research* (pp. 317–345). Hillsdale, NJ: Erlbaum.

Giel, R. (1990). Psychosocial processes in disasters. *International Journal of Mental Health, 19,* 7–20.

Gist, R., Lubin, B., & Redburn, B. G. (in press). Psychosocial, ecological, and community perspectives on disaster response. *Journal of Personal and Interpersonal Loss.*

Gist, R. & Stolz, S. B. (1982). Mental health promotion and the media: Community response to the Kansas City Hotel disasters. *American Psychologist, 37,* 1136–1139.

Gleser, G. C., Green, B. L., & Winget, C. (1981). *Prolonged psychological effects of disaster: A study of Buffalo Creek.* New York: Academic Press.

Greenberg, M. S. (1980). A theory of indebtedness. In K. Gergen, M. S. Greenberg, & R. Wills (Eds.), *Social exchange: Advances in theory and research* (pp. 3–26). New York: Plenum.

Greenberg, M. S., & Shapiro, S. P. (1971). Indebtedness: An adverse aspect of asking for and receiving help. *Sociometry, 34,* 290–301.

Greenberg, M. S., & Westcott, D. R. (1983). Indebtedness as a mediator of reactions to aid. In J. D. Fisher, A. Nadler, & D. M. DePaulo (Eds.), *New directions in helping: Vol I. Recipient reactions to aid* (pp. 85–112). New York: Academic Press.

Hanson, R. F., Kilpatrick, D. G., Freedy, J. R., & Saunders, B. E. (1995). Los Angeles County after the 1992 civil disturbances:. Degree of exposure and impact on mental health. *Journal of Consulting and Clinical Psychology, 63,* 987–996.

Hatfield, E., & Sprecher, S. (1983). Equity theories and recipient reactions to aid. In J. D. Fisher, A. Nadler, & D. M. DePaulo (Eds.), *New directions in helping: Vol I. Recipient reactions to aid* (pp. 113–141). New York: Academic Press.

Heider, F. (1958). *The psychology of interpersonal relations.* New York: Wiley.

Herbert, T. B., & Dunkel-Schetter, C. (1992). Negative social reactions to victims: An overview of responses and their determinants. In L. Montada, S. H. Filipp, & M. Lerner

(Eds.), *Life crises and experiences of loss in adulthood* (pp. 497–518). Hillsdale, NJ: Erlbaum.

Hobfoll, S. E. (1989). Conservation of resources: A new attempt at conceptualizing stress. *American Psychologist, 44*, 513–524.

Hobfoll, S. E., & Lerman, M. (1989). Predicting receipt of social support: A longitudinal study of parents' reaction to their child's illness. *Health Psychology, 8*, 61–77.

Hodgkinson, P. E., & Shepard, M. A. (1994). The impact of disaster support work. *Journal of Traumatic Stress, 7*, 587–600.

Horowitz, M. J., Stinson, C., & Field, N. (1991). Natural disasters and stress response syndromes. *Psychiatric Annals, 21*, 556–562.

Janoff-Bulman, R. (1992). *Shattered assumptions: Towards a new psychology of trauma.* New York: Free Press.

Joseph, S., Williams, R., & Yule, W. (1993). Changes in outlook following disaster: The preliminary development of a measure to assess positive and negative responses. *Journal of Traumatic Stress, 6*, 271–279.

Kaniasty, K., & Norris, F. (1993). A test of the support deterioration model in the wake of a natural disaster. *Journal of Personality and Social Psychology, 64*, 395–408.

Kaniasty, K., & Norris, F. (1995). In search of altruistic community: Patterns of social support mobilization following Hurricane Hugo. *American Journal of Community Psychology, 23*, 447–477.

Kaniasty, K., Norris, F., & Murrell, S. A. (1990). Received and perceived social support following natural disaster. *Journal of Applied Social Psychology, 20*, 85–114.

Katz, I. (1981). *Stigma: A social psychological analysis.* Hillsdale, NJ: Erlbaum.

Kelley, H. H. (1973). The processes of casual attribution. *American Psychologist, 28*, 107–128.

Kessler, R. C., Sonnega, A., Bromet, E., Hughes, M., & Nelson, C. B. (1995). Posttraumatic stress disorder in the National Comorbidity Survey. *Archives of General Psychiatry, 52*, 1048–1060.

Krause, N. (1987). Chronic strain, locus of control, and distress in older adults. *Psychology and Aging, 2*, 375–382.

Krause, N., Herzog, A., & Baker, E. (1992). Providing support to others and well-being in later life. *Journal of Gerontology: Psychological Sciences, 47*, 300–311.

LaGreca, A. M., Silverman, W. K., Vernberg, E. M., & Prinstein, M. J. (1996). Symptoms of posttraumatic stress in children after Hurricane Andrew: A prospective study. *Journal of Consulting and Clinical Psychology, 64*, 712–723.

Latané, B., & Darley, J. M. (1970). *The unresponsive bystander: Why doesn't he help?* New York: Appleton-Century-Crofts.

Lazarus, R. S. (1966). *Psychological stress and the coping process.* New York: McGraw-Hill.

Lazarus, R. S., & Folkman, C. S. (1984). *Stress, appraisal, and coping.* New York: Springer.

Lechat, M. F. (1979). Disasters and public health. *Bulletin of the World Health Organization, 57*, 11–17.

Lerner, M. J. (1980). *The belief in a just world.* New York: Plenum.

Levav, I., Kohn, R., Flaherty, J. A., Lerner, Y., & Aisenberg, E. (1990). Mental health attitudes and practices of Soviet immigrants. *Israel Journal of Psychiatry and Related Sciences, 27*, 131–144.

Lima, B. R., Santacruz, H., Lozano, J., Chavez, H., Samaniego, N., Pompei, M. S., & Pai, S. (1990). Disasters and mental health: Experience in Columbia and Ecuador and its relevance for primary care in mental health in Latin America. *International Journal of Mental Health, 19*, 9–20.

Lima, B. R., Pai, S., Santacruz, H., & Lozano, J. (1991). Psychiatric disorders among poor victims following a major disaster: Armero, Columbia. *The Journal of Nervous and Mental Disease, 179*, 420–427.

Linville, P. W. (1985). Self-complexity and affective extremity: Don't put all your eggs in one cognitive basket. *Social Cognition, 3*, 94–100.

Linville, P. W. (1987). Self-complexity as a cognitive buffer against stress-related illness and depression. *Journal of Personality and Social Psychology, 52*, 663–676.

McCrae, R. R. (1984). Situational determinants of coping responses. *Journal of Personality and Social Psychology, 46*, 919–928.

McKinlay, J. B. (1975). The help-seeking behavior of the poor. In J. Kosa & I. K. Zola (Eds.), *Poverty and health: A sociological analysis* (rev. ed.). Cambridge, MA: Harvard University Press.

Mechanic, D. (1972). Social psychological factors affecting the presentation of bodily complaints. *The New England Journal of Medicine, 286*, 1132–1139.

Mechanic, D. (1982). The epidemiology of illness behavior and its relationship to physical and psychological distress. In D. Mechanic (Ed.), *Symptoms, illness behavior, and help-seeking* (Vol. 3, pp. 1–24). New Brunswick, NJ: Rutgers University Press.

Mileti, D. S., & O'Brien, P. W. (1992). Warnings during disaster: Normalizing communicated risk. *Social Problems, 39*, 40–57.

Miller, D. T., & McFarland, C. (1991). When social comparisons go awry: When similarity is interpreted as dissimilarity. In J. T. Suls & T. Wills (Eds.), *Social comparison: Contemporary theory and research,* (pp. 287–313). Hillsdale, NJ: Erlbaum.

Miller, D. T., & Prentice, D. A. (1994). Collective errors and errors about the collective. *Personality and Social Psychology Bulletin, 20*, 541–550.

Mirowsky, J., & Ross, C. E. (1989). *Social causes of psychological distress.* Hawthorne, NY: Aldine de Gruyter.

Morgan, H. J., & Janoff-Bulman, R. (1994). Positive and negative self-complexity: Patterns of adjustment following traumatic versus non-traumatic life experiences. *Journal of Social and Clinical Psychology, 13*, 63–85.

Murphy, S. A. (1988). Mediating effects of intrapersonal and social support on mental health 1 and 3 years after a natural disaster. *Journal of Traumatic Stress, 1*, 155–172.

Nadler, A. (1991). Help-seeking behavior: Psychological costs and instrumental benefits. In M. S. Clark (Ed.), *Prosocial behavior: Review of personality and social psychology* (pp. 290–311). New York: Academic Press.

Newsom, J. T., Knapp, J. E., & Schulz, R. (1996). Longitudinal analysis of specific domains of internal control and depressive symptoms in patients with recurrent cancer. *Health Psychology, 15*, 323–331.

Norris, F. H. (1992). Epidemiology of trauma: Frequency and impact of different potentially traumatic events on different demographic groups. *Journal of Consulting and Clinical Psychology, 60*, 409–418.

Norris, F. H., Kaniasty, K. Z., & Scheer, D. A. (1990). Use of mental health services among victims of crime: Frequency, correlates, and subsequent recovery. *Journal of Consulting and Clinical Psychology, 58*, 538–547.

Norris, F., & Uhl, G. A. (1993). Chronic stress as a mediator of acute stress: The case of Hurricane Hugo. *Journal of Applied Social Psychology, 23*, 1263–1284.

Ormel, J., & Tiemens, B. (1995). Recognition and treatment of mental illness in primary care: Towards a better understanding of a multifaceted problem. *General Hospital Psychiatry, 17*, 160–164.

Parson, E. R. (1995). Mass traumatic terror in Oklahoma City and the phases of adaptational coping, Part II: Integration of cognitive, behavioral, dynamic, existential, and pharmacologic interventions. *Journal of Contemporary Psychotherapy, 25*, 267–309.

Peralin, L. I., Lieberman, M. A., Menaghan, E.G., & Mullan, J. T. (1981). The stress process. *Journal of Health and Social Behavior, 22*, 337–356.

Pearlin, L. I., & Schooler, C. (1978). The structure of coping. *Journal of Health and Social Behavior, 19*, 2–21.

Poulshock, S. W., & Cohen, E. S. (1975). The elderly in the aftermath of a disaster. *The Gerontologist, 15*, 357–361.

Price, J. (1978). Some age-related effects of the 1974 Brisbane floods. *Australian–New Zealand Journal of Psychiatry, 12*, 55–58.

Prince-Embury, S. (1992). Psychological symptoms as related to cognitive appraisals and demographic differences among information seekers in the aftermath of technological disaster at Three Mile Island. *Journal of Applied Social Psychology, 22*, 38–54.

Quarantelli, E. L. (1985). An assessment of conflicting views on mental health: The consequences of traumatic events. In C. Figley (Ed.), *Trauma and its wake: The study and treatment of post-traumatic stress disorder* (pp. 173–215). New York: Brunner/Mazel.

Ray, D. C., Raciti, M. A., & MacLean, W. E. (1992). Effects of perceived responsibility on help-seeking decisions among elderly persons. *Journal of Gerontology, 47*, 199–205.

Resnick, H. S., Kilpatrick, D. G., Best, C. L., & Kramer, T. L. (1992). Vulnerability-stress factors in development of posttraumatic stress disorder. *The Journal of Nervous and Mental Disease, 180*, 424–430.

Rickwood, D. J., & Braithwaite, V. A. (1994). Social-psychological factors affecting help-seeking for emotional problems. *Social Science Medicine, 39*, 563–572.

Robbins, J. M. (1981). Lay attributions of personal problems and psychological help-seeking. *Social Psychiatry, 16*, 1–9.

Rochford, E. B., & Blocker, T. J. (1991). Coping with "natural" hazards as stressors: The predictors of activism in a flood disaster. *Environment and Behavior, 23*, 171–194.

Ross, C. E., & Mirowsky, J. (1989). Explaining the social pattern of depression: Control and problem-solving: Or support and talking? *Journal of Health and Social Behavior, 30*, 206–219.

Rubonis, A. V., & Bickman, L. (1991a). Psychological impairment in the wake of disaster: The disaster–psychopathology relationship. *Psychological Bulletin, 3*, 384–399.

Rubonis, A. V., & Bickman, L. (1991b). A test of the consensus and distinctiveness attribution principles in victims of disaster. *Journal of Applied Social Psychology, 21*, 791–809.

Shapiro, E. G. (1980). Is seeking help from a friend like seeking help from a stranger? *Social Psychology Quarterly, 43*, 259–263.

Sims, J. H., & Bauman, D. D. (1972, June 30). The tornado threat: Coping styles of the North and South. *Science, 176*, 1386–1392.

Solomon, S. D. (1986). Mobilizing social support networks in times of disaster. In C. R. Figley (Ed.), *Trauma and its wake: Vol. 2. Traumatic stress theory, research, and intervention* (pp. 232–263.). New York: Brunner/Mazel.

Solomon, S. D., Bravo, M., Rubio-Stipec, M., & Canino, G. (1993). Effect of family role on response to disaster. *Journal of Traumatic Stress, 6*, 255–269.

Solomon, S. D., Regier, D. A., & Burke, J. D. (1989). Role of perceived control in coping with disaster. *Journal of Social and Clinical Psychology, 8*, 376–392.

Solomon, S. D., Smith, E. M., Robins, L. N., & Fischback, R. L. (1987). Social involvement as a mediator of disaster-induced stress. *Journal of Applied Social Psychology, 17*, 1092–1112.

Stevens, W. K. (1997, June 3). Storm warnings: Bigger hurricanes and more of them. *The New York Times*, pp. C1, C10.

Taylor, S. E. (1983). Adjustment to threatening events: A theory of cognitive adaptation. *American Psychologist, 38*, 1161–1173.

Taylor, S. E., & Brown, J. D. (1988). Illusion and well-being: A social psychological perspective on mental health. *Psychological Bulletin, 103*, 193–210.

Taylor, S. E., & Lobel, M. (1989). Social comparison activity under threat: Downward evaluation and upward contacts. *Psychological Review, 96*, 569–575.

Taylor, S. E., Wood, J. V., & Lichtman, R. R. (1983). It could be worse: Selective evaluation as a response to victimization. *Journal of Social Issues, 39*, 19–40.

Tellen, S. (1990). Parental beliefs and help seeking in mothers' use of a community-based family support program. *Journal of Community Psychology, 18*, 264–276.

Tessler, R., & Mechanic, D. (1978). Psychological distress and perceived health status. *Journal of Health and Social Behavior, 19*, 254–262.

Tessler, R. C., & Schwartz, S. H. (1972). Help-seeking, self-esteem, and achievement motivation: An attributional analysis. *Journal of Personality and Social Psychology, 21*, 318–326.

Thoits, P. A. (1986). Social support as coping assistance. *Journal of Consulting and Clinical Psychology, 54*, 416–423.

Thompson, M. P., Norris, F. H., & Hanacek, B. (1993). Age differences in the psychological consequences of Hurricane Hugo. *Psychology and Aging, 8*, 606–616.

Van Den Bout, J., Havenaar, J. M., & Meijiler-Iljina, L. I. (1995). Health problems in areas contaminated by the Chernobyl disaster. In R. Kleber, C. Figley, & B. Gersons (Eds.), *Beyond trauma: Cultural and societal dynamics* (pp. 213–232). New York: Plenum Press.

Veroff, J., Kulka, R. A., & Douvan, E. (1981). *Mental health in America: Patterns of help-seeking from 1957–1976.* New York: Basic Books.

Waxman, J., Larner, E., & Klein, M. (1984). Underutilization of mental health professionals by community elderly. *The Gerontologist, 24*, 23–30.

Weisæth, L. (1989). A study of behavioral responses to an industrial disaster. *Acta Psychiatrica Scandinavica (Supplement 335)*, 13–24.

Weiss, D. S., Marmar, C. R., Metzler, T. J., & Ronfeldt, H. M. (1995). Predicting symptomatic distress in emergency services personnel. *Journal of Consulting and Clinical Psychology, 63*, 361–368.

Wells, J. E., Robins, L. N., Bushnell, J. A., Jarosz, D., & Oakley-Brown, M. A. (1994). Perceived barriers to care in St. Louis (USA) and Christchurch (NZ): Reasons for not seeking professional help from psychological distress. *Social Psychiatry Psychiatric Epidemiology, 29*, 155–164.

Wills, T. A. (1983). Social comparison in coping and help-seeking. In B. M. DePaulo, A. Nadler, & J. D. Fisher (Eds.), *New directions in helping: Vol. 2. Help seeking* (pp. 109–143). New York: Academic Press.

Wills, T. A. (1987). Help-seeking as a coping mechanism. In C. R. Snyder & C. E. Ford (Eds.), *Coping with negative life events: Clinical and social psychological perspectives* (pp. 19–50). New York: Plenum Press.

Wills, T. A. (1991). Social support and interpersonal relationships. In M. S. Clark (Ed.), *Prosocial behavior: Review of personality and social psychology* (pp. 265–289). New York: Academic Press.

Wills, T. A., & DePaulo, B. M. (1989). Interpersonal analysis of the help-seeking process. In C. R. Snyder, R. Donelson, & D. R. Forsyth (Eds.), *Handbook of social and clinical psychology* (pp. 350–375). New York: Pergamon Press.

Wood, J. V. (1989). Theory and research concerning social comparisons of personal attributes. *Psychological Bulletin, 106*, 231–248.

Wood, J. V. (1996). What is social comparison and how should we study it? *Personality and Social Psychology Bulletin, 22*, 520–537.

Wortman, C. B., & Dunkel-Schetter, C. (1979). Interpersonal relationships and cancer: A theoretical analysis. *Journal of Social Issues, 39*, 120–155.

Wortman, C. B., & Silver, R. (1987). Coping with irrevocable loss. In G. R. VandenBos & B. K. Bryant (Eds.), *Cataclysms, crises, and catastrophes: Psychology in action* (pp. 189–235). Washington, DC: American Psychological Association.

Yates, S. (1992). Lay attributions about distress after a natural disaster. *Personality and Social Psychology Bulletin, 18*, 217–222.

Yates, S. (in press). Attributions about the causes and consequences of cataclysmic events. *Journal of Personal and Interpersonal Loss, 3*, 7–24.

Yates, S., Axsom, D., Bickman, L., & Howe, G. (1989). Factors influencing help seeking for mental health problems after disasters. In R. Gist & B. Lubin (Eds.), *Psychosocial aspects of disaster* (pp. 163–189). New York: John Wiley & Sons.

Chapter 7

Coping with Disastrous Events: An Empowerment Model of Community Healing

Julie van den Eynde and Arthur Veno

INTRODUCTION

Finding clarity of ideas within the disaster literature is a difficulty. Definitions and typologies seem fraught with contradictions. Underpinning these definitional attempts, values emerge, defining the language and flavor of the conceptualizations and the motivations of the researcher. Research yields seemingly antithetic outcomes.

These issues will be examined in a bid to clarify and to direct our experiences of working with a small rural town in Australia (Banksia).[1] Finally, an alternative method of community intervention is proposed, couched in the principles and values of community psychology, which was taught, demanded, and driven by community members in Banksia.

DEFINITIONS OF DISASTERS

If an earthquake strikes the center of Australia's outback, it is unlikely to be defined as a disaster. If an earthquake occurred with the same force in a major Australian city, a disaster would likely be defined and declared. An

[1]The town name Banksia is a pseudonym.

earthquake that affected an aboriginal community's sacred place in the outback, however, would likely be considered a disaster by the aboriginal people concerned. Disaster then, requires a social context and, as such, qualifies as a worthwhile area for psychological study. Disasters also illustrate the interaction between nature and community. Many authors have attempted more detailed definitions of disasters, both to narrow the scope of inquiry and to differentiate impact from hazards (Whittow, 1980) and crisis (Rosenthal, Charles, & Hart, 1989).

Definitions and assumptions

Consideration of the definitions below is an illuminating exercise, and indicates the slightly different foci of each quoted author. Disaster has been variously defined as: "a crisis event in which the demands being placed on a human system by the event *exceed the systems capacity to respond*" (italics added for emphasis; Bolin, 1989, p. 62); "a category of environmental events that periodically, and with varying degrees of intensity, *subject human systems to a wide range of disruptions and stress*" (italics added for emphasis; Bolin, 1989, p. 61); "collective stress situations that happen (or at least manifest themselves) relatively suddenly in a particular geographic area, involve some degree of loss, *interfere with the ongoing social life of the community*, and are subject to human management" (italics added for emphasis; Tierney, 1989, p. 12)

These definitions illustrate a set of assumptions that reflect the dominant value position in the disaster literature and are worthy of some reflection and debate. Those assumptions would seem to include the elements listed below:

1 A disaster is perceived by the community as negative.
2 A disaster renders the community incapable of coping.
3 The goal of intervention is that communities should be restored to previous functioning level.

The first and second assumptions—that communities will perceive a disaster as a negative impact and that communities cannot cope with the aftermath of a disaster—are discussed by Kreps (1984) and by Kaniasty and Norris (1995). Both discuss inconsistent research outcomes and note that community impacts from disaster seem to be distributed along continua. It is argued at one end of the debate that disasters produce minimal distress, whereas the other end of the debate holds that disasters produce severe distress. Although it is a well-held notion that disasters cause some distress in our communities, research suggests that this is *not always* true. This is a critical finding that should clearly impact on the intervention strategies used. It is from this perspective the research findings below are examined.

A torrential downpour in 1985 caused widespread flooding and dangerous mud slides in Puerto Rico, inflicting housing dislocation and widespread property damage. Residents had, within the previous year, completed a mental health survey, allowing researchers a unique opportunity for a prospective and retrospective research design. Interviews were gathered both from residents who were affected by the events and from those unaffected, thus controlling for degree of exposure to the disaster. Results indicated some evidence of trauma experienced by those who were exposed to the disaster, with such residents displaying signs of depression, posttraumatic stress, and somatic symptoms; these did not, however, differ at statistically significant levels when compared to unaffected residents. Bravo, Rubio-Stipec, Woodbury, and Ribera (1990) argued that these results support a "strengths" perspective that "suggest(s) that people can be very resilient to the development of new psychological symptoms even in the presence of such strong stressors as life threats, heavy personal or material losses, as well as evacuation and relocation" (p. 647).

Such a "strengths" perspective seems to strongly suggest that psychological hardiness or resilience buffered the residents from the effects of disaster. This disaster was uncontrollable and unexpected; was associated with high impact, high exposure, and terror; and had long-lasting physical impact on the residents. Similarly, Taylor, Ross, and Quarantelli (1976, cited in Kreps, 1984) found that although residents of a tornado effected area exhibited some stress symptoms, no longer term psychological problems tended to evolve—in fact, some residents reported positive reactions to the disasters.

Powell and Penick (1983) found comparable results among U.S. residents who experienced widespread flooding in the Mississippi Valley in 1973: Their responses were sought 8 to 12 weeks after flooding had occurred, and residents were asked both how they felt before the flood and how they felt at the time of the survey. They were recontacted 11–15 months after the initial interview to inquire regarding long-term effects of the disaster. Results included a significant increase in general tension and anxiety after the disaster. Further, residents with previous psychological problems were especially vulnerable to being affected by the disaster, whether shortly after the occurrence or 1 year later. None in the sample, however, required psychiatric hospitalization and none developed new psychopathological illness. Interestingly, "most victims described their reactions as distressful but 'natural'; they typically did not regard themselves as psychiatrically ill or in need of psychiatric care" (Powell & Penick, 1983, p. 275).

Further support for the community "strengths" hypothesis (Bravo et al., 1990) comes from examination of social reintegration, social support, and bonding after the dissolution and breakdown of communist East Germany (Schwarzer, Hahn, & Schroder, 1994). The authors argue that these political and social events represented both a critical life event and a stress inducing event, as major life changes occurred for many people. Many German people reframed their lives, changed their life courses and disrupted their social and network ties as they relocated into new social and political climates. Schwarzer et al. (1994) conducted a 2-year longitudinal study, controlling for life change and disruption, with 418 East German people, testing for psychological readaptation. Results confirmed that most of the immigrants were not "passive or helpless victims" overwhelmed by environmental events, but were active change agents who displayed clear abilities to restructure and take control of their lives in a constructive manner.

Parallel findings have been reported from residents in Israel during the Gulf War who were experiencing SCUD missile attacks on their homeland. Omer and Alon (1994) reported orderly, calm, and resolute patterns of behavior from the residents. Panic, shock, and looting did not occur. The authors discussed the efforts of news media and authorities to redefine residents' courteous and orderly behavior as shock reactions, possibly as a means to justify treatment, intervention, and relocation of residents for their own safety.

Omer and Alon (1994) coin the term *abnormalcy bias* to explain this behavior and attitude set, which reflects experts "underestimating the ability of people to function adequately in the face of a disaster" (p. 275). The researchers muse in their conclusions the possibility of zero intervention in some community disasters, and certainly posit the notion of minimalist intervention.

The studies and reports listed above were intentionally chosen to highlight the political conflicts that often occur in disaster work. Definition of disaster may be dependent on our subjective and objective views of events (Rosenthal et al., 1989), and may well depend on the type of community we are discussing, where our political views lie, and other similar and often subliminal features. The bombings of buildings in London may be viewed by English people as a disaster, whereas the initiators may well view these activities as a moral victory—disaster may well rest in the eye of the beholder.

Disaster as a concept is clearly dependent upon social and political factors; it may therefore be argued as a perception. As such, it is essentially a social construction. We generally construct events to be consistent with our world view. However, when a disaster is declared, the authorities and subsequently the media portray the event as powerful, devastating (at least to the powerful and propertied), and engendering of a trail of destruction throughout the community. Media tend to amplify the impact of the event, as this tactic is in their interest: The bigger the destruction, of course, the bigger the news. These factors serve to reinforce the perceived "impact" of the event and to provide a script as to how to respond to the event, now labeled as and known to be a "disaster."

The research above arguably raises questions regarding the first assumptions inherent in previous definitional attempts. The *community strengths hypothesis* (Bravo et al., 1990) and the *abnormalcy bias* (Omer & Alon, 1994) hint at the possibility of communities being capable of managing their own affairs and drawing on their own resources to overcome environmental events. Indeed, at least in some instances, outside "helpers" are viewed as a hindrance rather than as facilitators of rehabilitation (Omer & Alon, 1994; Toubiana, Milgram, Strich & Edelstein, 1988; Webb, 1989). Caution should prevail in our assumptions of a "needy community in distress," lest we fall into the victimological–medical-model trap (e.g., Brickman, Rabinowitz, Karusa, Coates, Cohn, & Kidder, 1982; Durrant & Kowalski, 1990; Ryan, 1971).

The remaining assumption initially posed considered a return to the former operating state of the community as the desired goal (see Omer & Alon, 1994). We suggest that communities, like people, cannot return to a previous state of operation once an event occurs. The event becomes incorporated into the community life and a new reality is formed.

Change in society is pervasive (e.g. Moore, 1974; Smith, 1976). The important questions about social change involve the rate and the direction of change. In this context, the role of the psychologist in the social change process is *the facilitation of change*, which provides a better quality of life for the greatest number of citizens. This statement reflects a value position quite consistent with ecological and community perspectives.

CONCEPTIONS ABOUT SOCIAL CHANGE

Two common myths or misconceptions about change, especially as related to disaster, cast it as a deviant or atypical phenomenon, and as one that is of necessity traumatic or stressful.

Change as deviant

One conservative argument for avoiding change is that change itself is essentially deviant, hence no change is truly normal. Some structural-functionalists have maintained this position for many years (see Demerath & Peterson, 1967; Parsons, 1951). This perception that persistence rather than change is normal for society seems to be associated with the pace of social change (Lauer, 1982).

Overall, however, change is neither unusual nor atypical. The change process is ubiquitous. Research questions relevant to investigation of change include societal and temporal differences in rates of change; factors affecting rates of change and the effects thereof, and optimum rates of change for maintenance of human well-being. In this context, disaster may be seen as unusually fast, unplanned social change occurring in the context of specific communities.

Change as traumatic or stressful

The notion that change is abnormal is often associated with the second questionable presumption: that change is of necessity traumatic. Change has been called an "ordeal" (Hoffer, 1952), a "crisis" (Nisbet, 1969), and a "foreign unwanted agent" (LaPierre, 1965). This conceptual cast might seem substantiated by evidence that suggests mental hospital admissions to be highly correlated with social change, for example, rates of hospitalization increase for people who migrate between countries (Francis, 1988), during times of economic stress (Dohrenwend & Dohrenwend, 1974), and for people undergoing life transitions (Holmes & Rahe, 1967). However, lower rates of admission to mental hospitals are reported during transitions from war to peace and peace to war (Murphy, 1961). Suicide rates similarly reflect this anomaly, as suicide rates have been shown to increase during economic depressions, and reduce at times of world wars (Australian Bureau of Statistics, 1983). Moreover, the disaster literature indicates varying levels of distress after the initial event (Bravo et al., 1990; Omer & Alon, 1994; Powell & Penick, 1983; Schwarzer et al., 1994).

The impact of social change, of course, is neither uniform nor universal across social or demographic strata. American epidemiological studies have shown that increases in unemployment rates are highly related to mental ill health, including all hospital admissions (Catalano & Dooley, 1977). These studies have also demonstrated that women and low-income groups were most likely to be negatively effected. Change did not lead to a generally increased probability of admission to mental hospitals for all members of the society, but instead differentially effected disadvantaged segments of society.

Change, including disaster (Kaniasty & Norris, 1995), appears to distribute its impacts—including its "traumatic" effects—selectively. Generally, those most at risk for negative impact affected are people who have the least power and least access to resources. Those who have least control over life events (such as the poor and the powerless) are most likely to be negatively affected (Peterson & Seligman, 1984). Thus, change per se does not necessarily lead to trauma, unless people have few economic resources, little power, and little social support. These conditions may accentuate traumatic impacts associated with disasters (Bravo et al., 1990; Omer & Alon, 1994; Schwarzer et al., 1994).

CONCLUSIONS ABOUT CHANGE AND DISTRESS

Toffler (1970) coined the term *future shock* to describe psychological disruption resulting from the experience of too much change too quickly. Both positive or negative life events have been reported to be related to higher risk of physical illness (Dohrenwend, 1978; Holmes & Rahe, 1967). Consistent with Vinokur and Seltzer (1975) is a construction that explains this seeming paradox as due to the perceived *rate* of change being stressful, not the experience of positive and negative change by itself. Change that is either too rapid or too slow is said to yield stressful impacts, with change seen to be imposed from outside and not under the control of people most affected by it yielding particularly negative impacts. Similarly, if communities develop expectations that the removal of oppressive or otherwise undesirable life conditions is imminent, the absence of desired changes may be experienced as stressful. What is perceived as disaster to a putatively oppressive segment of a society may be seen very differently by the oppressed.

Change per se, then, is not of necessity the traumatogenic agent. There is convincing evidence, however, to suggest that too rapid or too slow a pace of change may be traumatic. Rapid and undesirable change seems to produce the greatest incidence of negative psychological effects, and this would certainly include most incidents alluded to in the disaster literature.

IS THERE UNIVERSAL RESISTANCE TO CHANGE?

A number of impediments to social change have been identified in the literature, including both social and psychological factors (Rogers, 1983). Psychologists acting as change agents face a wide array of resistance when trying to facilitate change. The sources of this resistance may include value systems, social stratification, and opposition to the goals of change.

People have resisted many forms of change at virtually every level of society. Innovations that have been resisted include railroads, automobiles, typewriters, computers, alternating electric current, tractors, umbrellas, street lighting, and even potatoes (Barber, 1952). Spicer's (1952) analysis of resistance to social change indicates that people are constantly changing their ways, but will resist change under at least three circumstances: when the change is perceived to be a threat to their basic security, when the change is not understood, and when the change is imposed on them. This, of course, has enormous relevance to understanding the effects of disasters, as all disasters certainly share at least one of these properties.

Change also may be resisted when a calculation of risks based on value judgments makes the new direction seem unsafe. A good example of this

resistance is the anti-nuclear (No Nukes) movement that opposes development of nuclear power facilities and production and storage of nuclear
weapons.

SOCIAL SUPPORT

Many authors (e.g., Orford, 1992) consider social support as a critical
social resource central to, and providing a link between, individual and
community well-being. Table 1 presents five main functions of social
support as suggested by Oxford.

Kaniasty and Norris (1993) posited that social support helps buffer
stress, including that induced by disaster, in two highly interdependent
ways: First, support from others in times of crisis acts as a buffer to stress;
and second, such support is associated with psychological and physical
health, independent of stress conditions. According to Gordon (1991), a
disaster can be analogous to an instrument piercing the body of the
community. He described this process as a debonding of community
structures that disrupts the warp and weft of the community, sending its
members adrift from their bonded established relationships. In this model,
disasters may devastate community structures and community members'
perceptions, with wide impact on the community. Figure 1 illustrates this
phenomenon as described by Gordon.

Gordon (1991) argued that impact would be felt throughout the
community, although the strength of the impact would depend on community members' proximity to the disaster and the level of remaining and
provided support. Some supporting evidence comes from Kaniasty and
Norris (1993), who found that a disaster reduced community embeddedness, kin support, and nonkin support.

To examine the role of social support in a hurricane-affected area in
the United States, Kaniasty and Norris (1995) established a well-controlled
methodology, with a representative sample set by socioeconomic status and

Table 1   Types and functions of social support.

Type of social support	Function of social support
Material support	Practical aid, goods, and services
Emotional support	A feeling of being a trusted and worthy person, empathy, support, caring, and concern
Esteem support	A confidant relationship, encouraging expressive outlets
Informational support	The giving of advice, guidance, and information
Companionship support	Spending time with others in leisure activities, affiliating with others, and interacting in diversionary tactics

Figure 1 Debonding of community structures after an event disaster
Source: Gordon (1991), p.14.

race. Results indicated that most citizens both received help and gave help and support in the first 2 months after the hurricane. Disaster victims received and gave more help than non-disaster victims, and high-loss victims received more help than low-loss victims. Tangible support was given more frequently (money, transportation, shelter), followed by informational support. Interestingly, emotional support was also given and received, but remained constant across both disaster and non-disaster groups, indicating emotional support may be independent of direct experience of a disaster.

Kaniasty and Norris (1995) also found that social support was *not* distributed equitably in times of disasters. A "pattern of neglect" was detailed, where men received less emotional help than women, married people received more informational and emotional support than single people, Black people received less tangible, informational and emotional help than White people similarly affected, and people with less education received less emotional support. Further, age and received support were inversely related, highlighting concerns for those aged 66 years and older.

Consideration of both assumptions and limitations underlying the disaster literature begs review of essential constructs and definitions. It would seem advantageous at the very least, to view communities as capable, strong, and resilient, rather than as "victims who are unable to respond to challenge and change." Examination and explication of motivations and values contributing to the social construction of disaster should combine with cautious avoidance of any attribution of a victim–community "mental set." The following definition of *disaster*, given the above considerations, is "Disaster is a perception and a social construction of an act or physical event which holds the possibility of creating rapid, unwanted, and unplanned social change in a community."

Classification of disasters

Clsssification and categorization of disasters into some convenient typology has eminent appeal. To arrange disaster events together and to identify commonalities within each category makes for scholarly logic, holds promise for further understanding, and eventually enables more precision in intervention methodology. Berren, Santiago, Beigel, and Timmons (1989) proposed an engaging model based on dimensions of residents' psychological symptoms, social symptoms, and the emotional stages through which victims proceed. Disasters are classified under two categories, either as natural disasters or as human-induced disasters. *Natural disasters* include those events that are largely caused by the forces of nature, like earthquakes, floods, tornadoes, and volcanoes. *Human induced disasters* include all events that are not a result of natural causation. Berren et al. (1989) further divided this section into acts of omission and acts of commission. *Acts of omission* are those events that are caused by poor planning, attempts to save money, resources, and time, and by negligence. Toxic waste dumps are a prime example of this type of disaster. *Acts of commission* include events like terrorism, mass kidnappings, and other purposeful violence.

Although the simplicity of this typology is attractive, closer scrutiny suggests the categories to be largely capricious and to lack both definitional rigor and explanatory power. Consider the Vaiont Dam disaster in the Italian Alps in 1963 where a large dam was built on unstable bedding. There was evidence of earlier landslides, and new large fissures in the slopes above the reservoir suggested further landslides were forthcoming. Predictably, rock falls caused a major wave that burst the Vaiont Dam and inundated the village below, drowning 2,000 people. In a similar way, landslides in Hong Kong occurred in 1966, 1972, and 1976 that caused multiple deaths, urgent evacuation of residents, and destruction of many buildings erected on the terraced mountains. Causation was attributed to a combination of new housing constructions and new road cuttings, in conjunction with severe tropical cyclones (Waltham, 1978; Whittow, 1980).

The Aberfan disaster in South Wales in 1966 is yet another example where simple typologies prove unproductive in understanding the complexity of the event and its sequelae. A 250-meter coal tip collapsed and flowed onto the village, suffocating 144 people. Deaths included 116 children in the local school, which represented almost the entire young population. Virtually every family in the community had a relative who died in the school building. Mine managers, driven by economic factors, had ignored earlier warnings, and mine waste was still being dumped on the tip the day the disaster occurred. Subsequent investigations found that colliery waste had been dumped across a course of natural springs, which saturated the coal waste, causing the foundations to liquefy and destabilize when a critical mass had been reached (Couto, 1989; Whittow, 1980).

Landslides and tropical cyclones are considered to be natural occurrences, but their classification as natural disasters in these cases neither (a) reflects the complexities of the incidents, (b) recognizes the element of human error as acts of omission, nor (c) recognizes the systemic errors inherent in economically driven decisions that placed cost factors above human risk.

This mix of causes is equally obvious in many other disaster events, for example:

1   A combination of technological failure, management and staff breaches of safety policies and procedures, and poor industrial infrastructure, caused a Methyl Isocyanate (MIC) gas leakage from an underground storage tank at the Union Carbide Corporation, killing nearly 3,000 people in Bhopal, India (Shrivastava, 1989).

2   The West-Gate bridge collapse (Victoria, Australia) was attributed to management neglect, undue political pressure, and engineering short-cuts (Kouzmin & Jarman, 1989).

3   Institutional failure and management risk-taking behavior were seen as key factors in the Granville-Train Crash, in New South Wales, Australia (Kouzmin & Jarman, 1989).

Finally, classification systems seem to ineffectively classify disasters that have a historical context based on a social interaction occurring in a community. For example, in Dunblane, Scotland, a resident of the town was identified as a pedophile some 30 years ago. He was subject to increasing isolation, shutting off from the community. He was "fair game" for the parents to deride and even assault with rocks. This led to even further isolation, culminating in his murder of 16 children in a gym class at the school and his subsequent suicide (Deegan, 1996).

Classification and categorization becomes increasingly tenuous with the recognition that disasters are caused by dynamic interacting factors that may then interact with a series of environmental factors. If the aim of classification systems is to enable precise and accurate interventions, caution must prevail in assuming commonalities between events or similarities in symptoms. Additionally, it may seem wise to desist from attempts to force events into neat categories. Regardless of type, duration, or size of the disaster, it remains necessary to maintain an awareness of both individualistic responses to disasters (Berren et al., 1989) and to recognize differences in communities responses to disasters. Accordingly, typologies, at least to date, have proven of limited value in attempts to simplify and target helpful practices for people experiencing disasters.

The following case study is offered to illustrate the difficulties in typologies and the social/contextual impact of disaster on the warp and weft of communities. The case selected is Victoria, Australia's most recent Displan declaration. ("Displan" is the State Emergency Plan where a locality is declared by the State to have entered disaster status.)

CASE STUDY: BANKSIA VILLAGE — TRAUMA IN PARADISE

Some 50 years after the colonization of other parts of Victoria, European settlers arrived in the Banksia region. Early visionaries (ca. 1870) used draught horses pulling scoops to dredge deep channels on the side of the valley, which drained the excess water and rendered the land usable for forestry and subsequently dairy farming. This led to the establishment of Banksia. The village expanded, producing timber and dairy products as an economic base. Churches, schools, bush hospitals, and small businesses were built to service the families from the burgeoning cattle, forestry, and dairy industries.

Vast deposits of brown coal were discovered nearby in the late 1880s. These deposits supported the growth of largely industrialized towns whose main industry was coal mining and generation of electricity. Banksia village is situated away from the nearby coal mines, electricity stations, labor unions, and workers. Banksia residents felt protected from concomitant social problems in the other nearby industry towns, and often talked about the imaginary "wall of safety" they had constructed around their perimeter. Burglaries, assaults, domestic violence, drug and alcohol abuse, racial problems, wild teenagers, and gangs occurred in other nearby towns, but not in Banksia. The sanctuary illusion was reinforced by parents from nearby industrialized towns who bussed their children into Banksia, searching for a traditionalist enclave and notions of discipline, order, and safety in the local schools. Professionals were also recent arrivals, who chose to live there and commute to their work.

This set of dominant values and self-definition as a bastion of traditional agrarian values in the midst of industrial environments led the population to grow to 2,500 residents by 1994. Though Banksia's metaphorical "security wall" protected its population from the social evils of the outside, pending disaster was already within their own walls.

The problem

A newly appointed parish minister began receiving reports from parishioners of sexual molestation of children within her church. The suspected perpetrator was the Sunday school teacher. The minister, herself a mother of a young child and pregnant again, contacted the Community Police.

The Community Police in Victoria is the agency assigned to deal with cases involving family violence and sexual matters. The Senior Constable appointed as the investigating officer for the case was initially puzzled by the report. The alleged perpetrator was an invalid, confined to a wheelchair since the 1960s. He had lived in the town most of his life and was now almost 60 years of age with no previous convictions or recorded police history. His family had been respected in the community for decades. He was married with two children.

On the other hand, the activity profile of the suspect seemed to suggest a person who structured his life to be around children. He was a Boy Scout leader, a church elder, a Sunday school teacher. These facts alone led the constable to think that the allegations might have substance.

While the constable was considering the complexities of this case, she received a telephone call. An adult male reported that the alleged perpetrator had raped him over the bonnet of a car in the 1950s. He now wished to bring the matter to the attention of the authorities to stop the perpetrator and others like him from hurting more children. The police constable slowly realized that she was faced with two sexual assault charges against the same perpetrator, some 40 years apart. If both allegations were true, what might have happened in the intervening years?

The investigations progressed cautiously and slowly. The net effect of the investigations was to create a small cadre of complainants who were bound together by a conspiracy of silence. Children were instructed to wave and greet the alleged perpetrator as he drove by; neighborhood children took a birthday cake to his house as they normally would. The accusers' unity was galvanized into supporting the police investigations, and they provided intelligence on the accused's activities and whereabouts on a very frequent basis.

The initial tension was released when the alleged assailant was arrested and charged with numerous sexual offenses. There were 45 residents willing to press charges regarding a series of 219 alleged events spanning four decades. Earlier victims were now in their fifties while the youngest was a little girl four years of age.

The news spread through the community like a bush fire. It emerged that the perpetrator had begun pedophile activities when 15 years old, some 40 years previously. He initially preferred prepubescent boys and accessed them through his involvement in the Scouting movement and as a Sunday school teacher. In later years, he attracted boys by using his disability, their fascination with his wheelchair, his coin collection, and his computer games. He manipulated their silence with appeals to their Christian beliefs and threats of exposure. He carried a gun, and ensured the children's silence with threats of murdering their families.

After the birth of his daughter, his sexual orientation turned to girls as well as boys. His niece, his neighbors, and girls as young as 4 at the Sunday school picnic fell prey to him. His own daughter was raped and assaulted repeatedly. He became so confident of his abilities to manipulate children and parents that he would visit young boys' homes for the expressed purpose of sex, and at other times he would lure children away from their mothers while they were visiting his wife and assault them in his study or bedroom. In the parlance of policing, the perpetrator was an experienced "groomer" of parents: He would target his desired children and then proceed to manipulate the parents of these children to place himself in trusted positions with the explicit goal of having sex with the child.

Community reactions varied as more violations became public. Some gatekeepers in the town reported an overwhelming "wall of denial and silence" from community members, while local counselors and psychotherapists were inundated with requests for help, many who from families unable to pay for the services they felt they needed. Counselors reported being approached in supermarkets, at local meetings, after church services, and at school activities by residents who needed to talk. Those seeking help included current children who had been sexually abused, past victims who had never spoken out, people who had been told by their children but who had done nothing, and those who had told the police but reported that nothing had been done.

The general illusion of sanctuary and safety had been dashed. Banksia was not, and never had been, a safe place to raise children. The values of respectability and conservatism had inadvertently supported the activities of the pedophile for four decades. Notions of family life and trusting neighbors, the church, Sunday school, and the scouting movement had all failed to provide a safe haven for Banksia's children. Overwhelmed by the strength, magnitude, intensity, and veracity of community reactions, the minister and a local psychologist contacted community psychologists based at a nearby university for advice.

In the context of the magnitude of the case, the State Government declared the situation a disaster. A town meeting was called by the besieged counselors, clergy, and general practice physicians in the town, with the goal of establishing a committee to manage the healing process of the community.

An empowerment orientation for the problem and intervention

Table 2 demonstrates competing approaches taken by varied community workers and governmental agencies in community work, separated along assumptions regarding competence and resiliency.

Table 2 Conflicting approaches to community intervention.

Victim community	Competent community
1. Outside agencies are experts holding special knowledge regarding healing to which the community should submit.	1. The community is expert in its life, and has the ability to determine its best healing approach.
2. The community is viewed as damaged or broken by the disaster.	2. The community is viewed as oppressed by and struggling with the effects of the disaster.
3. Deficit model: Agencies seek to 'fix' the community.	3. Resource model: Agencies seek to build on strengths and resources of the community.
4. Insight into the dynamics of the disaster is the key goal of treatment.	4. Goals of treatment are the community viewing itself as competent and as having control over the intervention.
5. A cathartic or corrective experience is necessary to produce community change.	5. Best "corrective experience" is the getting on with life in a way which best suits the community, and change will be promoted by experiencing this possibility.

Note. Information from Durrant & Kowalski (1990, p. 67).

Victim–community interventions are described as those in which problems are identified within a community by professionals, the community is viewed as incapable of managing their problems, and the community is expected—whether implicitly or explicitly—to acquiesce to the holders of expertise for treatment of its problems. Alternatively, *competent-community interventions* are self-help focused, where the community uses its own resources and abilities to manage the challenges it faces through self-determination. Similar concepts can be found in discussions of the merits of a "compensatory model" of intervention compared with a "medical model" (e.g. Brickman et al., 1982).

After consultation with the community gatekeepers, both psychologist and minister were clear that the use of victim models would prove counter productive if not overtly harmful. They did not view their community as comprised of victims who were broken and damaged; they viewed their community as competent with existing strengths and resilience, and wanted respectful treatment *if* the community psychologists were *allowed* entry into their community. A contract encapsulating these values was developed between researchers and the community gatekeepers. The researcher/consultants were then invited into a steering meeting at the local Sunday school hall, whose purpose was to activate plans of action for the rehabilitation of Banksia Village. In contrast to Young's (1989) assertion that local residents may be ineffective in dealing with emotional injuries, it was clear from our initial contact that Banksia held the possibility of a competent community, well able to work through its own problems with minimal assistance from psychologists. Rather than gatekeepers receiving training in crisis intervention, listening techniques, and coping skills (Young, 1989), a model based on support, facilitation, and empowerment was seen as more appropriate.

EMPOWERMENT AND GRASS-ROOTS COMMUNITY GROUPS

Rappaport (1981) proposed "empowerment" as a central tenet of community psychology. He claimed that the logic and imagery of empowerment demand "that we look to many diverse local settings where people are already handling their own problems in living, in order to learn more about how they do it" (p. 15). Kieffer (1984) and Saegert (1989) have provided examples of where empowered people might be found and who they might be.

Saegert (1989) gained the stories of 37 residents of tenement housing in the Harlem section of New York City who had faced a housing crisis after previous landlords relinquished ownership by defaulting on taxes. In response to this emergency situation, a housing cooperative formed who collectively organized to rehabilitate, manage, control, and often, purchase their buildings. Saegert was surprised to find an empowered group of housing co-op leaders who were people of color, predominantly women, sole heads of their own households, most aged in early 60s to early 80s with sketchy education and work records. Additionally, none had previous leadership roles in other organizations but most were active members in their churches.

Similarly, Kieffer (1984) reported on members of varied grass roots organizations who had undergone a transformation from relative powerlessness to relative empowerment, and suggested a four-stage developmental process, including (a) an era of entry, (b) an era of advancement, (c) an era of incorporation, and (d) an era of commitment. Kieffer's (1984) typology can be used to track the developmental process of the Banksia's Recovery Community Group's (BRCG) empowerment, and corollaries can be drawn from Saegert's (1989) empowered women.

Stage 1: The era of entry

At the entry stage of the empowerment process, Kieffer (1984) postulated that participants are aware of their powerlessness, their silence, and their acquiescence to societal institutions. These are described as consequences of learned behavior and functions as the need to survive in the particular social context. Kieffer noted that "despite the sense of powerlessness which characterized the prior life-worlds of all participants, these individuals also shared a common sense of "integrity" in their sensed self-identity and daily lives," which included "a strong sense of pride and determination, a deeply felt rootedness in community, a commitment to self reliance, and feelings of attachment and support within a caring community of peers" (p. 18). These attributes of connectedness to their community, and an overriding care and concern for the residents and town generally, were consistently displayed by the Banksia residents in the early meetings at BRCG.

Banksia residents had a clear vision of how the community group should operate. To defend against further abuse of the townspeople, they decided meetings should be positive experiences for town members. They were defining a bottom-up process of community participation, which had the potential of increasing the participants' feelings of control and allowed the opportunity to develop or select programs that matched their needs and values (Wandersman, 1979, 1984). The decision-making process also received considerable attention. A consensus model was preferred (where the group held authority rather than an executive), no roles would be assigned, and no agenda nor formal meeting procedure would be prescribed (Rothschild-Whitt, 1979).

These notions were intended to ensure that all community members had opportunity for input in the town's rehabilitation. Of equal importance was the opportunity for those community members who had held their silence and acquiesced to abuse of their children to find a voice and be a part of their towns' recovery. Under these conditions, the group could not only evolve into an empowering organization and provide healing for community members, it could also develop into an empowered organization with the capacity to influence the larger social system (Israel, Checkoway, Schulz, & Zimmerman, 1994).

Early meetings of the rehabilitation group were held in a local church, where the psychologist and the minister explained to those attending the purpose of the group, the reasons for the consensus mode of practice, and their underlying philosophy of a "competent community." Community members from the churches, schools, and medical professions were present, as well as regional welfare agencies. These early meetings were labored and exhausting, with little apparent progress made on the task of rehabilitation. Expressions of guilt and confusion were evident in some of the towns' people. Denial was frequent as some argued there was not a problem in their town. The community psychologists were largely silent observers at these early meetings, watchful of the group dynamics at work, and wary of their role in the proceedings.

Against this backdrop of disquiet, regional welfare agencies made a move to establish a "victim–community" model of treatment of Banksia. Seemingly motivated by the need for action and quick resolution, and incorrectly perceiving a power vacuum within the group, they attempted to formalize procedures and implant structures within the group, appoint themselves to roles and tasks, and take independent action on behalf of the group. The community recoiled with shock, and reacted with passive resistance to all suggestions and ideas. Frustrated by the inaction, the regional welfare agencies apparently felt their suspicions confirmed that this was an incompetent community. Without consultation with the community people, the welfare agencies attempted to bring in State government agencies to take over the recovery program in Banksia.

Kieffer (1984) stated that, nearly universally, some provocative event is needed as the catalyst for individual mobilization and progress beyond the era of entry. The event must be of sufficient force to offend the personal integrity of the participants and threaten family or self-interests. The developmental tasks of the facilitators in the entry stage are to redefine the power relationships with authority, to demystify the symbols and rituals of the powerful, and to "reorientate the self, in relation to authority" (p. 18). The actions of the regional welfare agencies and State government agencies, coupled with their apparent victim–community philosophy, provided the provocative event for action. This catapulted the community group into the next stage of Kieffer's developmental view of empowerment.

Stage 2: The era of advancement

For this stage to proceed, Kieffer (1984) stated that three new developmental tasks would need to be present.

   1   The involvement of a mentor who acts as a role model, ally, and friend. This enabler can provide emotional support and experience, encourage strengths and support autonomous political experimentation.
   2   Involvement by community members in an organization that provides mutual support and opportunities to develop political skills.
   3   Reconceptualizing the process with a more critical understanding of social, economic, and political relations that have caused their alienation and exploitation. This new-found knowledge deepens awareness and generates an earnest commitment to political action.

All Kieffer's (1984) requisites were present for the community. The community psychologists provided the necessary mentor and supportive friendship function, a supportive community group was activated, and the take-over tactics of the professionals deepened political awareness and reconceptualization. The local psychologist and minister were aghast at the politicalization of events but were also aware of the ramifications for their town if action was not taken. Options were discussed in detail, clear goals were defined, actions and time lines were developed. With encouragement and support, these town leaders decided on a community action approach (e.g., Alinsky, 1972).

The outside agencies were working under an assumption that the community was "needy," "injured," or "sick." This underestimated the commitment of the community, undervalued the community they were trying to "fix," and disregarded the hidden but powerful supportive networks operating in helping organizations in the area. Spontaneously, intelligence on the regional welfare agencies activities was reported to local leadership and confirmation was received concerning the take-over tactics of the State government agencies. Discussions were held with key people in the State government agencies, and agreement was reached that the meeting would not proceed until proper community representation could be organized. Satisfaction was short-lived, as "moles" within the government departments telephoned the local psychologist and reported the meeting was to proceed despite their assurances, without any community representation. This ignited the community into action, and galvanized the community into a common cause: reclamation of their right to determine their own healing.

Before the appointed time of the professionals' meeting, the community group assembled in the meeting place, tables were removed, and chairs were arranged in a circle. Shock and confusion was evident on the faces of the government representatives as they arrived in the hall and noticed the uninvited residents, and as their attempts at securing powerful seating positions were thwarted by community members seated at regular intervals around the circle. More community people arrived, several obviously coming directly from their milking sheds, resplendent in Wellington boots, beanies, gloves, and scarves. Others had made last minute baby-sitting arrangements and rushed to the hall. A nervous silence settled into the room, and the local leadership began to address the group.

State government groups were asked to explain their presence in Banksia after a clear understanding had been struck to cancel any meetings. The government agencies retorted angrily, stating they held a mandate to work in the area. They were reminded that if they were to undertake any intervention work in the town, they would need community support that risked nullification by their present actions. It was noted that the government agencies were acting in an imperialistic manner, which indicated grave concerns for future treatment of the community. Local leaders asked for the meeting to be closed, and stated that the Banksia group would invite agencies to work in the town if their services were needed.

One by one, community members took turns to state their case, making it clear that the organizations represented might have many useful resources but the healing of Banksia should be done by community members, run by the community, and driven by the community. During these exchanges, outside organizational leaders sat in their seats silently.

Some agencies apologized to the residents of Banksia, stating they were not aware they were not welcome in the town and offered to leave. Others angrily continued to instruct the community group in how they should proceed, with recommendations as to the need to establish guidelines, set agendas, elect positions of responsibility, and set "achievable" outcomes. At this point the meeting was closed, and the government agencies left the town.

Stage 3: The era of incorporation

Kieffer (1984) asserted that in Stage 3, participants incorporate their new-found sense of mastery and an acceptance of themselves as political actors into a sense of identity. Organizational skills are intensified, multiple role conflicts are balanced, and participants learn to contend with the permanence of institutional barriers. These factors serve to strengthen resolve and determination, and this sense of mastery heralds a newly developed sense of empowerment.

The Banksia group acted with strength and decisiveness after the expulsion of the government agencies. Gleefulness was mixed with trepidation—they were sufficiently "reality-based" to recognize that a payback would occur from publicly embarrassed government agencies. Their supportive network was still activated, and continued to gather intelligence on activities of government agencies. There were numerous reports of great anger at the Banksia community, and vehement personal attacks made against local leaders particularly. Government agencies held their own meetings concerning the disaster and tried to instruct the Banksia group on how they should proceed; co-option was attempted repeatedly, as if to break the power relations of the group. The Banksia group held firm, as none of the options provided by the State government agencies included full community consultation and most were directive and disempowering.

In the next few months, the Banksia community group began to flourish, and community participation increased considerably. Organizational skills were intensified, natural strengths of the community members were fostered and developed, and skills emerged and were realized as people began to take up informal roles within meetings. The consensus model held, with a different facilitator appointed each meeting. Consideration was given to the new members, who were encouraged to participate in decision-making processes.

The community group was now able to take action. Invitations were made to various agencies and to the community psychologists to present plans of action for the town's rehabilitation. The community psychologists' approach was selected, based on five criteria.

1 The community psychologists had become trusted members of the group and were committed to a long involvement in the town.

2 The Banksia community felt they had a degree of control over their activities, as the community psychologists were accountable directly to the university and their activity could be halted if community prerogatives were violated.

3 The proposed intervention included an evaluation, so that our model could be replicated in other towns with similar social disasters.

4 Townspeople were explicitly recognized as responsible for developing their own programs for healing, which the community psychologists would facilitate.

5 The community was responsible for the implementation of the program, although the researchers would consult and assist.

Information dissemination was begun with pamphlet drops advising residents of the variety of counseling services available and information stickers placed in key positions around the town. Free-call telephone counseling was organized and advertized. Relationships with media were fostered, and group activities were advertized to the community. The group felt sufficiently confident to invite some government representatives back to the meetings, although it was made clear that this time their roles were as advisors only.

A new distractor entered the group activities as government agencies managed to secure considerable funding to aid the recovery of Banksia. Government administrators held vested interests in securing control of the spending to maximize organizational credibility. Although the group was only vaguely interested in the funding, government agencies were trying to wield power by insisting that funds be spent. Subgroups were formed to decide what to do with the money. Government agencies again tried to set up an executive within this subgroup, who would silently run Banksia group activities. Community members' passive resistance was reactivated, and the subgroup meetings folded.

Stage 4: The era of commitment

While the community psychologists' rehabilitation intervention was proceeding with considerable support from the Banksia group, the perpetrator's trial and sentencing marked a considerable turning point in the nature and purpose of the group. Given the definition of disaster vied in this chapter, media can play a key role in amplification of the disaster, and can further entrench the victim–community perception. Extensive discussion and consideration was devoted to portrayal of events to the media. Spokespersons and media briefs were organized and prepared that portrayed Banksia as a community coping well with trauma. The focus by the spokesperson was that Banksia was unusual only in the strength of its community in the face of an adversity found in any community.

At the point of writing, the researchers have facilitated a search conference to establish a program for healing the town, composed mainly of townspeople. A community development officer had been appointed to implement the healing program. Surveys collected to date show significant improvements for the town's scores on the General Health Questionnaire, from the period just after sentencing to 1 year later (time of writing this chapter). No resident remains in psychotherapy for the events of the disaster. A community family "Band-Day" is planned to "mark the end" of the trauma.

The group has at times turned to wider political action and has become a pressure group aimed at changing laws to ensure prosecution of pedophiles and protection of children. The community has also been engaged in lobbying local councils to establish youth drop-in centers and facilities for the Community Development Officer. The group has begun to contact relevant national organizations for informational support and affiliation. These results will be carefully evaluated in the future and reported elsewhere.

BRCG began as a small collection of residents who invited outsiders for assistance. It has survived many attacks on its viability and independence from outside government agencies and from within its own ranks. With its passage through time, it has reflected the towns' pain and anguish while demonstrating its ability to resolve its problems constructively. It is a constantly evolving mechanism, with its mission clearly designated as community healing, but its future is unclear at this stage. This might be anticipated as Kieffer's (1984) *Era of Commitment*, which heralds a necessity to integrate a new political identity into the realities of everyday life, and as the participants search for meaningful roles in which to apply their new found skills and self concepts.

CONCLUSION

'**empower**' 1. to give power or authority, to authorize. 2. to enable or permit (Macquarie Dictionary, 1982)

This case study illustrated that the concept of empowerment in community psychology may be used inappropriately or inaccurately in many current applications. Kieffer's (1984) conceptualization that empowerment cannot be "given"; that power must be *seized* for empowerment to be effective. This lies closer to another concept from which psychologists, and community psychologists in particular, generally shy away.

Rather than accepting the dictates of authority and letting the "experts" delegate healing in their town, the Banksia community chose "to rise against constituted authority." This is a consistent theme in empowerment literature. Both Kieffer (1984) and Saegert (1989) noted this feature as essential in the empowerment process.

'**revolt**' 1. To break away from or rise against constituted authority. (Macquarie Dictionary, 1982)

The fundamental concept of empowerment expressed by Rappaport (1977, 1981) and subsequently accepted by the field of community psychology as a dominant value calls for an act of revolution. Although this may offend the sensitivities of some colleagues, this is, in fact, what is done by groups such as the BCRG.

Rather than delegation of authority, empowerment as used in the community psychology literature refers at least metaphorically to revolution. Is this a sensible "therapeutic" goal? We argue affirmative, but suppose that it depends, yet again, on one's values. The traditional authority in Kieffer (1984), Saegert (1989), and Banksia are core causes of the various groups' problems, and are therefore oppressors of sorts to be overthrown by the "empowered" group. Overthrow of oppressor would logically lead to a sense of power and control, thus increasing any group members sense of personal efficacy and reducing stress for members of the empowered groups.

If we can take heed from the unique research of Kieffer (1984), Saegert (1989), and the community of Banksia, community psychologists' involvement must be carefully considered so as to not override or brutalize the empowerment/revolution development in community members. Our role must be embedded within the boundaries of acting as mentors, facilitators, and enablers to those progressing through their development; by assisting in organizational development and understanding group processes; by developing our own critical awareness of the stages of empowerment; and by reacting appropriately and sensitively to developmental tasks with which communities and their individual members must struggle.

This chapter has argued for a new definition of disaster, and for discard of existing typologies of disastrous events. We contend that definitions contain value sets that need explication to develop effective interventions. Further, typologies appear not only to be inadequate in explaining the multi-causes implicit in many disasters, but also fail to account for disasters experienced in communities like Banksia, Australia, or Dunblane, Scotland.

Lessons from working with the Banksia community have clarified and confirmed notions of community strengths and capabilities. The grass-roots community has driven its own rehabilitation program and maintained ownership of this process with minimal intervention from community psychologists or other outside experts. The role we have advocated has been to facilitate rather than direct, to encourage the development of new political and organizational skills, and to support community action. In short, the approach has been to facilitate an empowerment model of rehabilitation with minimal intervention, and to explicitly resist a victim–community approach.

REFERENCES

Alinsky, S. (1972). *Rules for radicals*. New York: Harper Row.

Australian Bureau of Statistics. (1983). *Suicides Australia, 1961–1981*. Cat. 3309.0.

Barber, B. (1952). *Science and social order*. Glencoe, IL: Free Press.

Berren, M. R., Santiago, J. M., Beigel, A., & Timmons, S. A. (1989). A classification scheme for disasters. In R. Gist & B. Lubin (Eds.), *Psychosocial aspects of disaster* (pp. 40–58). New York: John Wiley & Sons.

Bolin, R. (1989). Natural disasters. In R. Gist & B. Lubin (Eds.), *Psychosocial aspects of disaster* (pp. 61–85). New York: John Wiley & Sons.

Bravo, M., Rubio–Stipec, M., Woodbury, M. A., & Ribera, J. C. (1990). The psychological sequelae of disaster stress prospectively and retrospectively evaluated. *American Journal of Community Psychology, 18*, 661–680.

Brickman, P., Rabinowitz, V. C., Karusa, J., Coates, D., Cohn, E., & Kidder, L. (1982). Models of helping and coping. *American Psychologist, 37*, 368–384.

Catalano, R., & Dooley, D. (1977). Economic predictors of depressed mood and stressful life events. *Journal of Health and Social Behavior, 18*, 292–307.

Couto, R. A. (1989). Catastrophe and community empowerment: The group formulations of Aberfan's survivors. *Journal of Community Psychology, 17*, 236–248.

Deegan, L. (1996, March 20). The day mothers tackled a monster. *Herald-Sun*, p. 3.

Demerath, N. J., & Peterson, R. A. (1967). *System change and conflict*. New York: Free Press.

Dohrenwend, B. S. (1978). Social stress and community psychology. *American Journal of Community Psychology, 6*, 1–14.

Dohrenwend, B. P., & Dohrenwend, B. S. (1974). Social and cultural influences on psychopathology. *Annual Review of Psychology, 25*, 415–452.

Durrant, M., & Kowalski, K. (1990). Overcoming the effects of sexual abuse: Developing a self perception of competence. In M. Durrant & C. White (Ed.), *Ideas for therapy with sexual abuse* (pp. 65–110). South Australia: Dulwich Centre Publications.

Francis, R. (1988, October). *Migration and incarcaration in Australia*. Paper presented to the 2nd biennial meeting of Researchers in Australian Criminology. (Available from the Australian Institute of Criminology, Canberra.)

Gist, R., & Lubin, B. (Eds.) (1989). *Psychosocial aspects of disaster*. New York: John Wiley & Sons.

Gordon, R. (1991). *Engineering aspects of disaster recovery. Local Government Guide to Disaster Management*. Melbourne, Australia: State Government Printing Office.

Hoffer, E. (1952). *The ordeal of change*. New York: Harper and Row.

Holmes, J. H., & Rahe, R. H. (1967). The Social Re-adjustment Rating Scale. *Journal of Psychosomatic Research, 11*, 213–218.

Israel, B. M., Checkoway, B., Schulz, A., & Zimmerman, M. (1994). Health education and community empowerment: Conceptualising and measuring perceptions of individual, organizational and community control. *Health Education Quarterly, 21*, 149–170.

Kaniasty, K., & Norris, F. H. (1993). A test of the social support deterioration model in the context of natural disaster. *Journal of Personality and Social Psychology, 64*, 395–408.

Kaniasty, K., & Norris, F. H. (1995). In search of altruistic community: Patterns of social support mobilization following hurricane Hugo. *American Journal of Community Psychology, 23*, 447–478.

Kieffer, C. (1984). Citizen empowerment: A developmental perspective. *Prevention in Human Services, 3*, 9–36.

Kouzmin, A., & Jarman, A. (1989). Crisis decision making: Towards a contingent decision path perspective. In U. Rosenthal, M. T. Charles, & P. Hart (Eds.), *Coping with crisis: The management of disasters, riots and terrorism* (pp. 397–435). Springfield, IL: Charles C. Thomas.

Kreps, G. A. (1984). Sociological inquiry and disaster research. In R. H. Turner & J. M. Short (Ed.), *Annual Review of Sociology, 10*, 309–330.

LaPierre, R. T. (1965). *Social change*. New York: McGraw Hill.

Lauer, R. H. (1982). *Perspectives on social change*. Boston: Allyn & Bacon.

Macquarie Dictionary (1982). NSW Australia: Macquarie Library.

Moore, W. E. (1974). *Social change* (2nd ed.). Englewood Cliffs, NJ: Prentice–Hall.

Murphy, H. M. B. (1961). Social change and mental health. *Milbank Memorial Fund Quarterly, 39*, 385–445.

Nisbet, R. A. (1969). *Social change and history*. New York: Oxford University Press.

Omer, H., & Alon, N. (1994). The continuity principle: A unified approach to disaster and trauma. *American Journal of Community Psychology, 22*, 273–287.

Orford, J. (1992). *Community psychology: Theory and practice*. London: John Wiley and Sons.

Parsons, T. (1951). *The social system*. Glencoe, IL: Free Press.

Peterson, C., & Seligman, M. E. P. (1984). Causal explanations as a risk factor for depression: Theory and evidence. *Psychological Review, 91*, 347–374.

Powell, B. J., & Penick, E. C. (1983). Psychological distress following a natural disaster: A one year follow-up of 98 flood victims. *Journal of Community Psychology, 11*, 269–276.

Rappaport, J. (1977). *Community psychology, values, research and action*. New York: Holt Rinehart & Winston.

Rappaport, J. (1981). In praise of paradox: A social policy of empowerment over prevention. *American Journal of Community Psychology, 9*, 1–25.

Rappaport, J. (1984). Studies in empowerment: Introduction to the issue. *Prevention in Human Services, 3*, 1–7.

Rogers, E. M. (1983). *Diffusion of innovations* (3rd ed). New York: Free Press.

Rosenthal, U., Charles, M. T., & Hart, P. (Eds.) (1989). *Coping with crisis: The management of disasters, riots and terrorism*. Springfield, IL: Charles C. Thomas.

Rothschild–Whitt, J. (1979). The collectivist organization: An alternative to rational-bureaucratic models. *American Sociological Review, 44*, 509–527.

Ryan, W. (1971). *Blaming the victim*. New York: Random House.

Saegert, S. (1989). Unlikely leaders, extreme circumstance: Older black women building community households. *American Journal of Community Psychology, 17*, 295–316.

Schwarzer, R., Hahn, A., & Schroder, H. (1994). Social integration and social support in a life crisis: Effects of macrosocial change in East Germany. *American Journal of Community Psychology, 22*, 685–706.

Shrivastava, P. (1989). Managing the crisis at Bhopal. In U. Rosenthal, M. T. Charles, & P. Hart (Ed.). *Coping with Crisis: The Management of Disasters, Riots and Terrorism*. (pp. 92–176). Springfield, IL: Charles C. Thomas.

Smith, A. (1976). *Social change*. London: Longman.

Spicer, E. H. (1952). (Ed.) *Human problems in technological change*. New York: Russel Sage Foundation.

Taylor, V. A., Ross, G. A., & Quarantelli, E. L. (1976). Delivery of mental health services in disasters: The Xenia tornado and some implications (Disaster Res. Cent. Monogr. Ser. 11). Columbus: Ohio State University. Also in R. H. Turner & J. M. Short (Ed.), *Annual Review of Sociology, 10*, 309–330.

Tierney, K. J. (1989). The social and community contexts of disaster. In R. Gist & B. Lubin (Ed.), *Psychosocial aspects of disaster* (pp. 11–39). New York: John Wiley & Sons.

Toffler, A. (1970). *Future shock*. New York: Random House.

Toubiana, Y. H., Milgram, N. A., Strich, Y., & Edelstein, A. (1988). Crisis intervention in a school community disaster: Principles and practices. *Journal of Community Psychology, 16*, 228–240.

Vinokur, A., & Seltzer, M. (1975). Desirable versus undesirable life events. Their relationship to stress and mental distress. *Journal of Personality and Social Change, 32*, 329–337.

Waltham, A. C. (1978). *Catastrophe, the violent earth*. New York: Crown Publishers.

Wandersman, A. (1979). User participation: A study of types of participation, effects, mediators and individual differences. *Environment and Behavior, 11*, 185–208.

Wandersman, A. (1984). Citizen participation. In K. Heller, R. Price, S. Reinharz, S. Riger, A. Wandersman, & T. D'Aunno (Eds.). *Psychology and community change, challenges of the future* (pp. 337–379). Belmont, CA: Brooks/Cole.

Webb, D. B. (1989). PBB: An environmental contaminant in Michigan. *Journal of Community Psychology, 17*, 30–46.

Whittow, J. (1980). *Disasters: The anatomy of environmental hazards*. London: Penguin.

Young, M. A. (1989). Crime violence and terrorism. In R. Gist & B. Lubin (Eds.), *Psychosocial aspects of disaster* (pp. 140–160). New York: John Wiley & Sons.

Chapter 8

Children's Responses to Disaster: Family and Systems Approaches

Eric M. Vernberg

INTRODUCTION

Although children's psychological and behavioral responses to disasters have been described in case studies as early as the 1950s, systematic research on the nature of these responses remains sparse. Recent reviews of literature on children and disasters report fewer than 10 longitudinal studies, and these vary widely in terms of the types of disasters and the conceptual framework guiding the studies (Green, 1991; Vogel & Vernberg, 1993). Almost no systematic research has been published on the efficacy of post-disaster interventions with children, although numerous case studies exist. Despite the lack of empirical evidence for efficacy of interventions and the sparse research on the nature of children's responses to disasters, several models for intervention with children following disasters have emerged (e.g., Klingman, 1987, 1993; La Greca, Vernberg, Silverman, Vogel, & Prinstein, 1994; Eth & Pynoos, 1985; Pynoos & Nader, 1988; Yule & Williams, 1990; see Vernberg & Vogel, 1993, for a recent review). These interventions represent "best guesses" regarding children's needs after disasters, and are based on practical experience and conceptual models (e.g., psychodynamic, cognitive-behavioral) of children's probable psychological reactions to traumatic experiences.

The purpose of this chapter is to take stock of current practices in disaster response with children from a family and systems perspective, with the goal of identifying those issues most in need of clarification and intensive study in the coming generation of disaster research and intervention with children. This process is organized using a conceptual model that has proved useful in guiding research on children's reactions to disasters, accounting for over 60% of the variance in children's self-reported post-traumatic stress symptoms at 3-months post-disaster (Vernberg, La Greca, Silverman, & Prinstein, 1996) and almost 30% by 10 months post-disaster (La Greca, Silverman, Vernberg, & Prinstein, 1996; see Figure 1). This model directs attention toward five broad, multi-dimensional factors. Of these, three factors represent features of the environment or dispositional characteristics: characteristics of the disaster, characteristics of the child at the time of the disaster, and characteristics of the post-disaster environment. These factors are posited to influence the child's attempts to process traumatic events cognitively and affectively, which in turn are posited to influence the child's psychological and behavioral adaptation to disasters. This discussion is organized by these three environmental/dispositional factors, with consideration of the interplay between these factors and the more intrapsychic factors. Relationships among these factors are assumed to be multiple, complex, and dynamic. Because several aspects of each factor seem likely to influence children's reactions to disasters, identifying target populations for disaster mental health programs requires a comprehensive approach that asks about relevant aspects of each factor.

CHARACTERISTICS OF DISASTERS: EXPOSURE TO TRAUMATIC EVENTS

As noted elsewhere in this volume, categorizing disasters is far from straightforward. For ease of presentation, characteristics of disasters are described here in terms of the elements of traumatic exposure that occurred during a disaster (as proposed by Green, 1990), leaving aside thorny questions related to the categorization of disasters themselves (e.g., natural vs. technological, predicted vs. unexpected). The model that organizes this presentation conceptualizes these under the rubric of exposure to traumatic events. Note that characteristics of the post-disaster recovery environment are described later, although the link is often strong between events that occurred during the disaster experience and features of the recovery environment. Indeed, additional traumatic events often occur in the months or years following disasters, and some of these may have been set in motion by the disaster itself. Keeping with the focus on family and system characteristics, exposure is described in terms of variations related to these characteristics.

Threat to one's life or bodily integrity

Judging threat to one's life is at times rather subjective, and several issues bear comment in relation to children. The first involves children's level of understanding of events, and age-related changes in children's reliance on the reactions of others as a basis for judging threat. Certainly, dramatic expressions of fear of death by family members are likely to influence children's judgments of threats to themselves, and this influence may be profound for younger or more cognitively limited children who may have difficulty making independent judgments of threat. Careful exploration of expressions of fear of death by family members or others present during traumatic experiences is therefore warranted.

Our studies of elementary school children's reactions to Hurricane Andrew found that a child's perception that death was imminent at some point during the storm continued to be a meaningful predictor of distress throughout the year after the storm (La Greca et al., 1996). It was also noteworthy that 60% of the children in this sample held this perception, even though few people actually died during the storm (Vernberg et al., 1996). Most children reporting this perception also reported one or more relatively objective events that might validate the perception, such as windows or doors giving way or being hit by flying or falling objects. However, some children reported these objective events without believing their lives were in imminent danger, and some children thought their death was imminent even though they did not report more objective evidence of threat.

One implication of these findings is that it is important to inquire about perceived life threat among children following disasters. Some information about children who experienced serious life threat may be available from emergency medical services records. However, those who were seriously threatened but not seriously injured are unlikely to be included in such records. Moreover, children who thought they were seriously threatened but in reality were not may still be quite troubled by traumatic events.

Direct questions about exposure to life threat generally take one of two strategies. First, it is possible to ask about relatively objective events during a disaster that seem likely to indicate potential life threat. These events vary by type of disaster. After a flood, for example, it may be appropriate to ask whether individuals had to climb onto a roof or swim to escape drowning. For a tornado, being hit by flying debris may be a more appropriate question. The second possibility is to ask about perceived or subjective life threat. A specific question, used in the Diagnostic Interview Survey–Disaster Supplement (DIS/DS; Robins & Smith, 1993), is "At any time during the disaster, did you think you might die?"

Under optimal circumstances, it seems preferable to ask about both objective events and perceived life threat. When extreme brevity is required, there is some evidence to indicate that perceived life threat may be a more potent predictor of PTSD symptoms than objective events (La Greca et al., 1996; Vernberg et al., 1996).

Physical harm or injury to self

Injuries to children during traumatic events take many forms, and raise concern regarding problematic psychological sequelae. Injuries that cloud mentation may delay a child's ability to understand the nature of events (Fornari, 1991). Ironically, memory of the actual event may not be stored when a moderate or severe head injury occurs during the event, thus limiting certain types of exposure (e.g., exposure to the grotesque, perceived life threat). One complicating factor related to physical injury is that this may delay the child's resumption of normal roles and routines, which seems to be an important factor in recovering from traumatic events (Vernberg & Vogel, 1993). Certainly, the family's response to an injured child deserves careful scrutiny, and recommendations to parents about appropriate responses should be a regular component of medical treatment for traumatic injury.

Receipt of intentional injury or harm

The issue of intentionality provides an additional level of complexity to injuries to children during disasters. Intentionality is widely believed to pose a substantial additional obstacle to recovery (Pynoos & Nader, 1988). Family anger is likely to be intense, and the task of making sense of a traumatic experience may be particularly difficult, when children are the intentional objects of harm, such as in school sniper shootings and kidnappings (Pynoos & Nader, 1988; Terr, 1983). Moreover, younger children who have limitations in causal reasoning may be particularly susceptible to acquiring fears and phobias regarding activities that preceded the trauma or stimuli present during the event (Pynoos & Nader, 1988). Once again, sensitivity to specific developmental issues is needed on the part of families, helpers, and schools.

Exposure to the grotesque

Exposure to grotesque scenes is problematic for many individuals, regardless of age. There is preliminary support for an exposure-effect gradient, such that direct observation of grotesque scenes provokes stronger, more persistent reactions than simply being in the vicinity of a traumatic event or learning about an event later (Yule, 1993). Explanations for this effect often center around the difficulty of processing disturbing visual images. Indeed, recurrent, intrusive thoughts and images were the most commonly reported and most persistent symptoms of posttraumatic stress in several studies of children's recovery from hurricane-related trauma (La Greca et al., 1996; Shannon, Lonigan, Finch, & Taylor, 1994; Vernberg et al., 1996). One obvious implication of these findings is to limit children's exposure to grotesque scenes as much as possible. If the visual media cannot provide such limits voluntarily, parents and other caretakers would be well advised to do so.

Violent/sudden loss of a loved one

Loss of life of a family member or close friend poses obvious challenges to children after disasters. From a research perspective, evidence on children's reactions to death remains sparse, and available studies are inconsistent in their conclusions. For example, a study of children who lost fathers because of war concluded that sudden parental death causes "marked psychological impairment and severe emotional disturbance" in most instances (Elizur & Kaffman, 1983). In contrast, the Harvard Child Bereavement Project concluded that, although the death of a parent is a stressful event, most children did not seem too overwhelmed across the 2 years after the parent's death (Silverman & Worden, 1993). It seems important to understand from these contrasting findings that additional circumstances might make bereavement more problematic for children, such as qualities of the family environment, characteristics of the child, and specific responses to children's concerns or reactions to the death.

Witnessing or learning of violence to a loved one

Seeing a loved one hurt, or learning of such violence, has potential to spur a host of troubling thoughts and feelings, ranging from fear to disgust to anger. Issues here to some extent are similar to those involved in exposure to the grotesque. Indeed, some have argued against disclosing or discussing traumatic events involving family members in detail with children who have no direct knowledge of the events for fear of producing iatrogenic psychological problems (Figley, 1988). In instances where violence has been witnessed directly, some have argued in favor of an intensive, rather confrontive interview soon after the traumatic events in an effort to promote emotional processing of the experience before psychological defenses make processing difficult (Eth & Pynoos, 1985). Solid research evidence is sorely lacking to aid decision-making on this issue.

Exposure to toxins with long-term effects

This type of exposure occurs only with a subset of disasters, and it is not clear how much children of varying ages may be concerned about this type of exposure. For adults, exposure to toxins has been measured by objective methods, such as the distance between a residence or job site and a known toxin contamination location (e.g., site of a chemical spill). Perceived exposure has also been assessed in some studies (e.g., Bromet, Parkinson, & Dunn, 1990), and, in terms of arousing anxiety or anger, perceived exposure may be as influential as objective exposure. It is certainly plausible that some children may show similar reactions of anxiety and anger, and this seems particularly likely when adults in the household also have such reactions.

Causing death or severe harm to another

The issue of causality is complicated for children. As noted earlier, preschool children are in many respects "precausal" in their reasoning. It is quite possible for younger children to believe that their behavior influenced the course of a traumatic event even when this is clearly implausible. It is also possible for a child to initiate a chain of events leading to harm to another person.

Older children may have sufficient guilt to harm themselves: In my own childhood, a 12-year-old friend helped build a tunnel in the sand, which later claimed the lives of two younger boys. This friend committed suicide within 6 weeks of the tunnel collapse, leaving a concise note that his guilt regarding these deaths motivated his action. Clearly, concern for children's beliefs about why disaster events occurred is warranted, especially when there is reason to believe that a child may hold himself or herself in some way responsible.

PREEXISTING CHILD CHARACTERISTICS

Characteristics of children at the time of exposure to traumatic events possibly influence children's reactions to disasters, yet research remains limited (Vogel & Vernberg, 1993). In the disaster field, more research information is available regarding demographic characteristics of children, such as age, gender, and ethnicity than for psychological characteristics such as temperament, general anxiety, or prior experiences with trauma. This situation occurs because the unpredictable nature of disasters seldom allows the collection of valid information about children's predisaster psychological functioning, whereas demographic information can easily be collected ex post facto.

Gender

The rationale for possible gender differences in reactions to traumatic events is typically based on variations in the acceptability of different expressions of psychological distress for boys and girls (Vogel & Vernberg, 1993). The tendency for boys to exhibit greater externalizing symptoms than girls in response to stressful events, and for girls to experience more internalizing symptoms, is well-documented for several classes of stressors, including divorce and exposure to parental discord (Emery, 1988). This pattern appears to hold for disasters as well.

Several studies of disasters found that girls reported more overall symptoms of post-traumatic stress than did boys (Green et al., 1991; Lonigan, Shannon, Finch, Daugherty, & Taylor, 1991; Shannon et al., 1994; Vernberg et al., 1996; Yule, 1993), and also more symptoms of anxiety, depression, and specific fears. When boys do report post-traumatic stress symptoms, there is some evidence that they are more likely to acknowledge behavioral symptoms (e.g., sleep difficulties, reckless behavior) or cognitive symptoms (attentional or memory difficulties) than to report emotional symptoms (e.g., fear of recurrence, emotional numbing). Evidence for greater externalizing symptoms among boys after disasters is sparse, although it is important to note that internalizing symptoms are more commonly the focus of disaster research with children.

The magnitude of gender differences is typically small, and overall effects for gender typically pale in comparison to effects for exposure and characteristics of the postdisaster recovery environment. Nonetheless, the signs of distress that boys typically show may be somewhat different than for girls. Sensitivity to these differences by parents, teachers, and helpers is needed to prevent minimization of boys' psychological reactions to disasters.

The negative scenario found in divorce studies may be instructive here. Boys' disruptive behavioral reactions to divorce often led to punitive, angry responses from adults, whereas the sadness and tearfulness more typically shown by girls led to comforting and nurturance (Hetherington, 1981). Awareness of this possible gender difference in the manifestation of distress following disasters may counteract the tendency of adults to respond punitively to problem behaviors that appear on the surface to be only loosely related to a child's disaster experiences.

Age

A number of age-related differences in post-traumatic stress symptoms following disasters have been proposed, based on developmental differences in children's abilities to comprehend the nature of traumatic events, age-related changes in coping repertoires, and greater involvement of older children in extra-familial community systems (Eth & Pynoos, 1985; Terr, 1989; Vogel & Vernberg, 1993). Thus far, age-related differences in post-traumatic stress symptoms have primarily been found in comparisons between youngsters in early versus middle childhood or adolescence (Green et al., 1991; Nader, Pynoos, Fairbanks, & Frederick, 1990; Schwarz & Kowalski, 1991).

Among the more reliable age differences in reactions, preschoolers and young elementary school children, compared with older children, show more specific fears, separation difficulties, enuresis, and overt behavior problems (Vogel & Vernberg, 1993). Older children and adolescents are often reported as showing more internalizing symptoms such as post-traumatic stress disorder (PTSD), depression, and anxiety than do younger children. However, measurement difficulties give reason for caution: Children are typically not viewed as reliable reporters of internalizing symptoms until their early elementary years (La Greca, 1990), and external reporters (parents, teachers) almost always report fewer symptoms for children than children report for themselves.

Perhaps the most conservative stance at present is that the manifest form of postdisaster reactions changes some with age, yet both younger and older children may indeed struggle in terms of psychological adjustment after disasters. Infants and toddlers are often very sensitive to disruptions in caretaking, and may show increases in feeding problems, irritability, and sleep problems when such disruptions occur (Vernberg & Field, 1990). These behavioral problems in turn place increased demands on caretakers, who may themselves be highly distressed by a disaster.

Preschool children are beginning to use language in relatively sophisticated ways but are very limited in their understanding of disaster-related events. This limited understanding often leads to fears that may seem unwarranted to older children and adults (e.g., extreme fears during thunderstorms that occur after a flood or tornado). These fears may lead to dramatic reactions to relatively harmless post-disaster events.

Elementary school-age children understand the physical environment much better than preschoolers, but they may be very preoccupied by the loss of possessions or pets, or by memories of traumatic events. Elementary school-age children also are often able to recognize distress in their caretakers, and may be quite worried about the safety and security of their families (Pynoos & Nader, 1988). Children of this age can do relatively little to actively help in the recovery process, however, which may increase feelings of isolation and helplessness.

Adolescents are more competent to help with recovery and are less dependent than younger children. At the same time, adolescents may engage in greater risk-taking behavior after disasters, and may also show intense feelings of being cheated out of expected experiences (e.g., athletic and social events that are canceled or postponed).

Ethnicity

Differences in PTSD symptoms among adults have been reported between communities following similar types of disasters (Steinglass & Gerrity, 1990). These differences may reflect cultural norms for responding to traumatic events, including those governing the expression of emotions, selection of coping responses, and social-support seeking (Steinglass & Gerrity, 1990).

Variations in PTSD symptoms among school-age children of different cultures seem possible, and a recent study of Hurricane Hugo reported higher scores for African American children on several symptoms (attentional difficulties, sense of foreshadowing, engaging in reckless behavior) compared with European American children and other minority children (Shannon et al., 1994). However, African American children also were exposed to more trauma than other ethnic groups, and this difference in exposure may have contributed to these ethnic differences in symptom severity. Studies of children following Hurricane Andrew found that ethnic differences in symptoms did not emerge 3-months postdisaster after controlling for differences in exposure to trauma, but were found 7- and 10-months post-disaster (La Greca et al., 1996; Vernberg et al., 1996). Here, both African American and Hispanic American children reported more post-traumatic stress symptoms than European American children.

Several possible reasons for these differences exist. Perhaps the most parsimonious explanation involves differences in economic and educational resources of parents of children of different ethnic groups. These differences may be particularly pronounced following mass destruction of housing and job losses, in that limited (or nonexistent) economic reserves place extreme stress on families that reverberates through the child's social environment.

Education may influence a parent's ability to cope with the demands for documentation and careful completion of applications for disaster assistance. Education is also linked to skills in seeking information regarding resources, including mental health resources. Financial status exerts multiple possible influences on post-disaster functioning. In terms of increased exposure to traumatic experiences during disasters, housing built of less durable materials (e.g., mobile homes) or in less desirable locations (e.g., flood-prone land) is more likely to be damaged by disasters in the first place. This places poorer individuals, on average, at greater risk for loss of personal possessions and exposure to life-threatening circumstances.

Following disasters, individuals with few financial resources (including personal property insurance) may find it virtually impossible to repair or replace lost belongings. Even for poorer families with some insurance, months may be required before claims are settled, placing extreme financial pressures on those with few financial reserves. Note also that many lower paying, lower occupational status jobs offer little in the way of paid personal leave or scheduling flexibility. This may further complicate post-disaster recovery by making it difficult for parents to find the time to pursue aid or repairs.

Dispositional characteristics

Prior experiences with trauma and pre-existing psychological characteristics such as anxiety or temperament certainly seem likely to influence children's reactions to disasters, yet the limited research available on this issue is equivocal (Vogel & Vernberg, 1993). Retrospective reports of predisaster functioning have sometimes suggested such influences (e.g., Earls, Smith, Reich, & Jung, 1988), but others have not (Dollinger, 1985). A recent study of children following Hurricane Hugo argued that Revised Children's Manifest Anxiety Scale (RCMAS) scores represented trait anxiety, even though the measure was given after the hurricane (Lonigan, Shannon, Taylor, Finch, & Sallee, 1994). Post-traumatic stress symptoms were strongly related to RCMAS scores: Over 75% of children classified as exhibiting post-traumatic stress syndrome also scored in the upper quartile of the RCMAS, and very few children scoring below the median on the RCMAS met criteria for post-traumatic stress symptoms. Still, a conservative evaluation of the evidence suggests that the issues of pre-existing psychological characteristics and children's reactions to disasters have yet to be addressed in a powerful manner.

Psychological resources

Several psychological resources have been linked to resolution following traumatic events of varying types. Although not yet studied in children, religious faith or philosophical perspectives that in some way enable individuals to make sense of their disaster experiences appear to be important resources for many adults following disasters (e.g., North, Smith, McCool, & Lightcap, 1989). A second set of psychological resources has been articulated in the concept of "resilience," as developed in research on children who seemed to function well despite living under very adverse circumstances (see Garmezy, 1993, for a recent review). These resources include at least average intelligence, good communication skills, and strong beliefs of self-efficacy (i.e., believing oneself to be capable of overcoming most of life's obstacles through one's efforts). Direct study of children's psychological resources in relation to disaster recovery seems a promising and needed direction for the next generation of disaster research.

CHARACTERISTICS OF POST-DISASTER RECOVERY ENVIRONMENT

The post-disaster recovery environment seems likely to exert powerful effects on children's reactions to disasters. It is important to note that children are not passive entities in this environment. Rather, they influence some aspects, such as the quality of their social relationships, quite directly through their own behaviors and responses to others. Indirect, evocative effects also occur through children's stimulus qualities, such as age, gender, and ethnicity. At the same time, numerous aspects of the environment are influenced little by individual children, such as the pace of rebuilding or economic opportunity for parents.

In terms of disaster response planning, it is important to recognize the distinction between uncontrollable external forces and elements of the environment that are responsive to child behaviors or characteristics. The former calls for coping strategies that are more emotion-focused (i.e., managing emotional response to unchangeable circumstances), whereas problem-focused approaches (i.e., attempts to change the source of a problem) are appropriate for latter elements (Compas & Epping, 1993). If, as many have suggested, regaining a sense of control and predictability is a major psychological task following disasters, helping children recognize and act on opportunities to exert influence at appropriate moments may be among the more useful qualities of recovery environments.

The postdisaster recovery environment can be conceptualized at several levels of complexity, ranging from microsystems to entire societies. It may be useful for present purposes to consider the social environment at the level of microsystems, mesosystems, and community systems. *Microsystems* refer to specific social settings (e.g., occupational settings, recreational settings) or relationships in which an individual participates actively (e.g., family relationships, friendship networks). *Mesosystems* refer to linkages between an individual's microsystems, such as connections between work settings, educational settings, and the family system. *Community systems* are the context in which an individual's microsystems and mesosystems operate, and include larger social units such as government, schools, and religious or spiritual organizations.

Microsystem characteristics

Strong, supportive relationships with others have been found to play meaningful roles as protective factors against deleterious effects of many stressful events for children and adolescents, and it is at the level of microsystems that much of this support occurs. Although research on social support specific to disaster effects is scant, the limited data available suggest that these protective effects also operate following disasters (La

Greca et al., 1996; Vernberg et al., 1996). Conversely, greater tension, conflict, and hostility in one or more microsystems is believed to contribute to greater psychological distress and complicate recovery from disaster-related distress. Qualities of three microsystems seem particularly important to consider: family, friendships, and school.

Family Children, even into adolescent years, rely heavily on their parents for many types of support, including emotional support, instrumental aid, and companionship (Furman & Buhrmester, 1985). Forces that disrupt this family support complicate the recovery process. A central question thus becomes "What helps families perform these support functions, and what interferes?"

Several answers are readily apparent. First, physical disruption in the form of damage to a family's home and possessions diminishes the time and energy available to parents for attending to children's wants and needs. This appeared to account in part for the contribution of damage and disruptions after Hurricane Andrew to higher levels of psychological symptomatology among children, and lower support for children by parents in more seriously damaged homes (Vernberg et al., 1996). Major life events that appeared unrelated to the hurricane but occurred 3 to 7 months after the storm also had a measurable negative impact on symptom remission and social support (La Greca et al., 1996). The types of disruptions and events that seemed to diminish family support for children were numerous, ranging from damage to the primary family residence and dislocation to increased commuting time and loss of income. These daily hassles and stressors in turn produce a variety of negative emotions and behaviors in parents, most commonly including anxiety, depression, and somatic complaints (Green, 1991).

Prolonged disruptions that necessitate heroic demands on informal sources of support for families tend over time to produce a depletion of social resources (Kaniasty & Norris, 1993; Kaniasty, Norris, & Murrell, 1990). In terms of strengthening a family's ability to help their children, recovery efforts that focus on reducing financial, physical, and time demands on parents seem crucial. Recognition that informal social support resources often become depleted long before recovery from disasters is complete should lead to a greater policy emphasis on providing supportive services to severely disrupted families. This support should not just be offered in the first few weeks after a disaster, but considerably later (e.g., 6- to 18-months postdisaster) when informal support has often markedly decreased.

Friends Friends are also a significant source of support for children, serving the important functions of providing opportunities for pleasurable activities and communication with others operating at a similar level of understanding of disasters and their sequelae. In studies following Hurricane Andrew, support from friends seemed to contribute to diminished post-traumatic stress symptoms over time (La Greca et al., 1996; Vernberg et al., 1996). As with parental support, children who experienced greater postdisaster disruption and more major life events also reported lower levels of support from friends (La Greca et al., 1996; Vernberg et al., 1996).

The limited research available also suggests that friends provide opportunities for some types of activities that may be important for recovery from trauma but are rarely offered in parent–child or teacher–child relationships (Prinstein, La Greca, Vernberg, & Silverman, 1996). Specifically, children were more likely to play games related to the hurricane with friends than with parents or teachers. For disaster response efforts, providing encouragement and opportunities for trauma-exposed children to interact with friends seems important.

Schools Schools are believed to serve several important functions in children's recovery from disaster. Primary among these are providing an opportunity to return to normal roles and routines, allowing access to supportive friends and teachers, and giving factual information that may help with understanding the causes and consequences of disaster experiences (Klingman, 1987, 1993). Schools are also a potentially important site for addressing mental health issues related to disasters (Klingman, 1993; Vernberg & Vogel, 1993). Returning children to school as quickly as possible, even those who are quite distressed, seems highly desirable. This enables screening for difficulties and, perhaps more importantly, makes performance demands on children that may prevent them from assuming a role as damaged or ill (see Klingman, 1987, 1993, for a review of school-based postdisaster mental health strategies).

In terms of delivering mental health services, schools have numerous advantages over clinical settings. First, schools allow access to large numbers of children in the aftermath of widespread disasters. For example, Hurricane Andrew left 150,000 families without homes, and many of these families were in their homes as they were destroyed. Schools offered the only realistic possibility of direct contact regarding mental health issues for the immense number of children severely affected by the hurricane. Second, schools are a familiar, naturally occurring setting for children; services can be provided with minimal disruption and stigmatization.

Unfortunately, almost no research has evaluated the efficacy of school-based interventions, even though such interventions are frequently offered after disasters (see Galante & Foa, 1986, for one of the few exceptions). The lack of manualized interventions and difficulties in obtaining necessary approvals seriously impedes evaluations of post-disaster, school-based interventions (Vernberg, 1994). However, an intervention manual for school-based interventions after disasters was recently developed based on work with the schools in Dade County, Florida, after Hurricane Andrew (La Greca et al., 1994). The availability of a specific set of activities should enable progress in evaluating how well this form of intervention in fact works.

Mesosytem characteristics

It is clear that events in one microsystem can influence a child's performance in other microsystems (e.g., family conflict can affect a child's academic and behavioral performance at school, and vice versa). Linkages between microsystems can be helpful in adjusting expectations or demands in one setting to accommodate changing demands in another. Following disasters, significant additional stress may be added by the absence of effective linkages between settings or by a lack of accommodation. For example, occupational settings that are unable or unwilling to make temporary changes in scheduling or work load to accommodate increased home and family demands related to disasters may contribute to psychological distress. Research on these mesosystem characteristics in relation to children and disasters appears virtually nonexistent, but seems important to conduct.

Community characteristics

Communities vary in the strength of resources available to help disaster survivors. Poorer communities may lack the strong local leadership needed to muster resources after disasters or to distribute resources in an efficient, equitable manner. In severe, widespread disasters, the ability of existing community structures to perform even basic functions may be impaired, leading to increased demands on individual resources. Children and families who depend a great deal on such structures may be highly stressed by the diminished functioning of these structures (e.g., families receiving support from social services), especially if other segments of the community (e.g., informal helping networks) do not fulfill some of the lost functions. Smaller or more tightly knit communities with strong traditions of helping those in need may be able to fill the void left when more formal community structures fail, whereas communities characterized by great geographic dispersion or high levels of anonymity seem likely to be less able to develop informal structures quickly.

CONCLUSION

The interplay between traumatic experiences, child characteristics, and the broader recovery environment is intricate and complex. However, research on children and disasters seems to be accelerating, and support is accumulating for several basic propositions. First, traumatic events can be meaningfully conceptualized in terms of the nature of a child's exposure to disturbing or frightening circumstances. Understanding the extent and intensity of exposure is certainly a critical element in predicting psychological outcomes. Second, children vary in the types of responses they show following exposure. Some of this variation can be explained by demographic variables such as age, gender, and ethnicity. However, these variables serve as markers rather than explanations for differences in response. It is much more important to understand *why* these variables are related to differences in response than to simply note an association. It is in the understanding of this "why" that progress has been made in recent years.

Finally, the postrecovery environment plays a major role in shaping children's responses to disasters. Access to supportive social relationships appears to be a primary mechanism aiding children's recovery from disasters. The forces that diminish this access are becoming clearer, and it seems reasonable to concentrate policy efforts on counteracting the powerful forces that interfere with support processes after disasters. Some of these forces seem very likely to involve linkages across systems, although little research examining these linkages has been carried out in the context of children and disasters.

REFERENCES

Bromet, E., Parkinson, D., & Dunn, L. (1990). Long-term mental health consequences of the accident at Three Mile Island. *International Journal of Mental Health, 19*, 48–60.

Compas, B. E., & Epping, J. E. (1993). Stress and coping in children and families: Implications for children coping with disaster. In C. F. Saylor (Ed.), *Children and disasters* (pp. 11–28). New York: Plenum Press.

Dollinger, S. J. (1985). Lightning-strike disasters among children. *British Journal of Medical Psychology, 58*, 375–383.

Earls, F., Smith, E., Reich, W., & Jung, K. G. (1988). Investigating the psychopathological consequence of disaster in children: A pilot study incorporating a structured diagnostic interview. *Journal of the American Academy of Child and Adolescent Psychiatry, 27*, 90–95.

Elizur, E., & Kaffman, M. (1983). Factors influencing the severity of childhood bereavement reactions. *American Journal of Orthopsychiatry, 53*, 668–676.

Emery, R. E. (1988). *Marriage, divorce, and children's adjustment.* Newbury Park, CA: Sage.

Eth, S., & Pynoos, R. S. (1985). *Post-traumatic stress disorder in children.* Washington, DC: American Psychiatric Press.

Figley, C. R. (1988). Post-traumatic family therapy. In F. M. Ochberg (Ed.), *Post-traumatic therapy and victims of violence* (pp. 83–109). New York: Brunner-Mazel.

Fornari, V. (1991). The aftermath of a plane crash—helping a survivor cope with deaths of mother and sibling: Case of Mary, age 8. In N. Webb (Ed.), *Play therapy with children in crisis. A casebook for practitioners* (pp. 416–434). New York: Guilford.

Furman, W., & Buhrmester, D. (1985). Children's perceptions of the personal relationships in their social networks. *Developmental Psychology, 21,* 1016–1024.

Galante R., & Foa, D. (1986). An epidemiological study of psychic trauma and treatment effectiveness for children after a natural disaster. *Journal of the American Academy of Child Psychiatry, 25,* 357–363.

Garmezy, N. (1993). Developmental psychopathology: Some historical and current perspectives. In D. Magnusson & P. Caesar (Eds.), *Longitudinal research on individual development* (pp. 95–126). Cambridge, England: University Press.

Green, B. L. (1990). Defining trauma: Terminology and generic stressor dimensions. *Journal of Applied Social Psychology, 20,* 1632–1642.

Green, B. L. (1991). *Mental health and disaster: A research review.* Rockville, MD: Emergency Services and Disaster Relief Branch, Center for Mental Health Services.

Green, B. L., Korol, M., Grace, M. C., Vary, M. G., Leonard, A. C., Gleser, G. C., & Smitson-Cohen, S. (1991). Children and disaster: Gender and parental effects on PTSD symptoms. *Journal of the American Academy of Child and Adolescent Psychiatry, 30,* 945–951.

Hetherington, E. M. (1981). Children and divorce. In R. Henderson (Ed.), *Parent–child interaction: Theory, research, and action* (pp. 233–258) New York: Academic Press.

Kaniasty, K. Z., & Norris, F. H. (1993). A test of the social support deterioration model in the context of natural disaster. *Journal of Personality and Social Psychology, 64,* 395–408.

Kaniasty, K. Z., Norris, F. H., & Murrell, S. A. (1990). Received and perceived social support following natural disaster. *Journal of Applied Social Psychology, 20,* 85–114.

Klingman, A. (1987). A school-based emergency crisis intervention in a mass school disaster. *Professional Psychology: Research and Practice, 18,* 604–612.

Klingman, A. (1993). School-based intervention following a disaster. In C. F. Saylor (Ed.), *Children and disasters* (pp. 187–210). New York: Plenum Press.

La Greca, A. M. (1990). *Through the eyes of a child: Obtaining self-reports from children and adolescents.* Boston: Allyn & Bacon.

La Greca, A. M., Silverman, W. K., Vernberg, E. M., & Prinstein, M. J. (1996). Symptoms of posttraumatic stress in children following Hurricane Andrew: A prospective study. *Journal of Consulting and Clinical Psychology, 64,* 712–723.

La Greca, A. M., Vernberg, E. M., Silverman, W. K., Vogel, A. L., & Prinstein, M. J. (1994). *Helping children prepare for and cope with natural disasters: A manual for professionals working with elementary school children.* University of Miami, Department of Psychology, Coral Gables, FL.

Lonigan, C. J., Shannon, M. P., Finch, A. J., Daugherty, T. K., & Taylor, C. M. (1991). Children's reactions to a natural disaster: Symptom severity and degree of exposure. *Advances in Behavioral Research and Therapy, 13,* 135–154.

Lonigan, C. J., Shannon, M. P., Taylor, C. M., Finch, A. J., & Sallee, F. R. (1994). Children exposed to disaster: II. Risk factors for the development of post-traumatic symptomatology. *Journal of the American Academy of Child Psychiatry, 33,* 94–105.

Nader, K., Pynoos, R. S., Fairbanks, L., & Frederick, C. (1990). Children's PTSD reactions one year after a sniper attack at their school. *American Journal of Psychiatry, 147,* 1526–1530.

North, C. S., Smith, E. M., McCool, R. E., & Lightcap, P. E. (1989). Acute postdisaster coping and adjustment. *Journal of Traumatic Stress, 2,* 353–360.

Prinstein, M. J., La Greca, A. M., Vernberg, E. M., & Silverman, W. K. (1996). Children's coping assistance: How parents, teachers, and friends help children cope after a natural disaster. *Journal of Clinical Child Psychology, 25,* 463–475.

Pynoos, R. S., & Nader, K. (1988). Psychological first aid and treatment approach to children exposed to community violence: Research implications. *Journal of Traumatic Stress, 1,* 445–473.

Robins, L. N., & Smith, E. M. (1993). *Diagnostic Interview Schedule. Disaster Supplement.* St. Louis, MO: Washington University School of Medicine, Department of Psychiatry.

Schwarz, E. D., & Kowalski, J. M. (1991). Malignant memories: Posttraumatic stress disorder in children and adults following a school shooting. *Journal of the American Academy of Child and Adolescent Psychiatry, 30*, 936–944.

Shannon, M. P., Lonigan, C. J., Finch, A. J., & Taylor, C. M. (1994). Children exposed to disaster: I. Epidemiology of post-traumatic symptoms and symptom profiles. *Journal of the American Academy of Child Psychiatry, 33*, 80–93.

Silverman, P., & Worden, J. W., (1993). Children's reactions to the death of a parent. In M. Stroebe, W. Stroebe, & R. Hansen (Eds.), *Handbook of bereavement. Theory, research and intervention* (pp. 175–195). New York: Cambridge University Press.

Steinglass, P., & Gerrity, E. (1990). Natural disasters and post-traumatic stress disorder: Short-term versus long-term effects in two disaster-affected communities. *Journal of Applied Social Psychology, 20*, 1746–1765.

Terr, L. C. (1983). Play therapy and psychic trauma: A preliminary report. In C. Schaefer & K. O'Connor (Eds.), *Handbook of play therapy* (pp. 308–319). New York: Wiley.

Terr, L. C. (1989). Treating psychic trauma in children: A preliminary discussion. *Journal of Traumatic Stress, 2*, 3–20.

Vernberg, E. M. (1994). Evaluating the effectiveness of school-based interventions after large-scale disasters: An achievable goal? *Child, Youth, and Family Services Quarterly, 17*(3), 11–13.

Vernberg, E. M., & Field, T. (1990). Transitional stress in children and adolescents moving to new environments. In S. Fisher & C. L. Cooper (Eds.), *On the move. The psychology of change and transition* (pp. 127–151). Chichester, England: John Wiley & Sons.

Vernberg, E. M., La Greca, A. M., Silverman, W. K., & Prinstein, M. J. (1996). Prediction of posttraumatic stress symptoms in children after Hurricane Andrew. *Journal of Abnormal Psychology, 105*, 237–248.

Vernberg, E. M., & Vogel, J. (1993). Interventions with children following disasters. *Journal of Clinical Child Psychology, 22*, 485–498.

Vogel, J., & Vernberg, E. M. (1993). Children's psychological responses to disasters. *Journal of Clinical Child Psychology, 22*, 464–484.

Yule, W. (1993). Technology-related disasters. In C. F. Saylor (Ed.), *Children and disasters* (pp. 105–122). New York: Plenum.

Yule, W., & Williams, R. M. (1990). Post-traumatic stress reactions in children. *Journal of Traumatic Stress, 3*, 279–295.

Chapter 9

There Are No Simple Solutions to Complex Problems: The Rise and Fall of Critical Incident Stress Debriefing as a Response to Occupational Stress in the Fire Service

Richard Gist and S. Joseph Woodall

A battalion chief in a large metropolitan fire and rescue agency, writing in a trade letter about the ascendance of the "critical incident stress debriefing" (CISD) movement in his industry, noted a comment made decades earlier by a hook-and-ladder captain: "We used to have steel men and wooden wagons; now we have steel wagons and wooden men" (Tvedten, 1994, p. 7). Like most of his counterparts, he expressed full recognition that remarkable changes in the nature of the enterprise had yielded dramatic alterations in the frequency, content, structure, purpose, and impact of the daily contacts between firefighters and the citizens and communities they served; he also voiced full recognition that these had, in their turn, yielded equally dramatic changes in the types of persons entering the service, the goals and motivations they brought to the job, and

COMMUNITY STRATEGIES FOR INTERVENTION

the impact the work held for them. Like an increasing number of his peers, however, he also expressed a gnawing reservation that the trend he perceived toward aggressive, nearly reflexive application of rigid and routinized quasi-therapeutic protocols in essentially any situation that might seem stressful could, in fact, inadvertently undermine the natural support and adaptation processes that had long provided firefighters resilience and growth.

Those colloquial concerns have proven ever more prophetic as serious empirical research has accumulated regarding the efficacy of CISD and the veracity of its constructs and presumptions. Indeed, it is quite fair to say that current questions regarding the debriefing paradigm and the movement it spawned no longer center on the efficacy of the principal intervention; those issues can now be addressed in reasonably short summary (Gist et al., 1997; Gist & Woodall, 1998):

1 There is no reliable empirical evidence indicating demonstrable preventive effect (cf. Bisson & Deahl, 1994; Foa & Meadows, 1997; Gist, 1996a, 1996b; Gist & Woodall, 1995; Kenardy & Carr, 1996; Kenardy et al., 1996; Meichenbaum, 1994; Raphael, Meldrum, & McFarlane, 1995; Stephens, 1997).

2 What palliative effect may be derived is no greater than that afforded by more traditional venues of discussion and social support (cf. Alexander & Wells, 1991; Hytten & Hasle, 1989; Gist, Lubin, & Redburn, 1998; Stephens, 1997; Thompson & Solomon, 1991).

3 There have been no systematic data reported that suggest any superiority of the "Mitchell model" of debriefing compared with any other method or approach to occupational stress or exposure.

4 Paradoxical effects, very possibly of iatrogenic origin, have been noted in several independent studies (Bisson, Jenkins, Alexander, & Bannister, 1997; Gist et al., 1998; Griffiths & Watts, 1992; Hobbs, Mayou, Harrison, & Worlock, 1996; Kenardy et al., 1996; McFarlane, 1988).

5 The more rigorous the study, the more objective its measurements, the more independent the researchers from the "movement" itself, and the more discerning the venue of publication, the more likely has been a neutral to negative assessment (Gist et al., 1997; Gist & Woodall, 1998).

The theoretical and scientific questions now active go beyond CISD itself to consider the implications of such findings for fundamental assumptions long accepted as postulates in the arena of immediate crisis response and "one off" intervention programs. Bisson et al. (1997) questioned the principal assumption of immediate intervention, suggesting that such early intrusion may effectively inhibit distancing needed in the immediate aftermath of traumatic disruption. Gist et al. (1998; see also introduction) have similarly questioned this fundamental tenet, noting particularly that models who can provide effective social comparison and facilitate both salutagenic social constructions of the problem and selection of productive solution schemata may prove directly helpful, while attempts at emotional catharsis prior to such constructions gaining a stable focus may, in fact, disrupt these essential elements of adaptive resolution.

Charlton and Thompson (1996) reported that persons exposed to the novelty and intensity of traumatic experiences tend initially to attempt a very wide range of coping strategies, but they found that only cognitive reframing and psychological distancing tended to prove beneficial as effective coping strategies—both these coping mechanisms stand specifically contrary to the presumption inherent in CISD and related intervention protocols that early excursions into emotional venting and other forms of emotion-based coping are somehow essential to resolution. Gump and Kulik's (1997) demonstration of social contagion in settings characterized by shared traumatic exposure may further suggest how early forays into group interventions might just as readily promote paradoxically maladaptive responses as encourage constructive coping.

Taken together, these findings have pointed with progressively greater emphasis to but one scientifically and ethically defensible position regarding the popularized debriefing movement: Suspend immediately the rampant and virtually indiscriminate application of the debriefing paradigm and explore instead such alternatives as the enhancement of essential resiliency in individuals, communities, and organizations; the facilitation of avenues of instrumental aid and social support, especially through those vehicles inherent in the ordinary functioning of the persons and systems affected; and increased reliance on "invisible interventions" that restore personal and collective autonomy. Programs that harbor, whether implicitly or explicitly, goals of promoting interventionist causes through the sort of highly promoted "trauma tourism" ventures that ultimately risk what social psychologists have sometimes dubbed "overhelping" (Gilbert & Silvera, 1996) may ultimately disempower those they purport most to aid by depriving them, to greater or lesser degrees, of the very esssence of resilient resolution—the sense of personal mastery that flows from standing to threat and challenge and prevailing under duress.

CONTEMPORARY VIEWS OF FIREFIGHTER STRESS

Recognition of stress as a significant factor affecting firefighter health and safety no longer meets "macho" resistance within the industry; no longer do stress management or behavioral wellness programs encounter denial so intense as to demand or justify missionary zeal to secure their endorsement or adoption. Behavioral wellness, including personal and occupational stress management, was accorded direct recognition and standing in the Joint Wellness Initiative of the International Association of Fire

Fighters, AFL-CIO, and the International Association of Fire Chiefs (IAFF/IAFC, 1997, Chapter 5); these are also recognized components within the National Fire Protection Association standards regarding occupational health and safety for firefighters (NFPA, 1997, Standard 1500). References to stress and stress management in fire service trade literature and instruction have gone in little more than a decade from an avant garde rarity to what would seem now a nearly gratuitous frequency; however, little in the way actual research or empirical data have been reported.

Most of the upsurge seen in trade venues has remained focused on a relatively singular and narrow construction of occupational stress and occupational stressors (i.e., "critical incident stress") and a specific popularized model of "peer" intervention (CISD); most all have demonstrated a peculiar, nearly exclusive reliance on a single author whose work has remained well outside the refereed literature of psychology and its related disciplines (Mitchell, 1983, *et seq.*). Much like the suicide prevention and crisis intervention movement of a quarter-century ago (cf. Echterling & Wylie, 1981), the CISD phenomenon has arisen primarily as a "grass-roots" amalgam of a self-anointed laity, self-generated paraprofessionals, and semiprofessionals from the more distal end of the education and practice continuum, spurred by a few charismatic leaders—highly revered within the movement itself, but largely unrecognized and unestablished outside its boundaries. It has only been very recently, well after its growth into a substantial cottage industry with a disturbingly strong foothold in the fire and rescue professions, that this phenomenon has attracted solid academic scrutiny.

The core contentions on which the enterprise has been erected derive from an essential assumption that occupational events function on an individual level as psychic traumata, "wounding" the psyche of individuals confronting them in such fashions as to disrupt the capacity of these persons to function normally in the aftermath (cf. Mitchell, 1983, 1988b; Mitchell & Bray, 1990; Mitchell & Everly, 1993). The premise that these exposures, if not contravened through direct and focused rapid interventions, will lead to post-traumatic stress disorder and related psychiatric maladies (cf. Mitchell, 1992) has become so ubiquitous as to be presumed axiomatic, and has become central to arguments supporting ever-more elaborate and expansive intervention schemata.

Despite ease with which this popular model has been assimilated and the seemingly facile congruence of its loosely specified but rigidly espoused causal presumptions to colloquial constructions of traumatic reactivity, direct attempts to specify and test its component constructs have consistently suggested that such facile pictures of reactions and resolution are far too shallow to prove robust (see discussion above). Particularly with respect to occupational and organizational events, context and circumstance may prove much more determinant of impact than any aspect such as the mere nature or magnitude of a given incident (Alexander & Wells, 1991; Gist et al., 1998), while individual circumstances and proclivities pre-extant to the event have proven decidedly more predictive of lasting sequelae than have such features as proximity and exposure alone (Cook & Bickman, 1990; McFarlane, 1988, 1989). Simplistic arguments make, perhaps, for easy sales of intervention packages, but they often belie shallow and shoddy scholarship.

The growing criticism and increasingly frequent calls for caution from research and academic arenas have not seemed to impede continuing efforts of CISD principals to further market their intervention product. Arguments from proponents have now shifted from attempts to assert unique and phenomenal efficacy (cf. Mitchell, 1992) to contentions that no component can be tested outside total and complete adherence to a labyrinthine conglomerate of equally unverified activities and interventions that Mitchell and Everly (1997) now dub CISM to denote "critical incident stress management." Claims have been made of extensive "scientific evidence for CISM" (Mitchell & Everly, 1997), though citations offered to support these claims have been composed principally of unpublished presentations from proprietary conferences, unpublished theses (many from programs of uncertain rigor or reputation), articles from nonjuried trade magazines, and trade books authored by CISM principals and published by their wholly owned Chevron Publishing subsidiary (see Gist & Woodall, 1998, for a more detailed discussion). When salesmanship is forced to give way to scholarship, however, entirely different constructions begin to emerge.

ALTERNATIVE CONSTRUCTIONS OF OCCUPATIONAL STRESS AND OCCUPATIONAL STRESSORS

Taylor (1983) posited more than a decade ago that cognitive adaptation to stressful events might be more effectively characterized from a salutagenic, developmental perspective rather than being presumed pathognomonic of psychopathologic risk. A rigorous and very productive line of empirical research emerging since that time (see, e.g., Taylor & Brown, 1988; Taylor & Lobel, 1989) has affirmed and refined these propositions, and they have been melded into an alternative, more discernable and testable construction of the operation of such stressors in both individual and collective adjustment to negative events (Taylor, 1991). More intriguingly, perhaps, it has helped to provide constructions that recognize the unique salience and impact of extraordinary threat as a stressor while still embracing the long-standing conventional wisdom that adversity can, and in fact most commonly will, provide challenges from which character and resilience are built.

Exposure to "critical incidents" is not only unavoidable in fire and rescue work, it is in fact the essence of the enterprise. For most providers in most situations, these encounters are not sources of *threat* or *loss* but are rather episodes of *challenge* in which skills and effort central to one's personal and professional role identity are focused on a legitimate demands of the occupation (see McCrae, 1984, for an overview of situational determinants of coping strategy). The organization may be argued to hold a range of responsibilities to ensure that personnel are adequately prepared, equipped, deployed, and configured for effective response, and for ensuring that the impact of equivocal events is effectively addressed in organizational and operational review (Gist & Taylor, 1996), but individual decisions, actions, coping patterns, and responses are also highly determinant of adjustment. These interact with organizational determinants in complex and sometimes unpredictable ways that render uniform approaches to remediation suspect, if not overtly dangerous (Moran, 1998). Accordingly, appropriate strategies for intervention and assistance must separately and distinctly address organizational, situational, and individual factors and determinants, and must be capable of effectively addressing both the unique contributions of each and the interactions between them.

Distinction must also be drawn between approaches focused on issues and assumptions related to presumed vulnerability factors versus those focused on building and enhancing resilience. Despite the presumptions of the debriefing movement and its conceptual cousins in disaster response regarding exposure, risk, and causation, an increasing body of empirical research has focused on consistent findings of remarkable resilience in a sizable, often strongly dominant portion of those exposed to ostensibly traumatizing events. The distinctions between these competing views reach much further than simple twists of title or subtle shifts of attention, and became a principal focus of the National Institute of Mental Health's proposed plan for basic behavioral science research (Basic Behavioral Science Task Force, 1996).

Constructions built on pathogenetic assumptions regarding trauma and exposure have tended to spawn "case finding" approaches that assume dysfunctional and/or debilitating reactions to be a relatively natural consequent of the experience, and which further assume that prevalence and severity are generally understated and underestimated (see Solomon & Canino, 1990, as an example). Constructions built on assumptions of resiliency are more likely to generate "case exclusionary" rubrics that promote more conservative approaches to establishing "caseness" and assume that the presence of various forms of subjective discomfort are generally to be seen as signs of disequilibrium attendant to and essential for salutagenic processes of adaptation and accommodation (rather than as "symptoms" viewed as somehow pathognomonic of maladjustment and prognostic of disorder and dysfunction). These disparities have contributed to sometimes remarkable differences in estimation of pathology following traumatic exposure (Rubonis & Bickman, 1991), and have fueled substantial differences in such things as the nature, scope, visibility, and intrusiveness of intervention modalities.

Much literature directly examining resiliency has focused on specific populations such as high-risk children (Garmezy, 1993; Werner, 1995) or older adults (Foster, 1997; Staudinger & Fleeson, 1996), or on specific risk factors such as parental alchololism (Wolin & Wolin, 1997). Although there has been some extension of these studies to examine survivors of trauma and violence (see Masten, Best, & Garmezy, 1990, for an overview; see Holaday & McPhearson, 1997; Howard, 1996; Liem, James, O'Toole, & Boudewyn, 1997, for specific examples), the integration of posited determinants of resiliency into intervention and prevention strategies has been far less than extensive or systematic.

The essential characteristics associated with resilience have included dispositional features, especially certain protective factors demonstrated to offset the negative impacts of life experiences; emotional ties to family and primary social relationships; and both the extent and the quality of external support systems that can serve to buffer the impact of negative life events and reinforce the election and successful execution of positive coping strategies (Basic Behavioral Sciences Advisory Board, 1996; Garmezy, 1991; Masten et al., 1990; Werner, 1994a, 1994b). Conversely, the characteristics of negative events themselves have proven notoriously nonpredictive of outcome among resilient individuals; indeed, many of the very experiences that would commonly be expected to induce decompensation and dysfunction become for them—despite conjunction with very real and sometimes overwhelming personal distress at various points in the longitudinal process of adaptation—benchmarks of character, perseverance, and meaning rather than indelible impediments to resolution. Effective strategies for intervention and assistance, then, must begin with strategies to enhance resilience, and must integrate these strategies with approaches that supplement and reinforce resilient responses of individuals and organizations. When specific interventions are undertaken, they must occur without supplanting or replacing natural contacts and supports that promote autonomy and resilience with artificial structures that may instead reinforce vulnerability or encourage reliance on inappropriate, ineffective, or ill-timed strategies of coping and resolution.

A SYSTEMATIC VIEW OF OCCUPATIONAL STRESS

Motowidlo, Packard, & Manning (1986) offered an interactive schematic suggesting how several factors might interact to result in perceptions of occupational stress and influence attitudinal and behavioral concomitants

OCCUPATIONAL STRESS

Figure 1 Schematic model of occupational stress and workplace impacts (from Motowidlo et al., 1986).

to those perceptions (see Figure 1). Job conditions provide one set of influencing factors, but certain personal characteristics—particularly job experience, Type A characteristics, and fear of negative evaluation—also strongly influence how events in one's working life will be experienced and interpreted. These factors interact at any given juncture with both the frequency and the intensity of stressful events to influence the subjective reactions of the worker and the affective experience of the events and their contexts. These influences, in sequence, affect aspects of job performance that translate readily to behavioral and attitudinal conditions colloquially associated with monikers like burnout.

Once again, it is not some specific and conceptually isolated set of "critical incidents" that can be posited to determine the most salient links in the processes of reaction and resolution; it is, in fact, the backdrop of "daily hassles" in the form of personal and organizational strain that can ultimately be said to define the relative impact of a given stressor. This was highlighted in a thorough study of more than 200 firefighter/paramedics and firefighter emergency medical technicians (EMTs) in the State of Washington (Beaton & Murphy, 1993), wherein past "critical incidents" ranked well below such obvious concerns as sleep disruption, wages and benefits, labor/management issues, personal safety, equipment, job-skill concerns, and family/financial strains as elements of perceived job stress. Indeed, past "critical incidents" failed to significantly enter regression equations predicting job satisfaction and morale for paramedic firefighters and barely achieved significance for firefighter/EMTs. Moreover, Wright (1993) reported in a preliminary study of successful career paramedics that the principal factors influencing perceptions of stress in a series of hypothetical calls hinged not on the manifest content of the encounter or even on patient outcome, but were rather driven by perceptions of personal and organizational success in the address of component evolutions.

The first strategy for effective occupational stress interventions in these professions, then, must deal with enhancing those features of organizational performance, personal conditioning and development, and social support that provide effective response and promote personal and organizational resilience. Similarly, strategies for incident-specific interventions must look to support the operation and, if necessary, the regeneration of these same factors through the least intrusive vehicles consistent with the given circumstance, while carefully considering and evaluating the interactions between individual circumstances of the affected individuals and broader organizational impacts and needs. Moreover, inherent conflicts between individual and organizational interests cannot be avoided, and separate routes of intervention with clearly specified client relationships will generally be required for the system to operate ethically and effectively.

LIMITATIONS OF THE CISD MODEL

The cornerstone of the critical incident model has been the embodiment of its social movement features in the form of the CISD team—generally construed (see Mitchell, 1988a; Mitchell & Bray, 1990; Mitchell & Everly, 1993) as a separately chartered volunteer collegium, again strikingly reminiscent in both structure and tone to the crisis intervention centers, telephone hotline programs, and the like that proliferated during the early 1970s (see Echterling & Wylie, 1981). The CISD movement has shared with these progenitors both an inability to demonstrate in concrete and empirical ways any level of significant preventive impact, and the peculiar array of social and political machinations that came to characterize the former movement across the decade or so of its longevity.

Basically, CISD teams have tended to be composed of self-selected personnel who have declared an interest in this enterprise and who have attended at least two consecutive days of training, either directly from the originator of this approach or from an "approved" vendor (essentially a franchisee). That initial training program has now grown to include a 2-day "advanced" program, a "peer counseling" program, and a "family support" program, each similarly distinguished by its fiduciary relationship to a principal franchising agent. Whereas attendance at these programs is declared as mandatory of one is to provide the "right kind of help" (cf. Mitchell, 1992, or Dernocoeur, 1995) and "certification" is offered (for a fee) by the franchising agent, there are no requirements for examination or other verification of skill or competence connected to these enterprises, nor has there been any report of credible evidence for any particular or peculiar adequacy of the approaches taught with respect any specific application or outcome, nor has there has been any presentation of empirical data in any reliable venue that would justify the intemperate claims, both explicit (Mitchell, 1992) and implied (Dernocoeur, 1995), that other approaches are somehow harmful.

Much as occurred with the crisis center movement (Echterling & Wylie, 1981), the politics of the CISD social movement have begun to raise questions and conflicts of their own, both within these teams and their affiliates, between these teams and the public safety organizations whose employees are the intended recipients of their ministrations, between CISD teams themselves, between the teams and their parent organization, and between principals of the "movement" and established loci of research, practice, and training within the psychological and academic communities (see Woodall, 1994, for an overview of these points). Many of these matters may well be influenced by the subprofessional (or, at best, paraprofessional) nature of much of the CISD enterprise, and from the lack of clear definition regarding roles, relationships, boundaries, and expectations that often plagues movements that veer away from established professional arenas and the standards they carry.

Though this may work in the early stages of a movement to preserve for its founders levels of influence and deference that would be subject to increasing challenge in circles where formal training, codified standards, and refereed research displace charisma, rhetoric, and ad vericundium authority as the harbingers of status and standing, the transition from social movement to social institution nonetheless forces those enterprises that survive further into the spotlight of objective scrutiny. It is in that light that difficulties once easily waved away become persistent and sometimes glaring.

PROFESSIONAL ISSUES, CLIENT RELATIONSHIPS, AND ETHICAL DILEMMAS

Client relationships, definitions of roles and expectations, and the legal and ethical responsibilities that these imply and define are critical issues to competently practicing professionals. Social movements often hold particular disdain for these sometimes subtle and often prickly questions, purporting that helping those perceived to be in need should simply supersede such abstractions and tossing glaring ad hominem aspersions at any who would deign to argue otherwise. Yet these boundaries and definitions can become particularly difficult where employer/employee relationships must be factored into the matrices of roles, responsibilities, and relationships, and can hold very serious consequences if not appropriately managed at all stages of interaction.

Specific identification of client relationships for CISD teams and their interventions has proven elusive at very best. Although identification of the client relationship is arguably the most fundamental question in any professional encounter and is absolutely critical to any meaningful approach to such bedrock matters as informed consent or outcome assessment, this crucial issue finds no satisfactory address in the rubrics of the CISD movement. Indeed, despite the lack of such declarations, it has become increasingly commonplace to hear both arguments that blanket debriefing participation should be "mandatory" for certain types of events, and to hear reports that indicate, usually quite proudly, that such measures were in fact implemented (e.g., Hansen, 1995). Given the potential for paradoxical outcomes and the growing implication of iatrogenesis for certain participants (Bisson et al., 1997; Gist et al., 1998; Griffiths & Watts, 1992; Hobbs et al., 1996; McFarlane, 1988), such mandates work to ensure that those at risk of negative outcomes will in fact be exposed to the intervention, and are in that context a cause for grave concern.

The ethical dilemmas presented regarding client relationships and informed consent should be immediately self-announcing to any competent professional, and the fact that they lie essentially unaddressed accordingly becomes deeply disturbing—especially to the extent that it may indicate failure even to recognize the problem among the practitioners of this and other self-help movements (see Dawes, 1994; Kaminer, 1992; Peele, 1989, for discussions of this problem and its implications in other self-help enterprises). Questions of where and with whom responsibility and authority for matters impacting individual and organizational welfare shall be vested and the standards for execution and evaluation of the various decisions entailed, actions taken, and interventions attempted are also elements critical to ethical and effective professional relationships. All these matters seem to receive more evasion that definition in the standard protocols and prescriptions of the CISD enterprises. Wide areas remain for potential conflict, miscommunication, and liability with little or no competent guidance through which to navigate these sometimes treacherous straits.

Mitchell's approach to CISD (cf. Mitchell & Bray, 1990, Chapter 7) envisioned a volunteer team of peer responders and counselors, hosted by a specified "lead" agency but under its own direction and operating within its own protocols and structure. This is again strongly reminiscent of the semiamorphous ad hocracy but paradoxically rigid hierarchies described by Echterling and Wylie (1981) for crisis centers, by Kaminer (1992) for recovery groups and 12-step programs, by Peele (1989) for addiction groups, or by Dawes for a variety of self-help groups and self-proclaimed therapies, movements, and seers. Whether the ministrations of CISD teams are organizational interventions geared toward preservation of work team integrity or group interventions geared toward maintaining psychic integrity in the individual members of some collection of workers connected to some specific event or incident is not entirely clear, though operational suggestions and reported practices—which include the simultaneous address of representatives from differing agencies and professions who may have experienced duty in the same basic event (Mitchell, 1988a; Mitchell & Bray, 1990)—would strongly suggest the latter. Either way, the emphasis given prevention of post-traumatic stress disorder and other presumably consequent psychiatric maladies clearly defines this application as a therapeutic enterprise, despite whatever semantic manipulations might be offered in an effort to finesse the process outside the realm of regulated activity. Any such application should accordingly require appropriate licensure, informed consent, clear definition of client relationships, and full documentation on an individual basis of services rendered and results derived. None of these factors, however, has been routinely exercised in protocols we have reviewed, and some (e.g., documentation) have been specifically eschewed (cf. Mitchell, 1983; Mitchell & Bray, 1990).

Perhaps even greater pause should be taken from an increasing tendency for CISD teams and their members to extend their "services" into the civilian population, particularly when those contacts initiate under the auspices of an emergency response provider agency or other government or quasi-governmental entity. The client relationship established through 911 contact clearly does not extend to psychological intervention of any more broadly therapeutic nature, nor do immunities and protections (or liability coverages) necessarily apply—especially when extended beyond crisis intervention assistance with propinquity in both time and location to the precipitating emergency event. The potential for therapuetic misadventure, including iatrogenic consequences of such encounters, is not inconsequential (see discussions above) and merits serious consideration of the legal and ethical implications of "inflicting a painful risk intervention of unproven effectiveness to prevent something that may not happen" (Grollmes, 1992, p. 153).

PURSUING A MORE REASONED COURSE

Gist & Taylor (1996) outlined a series of organizationally based strategies that, they argued, should be considered before, during, and after particularly stressful operations to promote maximum resilience within both the formal and the informal organizations of the workplace, which, in turn, would help to support maximum resiliency in individuals exposed to stressful occupational events. Rather than proposing any elaborate structure or designated cadre of "peer counselors" and therapists as the focal point for organizational preparedness and response, they focused on the incorporation of enhanced information and more effective practices into existing organizational relationships affecting management, command, supervision, and human resource support, and on the addition of skills and resources to supplement existing patterns wherever deficits might exist or develop. Moreover, they specifically advocated approaches based on empowerment in daily activities and responses over remedial interventions—

opting, metaphorically, to promote flood control engineering rather than sand bagging as the better strategy for risk management.

Woodall (1994) reported detailed evaluation data from preliminary presentations of a pilot program designed to incorporate the essential components of this strategy into an organizationally integrated, theoretically grounded approach to issues identified as affecting both organizational and individual resilience in the workplace (Gist, Taylor, Woodall, & Magenheimer, 1994). The approach taken was to explore an alternative to the pathogenetic assumptions of existing event-driven, rigidly technologic models of response to occupational stress in the career fire service. The approach was also to concentrate first on identification, development, and consistent reinforcement of workplace dynamics and structures that held demonstrated capacity to enhance such resilience—including programs and systems to support development and maintenance of individual resilience factors. The subsequent combination of these with postexposure strategies designed to minimize intrusion and visibility of the intervention while mobilizing and enhancing the capacity of existing roles and relationships was intended to provide whatever "boosts" might be necessary to bolster buffering characteristics during times of uncommon duress.

While the pilot presentations were compressed into the 2-day, 16-hour format that had become associated with the "traveling seminar circuit" of CISD enterprises, it was prepared and presented as a collection of 2-to-3-hour modules to preserve the possibility of offering components at different times to varying segments of an organization, depending on interest, need, and organizational proclivities. Moreover, the entire design was built to encourage tailoring the program to the social and organizational profile of the individual organization, rather than creating a separate external entity that would, in effect, expect to tailor the practices of one or more existing organizations to meet its own protocols and designs. The relative implications of these alternative strategies of presentation and configuration were also explored as components of the evaluation.

Component modules, their rationales, and the routes of address adopted are briefly summarized below:

1 *Overview of occupational stress, organizational strain, and personal reactivity.* This module used case studies, literature review, and operational analyses to introduce the premises and arguments that provided the foundations for psychosocial, ecological, and community treatments of occupational stress and its management.

2 *Building healthy baseline behaviors.* This component, which had been routinely presented in fire recruit training and as a recertification class for EMTs, reviewed implication of the model suggested by Motowidlo et al. (1986, see discussion above) and discussed individually based elements associated with resiliency at each point in the schematic.

3 *Contributing to and working within an effective organizational climate.* It is the daily interactions and issues of the workplace (cf. Beaton & Murphy, 1993), sometimes called "organizational strain," that largely determine the stressor impact of any given event. This presentation discussed elements of leadership from working and operating levels of professional service delivery organizations, with particular emphasis on team building and effective supervision.

4 *Controlling CIS (critical incident stress) through ICS (Incident Command System).* This module, again adapted from material routinely used in recruit training and officer development, sought to prepare personnel to work effectively within the Incident Management System built to ensure safe, focused, and effective partitioning of incident components and responsibilities, and to develop a broader understanding of its implications in the daily operation of the enterprise as well as in the delineation of capacity, capability, and accountability factors in effective incident response.

5 *Family, peer, and professional support systems.* This component emphasized the importance of social support to resilience and concentrated on such issues as boundaries and relationships in the often compartmentalized lives of the professional fire service responder. Given that it is often the backdrop of these "daily hassles" that defines the stressor impact of major events (Wagner, Compas, & Howell, 1988), the management of life strain outside the job was postulated as a crucial element in maintaining the buffering capacity of these essential support systems. Also addressed were the roles of such human resource support services as employee assistance programs and agency chaplains, and their effective use to assist with the various problems in living that can complicate progress in any professional career—as well as those problems made especially prominent by the unique nature of fire and rescue service.

The second day of the program centered on specific applications and techniques, divided into four component modules defined by level of work team involvement and the formality of the response set contemplated. Routine, consistent consideration and discussion of personal impacts of daily human services delivery were defined as role responsibilities of immediate supervisors (company officers), whereas broader and somewhat more formal strategies were contemplated at the management level (e.g., battalion chiefs) for events that produced impacts and required participation beyond the basic unit of the system. The more formal responses were reserved for those things that reached beyond the ordinary organizational unit, whereas other paths for involvement of the informal system to facilitate instrumental and emotional support of individuals and their families were also presented.

The group process model used for the most formal version of post-incident intervention stands, in many respects, as parallel to, if not functionally indistinct from, Mitchell's debriefing format, and reflects a specific but relatively direct application of a very general group counseling format diffused throughout the various counseling professions for many years (Corey, 1995). The placement and conduct of such formal exercises, their centrality to the overall program, and the parameters surrounding use and deployment, however, are almost orthogonally distinct.

Mitchell's (1983, et seq.) paradigm has portrayed the group process as a focal intervention, essential for the prevention of individual decompensation resultant of personal traumatization (cf. Mitchell, 1993; Mitchell & Everly, 1993). The alternative tested by Woodall afforded a much less critical role to any specific intervention set or technique, being organized instead along a continuum from least formal, structured, and intrusive approaches (given declarative precedence) to the most visible and the most structured. Where the Mitchell techniques have been presented as protocol bound and driven, with highly mechanized strategies proposed for description and application, the alternative system was designed to instead promote fluid adaptation of a range of process and provider options to meet specific needs of the organizational circumstance, favoring always the least formal, least intrusive, and more conservative of available options.

COMPARATIVE TESTS OF THE MODELS

Woodall (1994) sought to directly compare this organizationally based model (Gist et al., 1994; see description above) against the dominant "Mitchell model" of critical incident stress management among groups of law enforcement, fire service, EAP, and education professionals directly acquainted with the latter approach. Participants were asked to complete detailed questionnaires at the conclusion of each module, and for the entire program as a package; these were then analyzed to assess suitability and impact at both component and package levels.

Participants reported the program's objectives as highly salient to workplace goals and showed strong preference for its construction, strategies, and grounding; these preferences were nearly universal among career fire service participants for whose organizations and processes the approach had been specifically designed. Moreover, it became immediately clear that the nearly amorphous mixtures of organizations, disciplines, jurisdictions, and propinquity characteristic of the Mitchell program would simply be unworkable and unreasonable in practice. The approach finally recommended included selective use of modules to fit an overall design specifically tailored to each individual organization and circumstance; it also clearly delineated the need to construe organizational intervention as a specific set of procedures developed for uniquely designated organizational clients and to distinguish these from individual-level interventions where the client relationship must be unique to the employee and all intervention based on thorough individual assessments (Moran, 1998).

BACK TO THE BASICS

These findings ultimately drove a much broader and much more fundamental reconsideration of the most basic assumptions and foundations regarding adjustment of these professionals to the experiences of their careers. Woodall (1996, 1997), after several years of progressive and incremental deconstruction of the CISD rubric and thorough exploration of the mounting empirical evidence of its inherent shortcomings, turned instead to an ethnographic strategy to explore afresh the views held by contemporary fire and rescue professionals of their work and its impact, and to examine their reported strategies for accommodating those impacts into the fabric of personal and occupational adjustment.

Firefighters from across the United States were contacted and requested to participate in extensive ethnographic interviews to explore several questions that had stood as axiomatic but unsubstantiated assumptions in the social evolution of the CISD movement:

1   What emotions are commonly experienced by firefighters in emergency situations, both critical and routine?

2   What emergency situations or circumstances commonly elicit the strongest emotional reactions?

3   How are those emotions managed, both in the immediate situation and in the processes of personal and occupational resolution?

4   How might their personal and colloquial descriptions of coping strategies be digested to provide a preliminary set of constructs and hypotheses from which to develop a more grounded picture of occupational adjustment in the contemporary enterprise?

The first and, in some ways, most striking finding was the wide diversity of personality and views in the contemporary profession. While strong bonds united them on professional levels, derived of both common challenges and shared loss, the contexts of their lives were as varied as the populations they served. This emerged as a critically important factor that had been seriously misassessed and hence misrepresented in the foundational arguments of the CISD movement.

Mitchell has claimed for many years (see, e.g., interview by Hopper, 1988, p. 7) that emergency services personnel could be distinguished by the presence of characteristic personality traits that rendered them uniquely similar, and that these had been demonstrated through definitive empirical research, to wit: "Our recent study using the Milan (sic) Personality Inventory clearly shows that the police officer/firefighter/paramedic personality is significantly, statistically different from the average population" (quoted by Hopper, 1988, p.7). This same contention had been repeated time and again in a variety of venues, but no data have ever accompanied those claims (see Gist & Woodall, 1998, for discussion). Indeed, when pressed to provide the data claimed but never presented, Mitchell finally acknowledged that these contentions came not from analysis of an organized database, but from his own personal observations and speculations (J. T. Mitchell, personal communication, 1993).

Despite the glaring absence of data to support this contention, the construct continues to receive central play in Mitchell's CISD training (International Critical Incident Stress Foundation, 1998) and is used to argue that uniform and routinized strategies for intervention are not only apt for this population, but are mandated by their homogeneity of personality and coping. The findings of Woodall (1996, 1997), especially when combined with the reports of Gist et al. (1998) and Fullerton, Wright, Ursana, & McCarroll (1993) regarding the dominant role of support systems outside the occupational context, suggest that sound systems of support will need instead to reflect the wide array of values, affiliations, and coping styles that a diversified and diversifying provider population may reflect at any particular juncture.

More significantly still, the coping strategies reflecting greatest success appear more reflective of what we learned from our grandmothers than what we learned from grad school. The processes involved, not surprisingly, strategies to provide both the distance needed to gain or maintain some level of objectivity in the performance of one's social roles, and the perspective needed to incorporate such proximal participation in difficult and disconcerting life events with some level of meaning and equanimity. When one asks not why the wounded fall but how the valiant continue to march, one seems to find a wholly different picture. Woodall (1997) described it like this:

> ...it is the very nature of a firefighter's journey, the seemingly endless exposure to human pain and suffering, that has afforded them the opportunity to appreciate the joys of life by knowing and understanding human tragedy. By experiencing, although most times vicariously, the emotional and physical pain of the sick, injured, and dying, they become capable of experiencing the true meaning of life. These resilient emotional skills serve them both at home and on the job. Their experiences afford them the emotional skills required to function in dangerous and tragic environments. By the same token, these skills also afford them the opportunity to take that little extra moment to appreciate the joys of life, understanding all the while just how fleeting those joys can be. (p. 160).

A pass through the various interviews and cases collected presents some striking and extraordinarily salient hypotheses regarding debriefing and its conceptual cousins that may make the troubling questions of selective iatrogenesis and pervasive noneffects clear and simple—especially when reviewed in the context of existing empirical work in applied social psychology (see Gist et al., 1998, for discussion of key research lines and their possible implications). Distancing, boundaries, and reframing are critical to the processes of integration and resolution; these essential components are too often directly (and probably paradoxically) countered by the most basic premises of the debriefing rubric. Focusing on the needs of others is salutagenic; focusing instead on making the loss personal invites instead pathogenetic identification. Finding comfort, solace, and support in the context of the informal society of the workplace casts the experience as disequilibrium in the service of personal and career growth; seeking ministration and intervention in the context of some "mental health" procedure casts it instead as treatment to fend off occupational injury and disease.

Most salient, though, is the observation that the principal product delivered by the contemporary fire and rescue system is no longer found in technologically based tasks and activities, but reflects instead the emotional connections created between citizen and responder at critical moments in the former's life (cf. Gist, 1997). These thrust the fire and rescue provider into the arena described by Hochschild (1983) as the realm of the "comodified emotion" and the "managed heart." Gist (personal communication, 1997) captured some of the essence of this transition in an essay written in response to an e-mail posting on a fire service mail list; the original correspondent (E. Shanks, personal communication, 1997) had written "Actually, even before political correctness reared its ugly head, what someone who fights fires was/is called is "firefighter." A "fireman" is the guy who shovels coal into the boiler of a steam locomotive." Gist, in turn, responded:

> Well, if you're gonna' be *that* picky about it, we'll have to admit that most "firefighters" don't fight that much fire—especially in the modern service organization. It's our genesis, our tradition, and for many our calling—but it hasn't been our principal occupation for quite some time. Don't get me wrong...it's critical, essential, and worthy of reverent focus—but it ain't the "bread and butter" of today's business or what necessarily gives it greatest value to the people we serve
>
> Just as an item of interest, by the way, it's not EMS, either—at least, not as we usually think of that enterprise. We tracked a decade of Kansas City Fire Department (KCFD) data to discover several very important things. First, our fire activity (which everyone thought was decreasing) hasn't dropped at all in that period. It's down radically across the preceding generation, to be sure, but those reductions resulted from changes in technology and regulation much more than from changes in tactics or deployment. Those changes were pretty well exhausted by even the mid-1980s, and even what new technology we have available is hard to extend into further decreases.
>
> We have the technology to virtually eliminate residential fires, for example, and could do so *technologically* through mandated retrofitting of residen-

tial sprinklers. It ain't gonna' happen, though... it's a social, economic, and political matter now, not simply an issue of technology. The current level of suppression activity can be expected to remain quite constant, but that presents its own set of demands—the fires now encountered are quite different in many critical respcts from the fires of a generation past, are often complicated by social conditions, are fought by persons with considerably less "hands-on" exposure, and are engaged under much different tactics, priorities, and performance standards. If anything, we have to work harder and invest more effort in being more prepared than ever.

EMS, however, has so accelerated as to dwarf fire suppression in terms of service volume. What is interesting in that same data set is that "life saving" EMS activity hasn't increased even a smidgen in that time. Almost all the increase in the agency's activity—and that's better than 60% increase overall —has come from what we've taken to calling "social service EMS"... basic EMT skills in nonthreatening circumstances; putting Grandma back into bed, putting band-aids on boo-boos, or simply holding a hand. Some might call this "system abuse"—others, though, are starting to see it as our most essential service product. Through that service, we touch in about five years every citizen we serve, directly or indirectly, with an "up-close and personal" exemplar of who we are and what we do.

That's a very different brand of contact. Major fires are, in many ways, distant and impersonal incarnations of the Roman circus, where clusters of costumed gladiators engage in mob violence directed toward inanimate objects while crowds of folks watch from the bleachers. This other stuff takes place one customer at a time, one company at a time—on their turf, in their living rooms, in their autos and workplaces at the most frightening moments of life. We're right there talking to them, touching them, treating them—so close that they can count the hairs on our noses and the vessels in our eyes. Their judgments of what we're doing have surprisingly little to do with the technical or objective quality of care—they want to believe that it's the best there is, and we have to be pretty blatantly inept to convince them otherwise. They base their assessments on the concern, the focus, the compassion—they don't care how much we know, but they want to know how much we care.

Gist went on to describe how the contemporary agency has adapted to meet that challenge by returning, in effect, to its earliest roots as a harbinger of commonwealth and community:

A much smaller agency with which I also work realized this some years ago and tied it to their small town roots with awesome effectiveness. Although an advanced life support medical provider, they were quick to grasp that the somewhat romantic notion of the medic as the robotic eyes and hands of the trauma surgeon or cardiologist fell wide of the mark in reality—we were instead the social replacement for the country doctor making the house call, coming out to provide compassion and concern as much (or even more) than treatment itself. They've made that presence and service their central focus, and have quickly become the strongest positive force in the community they serve.

We set there as a strategic goal two years ago this simple objective: "When District residents are asked the three best things about living in their community, the fire department should be one of those three." This was, in turn, tied to a simple statement of purpose: "Enhancing the quality of life in the communities we serve by every means we can muster." What lies beneath this is a return to the essential fabric of the enterprise—the commitment not just to combat a neighbor's blaze, but to help protect and restore that person's presence within the community.

Face it; those early bucket brigades didn't stop much fire. Fortunately, those early firefighters didn't stop there, either. The same folk who tried to counter conflagration stayed to shelter, to comfort, to rebuild and to restore. They marshaled the resources of the commonwealth to provide for that effort and support, and added their own efforts to restoration as well as suppression. The purpose for which they banded together, after all, was driven not by fire itself, but by its consequence for individuals, families, commerce, and community.

Gist finished by reflecting on the elements of service that have begun to redefine the fire service itself, and which ultimately provide for the well-balanced provider the successes that ultimately offset those tragic losses that are, unfortunately, inescapable parts of the social enterprise it represents:

> This stuff we're now calling "customer service" has become the next hot buzzword on the conference and trade magazine circuit, but it wasn't invented yesterday. Where the largest and most modern departments in the nation write books and host conferences about such "innovations," the nation is filled with small agencies who still carry that tradition as the essential core of their existence. It's befuddling sometimes to watch these folks plunk down days of time and fistfuls of dollars to listen in rapt fascination as folks like me explain how we've "discovered" what they've known and done for generations.
>
> When you look to the future, you should always see your roots. The fire service, though, seems to hold an oddly circumspect view of its own place in the evolution of the American community. As we become more aware of those "social service" roles and their implications, and as we respond more systematically to their execution, we'll be having to see them in more structured and organized ways. But beneath it will always lie the most fundamental values of our proudest traditions—that's who we are, that's what we do; that's how we've chosen to live.

The matters that emerge as most significant to firefighter resilience are, in the final analysis, functions of characteristics that can't be taught, can't be trained, and cannot be created after the fact by any sort of pop-psych rituals or routines. These features of resilience include such intangibles as optimism and determination, commonwealth and commitment. Like the Wizard of Oz, it seems, the capacity to deliver them to those who stand seeking the solace such traits bestow is frustrated until the Wizard gives up his act, steps out from behind the curtains and mirrors, and helps folks see that what they need and seek most, they've always held inside.

As it was for the travelers to the Emerald City, the things that matter most to those in crisis and those struck by calamity or catastrophe are, in the end, simple and clear: Those things are for most, as they were for the characters of that enduring tale, *heart*, *brains*, and *courage*...and some means to find your way home. We'll always do better, we suspect, to point quietly and persistently toward their realization than to wave and shout about obstacles, real or imagined, that may sometimes block the path.

A deputy chief in a respected urban fire service agency (L. P. Gilchrist, personal communication, 1998) replied to an essay regarding how CISD responders have sometimes seemed to miss the boundary between provider and client once considered sacrosanct to both psychologists and firefighters —the realization that professional responders are, at least in the vast majority of cases, assisting in resolving the crisis of another, not participating in some trauma all their own. His response began by quoting Robert Louis Stevenson:

> Give us grace and strength to preserve. Give us courage and gaiety and the quiet mind. Spare to us our friends and soften to us our enemies. Give us the strength to encounter that which is to come, that we may be brave in peril, constant in tribulation, temperate in wrath and in all changes of fortune, and down to the gates of death, loyal and loving to one another.

He concluded with an observation of his own that captured the essence of what healthy firefighters have been telling us for some time now, if only we will listen:

> Mitchell makes his fortune by telling the world that he can make me whole by CISD. I prefer to believe that I am made whole by my fellow firefighters, my family, my friends and my faith in God. I am where I want to be, trying to make a difference in a world that revolves knowing full well that fire, accidents, medical emergencies and death are also part of that revolution.

REFERENCES

Alexander, D. A., & Wells, A. (1991). Reactions of police officers to body handling after a major disaster: A before and after comparison. *British Journal of Psychiatry, 159*, 547–555.

Basic Behavioral Science Task Force. (1996). Basic behavioral science .research for mental health: Vulnerability and resistance. *American Psychologist, 51*, 22–28.

Beaton, R. D., & Murphy, S. A. (1993). Sources of occupational stress among firefighter/EMTs and firefighter/paramedics and correlations with job-related outcomes. *Prehospital and Disaster Medicine, 8,* 140–150

Bisson, J. I., & Deahl, M. P. (1994). Psychological debriefing and prevention of post-traumatic stress: More research is needed. *British Journal of Psychiatry, 165,* 717–720.

Bisson, I. J., Jenkins, P. L., Alexander, J., & Bannister, C. (1997). A randomised controlled trial of psychological debriefing for victims of acute harm. *British Journal of Psychiatry, 171,* 78–81.

Charlton, P. F. C., & Thompson, J. A. (1996). Ways of coping with psychological distress after trauma. *British Journal of Clinical Psychology, 35,* 517–530.

Cook, J. D., & Bickman, L. (1990). Social support and psychological symptomatology following a natural disaster. *Journal of Traumatic Stress, 3,* 541–556.

Corey, G. (1995). *Theory and practice of group counseling* (4th ed.). Pacific Grove, CA: Brooks/Cole.

Dawes, R. M. (1994). *House of cards: Psychology and psychotherapy built on myth.* New York: Free Press.

Dernocoeur, K. (1995). Are we getting the help we need? *Journal of Emergency Medical Services, 20*(8), 30–36.

Echterling, L., & Wylie, M. L. (1981). Crisis centers: A social movement perspective. *Journal of Community Psychology, 9,* 342–346.

Foa, E. B., & Meadows, E. A. (1997). Psychosocial treatments for posttraumatic stress disorder: A critical review. *Annual Review of Psychology, 48,* 935–938.

Foster, J. R. (1997). Successful coping, adaptation, and resilience in the elderly: An interpretation of epidemiologic data. *Psychiatric Quarterly, 68,* 189–219.

Fullerton, C. S., Wright, K. M., Ursano, R. J., & McCarroll, J. E. (1993). Social support for disaster workers after a mass-casualty disaster: Effects on the support provider. *Nordic Journal of Psychiatry, 47,* 315–324.

Garmezy, N. (1991). Resilience and vulnerability to adverse developmental outcomes associated with poverty. *American Behavioral Scientist, 34,* 416–430.

Garmezy, N. (1993). Children in poverty: Resilience despite risk. *Psychiatry: Interpersonal and Biological Processes, 56,* 127–136.

Gilbert, D. T., & Silvera, D. H. (1996). Overhelping. *Journal of Personality and Social Psychology, 70,* 678–690.

Gist, R. (1996a). Dr. Gist responds (Letter to the editor). *Fire Chief, 40*(11), 19–24.

Gist, R. (1996b). Is CISD built on a foundation of sand? *Fire Chief, 40*(8), 38–42.

Gist, R. (1997, August). *The answers may seem simple, but the questions never are.* Keynote address, 14th biennial symposium on Occupational Health and Safety, John P. Redmond Foundation/International Association of Fire Fighters, Toronto, ON, Canada.

Gist, R., Lohr, J. M., Kenardy, J. A., Bergmann, L., Meldrum, L., Redburn, B. G., Paton, D., Bisson, J. I., Woodall, S. J., & Rosen, G. M. (1997). Researchers speak on CISM. *Journal of Emergency Medical Services, 22*(5), 27–28.

Gist, R., Lubin, B., & Redburn, B. G. (1998). Psychosocial, ecological, and community perspectives on disaster response. *Journal of Personal & Interpersonal Loss, 3,* 25–51.

Gist, R., & Taylor, V. H. (1996). Line of duty deaths and their effects on coworkers and their families. *Police Chief, 63*(5), 34–37.

Gist, R., Taylor, V. H., Woodall, S. J., & Magenheimer, L. K. (1994, July). *Personal, organizational, and agency development: The psychological perspective.* Phoenix, AZ: St. Luke's Behavioral Health System/Phoenix Fire Department.

Gist, R., & Woodall, S. J. (1995). Occupational stress in contemporary fire service. *Occupational Medicine: State of the Art Reviews, 10,* 763–787.

Gist, R., & Woodall, S. J. (1998). Social science versus social movements: The origins and natural history of debriefing. *Austalasian Journal of Disaster and Trauma Studies, 1998–1* Online serial at www.massey.ac.nz/ ~ trauma.

Griffiths, J., & Watts, R. (1992). *The Kempsey and Grafton bus crashes: The aftermath.* East Linsmore, Australia: Instructional Design Solutions.

Grollmes, E. E. (1992). Postdisaster: Preserving and/or recovering the self. *Disaster Management, 4*(2), 150–156.

Gump, B. B., & Kulik, J. A. (1997). Stress, affiliation, and emotional contagion. *Journal of Personality and Social Psychology, 72,* 305–319.

Hansen, J. (1995, August 28). The Alfred P. Murrah Federal Building bombing. Presentation delivered at 13th biennial symposium on Occupational Health and Hazards of the Fire Service, John P. Redmond Foundation of the International Association of Fire Fighters, San Francisco, CA.

Hobbs, M., Mayou, R., Harrison, B., & Worlock, P. (1996). A randomised controlled trial of psychological debriefing for victims of road traffic accidents. *British Medical Journal, 313,* 1438–1439.

Hochschild, A. R. (1983). *The managed heart.* Berkeley: University of California.

Holaday, M., & McPhearson, R. W. (1997). Resilience and severe burns. *Journal of Counseling and Development, 75,* 346–356.

Hopper, L. (1988, November). Stress recovery: An interview with Jeffrey Mitchell, Ph.D. *PM (Public Management),* 5–8.

Howard, D. E. (1996). Searching for resilience among African-American youth exposed to community violence: Theoretical issues. *Journal of Adolescent Health, 18,* 254–262.

Hytten, K., & Hasle, A. (1989). Firefighters: A study of stress and coping. *Acta Psychiatrica Scandinavia, 355*(Suppl.), 50–55.

IAFF/IAFC. (International Association of Fire Fighters/International Association of Fire Chiefs) (1997). *Joint initiative on wellness and safety.* Washington, DC: Author.

International Critical Incident Stress Foundation. (1998). *Course brochure and outline.* Ellicott City, MD. XXX: Author.

Kaminer, W. (1992). *I'm dysfunctional, you're dysfunctional: The recovery movement and other self-help fashions.* Reading, MA: Addison-Wesley.

Kenardy, J. A., & Carr, V. (1996). Imbalance in the debriefing debate: What we don't know far outweighs what we do. *Bulletin of the Australian Psychological Society, 18*(2), 4–6.

Kenardy, J. A., Webster, R. A., Lewin, T. J., Carr, V. J., Hazell, P. L., & Carter, G. L. (1996). Stress debriefing and patterns of recovery following a natural disaster. *Journal of Traumatic Stress, 9,* 37–49.

Liem, J. H., James, J. B., O'Toole, J. G., & Boudewyn, A. C. (1997). Assessing resilience in adults with histories of childhood sexual abuse. *American Journal of Orthopsychiatry, 67,* 594–606.

Masten, A. S., Best, K. M., & Garmezy, N. (1991). Resilience and development: Contributions from the study of children who overcome adversity. *Development and Psychopathology, 2,* 425–444.

McCrae, R. R. (1984). Situational determinants of coping responses: Loss, threat, and challege, *Journal of Personality and Social Psychology, 46,* 919–928.

McFarlane, A. C. (1988). The longitudinal course of posttraumatic morbidity: The range of outcomes and their predictors. *Journal of Nervous and Mental Disease, 176,* 30–39.

McFarlane, A. C. (1989). The aetiology of post-traumatic morbidity: Predisposing, precipitating, and perpetuating factors. *British Journal of Psychiatry, 154,* 221–228.

Meichenbaum, D. (1994). *A clinical handbook/practical therapist manual for assessing and treating adults with posttraumatic stress disorder.* Waterloo, Ontario, Canada: Institute Press.

Mitchell, J. T. (1983). When disaster strikes ... the critical incident stress debriefing process. *Journal of Emergency Medical Services, 8*(1), 36–39.

Mitchell, J. T. (1988a). Development and functions of a critical incident stress debriefing team. *Journal of Emergency Medical Services, 13*(12), 42–46.

Mitchell, J. T. (1988b). The history, status, and future of critical incident stress debriefing. *Journal of Emergency Medical Services, 13*(11), 49–52.

Mitchell, J. T. (1992). Protecting your people from critical incident stress. *Fire Chief, 36*(5), 61–67.

Mitchell, J. T., & Bray, G. (1990). *Emergency servcies stress.* Englewood Cliffs, NJ: Brady.

Mitchell, J. T., & Everly, G. S. (1993). *Critical incident stress debriefing: An operations manual for the prevention of traumatic stress among emergency services and disaster workers.* Ellicott City, MD: Chevron Publishing.

Mitchell, J. T., & Everly, G. S., Jr. (1997). The scientific evidence for critical incident stress management. *Journal of Emergency Medical Services, 22*(1), 86–93.

Moran, C. C. (1998). Individual differences and debriefing effectiveness. *Austalasian Journal of Disaster and Trauma Studies, 1998-1.* Online serial located at http://www.massey.ac.nz/~ trauma.

Motowidlo, S. J., Packard, J. S., & Manning, M. R. (1986). Occupational stress: Its causes and consequences for job performance. *Journal of Applied Psychology, 71,* 618–629.

NFPA (National Fire Protection Association). (1997). *National fire codes.* Quincy, MA: Author.

Peele, S. (1989). *The diseasing of America: Addiction treatment out of control.* Lexington, MA: Lexington Books.

Raphael, B., Meldrum, L., & McFarlane, A. C. (1995). Does debriefing after psychological trauma work? Time for randomised controlled trials. *British Journal of Psychiatry, 310,* 1479–1480.

Rubonis, A. V., & Bickman, L. (1991). Psychological impairment in the wake of disaster: The disaster-psychopathology relationship. *Psychological Bulletin, 109,* 384–399.

Solomon, S. D., & Canino, G. J. (1990). Appropriateness of the DSM-III-R criteria for posttraumatic stress disorder. *Comprehensive Psychiatry, 31,* 227–237.

Stephens, C. (1997). Debriefing, social support, and PTSD in the New Zealand police: Testing a multidimensional model of organizational traumatic stress. *Australasian Journal of Disaster and Trauma Studies, 1.* Electronic journal accessible at http://www.massey.ac.nz/~ trauma/issues/1997-1/cvs.htm

Staudinger, U. M., & Flesson, W. (1996). Self and personality in old and very old age: A sample case of resilience? *Development and Psychopathology, 8,* 867–885.

Taylor, S. E. (1983). Adjusting to threatening events: A theory of cognitive adaptation. *American Psychologist, 38,* 1161–1173.

Taylor, S. E. (1991). Asymmetrical effects of positive and negative events: The mobilization-minimization hypothesis. *Psychological Bulletin, 110,* 67–85.

Taylor, S. E., & Brown, J. D. (1998). Illusion and well-being: A social psychological perspective on mental health. *Psychological Bulletin, 103,* 193–211.

Taylor, S. E., & Lobel, M. (1989). Social comparison activity under threat: Downward evaluation and upward contacts. *Psychological Review, 96,* 569–575.

Thompson, J., & Solomon, M. (1991). Body recovery teams at disasters: Trauma or challenge. *Anxiety Research, 4,* 235–244.

Tvedten, J. (1994). Critical incident stress debriefing: What is it and how can you use it? *Commish, 4*(2), 7–8.

Wagner, B. M., Compas, B. E., & Howell, D. C. (1988). Daily and major life events: A test of an integrative model of psychosocial stress. *American Journal of Community Psychology, 16,* 189–205.

Werner, E. E. (1994a). Overcoming the odds. *Journal of Developmental and Behavioral Pediatrics, 15,* 131–136.

Werner, E. E. (1994b). Risk, resilience, and recovery: Perspectives from the Kauai Longitudinal Study. *Development and Psychopathology, 5,* 503–515.

Werner, E. E. (1995). Resilience in development. *Current Directions in Psychological Science, 4,* 81–85.

Wolin, S., & Wolin, S. J. (1997). The challenge model: Working with strengths in children of substance abusing parents. *Child and Adolescent Psychiatric Clinics of North America, 5,* 243–256.

Woodall, S. J. (1994). *Personal, organizational, and agency development: The psychological dimension. A closer examination of critical incident stress management.* (National Fire Academy Executive Fire Officer program). Emmitsburg, MD: National Emergency Training Center, Learning Resource Center.

Woodall, S. J. (1996). *Hearts on fire: Ethnographic exploration of the emotional world of firefighters* (National Fire Academy Executive Fire Officer program). Emmitsburg, MD: National Emergency Training Center, Learning Resource Center.

Woodall, S. J. (1997). Hearts on fire: An exploration of the emotional world of firefighters. *Clinical Sociology Review, 15,* 153–162.

Wright, R. M. (1993, May). Any fool can face a crisis: A look at the daily issues that make an incident critical. In R. Gist (Moderator), *New information, new approaches, new ideas.* Overland Park, KS: Johnson County Community College, Center for Continuing Professional Education.

Part Three

Contemporary Issues in Community Systems Research and Practice

Klein (Klein & Rabkin, 1984) began a chapter treating specificity issues in psychotherapy outcome research with a delightful—and most pertinent—anecdote regarding his grandfather:

> My interest in the roots of psychotherapy may stem from an old family tradition, since my great-grandfather was a wonder-working rabbi known from Minsk to Pinsk. His son, also a well-known practitioner of faith healing from the Ukraine, emigrated to New York where, during my childhood, he lived with my parents. My mother told me that her father had been a faith healer, which piqued my curiosity, so I asked him for details.
>
> Our communication was marred by linguistic difficulties. Finally, in an attempt to gain clarity, I asked him to tell me about a case. In later life, this approach has been generally useful in trying to bring clarity to issues of therapeutic theory or technique. We are, of course, presenting a reconstruction with narrative rather than historical truth.
>
> Becky was told she was going to marry Shloime, the lout. She started to cry, but my grandfather pointed out that they all cried. She cried for two

weeks, but this was expectable, even laudable behavior. She then cried for another two weeks, and this was considered excessive and somewhat self-indulgent. After six weeks of her loudly symptomatic malfunctioning, her distressed parents came to my grandfather for professional help.

"Bring me her handkerchief," said the rabbinical authority. "So they brought me her handkerchief and I said the right prayers over it and told them to place it under her pillow. In the morning, she woke up bright-eyed and cheerful and went forward with her marriage, which was no worse than most marriages."

"But," I inquired, "did she know that you had done this?"

"Of course," he said. "It doesn't work otherwise."

However, even at an early age, I was already pursuing the question of specificity.

"Zayda, did you have to say the right prayers?"

"That's what made her better."

"But let's say that you had not said the right prayers, but she thought you said the right prayers. What would happen then?"

"But you have to say the right prayers," he reiterated. However, for the next several weeks he was seen muttering to himself, "You have to say the right prayers," and viewed me with some diminished affection (pp. 306–307).

Nowhere, perhaps, has this become more evident than in the burgeoning trauma intervention industry. When we first began our work in this arena, shortages of qualified providers for psychologically related services were accepted as an inherent limitation of the service delivery system, and a variety of peer and paraprofessional forays into suicide prevention, crisis intervention, self-help for addictions, and the like were just cresting as social movements in a society ever more immersed in escalating technological influences. Psychology's unified professional and academic voice had begun to crack as if a visible indicator of the field's entry into adolescence —a prodromal sign, perhaps, of its impending split, in literal as well as metaphorical terms, into academic and applied camps. Enrollments in graduate programs pursuing the basic research components of scientific psychology began to dwindle as enrollment in clinical and counseling programs spilled out of the universities and into proprietary trade schools, free-standing professional training centers, and other "nontraditional" programs and settings. It was, some might say, both the twilight ebb of social and scientific modernism and the dawning of psychology's postmodern era.

Fifteen years later, counselors, therapists, and paraprofessionals of every description now seem to converge at the site of any catastrophe. Definitions of "secondary victimization" have become so expansive that telephone hotline programs have been implemented under the sponsorship of ordinarily responsible and conservative professional organizations to provide counseling intervention for any children who may have been "traumatized" simply by hearing of distant events. The World Wide Web is dotted with sites of self-anointed experts in "disaster mental health," and insular Internet mailing lists provide forums where practitioners of unproven "power therapies" regale one another with unbridled anecdote while critical academic voices have been shouted down or even expelled.

Perhaps the greatest concern, however, is to be found not so much in these swarms of would-be helpers or their sometimes ardent efforts to market and promote their ministrations, but rather in the suppositions so many of these nouveau providers seem to bear, often unwittingly, about the nature of these events and their impacts, and about the vectors and the venues they rush to construct in the full and fervent belief that these will be essential to resolution and recovery. Despite accumulating evidence that reactions are far from simple, that current models are far from robust, and even that outcomes from some currently ubiquitous approaches to intervention are neutral at best and iatrogenic for some, it has become disturbingly apparent that no amount of rigorous empirical analysis seems to dissuade a number of those who have vested their identities and their incomes in popularized interventions. In a thin, thin layer beneath even this, however, lies what is perhaps the most salient concern of all: a growing assertion that presumption, anecdote, personal belief, and other elements of subjective experience and judgment are somehow owed the same credence once earned only through the rigorous and skeptical testing of empirical hypotheses.

Despite the gravity of these concerns, we remain committed to the beliefs that first led us into these efforts. The community psychologist, we believe, holds a unique capacity to balance the rigor of science with the wisdom of ageless compassion, and to assist communities in the quiet, understated, and invisible ways that have characterized our enterprise as they attempt to rebuild, restore, and regain resilience in the wake of challenge and loss. As we reach toward the heavens, though, we must first replenish our roots.

The final section of this treatise completes our cycle of inquiry by returning our critical scrutiny to what we believe we have learned and, more importantly, to the questions that confront us still. O'Neill (chapter 10) offers first a thoughtfully illustrated elucidation of the ethical dilemmas that confront the community practitioner, which he attempts to reconcile with the codified principles of our discipline and profession. Gist, Woodall, and Magenheimer (chapter 11) then proceed to consider the "alphabet interventions" as social psychological phenomena, and to reflect on their implications for the scientist–practitioner ethos of the field. Lohr, Montgomery, Lilienfeld, and Tolin (chapter 12) next take as specific exemplars two of the popularized "power therapies" to demonstrate the influence of pseudoscience in the contemporary trauma industry. Echterling and Wylie (chapter 13) finish the section by revisiting issues of social construction in disaster and disaster response to suggest how practical, conservative approaches to assistance can be tailored at the intersections of sound research and solid practice.

REFERENCE

Klein, D. F., & Rabkin, J. G. (1984). Specificity and strategy in psychotherapy research and practice. In J. B. W. Williams & R. L. Spencer (Eds.), *Psychotherapy research: Where are we and where should we go?* (pp. 306–331). New York: Guilford Press.

Chapter 10

Ethical Issues in Working with Communities in Crisis

Patrick O'Neill

This chapter will be organized around four key ethical concepts that pose special problems in community work and are even more difficult to negotiate when a community is in crisis. Emergencies demand rapid response from human service professionals. The pressure to act may undercut important ethical values. The four concepts selected for discussion include informed consent, cost-benefit analysis, competence, and divided loyalties.

It is often noted by community psychologists that traditional views in psychology have concentrated on the individual rather than the group (e.g., Sarason, 1988). Behavior tends to be explained in terms of individual sorts of variables, whether they be a person's unconscious, biology, reinforcement history, or decision-making biases. As Gist and Lubin (1989b) put it, the organism has been seen primarily as a reactive element within its environment, its behavior composed of determined responses to events and experiences (p. 2). The community approach, in contrast, brings the context into focus and works at the group level.

I would like to thank two people who shared their experiences with me for use in this chapter: John Service, who was a leader of the Aberdeen team that responded to the explosion at the Westray coal mine, and Joan Hanley who was working for social services in the Yellowknife at the time of the Giant gold mine bombing. Joan also did research for this chapter on the ongoing calamity of the Innu people of Davis Inlet.

Working with whole communities, and working at times of tension or crisis, poses problems for the usual approaches to ethics. In the area of informed consent, how can adequate information be provided or consent obtained from those affected by our interventions—many of whom are unknown to us? Working with a community in crisis, do we have the time to collect the data needed to carry out an adequate cost-benefit analysis before acting? The requirement that psychologists work only within our realm of competence may be turned upside down in a disaster, when everyone is pressed to do whatever needs to be done. Finally, ethical guidelines about objectivity may not prove helpful in communities with cross-cutting loyalties and antagonisms where the service provider may be allied or seen to be allied with one group or another.

Each of the following four sections begins by reviewing the general ethical requirements that apply to psychologists (and whose general provisions are usually found in the codes of ethics of other service providers) concerning each topic, and then turns to discuss the ways in which trying to follow ethical injunctions, at least as they are usually framed in our codes, becomes complicated in community work, and in particular, in times of crisis.

INFORMED CONSENT

Our codes of ethics tell us to obtain informed consent for services we provide to our clients. The recent code adopted by the American Psychological Association states that, in general, "When psychologists provide assessment, evaluation, treatment, counseling, supervision, teaching, consultation, research, or other psychological services to an individual, a group, or an organization, they provide, using language that is reasonably understandable to the recipient of those services, appropriate information beforehand about the nature of such services and appropriate information later about results and conclusions (American Psychological Association [APA], 1992, Principle I.07). The Code does not deal with community interventions per se, and is generally silent on consultation activities. With regard to treatment interventions, the APA Code says in Principle 4.02(a) that "informed consent generally implies that the person (1) has the capacity to consent, (2) has been informed of significant information concerning the procedure, (3) has freely and without undue influence expressed consent, and (4) consent has been appropriately documented" (APA, 1992).

Other general notions about informed consent include the desirability of seeking as full and as active participation as possible from others in decisions that affect them, and further that the psychologist ought to respect and integrate as much as possible the opinions and wishes of people affected by interventions. The Canadian Psychological Association

[CPA], in its 1991 Code, takes into account emergency situations—something about which the APA Code is largely silent. According to CPA (1991, standard I.13), an exception to normal rules of obtaining informed consent can be made in circumstances of urgent need (e.g., suicidal gesture). In such circumstances, say the codemakers, fully informed consent would be obtained as soon as possible. Thus, although there is reference to emergencies, the focus is still at the individual level. The example of a suicidal gesture is one that lends itself to getting informed consent "as soon as possible." The problems may be much more complicated when the service provider is dealing with a community disaster rather than an individual's suicidal gesture.

Many other ethical standards are clearly designed for work with individuals, families, or at the largest, discrete organizations. For example, psychologists are expected to establish and use signed consent forms that specify the dimensions of informed consent, to achieve informed consent by a collaborative process, and to provide during the consent process as much information as a reasonable or prudent person (or family or group) would want to know before making a decision or consenting to an activity. The Canadian code includes "community" in its list of possible service recipients who should receive this information before consenting—but the number of situations in which such a consent procedure would be possible in the community context are limited and do not encompass disasters. Codes sometimes require that the service providers indicate to clients the alternative courses of action that might be followed and likely consequences of non-action. Sometimes they demand that the client have a clear option to withdraw at any time, and that the client expressly agree to the time period over which consent applies. Clients are also supposed to be told how to rescind consent. It is easy to imagine examples of community work, and in particular work with communities in crisis, in which many of these requirements would paralyze the service provider.

Authors of influential texts on ethical behavior in psychology also keep their focus at the level of psychotherapy, ignoring community practice. Carroll, Schneider, and Wesley (1985) recommended that during the informed consent process, "The person's environment must be such that he or she can calmly reflect on what is being explained so that a rational decision can be made as to whether to consent" (p. 29). Keith-Spiegel and Koocher (1985) recommended that clients be warned about foreseeable, though indirect, effects of interventions. This is clearly relevant to community practice, where there are often such indirect effects. Even in the realm of therapy, though, Keith-Spiegel and Koocher recognized that there are problems with including indirect effects within the parameters of consent: "Obviously no psychotherapist can anticipate every potential indirect effect of therapy" (p. 122). This becomes much more difficult in settings where there are potential indirect effects to unknown persons who, although they may be recipients of service, could hardly have given consent.

Before and after Nuremberg

Before turning to the problem of informed consent in community work, it may be worthwhile to consider the sorts of abuses that informed consent procedures were designed to correct. The impetus for contemporary concerns about informed consent may be traced to the Nuremberg war crimes tribunal and the subsequent Nuremburg Code (1964/1945). One focus of the tribunal was the issue of medical experimentation without consent and under coercion, with concentration camps as an horrendous example. The Nuremberg Code set forth the following rules for medical treatment and experimentation: The voluntary consent of the human subject is absolutely essential. The person involved should be so situated as to be able to exercise free power of choice, and should have sufficient knowledge and comprehension of the elements of the subject matter involved as to enable him to make an understanding and enlightened decision. In the spirit of the Nuremberg Code, professional bodies representing various human services—not just medicine—have adopted rules that require free and informed consent.

The Nuremberg Code, and the concerns it expressed, was a sea change in thinking about professional–client relationships in the helping professions. From the time of Hippocrates an "ethic of care" had been the overriding principle in professional ethics. In the Hippocratic oath, there is no mention of informed consent, or for that matter of *any* consent after the choice to engage the doctor in the first place. Physicians were told to do their best for their clients, and to keep all confidences as secrets. In Hippocrates's other writings, it is clear that physicians are to present themselves with such authority that they are not questioned; they are told, in Hippocrates's (1923) *Decorum*, to perform their tasks calmly and adroitly, *concealing most things from the patient* while attending to him. They were told to turn the patient's attention away from what was being done to him. Sometimes, these early physicians were told, it would be necessary to reprove the patient sharply and emphatically, and sometimes comfort with solicitude and attention, but all the while revealing *nothing of the patient's future or present*. In his *Precepts*, Hippocrates (1923) warned that some patients may ask for treatments other than those the physician is prepared to administer. He told physicians that such requests deserve to be disregarded, and "you must readily oppose them" (Hippocrates, trans. 1923, p. 299).

Two thousand years later, the situation was little changed. In its first code of ethics, in 1846, the American Medical Association (AMA) spent as much time on the obligations of *"Patients to their Physicians"* as the reverse. The AMA told patients their obedience to doctors should be prompt and implicit. He (the patient) "should never permit his own crude opinions" as to the appropriateness of the doctor's prescriptions to "influence his attention to them." The AMA wasn't keen on second opinions. "A patient should never send for a consulting physician without the express consent of his own medical attendant. He should never converse [with other physicians] on the subject of his disease, as an observation may be made...which may destroy his confidence" in his own physician.

Socially, we are supposed to have evolved from an ideology of extreme professional paternalism, where treatment depended on a professional's assessment of what was "good" for the patient, to a concern with the patient's autonomy and dignity, expressed in part by the right to make an informed choice. As Carroll, Schneider, and Wesley (1985) stated, "A psychologist may have good reason to believe that a certain [intervention] will be beneficial to a client who might, if informed, reject it...But to withhold the information is to show disrespect for the client as it denies the person's autonomy and the individual's right to decide what happens to him or her (p. 30).

This topic has produced an array of papers on the moral arguments for informed consent (Nuremburg Code 1964/1945), legal requirements (Rozovsky & Rozovsky, 1990), ethical standards (Sinclair, Poizner, Gilmour-Barrett, & Randall, 1986), inadequacies of some present consent procedures (Handelsman, Kemper, Kesson-Craig, McLain, & Johnsrud, 1986), and means of obtaining consent (Everstine et al., 1980). Despite this attention to informed consent, there remains a certain narrowness of focus: In the spirit of the Nuremburg Code, most work has been done on whether patients are being coerced, whether they are told clearly what treatment is being proposed for them, whether they understand the explanation, and whether they agree to the intervention. There has been, for example, excellent research on whether people understand what they read on consent forms (Ogloff & Otto, 1990) and whether various populations have the decision-making capacity required to make an informed choice (Tymchuk, Outlander, & Rader, 1986).

In court, professionals charged with violating informed consent and other ethical rules could traditionally defend themselves by showing that their behavior conformed to the standards of the profession. However, a major legal shift occurred in a 1972 case, *Canterbury v. Spence* (Murphy, 1976), a shift that has legal implications for all professionals who intervene in the lives of others and ought to have their consent to do so. In *Canterbury*, the physician was liable even when he could show that he conformed to the usual standards for obtaining informed consent. Although all cases have limited application outside their own jurisdiction, it should be noted that this American judgment was specifically endorsed by the Canadian Supreme Court in 1980.

What does the "reasonable person" want to know?

The difference before and after this landmark case concerns the ability of professionals to defend their informed-consent practice by referring to the ways in which other professionals behave. Prior to *Canterbury*, the reasonable person standard referred to the professional, but afterward it shifted to refer to the person whose life is affected by the intervention. Previously, the professional was expected to provide the sort of information, and to get the sort of consent, consistent with the manner and form of other "reasonable" professionals. But in *Canterbury* the court said that the professional was responsible for disclosing any information that could be material to someone's decision to refuse or consent to the intervention. Material information is that which a reasonable person would want to have in deciding whether to be subject to an intervention. Further, the professional was not only expected to give information about the proposed intervention, but also about alternatives.

Consider the case of the health professional working in a community where it is impractical to give full information and to get specific consent from each person affected by the proposed intervention. If the "reasonable person" refers to the professional, as it did before *Canterbury*, the professional could say to himself or herself, and to others, that the procedure was justified because it was the sort of thing that similar professionals tend to do in similar situations. But *Canterbury* removes this way of justifying one's actions. Instead, the question becomes: What would reasonable citizens who might be affected by the intervention want to know or need to know to decide whether they want to participate?

In community work it may be unclear who the client is, or how many people will be affected by an intervention. How, then, is one to know what reasonable people in those circumstances might want to know to agree to some intervention? Even if one did know, the scale of the intervention and the circumstances (for instance, a community disaster) might make the informed consent process virtually impossible.

Negotiation toward some sort of consent, if it is undertaken, is usually sought with the presumed leaders of a group or community. There may be no practical way to ensure that members of the group want the services the professional plans to provide. Even if such broad-based consent procedures were possible, engaging in them might be considered an affront to the authority of leaders sensitive to any challenge. Such is the situation, for example, in the increasing number of armed standoffs between native people and White authorities from Mexico to Canada. In crises, time pressure works against any thought of providing information or obtaining meaningful consent from all those who might be affected by an intervention. And, of course, crises disrupt the usual lines of communication by which such consent might be obtained.

Despite all these difficulties in obtaining informed consent in the context of a community in crisis, it is still the case that people ought to have as much say as possible about the services that will be provided for them. Inevitably, in community work, that will mean that we will deal with representatives—community leaders, group spokespersons—of the people most likely to be affected by the intervention. Our problem may then become, "To what extent do the representatives actually represent?" Formal authority is no guarantee that someone such as a major or police chief embodies the interests of community members. In less formal groups, such as a group of masked natives patrolling a makeshift barracade, the person who talks the loudest may be accorded an inappropriate degree of legitimacy.

An aspect of the consent procedure that might well be useful in community situations is the requirement that the service provider clarify the nature of multiple relationships while obtaining consent. Previously I (O'Neill, 1989) have provided examples in which part of the problem might be traced to uncertainty (on the part of the service provider as well as the "clients") about where the provider's primary loyalty lay. In any situation, including the most extreme crises, recipients of service could expect to know who the helper represents, and to whom the helper owes primary allegience.

It is unlikely during emergencies that people who need help will have the luxury of calling on the services of someone who is their advocate alone. More likely, they will find themselves offered help by some person or group acting at the request of some third party. People have every reason to be suspicious of helpers they may not know and did not specifically request. Riger (1989) pointed to the political nature of communities, and stated that "Psychologists become players in a political game when they intervene in community settings, whether they want to or not" (p. 380). It would be naive to think that this political dimension disappears when disaster strikes. It should become apparent from two examples to be offered later in this chapter, the mine explosions at Westray in Nova Scotia and the Giant gold mine in the NorthWest Territories, that crises can make community life much more political.

The next section considers an element of the informed consent process: Does the client know the risks? This usually calls for the professional to engage in, and to permit the client to participate in, some weighing of potential benefits against possible costs.

RISK-BENEFIT ANALYSIS

One of the oldest formal injunctions in the helping professions is Hippocrate's command: "Do no harm." It is clear from his writings that Hippocrates (1923) had in mind intentional wrongdoing by physicians, whose medicinal skills could easily be corrupted into the poisoner's arts: "I will use my treatment to heal the sick according to my ability and judgment but never with a view to injury and wrong-doing" (p. 164). Our modern code-makers take a more benign but much broader view of the matter, and set forth standards requiring the presumably well-intentioned service provider to weigh the potential benefits against the risks when considering an intervention.

Principle E of the American Psychological Association *Code* (1992), for example, requires that "In their professional actions, psychologists weigh the welfare and rights of their patients or clients...and other affected persons...When conflicts occur among psychologists' obligations or concerns, they attempt to resolve these conflicts and to perform their roles in a responsible fashion that avoids or minimizes harm." It is the "other affected persons" who pose a challenge for community practice, where interventions are intended to affect many people, some unknown to the service provider. In reference to therapeutic interventions, APA tells psychologists to take reasonable steps to minimize harm where it is foreseeable and avoidable.

Other codes make at least passing reference to the community. For example, the CPA (1991) asked psychologists to demonstrate an active concern for the welfare of any individual, family, group, or community with whom they relate in their role as psychologists. This concern includes both those directly involved and those indirectly involved in their activities. Although this code refers to the community and persons indirectly af- fected, it specifies that the psychologist's responsibility is greater to those directly involved than to those indirectly involved such as the general public. This distinction between the directly and the indirectly involved is blurred in community work; in crises, the general public may be the intended target of an intervention. Psychologists are generally expected to take responsibility for the consequences of their actions, correcting any harmful effects that have occurred as a result of their activities. Again, this emminently reasonable ethical notion may be hard to apply in work with communities in crises, where it is hard for the service provider to find out (if he or she has the time to find out) what effects—good or bad—their work had on anyone.

The problem goes beyond assessing and correcting unintended harm- ful consequences of our actions. Psychologists need also be mindful that we ought to take great care about putting people and groups at risk, whether or not harm actually occurs. A distinction needs to be made between harm and risk. The psychologist is not asked to engage in a *cost*-benefit analysis, but a *risk*-benefit analysis. Often we cannot tell the nature and extent of risks that our interventions may entail. Carroll et al. (1985) pointed out that psychologists are often uncertain about what constitutes risk: In psychology (unlike medicine) the risks are not usually life-threatening, but they are more difficult to measure and document.

Philosopher Judith Jarvis Thomson (1986) made some cogent points about risk, as opposed to actual harm. She pointed out that sometimes a person would choose a relatively minor harm over a major risk. Robbery victims, for instance, frequently take the harm of losing their pocket money and credit cards over the risk of being maimed or killed. Thomson pointed out that people's rights are infringed upon when they are subjected to unnecessary risks, even though no harm occurs. Her example is that of a person who decides to play Russian roulette with you, but knows that you will not agree. So he sneaks into your house at night and puts a gun to your head as you sleep, and pulls the trigger. As it happens, the firing pin falls on an empty chamber and the intruder departs. You do not know that you have been put at great risk, and no harm has occurred. But no one would consider such an act to be morally right (or neutral), nor assert that your rights had not been infringed.

Thomson's analysis may well apply to community interventions, in which people may be put at risk without their knowledge. The well-intentioned service system with power to act decisively—power enhanced by crisis situation—may well play the equivalent of Russian roulette with whole populations of people. The fact that no harm is done does not, in Thomson's view, absolve them from responsibility for putting people at risk —and risk carries legal as well as moral implications.

Risk-benefit analysis is difficult in community work where interventions have (and are intended to have) ripple effects, typically with unknown impact on unknown persons. The problem is even more severe in emergency situations where there is little time for reflection. And, as Carroll et al. (1985) pointed out, the less visible nature of psychological consequences makes benefit, harm, and risk all the more difficult to discern.

Problem definition and the barren land people

So far, risk and harm have been discussed as though consequences of the normal sorts of interventions that psychologists and others in the human services generally provide to people and groups. Problem definition—how the community problem is defined in the first place—has not been directly discussed. The way we think about problems, however, opens and closes possibilities for solving them (O'Neill, 1981; O'Neill & Trickett, 1982), and the solution is ordinarily nascent in the problem definition.

The way we think about a problem can also lead us to interventions that do no good, do more harm than good, or put people at risk. In the following example, the problem definition led to a well-intentioned intervention that, at best, did not solve the fundamental community crisis. Worse, by promising more than it could deliver, the intervention turned attention away from what really needed fixing.

In 1967, the province of Newfoundland in Canada moved 500 members of a native band called the Innu ("barren land people") to Davis Inlet in northern Laborador. The people had been nomadic caribou hunters, whose way of life was seriously undermined when the Hudson's Bay Company established a fur trade throughout the traditional territory of the Innu. The plight of the Innu on their remote island location has occasionally come to the attention of the public. In the winter of 1992, for example, five children died in a house fire when they were left alone, the fire was triggered by a hotplate that was used to heat the small house. The parents were sent to a native alcohol and drug treatment center in Alberta, after which they faced abandonment charges. The country learned, in the ensuing press coverage, that alcohol problems were endemic in the community, and that there had been many attempts—some completed—at suicide. After a time, however, the press turned to other matters.

Public attention turned to Davis Inlet again in January of 1993, when a rescue party discovered that six children had attempted suicide in an unheated shack. The six, aged 10 to 16, were nearly comatose when they were found; all were solvent abusers. By chance, one of the rescue party carried a video camera, and the children were filmed as they were revived. They shouted obscenities and made it clear that they wanted neither to leave nor to live. The videotape was played and replayed on national television, and it was so striking that the story was picked up internationally.

What was the problem, and how was it to be treated? Within weeks of the rescue, the Canadian government had arranged to fly the 14 children —the initial 6 and 8 other solvent abusers, along with their parents and interpreters (60 people in all)—to Poundmaker's Lodge in Alberta, the same native-run addiction center to which the parents of the children who died in the earlier house fire had been sent for their alcohol addiction. The children had been identified as chronic gasoline sniffers. They were to undergo a 90-day holistic program in a lodge thousands of miles and five provinces away from their own remote community. Their parents, many of them alcoholics, were also scheduled for treatment. The problem had been identified as one of addiction, and within that problem definition lay the seeds of a particular intervention: treatment for the victims.

In a culturally correct twist, the treatment was to be rooted in native rituals and traditions. Not much analysis was made of the fact that native rituals and traditions are not the same everywhere or for all native peoples. Poundmaker's Lodge incorporates the use of native ceremonies common to people of the central plains, such as the burning of sweet grass to symbolize kindness and native prayer and values. It was unclear how these are related to the Innu, whose legends and rituals had always been centered on the caribou herds on which they had depended for survival for centuries. Tanner (1995), describing these people, said that every part of the caribou was used; the skin was decorated with painted or quill designs to make clothing of many kinds. A caribou shoulder-blade, burned in a prehunt ritual, was believed to foretell the location of game. This belief in animal spirits played a major role in the hunt. Status was gained mainly through the ability to make gifts of meat to others. After the hunt a ceremonial feast of bone fat, makushan, was held. There was no obvious equivalent to any of this in the ceremonies of the Plains tribes used at Poundmaker's Lodge.

The Innu themselves had some doubts about a treatment based on mismatched traditions of distant peoples. They asked for a treatment center closer to home but, for the moment at least, their request was ignored. The Innu were reminded that Poundmaker's Lodge did not rely entirely on native ceremony. There was counseling, too, of the sort common in substance abuse centers in any community. But the Innu pointed out that they did not speak the same language as the counselors at Poundmaker's Lodge, and it was difficult to do serious counseling with interpreters. The 90-day program turned into a 6-month stay at Poundmaker's. The problem, it seemed, was even more difficult than anticipated.

But what *was* the problem? It had been defined as one of substance abuse by a small fraction of the community of 500. That was the aspect of the problem, after all, that produced such graphic images on television and that prompted a public outcry for some solution. This was considered to be the solution for that problem. However, as necessary as it was to do emergency intervention with the young solvent sniffers, there was certainly another way to conceive of the problem of Davis Inlet.

The Innu people were lured to the remote site in 1967 with promises of water and sewer services—promises that were never kept. One main purpose in removing them to a distant island was to stop them from complaining about low-level flights by US aircraft. Canada played host to these exercises as part of its commitment to NATO. The Innu complained that the flights disrupted the pattern of caribou migration. The bureaucratic solution was to remove the Innu as far as possible from the flights—and, incidentally, from the caribou.

A reporter for Canada's national newspaper, the *Globe & Mail*, described the community at the time of the rescue of the children: "Houses are not insulated; they are falling apart. There are no roads, running water or sewage system. Human waste is thrown outside. Dogs eat it. Children play in it. Clothes are thin and ragged; there are sores and scars on children's faces. An alcohol counselor estimates that half of the 500 people are contemplating suicide at any given time" (*Globe & Mail*, Jan. 29, 1993).

For years, the Innu have wanted to move back to the mainland where the expanding population would have room to grow, and where they would feel less isolated. They also want to be able to press land claims to great stretches of Labrador. Land claims settlements are solving problems of many other native groups in Canada. But the Innu have been left out; jurisdiction over them has been divided between the federal Canadian government and the province of Newfoundland since the early 1950s. Without knowing who has clear jurisdiction, the Innu have been unable to advance or negotiate land claims.

But these fundamental community problems were not addressed. Instead, in a continuation of the solvent-abuse intervention, Davis Inlet was getting a different sort of preparation for the returning children and their parents. According to the *Globe & Mail* (Aug. 30, 1993), members of the Davis Inlet community were planning regular sweat lodges where "the Innu children will be able to ponder spiritual matters and confer with elders" (p. 2). Could even limited and individual-focused intervention work in the absence of more substantial changes in the community? Those in charge put on a brave face. The *Globe and Mail* (Aug. 30, 1993) reported, "Six months after they were plucked out of the horror of Davis Inlet, where life had become so devoid of hope... the youth return tomorrow to try a fresh start. Many of the children are afraid to go back to Davis Inlet —terrified of the violence, sexual abuse, and emptiness. A counselor said 'Fear is healthy' " (p. 2).

Healthy or not, the children's fears were matched by those who conceived of this as the appropriate intervention. They were reluctant to drop the children back down into a community of unheated houses, rampant sexual abuse, hunger, and hopelessness. Re-entry was delayed. The children were sent first to a wilderness camp in Labrador, because, according to the *Globe & Mail*, counselors did not wish to immerse the children directly into the world they spent 6 months escaping. But the wilderness camp only delayed return to the pathogenic environment. Not long after their return to Davis Inlet, there were more videos of children—some of the same children—under the influence of solvents and threatening to kill themselves.

The example of the Innu of Davis Inlet moves our attention from the risk or harm of some individual psychological intervention, and moves it to the question of whether an intervention strategy can, itself, be so misguided as to be harmful. Sarason (1972), discussing interventions gone wrong, pointed to the way we think about issues as a common problem: "The problems... stem in large measure from the way we thought and the knowledge we did not use; it was not what was in our hearts but was missing in our heads" (pp. 12–13). In the case of the Innu of Davis Inlet, should this community problem have been understood as one of solvent abuse requiring individual counseling, or should it have been seen as a political matter requiring a political solution?

Bolman and Deal (1984) warned against ignoring the political framework when one is attempting to understand the problems of an organization—and, by extension, a community. In this framework, communities can be seen as "alive and screaming political arenas that house a complex variety of individuals and interest groups." (p. 109). Shifting coalitions compete for scarce resources, jockeying for positions and power. Looking at Davis Inlet in that way, the problems of the community take precedence over the problems of a few individuals. The telegenic solvent-abuse problem is like the identified patient in family therapy—thrust into the glare of publicity but essentially providing a protective cover for the festering problems that are less easy to talk about and to resolve. In this case, of course, it is not the Innu people who find the problems hard to talk about, but the political forces who have isolated them, all but abandoned them, and have put them in a jurisdictional puzzle box where they cannot press their legitimate claims.

In his influential work, *Exit, Voice, and Loyalty*, Hirschman (1970) noted that, in the marketplace, groups often have alternatives between exit and voice—between switching to another company, say, or complaining to the management. In the realm of politics there may be nowhere to go, and the only option is to gain voice and make one's demands heard. But choices can be made by the media about which demands are heard, and by the array of human services about which aspects of the problem are selected for treatment. That those choices are infused with politics makes them no less a matter of ethical concern and judgment.

COMPETENCE

Human service professionals have an array of competencies; they are supposed to know what they can and cannot do, and make appropriate referrals when cases reach beyond the limits of their knowledge and training. Sometimes the ideals of our Codes of Ethics seem to be based on a metropolitan community in which referral possibilities are plentiful. They may be harder to follow in rural areas, or when disaster strikes and the environment presses everyone to do what he or she can—trained or not.

Principle A of the American Psychological Association Code of Ethics (1992) requires that psychologists "provide only those services and use only those techniques for which they are qualified by education, training or experience." Referring to the boundaries of competence in Principle 1:04(a), the Code again tells psychologists to "provide service only within the boundaries of their competence." The CPA (1991) notes that psychologists need to know what their competencies *are* before they can practice within them, and stated that the psychologist considers incompetent action to be unethical per se.

Writers on professional ethics disagree about the priority they give "competence" in any hierarchy of ethical values. Carroll et al. (1985)

considered competence a fundamental duty "since being competent not only implies having professional expertise ... but also knowing what one *cannot* do. The absolute nature of competence makes it unique ... in no case would reason suggest that incompetence is acceptable." (p. 28). There is a difference, of course, between doing something incompetently and doing an adequate job of something for which you have little, if any, formal training; for example, cabbies deliver babies on the way to the hospital.

Keith-Spiegel and Koocher (1985) noted that "It has also been difficult to obtain a consensus on a definition of competence. In fact, competence is often difficult to prove" (p. 224). They cite a study in which faculty members and field supervisors evaluated more than 100 clinical doctoral students. The evaluators said the main quality of the outstanding students was "high intelligence," whereas the main problem with incompetent students was "lack of knowledge." They used this research finding to make the point that there is a broad range of competence. "By definition, not everyone can be above average. It is certainly desirable to be exceptionally competent, but it is not unethical to practice in an area in which one's competence is simply 'adequate,' assuming we know what adequate means" (p. 227).

Part of the problem in defining adequacy comes from the fact that, in the human services, different professions teach different ways of doing things. Then, as they learn from their work, the nature of any professional's particular set of experiences (psychiatry, for instance, vs. social work) further shapes their approach to problems. Even within one profession, such as psychology, the various specialties and subspecialties involve different modes of intervention. In fact, as Keith-Spiegel and Koocher (1985) pointed out, "Part of the difficulty involves controversy about what constitutes a specialty, subspecialty, or particular area of expertise in the practice of psychology" (pp. 224–225). In some relatively new areas, such as community psychology, we do not know what constitutes the basic qualifications needed to practice. And yet, as Keith-Spiegel and Koocher pointed out, "In virtually all cases, individual psychologists are expected to know and practice within their own areas of competence" (pp. 224–225).

Blurred roles in community practice

The whole notion that helping is the domain of the trained professional goes against the grain for most community psychologists. Settings are developed in which people play multiple roles according to their actual abilities rather than as dictated by their formal training. This model is well suited to rural communities where, as a practical matter, there is a paucity of referral options. It is also well suited to the community in crisis, where there is great pressure on people, whatever their credentials, to do whatever seems to need doing.

The blurring of formal roles in community psychology is not merely a matter of unfortunate necessity, but rather an active ideal that has been pursued vigorously from community psychology's inception. Seymour Sarason and his colleagues and students founded the Yale Psychoeducational Clinical in the mid-1960s, before "community psychology" was recognized as a division in the APA. From the outset, Sarason (1988) recalled, there was a deliberate de-emphasizing of professional credentials: "The clinic would have a variety of people, some with and some without academic credentials. They would be chosen according to their interests and skills. Up to an undetermined point, everyone would be doing what everyone else did, the opposite of what is termed 'differential staffing.' There were several people without academic credentials I knew could be valuable assets in whatever we did, and I would seek to get them" (p. 359).

This notion of everyone doing what everyone else did (at least, "up to an undetermined point") was emulated by Sarason's colleagues when they helped create their own settings. Goldenberg (1971), for example, in discussing the staffing of a Residential Youth Center that was also created in the 1960s, said that "the nature of one's formal background or training was relatively unimportant for the complex kinds of human services we wanted to provide. In order to undertake the venture at all, one had to assume that people could learn, could change, and could function in ways heretofore unexpected. Staffing [the RYC had] more to do with getting certain kinds of *people* than with getting certain kinds of *credentials*." (p. 135).

Note that Goldenberg (1971) equated de-emphasizing of formal training with increasing flexibility and ability to learn and change. This notion that one's professional training and credentials can inhibit such flexibility and learning has been a common theme in community psychology. For one thing, professional identity can cut one off from the insights that others outside the usual service delivery system may have to offer. As Gist and Lubin (1989a) put it, "mental health professionals have at least as many important lessons to learn from hairdressers, bartenders, and police officers as they might learn from the professionals" (p. 344). This notion has led some to study the sorts of help that people sought from hairdressers and bartenders and the like, and the advice and assistance they receive (Cowen, 1982).

Rappaport (1977), in the first and most widely used undergraduate textbook in community psychology, sought to undermine the whole notion of a specialty. He chose instead to regard community psychology as a social movement, again emphasizing flexibility. He claimed that a social movement would need to have available a variety of realistic strategies and tactics for social change; "persons engaged in this profession require flexibility, willingness to change, and to react to feedback, and continual reevaluation" (p. 389). All this was, he thought, undercut by "reification of roles which necessitate a 'protection of turf,' in favor of fostering problem-solving skills among active agents of social change" (p. 389).

Rather than relying on professional training, leaders in the community movement have tended to emphasize personal qualities. Kelly (1979), in an article with the fitting title "T'ain't What You Do, It's the Way That You Do It," said that when professionals put aside the issue of personal qualities, they ignore those features of ourselves that are actually central defining elements when doing our work. "Our personal qualities are the foundation for the choices we make when we select our tasks and give time to our work. Why is this so? It is so, because our work is largely unpredictable, certainly ambiguous, often tentative, and even indetermi- nate ... We rely upon our qualities and quirks and our premises about other people, for better or worse, to get us through when there are no clear or set guidelines." (p. 246).

One reason that the notion of flexibility is so prized in community psychology derives from the ecological theory that is part of the thinking of so many in the area. In changing environments, the flexible will adapt and the inflexible—no matter how well trained—will not. This has been recognized and reflected in previous articulation of a "resource-based approach" to intervention. From this point of view, training and personal qualities are all resources that communities can draw on in their dealing with a community psychologist (O'Neill & Trickett, 1982, p. 3).

Another reason for the emphasis on the current needs of the setting rather than on formal training is the belief that communities have existing networks that should be used rather than ignored in community work (e.g., Sarason, 1976). These networks are an important fact of life in any community, and can be a source of strength whether one is working to change the community or attempting to cope with a community crisis. With regard to the former, Glidewell (1976) emphasized the need to link networks within a social system. Again, the creating of links suggests that overlapping roles are considered valuable. People who serve different functions in different networks are themselves links between systems. As Glidewell put it, "The most intense of linking devices is overlapping roles. A person has a role in each of two systems, that is, two sets of rights and duties ... Community institutions and cross-community networks are often linked by overlapping roles" (p. 236).

What works for induced social change also works when a community is in crisis. It is essential to use existing networks to exchange information and to enlist helpers. In the words of Gist and Lubin (1989a) "natural roles and delivery systems are inherently more effective (than professionals, paraprofessionals) for many situations" (p. 344).

One concerned with professional competence would probably question the assumption that training makes one inflexible, or that people who work in their areas of competence cannot learn and grow. But Rappaport (1977) seemed to have history on his side when he claimed that reification of professional roles leads to turf wars. And once one is protecting one's turf, there is manifestly less opportunity of playing multiple roles and providing links between networks in a community. In addition, those who dwell on their professional credentials may be less likely to value the opinions of the hair dressers, the bartenders, and the cops on patrol. Finally, a shift in emphasis from formal training to personal qualities, as advocated by Kelly, makes the notion of judging interventions by formal criteria of professional competence more than somewhat problematic. Expanded roles mean expanded exposure: Professionals may find themselves held accountable in ways not dreamed of in their formal training.

DIVIDED LOYALTIES

The myth of the objective helper, like that of the objective researcher, is increasingly being challenged by the view that helping is value laden. Codes of ethics now tell us to be aware of our biases, rather than assuming that we can be free of them. Psychologists frequently live in, and have long histories with, the communities in which they intervene. Their ties, and their social identities, can ally them with one side or another when community crisis involves factional disputes.

Principle B (Integrity) of the Code of Ethics of the APA (1992) says that psychologists should strive to be aware of their own belief systems and values, and the effect of these on their work. The Canadian code (CPA, 1991) requires psychologists to "evaluate how their personal experiences, attitudes, values, social context, individual differences, and stresses influence their activities and thinking, integrating this awareness into all attempts to be objective and unbiased" (Principle III.10).

Professionals may find themselves with divided loyalties as they cope with community crises. Such crises may result from, or be aggravated by, conflicting interests of different community groups. The helping professional is often a member of the community with ties to one or more of those groups. Such group identification is perceived in the community as putting the professional in one camp or another. All members of the community, including professionals, are affected by their affiliations in the way they think about and respond to particular crises. In the words of Wilkinson and Vera (1989), cultural beliefs affect how people interpret the cause of the disaster and account for its aftermath.

Levine has remarked on the importance of values in establishing a relationship between the helper and the setting. "In many instances the community psychologist's goals are not only to provide a helping service, but also to modify aspects of the setting in which people live and work...community psychologists will obviously become deeply involved in value questions." He dismisses the ideal of the value-neutral professional. Instead, Levine argues that we must know our own values and understand how they affect our interactions with others. "The community psychologist is an agent of deviancy control in settings which he values, and he can be an agent of change in settings whose the goals he questions" (pp. 219–220).

An even more value-focused theory is offered by Riger (1989), who sees communities and organizations as completely infused with politics. She stated that actors in community settings often have different goals and interests. "Groups fight to obtain and preserve scarce resources. Once resources are obtained, a group fights to keep control of them" (p. 380). By this account, professionals who believe they can remain objective, be seen as objective, and can offer objective interventions, would seem to be deluding themselves. Where there is intergroup conflict, professional help becomes a part of that conflict.

Disaster underground: Westray

On May 9, 1992, at 5:18 a.m., a powerful explosion trapped 26 men working underground in the Westray Coal Mine in Plymouth, Nova Scotia, Canada. For 5 tense days rescue workers gingerly picked their way through the damaged tunnels, families prayed that the miners would be all right and people around the world watched the drama unfold on their television screens. I followed the disaster, which occured an hour's drive from my home, on television in France, where it was the lead story day after day.

Volunteer firefighters, police officers, and ambulance attendants began converging on the mine less than 30 minutes after the explosion. The quick response was the result of an "eerie coincidence" (Jobb, 1994, p. 47). The local Emergency Measures Organization had staged a mock disaster the previous weekend; the large exercise was based on the premise that a plane had crashed into a campground leaving many injured. The drill sharpened communications among the district fire departments, police forces, and medical services.

Psychological consultation and counseling was provided by Aberdeen mental health services. The Aberdeen team was involved in the disaster response from the outset. Family members spent the long days of waiting in a room at the local fire hall. Although the room was large, at times it was extremely crowded with as many as 100 people sitting at tables—each for a different family. Members of the Aberdeen clinic worked shifts so there was always someone available around the clock. The Aberdeen team had no difficulty making therapeutic links with the families: "Many miners, family members, volunteers and service providers knew the Aberdeen staff first or second hand...The years of community involvement by the mental health team make the staff accessible and approachable" (Service & Gerrior, 1995, p. 9). It also put the team firmly on the side of the families, and tended to make the team compliant to all the families' wishes, which turned out to have some drawbacks.

As the Aberdeen team kept vigil with the anxious families, underground the draegermen—miners skilled in rescue work—had not found survivors. After 5 days, the rescue effort was halted. The mine yielded 15 victims; the bodies of the remaining 11 were left underground.

Jobb (1994), who has written the definitive book on the disaster, put the matter succinctly: "There were no survivors but there were plenty of questions—and plenty of allegations that Westray had been a disaster waiting to happen." The mine had only been operating for 8 months. There were repeated warnings that the project faced serious technical and safety problems, and might not make money. According to Jobb, "In the rush to bring the mine into production, the warnings were either ignored or dismissed as troublemaking. Safety took a back seat as the company desperately tried to fulfill its coal supply contracts" (pp. v–vi). The explosion led to a provincial inquiry and to charges of manslaughter and criminal negligence causing death against the mine's developer and two Westray managers.

We cannot know the outcome of various legal proceedings and political fallout (the mine was located in the constituency of the then-premier of the province), but we do know some of the problems faced by the team of service providers. Some of those problems involved sorting out the team's role in a community maelstrom of charged emotions and recriminations.

Bryk (1983) approached organizational and community problems using "stakeholder analysis." From this perspective, multiple actors in a situation are expected to have conflicting goals and interests. The Aberdeen team found itself dealing with a number of groups, all of whom had different stakes in the outcome—not only the life or death of the trapped miners, but the legal and political fallout from the disaster.

First, there were the families of the miners caught by the explosion. They had all of the natural reactions to catastrophe that might be expected by mental health workers. They also had strong feelings about the mining company, since rumors and questions about mine safety were now in the foreground.

Then there was the company itself, which directed rescue operations underground. The company had a paramount interest in keeping safety problems from becoming public knowledge. To that end, they banned the Aberdeen team from mine property. Although the team could work with families gathered in the local fire hall, they could not help the rescue teams of draegermen who were coming from the depths—first trying to find and help their trapped comrades and later bringing up bodies. Although they, too, may have needed mental health services, the company would only allow a few selected clergymen onto company property.

There was the press (local, national and international) that descended on the town. Because a disaster deep in the shafts of a mine provides none of the photo and sound opportunities of an above-ground catastrophe (an Oklahoma City bombing, for example), the press became increasingly hungry for news during the 5 days of waiting to learn the fate of the trapped men. The company officials were not doing much talking. The obvious option for the press was to try to interview the family members or those who were in contact with them, such as counselors.

There were other assorted groups each with its own agenda. There were representatives of the Steelworkers Union, for example, who had been in the midst of an organizing drive at Westray at the time of the explosion. They felt these were "their men" in a sense, although they had no mandate yet to represent them. And there were the politicians, who seemed intent on using the disaster for their own purposes. A second memorial service for the dead men had to be held so it could be attended by national politicians, even though the families had not requested it and were not much consulted about it.

It is clear from this brief description that there were cross-cutting agendas as all these groups came together and dealt (or refused to deal) with one another. In the middle were members of the Aberdeen team. They saw their primary mission as one of helping the families cope with the disaster, and doing what they could to insulate them from external forces, such as the ever-present members of the media.

Early in the 5-day wait, the families declared a boycott of the press. Reporters were not allowed access to the fire hall where the families waited. They asked the counselors from the Aberdeen team to abide by the boycott, and the team agreed. That denied the press access not only to the families, but also to the only people who were in constant contact with the families.

The press saw this as a conspiracy of silence, designed by company officials to keep the public from learning about unsafe conditions in the mine. According to Jobb (1994), "In the hectic hours after the explosion a public relations strategy seemed to emerge" (p. 59). He claimed the company worked behind the scenes to drive a wedge between the media and families of the trapped men: "Many anxiously waiting...had been told horror stories about safety conditions in the mine. But company officials repeatedly warned them not to talk to journalists or listen to the news on radio and TV. Reporters were blowing the whole incident out of proportion, they said; the media were vultures trying to use the families' anguish to make money." (p. 59).

John Service, a psychologist who led the Aberdeen team's efforts, disagrees with this characterization of the reason for a boycott of the press (J. Service, personal communication, Dec. 21, 1995). According to him, the families themselves decided very early that they did not want to talk to the press. Moreover, he recalls that the families vigorously turned down offers to put televisions and radios in the fire hall. They had no interest in hearing press coverage that speculated constantly (in the absence of harder news) about the fate of the trapped miners.

But now, looking back, the Aberdeen team wonders whether their single-minded loyalty to the families did not foreclose some possibilities of operating with a broader scope. Service and Gerrior (1995) say that in retrospect they might have used at least the local media to give residents general information about disasters, crisis intervention strategies, post-traumatic stress disorder, available resources, and so forth. This strategy would have allowed for the sharing of important psychosocial information, answered specific questions and more directly involved the general public (cf. Gist & Stolz, 1982).

The team also wondered whether they might not have been more active in helping with some of the political and legal matters that were swirling about the families. Service noted that mental health training tends to focus practitioners on traditional modes of intervention such as counseling, rather than encouraging exploration of other ways in which clients need help. He suggested that the team could have been more assertive with the mine operators, who were clearly pursuing their own agenda with little regard for the worried, then grieving, families; he also suggested that the team could have intervened more directly with government officials to modify the degree to which the grief of families was showcased for political purposes (Service & Gerrior, 1995; J. Service, personal communication, Dec. 21, 1995). As Gist and Lubin note: "Psychologists cannot take the pain away or keep it from happening; they can only make it easier to experience and to grow beyond" (1989a, p. 342).

If questions of loyalty and of training limited some aspects of the mental health team's response at Westray, another Canadian mine disaster the same year pointed up the problems that occur when disaster strikes a community already deeply divided. In the case of the Giant gold mine in Yellowknife, the miners were in fact on strike and the disaster was considered a mass murder.

Murder underground: The Giant mine

The Giant gold mine is located on the outskirts of Yellowknife, capital of Canada's NorthWest Territories and a community of 16,000 residents. In May 1992, the 240 miners turned down a contract proposal from the company. They were concerned, among other things, about underground safety. Hours before they were due to strike, the company locked them out and from the first day the mine was kept running by strikebreakers. These were later augmented by about 40 union members who returned to work. An American security firm was hired to patrol the perimeter (*Globe & Mail*, Oct. 24, 1994; *Globe & Mail*, Jan. 21, 1995).

The strike/lockout lasted 19 months and became known as one of the most bitter and violent labor disputes in the country's history. Union miners who crossed picket lines to work with strikebreakers were scorned by the strikers. Long-standing friendships among miners and among their families were destroyed.

On the second day of the lockout, 2 miners were struck and injured by a truck attempting to cross the picket line to enter the mine site. On the third day, 20 Royal Canadian Mounted Police (RCMP) officers flew to Yellowknife to enforce a court injunction that ordered striking miners not to block access to the mine. During the lockout, there were attacks on police, rock-throwing incidents between miners and managers, and fires on the site. A satellite dish at the mine was bombed, and another bombing took place in an air vent shaft; neither of these explosions led to injuries. There were also about 20 power failures caused by sabotage. At one point, a full-blown riot broke out as union members fought with security guards and RCMP officers. More than 100 criminal charges were laid against locked-out miners.

According to Canada's national newspaper, the *Globe & Mail* (Oct. 24, 1994), "The dispute carved enormous social rifts in Yellowknife's tightly knit community of miners and their families. Lifelong friendships were destroyed as some men chose to cross the picket line and return to work while those loyal to the cause were left to live on meagre strike pay. Several lost their homes or gave up and moved away" (p. A10).

At 8:45 a.m., Friday, Sept. 18, 1992, nine men, six union members who crossed the picket line and three strikebreakers, were killed instantly when the rail car in which they were travelling on the mine's 750-foot level was blown apart by a bomb.

Young (1989) has remarked on the special trauma that occurs in a community when its crisis is caused by an act of deliberate violence—a terrorist act. She has found in her work that "the type of violence with the greatest potential to affect entire communities, occurs within communities in which people are strongly affiliated with each other, calls for numerous rescue workers or helpers, and attracts a great deal of media attention" (pp. 148–149). The Giant gold mine bombing had all these ingredients and another one: Before the bombing, the town had already been torn apart by a labor dispute that destroyed old friendships and turned long-time friends into enemies. Further, this was not a random act of violence. Few doubted that the bombing had been carried out by someone on the side of the striking miners.

Young (1989) identified the special problems associated with disasters shaped by intentional violence. For the community, she says, "violence is endured as unjust, terrifying, enraging victimization, one that creates an immediate crisis and often a long-term traumatic reaction" (p. 157). The normal crisis reaction and ensuing trauma are complicated, she adds, by a loss of a sense of justice and order in the world. All these characteristics marked Yellowknife after the bombing.

Although the strikers had enjoyed considerable support, city residents now turned against them, certain that one of the men on the picket line had rigged the fatal device. The city once prided itself on its tight community spirit, but that was almost gone. Most residents thought the crime was probably the work of a member or members of the union. For the miners themselves, and for their families, there was a strong sense of what Young (1989) has called a loss of a sense of justice and order in the world. Almost none of them (as it turned out) knew anything about the bombing or its perpetrator. They had had a strong world view in which they were right, and in which they were the victims. Now others were victims, and the strikers were being blamed. Worse, most assumed there was a murderer in their midst.

Immediately after the bombing, the *Globe & Mail* called the northern city a powderkeg. As news spread, fights broke out and there were reports of vandalism. Bars closed early that day, because of the possibility that violence might escalate. Some union members sent their families from Yellowknife to southern Canada. "Nobody trusts anybody here anymore," a shopkeeper was quoted as saying shortly after the explosion (*Globe & Mail*, Jan. 21, 1995, p. 1).

More than two years later, emotional aftershocks still rumbled through Yellowknife. According to the *Globe & Mail* (Oct. 24, 1994) the explosion "left an open wound that won't heal. A once-outspoken miner who is now reluctant to talk about the violent dispute said 'We'd like to put this behind us. We've had to live this nightmare every single day . . . we want to get on with our lives' " (p. A2)

It was in this atmosphere that the mental health team had to make whatever psychological interventions it could. A crisis line was set up through the hospital. People could speak anonymously, but they could also identify themselves and ask for follow-up services. Local media were used to identify potential sources of support. Many, though, were afraid to call and ask for help. This was a criminal matter, after all, and a dedicated police team was tracking down every lead in an attempt to identify the bomber or bombers.

A special problem involved providing services to strikers and their families. As in the Westray case, mental health workers took an immediate interest in the families and friends of the slain men—all of whom had been strikebreakers. But those on the "other side" also needed help. In some cases, there was history of friendship between families; although these friendships were ended by the choices men had made during the strike, there was still grief among the strikers for old friends and for families who had lost a member. In addition, there was collective guilt; some dealt with it by denial, but still it festered. Finally, there was the "pariah" status that had suddenly descended on the miners and their families. The sympathy with which they had been viewed was gone, and it seemed that the world looked at them with new eyes.

A final problem was the fact that mental health teams were, themselves, members of the community. They, too, had their histories; they had their views of the violent strike. No matter how even-handed they were in offering help, they could not fail to be seen as having biases.

Just over a year after the bombing, on Oct. 15, 1993, police charged a striking miner with nine counts of five-degree murder in the bombing. In his confession, the striker, who was an expert in handing explosives, said he acted alone. The trial itself was another traumatic event for the community. Many people did not believe (and to this day do not believe) his claim that no one helped him, and that he told no one what he was going to do or, later, what he had done. The strikers could not seem to escape the opprobrium that had haunted them since the bombing. Finally, in January 1995, the accused man was sentenced to life in prison.

The community hoped that the verdict would at last put an end to the pain. Yellowknife Mayor David Lovell was quoted by the *Globe & Mail* (Jan. 21, 1995) as saying, "I think now the important thing is that the community just get on with life. It's been a long hard time, first with the strike and later with the murders. It's something we have to put behind us." Families of the victims issued a statement that said "While our grief is not over, we feel we can now return to our homes and our families... The last two years has been a long and trying time." As if to put the final event in place to assist the healing process, the Labour Relations Board ruled that the mining company had bargained in bad faith, paving the way for an end to the dispute. A month later it was over.

The swirling conflicts of interest at Westray and the battle lines in Yellowknife are evidence of what Riger (1989) referred to as the intensely political nature of community problems. "The psychologist interested in community intervention must... be as aware as possible of the political struggles in a situation before intervening. Ignorance of the realities of power not only will hamper interventions but also may cause serious damage" (p. 381). She spoke of community psychologists as advocates for a position in which they believe. If so, they had better know in what they believe. "Recognizing the advocacy role is uncomfortable to some, who would rather see themselves as neutral experts. In a political world, however, the inevitable political effect of many interventions must, as much as possible, be brought to consciousness and treated explicitly" (p.

382). It is vital to figure out whose interests our work will further—because it always furthers someone's interests—and not only (or especially) the interests of the people we intend to help.

CONCLUSION

Many of the ethical issues discussed in this chapter apply to community work in general. These problems are exacerbated when the community is in crisis. High anxiety levels, which affect those who help as well as those who need help, have predictable negative effects on our ability to make decisions, including ethical decisions. Glidewell (1976) noted that "Confusion and anxiety inhibit exploration and problem solving in individuals and organizations" (p. 233); when events move quickly, as in crises, tensions mount. The helper, in Glidewell's view, may have no more urgent need than to engage in tension management, a way of helping others to live with tension while continuing to work and to think.

Psychologists working with a community in crisis must not only help others manage tension, but must manage their own. People who are trying to solve problems under conditions of high arousal lose much of the flexibility and adaptability earlier noted as an ideal for the professional in community practice. Weick (1984) has pointed out that highly aroused people—and there is no exemption for the community psychologist—find it difficult to learn a novel response, to brainstorm, to concentrate, to resist old categories, to perform complex responses, to delegate, and to resist information that supports their current attitudes.

In this crucible of community work, ethical standards can serve as valuable road maps. Weick (1984) noted that "High arousal can improve performance if it occurs after a person has decided what to do and after she or he has overlearned how to do it" (p. 41). This suggests that once key ethical principles have become thoroughly integrated into practice—have been overlearned—they will not interfere with our decision making in crises and may help us get the job done. These principles become the background of our action. When we depart from them, we know that we ought to do so for good and defensible reasons. Whatever the crisis, we still need to work with as much consent as we can get, to figure out what helps rather than harms, to minimize risk, to do what we know how to do, and to be as even-handed as possible when the community's inner tensions burst into the open.

REFERENCES

American Medical Association. (1846). Code of ethics. *Proceedings of the National Medical Convention 1846–1847, 83–106.*

American Psychological Association. (1992). Ethical principles of psychologists and code of conduct. *American Psychologist, 12,* 1597–1611.

Bolman, L. G., & Deal, T. E. (1984). *Modern approaches to understanding and managing organizations*. San Francisco: Jossey-Bass.

Bryk, A. S. (1983). *Stake-holder based evaluation*. San Francisco: Jossey-Bass.

Canadian Psychological Association. (1991). *Canadian code of ethics for psychologists*. Ottawa, Canada: Author.

Carroll, M. A., Schneider, H. G., & Wesley, G. R. (1985). *Ethics in the practice of psychology*. Englewood Cliffs, NJ: Prentice-Hall.

Cowen, E. L. (1982). Help is where you find it: Four informal helping groups. *American Psychologist, 37,* 385–395.

Everstine, L., Everstine, D. S., Haymann, G. R., True, R. H., Frey, D. H., Johnson, H. G., & Seiden, R. H. (1980). Privacy and confidentiality in psychotherapy. *American Psychologist, 35,* 828–840.

Gist, R., & Lubin, B. (1989a). Epilogue: Implications for research and practice. (pp. 341–344). In R. Gist & B. Lubin (Eds.), *Psychosocial aspects of disaster*. New York: John Wiley & Sons.

Gist, R., & Lubin, B. (1989b). Introduction: Ecological and community perspectives on disaster intervention. (pp. 1–8). In R. Gist & B. Lubin (Eds.), *Psychosocial aspects of disaster*. New York: John Wiley & Sons.

Gist, R., & Stolz, S. B. (1982). Mental health promotion and the media: Community response to the Kansas City hotel disaster. *American Psychology, 37,* 1136–1139.

Glidewell, J. C. (1976). A theory of induced social change. *American Journal of Community Psychology, 4,* 227–242.

Globe & Mail. (1993, Jan. 29). *Former glue sniffer one of the lucky ones at Davis Inlet*. Toronto, Canada. p. 1.

Globe & Mail. (1993, Aug. 30) *Davis Inlet children going home*. Toronto, Canada. p. 1.

Globe & Mail. (1994, Oct. 24). *Miner's deaths haunt Yellowknife*. Toronto, Canada. pp. A10, A12.

Globe & Mail. (1995, Jan. 21). *Warren found guilty in 9 miners' deaths*. Toronto, Canada. p. 1.

Goldenberg, I. I. (1971). *Build me a mountain*. Cambridge, MA: MIT Press.

Handelsman, M. M., Kemper, M. B., Kesson-Craig, P., McLain, J., & Johnsrud, C. (1986). Use, content, and readability of written informed consent forms for treatment. *Professional Psychology: Research and Practice, 17,* 514–518.

Hirschman, A. O. (1970). *Exit, voice, and loyalty: Responses to decline in firms, organizations, and states*. Cambridge, MA: Harvard.

Hippocrates. (1923). *Oath. Decorum. Precepts*. (W. H. S. Jones, Trans.). Loeb Classical Library, Vol. 1. Cambridge, MA: Harvard University Press.

Jobb, D. (1994). *Calculated risk: Greed, politics and the Westray tragedy*. Halifax, Canada: Nimbus.

Keith-Spiegel, P., & Koocher, G. P. (1985). *Ethics in psychology: Professional standards and cases*. New York: Random House.

Kelly, J. G. (1979). 'T'ain't what you do, it's the way that you do it. *American Journal of Community Psychology, 7,* 224–261.

Levine, M. (1969). Some postulates of community psychology practice. In F. Kaplan & S. B. Sarason (Eds.), *The psycho-educational clinic: Papers and research studies*. (pp. 209–224). Boston: Department of Health, Commonwealth of Massachusetts.

Murphy, W. J. (1976). Canterbury v. Spence—the case and a few comments. *The Forum, 11,* 716–726.

Nuremburg Code. (1964/1945). *Science, 143,* 553.

Ogloff, J. R. P., & Otto, R. K. (1990). *What information about research do students understand?* Paper presented at the American Psychological Association Annual Convention, Boston.

O'Neill, P. (1981). Cognitive community psychology. *American Psychologist, 36,* 457–469.

O'Neill, P. (1989). Responsible to whom? Responsible for what? Some ethical issues in community intervention. *American Journal of Community Psychology, 17,* 323–342.

O'Neill, P., & Trickett, E. J. (1982). *Community consultation.* San Francisco: Jossey-Bass.

Rappaport, J. (1977). *Community psychology: Values, research, and action.* New York: Holt, Rinehart, & Winston.

Riger, S. (1989). The politics of community intervention. *American Journal of Community Psychology, 17,* 379–384.

Rozovsky, L., & Rozovsky, F. (1990). *The Canadian law of consent to treatment.* Toronto, Canada: Butterworths.

Sarason, S. B. (1972). *The creation of settings and the future societies.* San Francisco: Jossey-Bass.

Sarason, S. B. (1976). Community psychology, networks, and Mr. Everyman. *American Psychologist, 31,* 317–328.

Sarason, S. B. (1988). *The making of an American psychologist: An autobiography.* San Francisco: Jossey-Bass.

Service, J. C., & Gerrior, P. (1995). Westray revisited: A community development perspective. *The Nova Scotia Psychologist, 10*(4), 9–10.

Sinclair, C. M., Poizner, S., Gilmour-Barrett, K., & Randall, D. 1987. The development of a code of ethics for Canadian psychologists. *Canadian Psychology, 28,* 1–8.

Tanner, A. (1995). Montagnais-Naskapi. *The Canadian Encyclopaedia Plus.* Toronto, Canada: McClelland & Stewart.

Thomson, J. J. (1986). *Rights, restitution, and risk: Essays in moral theory.* Cambridge, MA: Harvard University Press.

Tymchuk, A., Outlander, J., & Rader, N. (1986). Informing the elderly: A comparison of four methods. *Journal of the American Geriatric Society, 34,* 818–822.

Weick, K. E. (1984). Small wins: Redefining the scale of social problems. *American Psychologist, 39,* 40–49.

Wilkinson, C. B., & Vera, E. (1989). Clinical responses to disaster: Assessment, management, and treatment. (pp. 229–267). In R. Gist & B. Lubin (Eds.), *Psychosocial aspects of disaster.* New York: John Wiley & Sons.

Young, M. A. (1989). Crime, violence, and terrorism. (pp. 140–160). In R. Gist & B. Lubin (Eds.), *Psychosocial aspects of disaster.* New York: John Wiley & Sons.

Chapter 11

"And Then You Do the Hokey-Pokey and You Turn Yourself Around . . ."

Richard Gist, S. Joseph Woodall,
and Lynn K. Magenheimer

Our first introduction to the odd and insular world of postmodern *cyber-psych* came in the form of an announcement presenting a "treatment protocol" that, it was claimed, could revolutionize the treatment of post-traumatic stress disorder (C. R. Figley, personal communication, July 5, 1995). It went, in reasonable fidelity to the original, something like this:

1 First, think of a distressing event and "work up as much dis-comfort as you can" (though we were cautioned not to spend more than a few moments at this); rate your level of discomfort somewhere between 1 and 10.

2 Now, tap yourself with two fingers five times between your eye-brows.

3 Next, tap yourself five times under either eye.

4 Then tap yourself five times just below the collarbone.

5 If you're not at least two steps below where you started on your scale of 1 to 10, gently "karate chop" one hand with the other while reciting the following mantra: "*I accept myself, even though I still have this kind of anxiety.*"

Next, you spend a while tapping the back of your hand with your eyes open, then closed, then while looking in each direction, while rolling your eyes, while humming a tune, while counting to five... and then, we suppose, you do the Hokey-Pokey and you turn yourself around.

We at first thought that this was some kind of hoax, or perhaps a ploy to demonstrate just how greedy and/or gullible the profession has become. Not only was the transmitter of this information, whom we had heretofore assumed to be a reputable enough fellow, quite serious about all this, but he sent us across the Internet to the "inventor" of this treatment. That gentleman, in turn, wrote a rather expansive tome (R. J. Callahan, personal communication, July 12, 1995) relating that his marvelous new insight was a fundamental breakthrough, at least on a par with the quantum revolution in physics, and required an entirely new theory to accommodate it—which had, of course, been rejected by conservative science in the way that revolutionary innovators are always scorned. Science has had its share of renegade geniuses, to be sure, and their discoveries have sometimes been profound. But where you find an odd duck, you may also find a quack... so science always tends to look first for the more parsimonious explanations of any phenomenon.

The capacity of rituals to restore a sense of order, control, and equilibrium is certainly nothing new. We were taught a very similar and very effective procedure when we were kids: It, too, began with a tap on the forehead, followed by one tap at the solar plexus and one on each side of the sternum; we then placed our rosaries in one hand, moved our beads with the other, and recited comforting phrases. We whistled through graveyards, we bounced our basketballs three times before each freethrow, we knocked on wood—and we always felt better as a result. We just never pretended that this was science, or that our fears and anxieties were in fact some sort of disease.

It's no great secret that a number of us in the research and academic end of psychology have become increasingly skeptical of the popular movement toward "victimization" of life's losses, threats, and challenges that now seems to pervade everything from television talk shows to criminal trials. We've now reached the point where counselors swarming about any major disaster have begun to outnumber even lawyers and reporters, and where distressingly similar questions about motive and intent have become difficult to dispel. It's nice to know that there are safety nets when you're in precarious positions, but folks who shadow your every move with life nets seem sometimes to hold a disturbingly vested interest in watching someone fall. It's hard to see that as healthy.

We've been rather hesitant, though, to voice our criticisms and concerns too loudly or too harshly. Babies can all too easily be tossed with their bath water, and we feared that things that are truly important—things like acknowledging and talking about the human impact of disturbing experiences—might stand discredited simply because certain social movements, ego identities, and pecuniary enterprises built on them proved to be corrupt. But trivialities cloaked in pseudoscience and peddled through sometimes surreal seeming surrogates for the traditional venues of critical scientific intercourse are, to the ethical scientist or practitioner, the most dangerous form of deceit, whether perpetrated from malice or from naiveté. Eventually, the mask must be removed.

THE CLOAK OF SCIENCE

Anderson, Lepper, and Ross (1980) conducted a classic study of how beliefs become entrenched, which just happened to focus on a very pertinent subject—do risk-takers make better firefighters? Half their participants were given case studies of a risk-prone person said to be a good firefighter, and of a very cautious person said to have been a rather poor firefighter; each was asked to write an explanation of why this might be (e.g., risk takers are brave, whereas the cautious may be too timid to act). The remaining participants received case studies quite the opposite—a risk-prone person rated poorly as a firefighter and a cautious person rated quite highly; they, too, were to write an explanation (e.g., risk takers act before thinking, whereas cautious people use sounder judgment). Even after the factual basis of the initial information was thoroughly discredited, participants still clung to the explanations they had crafted and the beliefs those stories had created.

When given information with a seeming ring of truth—when it seems consonant with our personal experience or at least plausible from our own perspectives and observations—we easily accept it as reasonable. If we add to that surface credibility the aura that presumed "scientific" endorsement can bestow, the simply plausible quite readily becomes the definite. What better proof than scientific certainty?

Actual science, of course, is not about certainty at all. Indeed, the logic of science proceeds through the *disconfirmation* of hypotheses. We're neither equipped for nor disposed toward proving our theories "right"—the whole process is built instead on a determined effort to keep proving ourselves *wrong*. No assertion is ever left unchallenged; no finding is ever left unquestioned.

Done right and done well, science is a humble and a humbling enterprise. The bolder the claim, the more skeptical the response; the more arrogant or self-aggrandizing the claimant, the less convincing the rhetoric. When push comes to shove, the issue boils down to sound testing of discrete hypotheses through well-formed questions and cold, objective data—not to prove our theories right (it just can't be done!) but rather to find their flaws. To any truly accomplished scientist-practitioner, it's a world view, an epistemology, a way of life—it's just not subject to post-modern deconstruction, much less to simple disregard or dismissal.

THE SOCIALIZATION OF SCIENTISTS

It was not that long ago that a reasonably thorough and critical under-standing of the epistemology of science could be assumed to have been an essential element of the education given any competent, independent practitioner of a psychologically related enterprise. Such a review would generally have followed one or more comprehensive treatments (e.g., Marx & Hillix, 1987) and would have taken the practitioner-to-be through an extensive review of the history of science and the emergence of psychology as an empirical discipline; it would have held as a central objective the formation of clear and abiding distinctions between that which can be argued only from speculation, conjecture, or faith and that which can stand to the muster of skeptical scrutiny through rigorous empirical testing. The cornerstone of that education was the proud archetype of the "scientist-practitioner"—a critically honed, self-correcting buffer between theory and practice whose constant attention to both science and its application would ensure the highest quality of care for the consumer and the highest quality of knowledge for the enterprise.

The sterling visions and stellar designs of early psychology's saints and seers, like most such grand beginnings, failed to foresee a great number of social trends and interplays that would, in not much more than a decade, radically shift several presumptions so central to the core of those prog-nostications that it seemed, at least at the time, unnecessary even to articulate them. In the world of those forebears, psychology was, above and before all else, an academic discipline and a basic science; its exten-sion into application and practice was a beloved stepchild that, although embraced and even nurtured, was never allowed to wander abroad without stringent supervision. In that era, the first psychologist to venture into the realm of the "media personality" was met with censure and disavowal, not with reverence and envy; their world saw the currency of exchange for scientific information as the refereed empirical literature and the juried scientific symposium—certainly not as the popular paperback, the propri-etary seminar, or the afternoon talk show circuit.

A number of transitions that would forever alter the relationship between psychology's academic progenitors and its growing throng of applied derivatives had found footing by the mid-1960s, and many of those offshoots were becoming progressively less influenced by the epistemologi-cal foundations of scientific psychology as the social movement they came to represent continued its coalescence and growth. The fabric of that movement was woven from a collection of seemingly diverse threads, not all of which strike an obvious chord on first consideration. Some, like sweeping incorporation of a wide range of "alternative" practitioners[1] as relatively independent players in the unbridled egalitarianism of the community mental health movement of the 1960s, or the resurgence of certain elements of Beers's (1907) "mental hygiene" movement in the self-help movements of the 1970s, are easily seen as rather obvious features of that emergent tartan. Others threads, such as the displacement of roles once ascribed to shamans and later to clerics by the emerging caste of the "mental health practitioner" (Szasz, 1970, 1974) and the peculiar matrimony of their enterprise with New Age spirituality in a befuddlingly paradoxical amalgam born of postmodern psychological scientism (see, e.g., Sorell, 1991, for critical philosophical discussion) are perhaps more subtle and hence, at least to some, more elusive.

It is at certain points of nexus—like those inherent when dealing with socially constructed discomforts so universal as to be pandemic but now consistently defined through reified metaphors to disease—that the impact of these intersections first rises to much fuller awareness. So it has been with the ubiquitous notion of "psychic trauma," a central but principally rhetorical construct in Freudian thought that, due in part to the easy congruence of this facile medical metaphor to the universal experience of acutely distressing and disequilibrating life events, has been thoroughly embedded into both professional and colloquial lexicons. That notion now stands as the centroid around which a burgeoning cottage industry— calling itself, with all the hype and hubris conventionally associated with contemporary social scientism, *traumatology*—has constructed its constellation.

SOCIAL SCIENCE VERSUS SOCIAL MOVEMENTS

Echterling and Wylie (1981) provided an intriguing discussion of the growth of "crisis intervention centers" through the 1970s from the perspective of a social movement. They noted that social movements tend to arise as some more-or-less charismatic force brings coalescence to groups of dissatisfied and/or disenfranchised persons seeking solution to their perceived angst surrounding some reasonably discernible set of problems or issues. At first, such movements are seen as poorly organized spontaneous clusters but, as that coalescence develops, social organization, defined roles, and definite rules and hierarchies begin to emerge.

---

[1] That collection of "alternative" practitioners was originally limited to subdoctoral psychologists, nurses, and social workers; it quickly grew to embrace a range of loosely defined and marginally regulated counselors for everything from relationships to addictions, a ubiquitous but largely amorphous category sometimes dubbed "indigenous paraprofessionals," and various sorts of "peer" providers who often hold little more than exposure to a couple of days of color slides and hyperbole in the context of a traveling seminar as preparation for inserting themselves into propitious moments in the lives of others.

Many movements sputter and die at this juncture, because the very essence of those characteristics that sustain the effort beyond its initial charismatic stages challenge precisely those elements that drew the movement together. The transition from social movement to social institution dramatically alters the mechanisms through which stature, standing, and credence are earned and afforded, evolving from charisma and persuasion as the principal vehicles of influence, through progressively more contorted internal oligarchies, until such less malleable standards as formal credentialing and empirically tested data eventually emerge as the dominant standard. By this time, such movements have generally been absorbed into more established arenas, bringing immersion into established stratification systems as well. Quite often, it seems, the very personalities, assumptions, and constructions that propelled a social movement in its early charismatic and coalescent stages ultimately fall short of these new, more rigorous, and certainly less fluid demarcations.

Social movements and their originators, of course, do not always or even ordinarily fade gracefully into history as these transitions occur. Those who have ridden the crest of a movement to Andy Warhol's 15 minutes of fame tend to have accumulated many interests, from the egoistic to the economic, that are rarely relinquished with ease. Moreover, such movements attract in the process of their emergence an odd amalgam of individuals and interests, many of whom are wont to display certain classic characteristics associated with the "true believer" (Hoffer, 1951), and whose cohesion and conformity—especially as "establishment" forces begin to threaten those roles, hierarchies, and belief systems that have lent them status within their movement—may become even more entrenched through rubrics described by Janis (1972) as "groupthink." Paradoxically, it seems, such emotive allegiance at the core of a movement may become its most vehement just as the objective mortar of the movement begins, in fact, to crumble.

The *traumatology* movement sits today at such a juncture. On the one hand, it is more than fair to observe that the idea of rapid intervention to provide instant, on-scene counsel and support to any and all victims of any ostensibly traumatic stressor has permeated Western society to the point that any calamity of consequence will quickly muster its own prolific entourage of "mental health professionals"—a rather amorphous term seemingly coined to embrace addiction counselors with junior college certificates, school guidance counselors, and other arguably related groups of helpers as if equivalent in skill and contribution to doctorally prepared, independently licensed, clinically trained psychologists. These players can now certify themselves with such otherwise unrecognized monikers as C.T.S. ("Certified Trauma Specialist" through the Association of Traumatic Stress Specialists) or B.C.E.T.S. ("Board Certified Expert in Traumatic Stress" through the American Academy of Experts in Traumatic

Stress) by exchanging a bit of paper and more than a bit of cash. Any provider wishing to quickly expand his or her repertoire of "brand name" ministrations can easily learn one or more of the "alphabet interventions" that spring forth from proprietary vendors at the distal peripheries of the discipline (e.g., EMDR™ [Eye Movement Desensitization and Reprocessing], TFT™ [Thought Field Therapy], EFT™ [Emotional Freedom Techniques], TIR [Traumatic Incident Reduction], CISD [Critical Incident Stress Debriefing], etc.) through any of the burgeoning number of weekend workshops and two-day seminars actively competing for their CEU dollar.

On the other hand, a growing number of studies and analyses in the refereed academic press have begun to question these techniques, their foundations, their efficacy, their applications, and their aggressive marketing programs (see, e.g., Herbert et al., in press; Lohr, Tolin, & Lilienfeld, 1998; or Lohr, Lilienfeld, Tolin, & Herbert, in press, for recent reviews of EMDR; see Gist et al., 1997; or Gist & Woodall, this volume, for a review of current findings and issues regarding CISD; see also Dawes, 1994; Dineen, 1996; or Kaminer, 1992, for more generic reviews). More significantly still, more sophisticated empirical studies, including randomized controlled trials, are now being reported for some of these approaches (specifically, "psychological debriefing"); their findings are calling into serious question the very most basic axioms of "one off" crisis intervention —matters such as immediacy and propinquity of intervention or the presumed absence of iatrogenic risk from widely disseminated "shotgun" intervention sets (Rose & Bisson, 1999; Wessley, Rose, & Bisson, 1998). Meanwhile, what effects may be seen from these evermore popular rushes into formalized intervention appear more and more linked to what may well be the same common set of nonspecific and expectancy effects that has sustained such quasi-mystical approaches to psychic healing since a shaman first shook a serpent (see McNally, in press, for a truly fascinating exploration of the parallels between Anton Mesmer's promotion of his "animal magnetism" machinations and the current phenomena surrounding Eye Movement Desensitization and Reprocessing).

THE GROWTH OF "TRAUMA TOURISM"

A sound basic idea has an attraction all its own. But if carefully wrapped, progressively stretched, and cleverly marketed, it can become much more than it ever was or likely should have been. Given the illusion of science and precision, it readily transforms to something between a cottage industry and a New Age cult. Social psychologists call this the "Barnum effect" after the master showman who built an empire on the premise that a little gullibility can be taken a long way.

A major distinguishing characteristic of the patent remedies popularized at the fringes of the traumatology movement has been a peculiarly postmodern tendency to wrap these ministrations in the cloak of science while donning at the same time the pointed cap of the conjurer—to present these wares as if an extension of the widely esteemed and revered social stratum of the scientific while simultaneously casting the practitioner as if some sort of conduit for the mysterious power of the faith healer and the crystal gazer. Proponents typically argue that their various protocols hold established and demonstrated efficacy. When the empirical veracity of such claims meets definitive challenge, however, the rejoinder often devolves to an argument that "clinical experience and intuition" are somehow more valid indicators of a treatment's efficacy—and, of course, that those who raise such questions are but "ivory tower" academics whose criticisms should be discounted because of their presumed lack of contact with the "real world" of the practitioner.

Consider the specific case of CISD, a core element of the popular traumatology movement directed toward emergency service personnel on the presumption that certain inescapable contexts of their work prove inherently traumatizing, and that these effects can be ameliorated only through proximal and immediate intervention (cf. Mitchell, 1992). Though virtually unmentioned in the mainstream literature of the psychological disciplines throughout its first decade, and though still considered a relatively untested approach by most serious commentators in those venues (cf. Bisson & Deahl, 1994; Deahl & Bisson, 1995; Foa & Meadows, 1997; Kenardy & Carr, 1996; Meichenbaum, 1994; Raphael, Meldrum, & McFarlane, 1995), the claims made by CISD adherents in the less critical venues of trade journals, trade shows, and proprietary gatherings held under the sponsorship of CISD principals and proponents have unabashedly proclaimed this alleged "scientific" standing. As studies have accumulated in the refereed academic press showing no preventive effect (Deahl, Gillham, Thomas, Dearle, & Srinivasan, 1994; Hytten & Hasle, 1989; Kenardy et al., 1996; Lee, Slade, & Lygo, 1996; Stephens, 1997) and even suggesting adverse outcomes (Bisson, Jenkins, Alexander, & Bannister, 1997; Gist, Lubin, & Redburn, 1998; Hobbs, Mayou, Harrison, & Warlock, 1996), principals of the debriefing movement have attempted to counter their impact by producing counterclaims woven primarily of unpublished information, anecdote, testimonials, and rhetoric (Mitchell & Everly, 1997). This pattern, unfortunately, has been inherent since the earliest days of the CISD movement and permeates its very foundations.

The "rescue personality"

Mitchell has long offered as a central construct in his "model" the contention that "emergency personnel have very special personalities" (quoted by Hopper, 1988, p.7). He goes on to make an incontrovertible claim of a definitive basis in research, to wit: "Our recent study using the

Milan (sic) Personality Inventory clearly shows that the police officer/ firefighter/paramedic personality is significantly, statistically different from the average population" (quoted by Hopper, 1988, p. 7). This same contention has been repeated time and again in lectures, seminars, and writings.

The only references ever directly cited, however, led to an unrefereed trade magazine (*Firehouse*; see Mitchell, 1986) and an "unpublished study" that article was said to describe. The trade piece purported the study to have been associated with Loyola College and the University of Maryland, and made very specific claims regarding sample sizes and the like. The data, however, appeared nowhere, although a string of pronouncements imputed to have derived from these measurements occupied the next several pages: Firefighters were said to be risk takers (remember Anderson, Lepper, & Ross [1980]?), perfectionistic, activity driven, manually skilled, and such—all basically plausible and easily rationalized. But how could such conclusions have arisen from a scale designed for clinical diagnostic work and linked directly to the diagnostic nomenclature, and just where could these data be found?

Mitchell promised in his *Firehouse* piece to publish these data within the year, but more than a decade passed and no such publication ever appeared. Direct requests for the data were made after a paramedic instructor completing a thesis project (Wright, 1993) derived conclusions diametrically opposed to several of Mitchell's standing assertions. Several months of increasingly more pointed correspondence led to some interesting revelations—including an eventual concession that the conclusions reported were not principally the product of such a database but were rather Mitchell's personal speculations (Mitchell, personal communication, Dec. 6, 1993) and a denial by the purported coinvestigator of any complicity in the espousing of these "profiles" (Everly, personal communication, Sept. 13, 1993).

No data, however, have been produced and Mitchell (personal communication, Jan. 5, 1994) has indicated that, despite both accepted academic convention and specific ethical prescriptions regarding provision of data to support published claims, no data should be expected. Explanations offered for their unavailability have included "last seen in the possession of another" (Mitchell, personal communication, Dec. 6, 1993) and "misplaced in an office move" (Ostrow, 1996). Although those claims have been characterized by more skeptical observers (Brown, 1996, p. 10) as the rough equivalent of "the dog ate my homework," the "emergency services personality" construct continues to occupy a principal position in the outline for Mitchell's basic CISD course (International Critical Incident Stress Foundation, 1998).

Dickson and Kelly (1985), reporting a classic exemplar of the Barnum effect, offered a litany of examples in which persons adhered to phony personality descriptions that, much like a horoscope from the morning paper, had a little something to fit anyone but nothing so specific as to ever stand clearly erroneous—these were found especially convincing when said (falsely) to have been derived from psychological tests. Indeed, when given the choice between these phony descriptors and actual psychological profile data, people tended to report the bogus descriptions as more accurate! It should come as little surprise, then, to observe that exposure of the questionable derivation of this "construct" and the presence of directly disconfirming data have seemingly had no discernible effect on those who purvey that information within the confines of the "CISD circuit."

THE TIP OF THE ICEBERG

Barnum's genius as a showman and a marketer was cemented with a truly awesome discovery connected to his very first "scam" (Kunhart, Kunhart, & Kunhart, 1995). He and a confederate were displaying what they claimed to be a 161-year-old former slave who, they said, had helped raise George Washington. The scam was moderately successful, but ticket sales were dwindling. Barnum then composed an anonymous letter that exposed and debunked his attraction in the press—after which, people came in droves to see what they knew fully well to be groundless in fact. Barnum learned two important lessons: There is no such thing as "bad" publicity when out to sell a scam and, even more importantly, that people will gladly pay for a product they know fully well to be bogus if they see it as a rewarding encounter to experience.

Even if this were the only problem with the marketing of this intervention program, it would still be a very large one; accuracy and adequacy of data and attribution are critical matters to scientific psychology, and even the appearance of compromise or distortion in their respect must be seriously avoided. When the exploration of a simple technique takes on the proportions of a "movement," though, such compromise tends to become commonplace.

Like most of its conceptual cousins in the larger traumatology movement, the critical incident stress movement was spawned and nourished far outside the critical and conservative waters of scientific psychology, espoused instead through a cacophony of trade magazines, proprietary conferences, road shows, and workshops. It can be difficult in such venues to distinguish between rhetoric and research, and faith can sometimes hold more sway than fact. Mitchell and Everly's (1997) trade magazine piece, published as a purported rejoinder to growing criticism and given the rather presumptuous title, "*The* **Scientific Evidence** *for Critical Incident Stress Management*" (emphasis in original), provides many examples of the misrepresentations and misperceptions that can so easily result.

Not all data are created equal

The vast majority of pieces on critical incident stress management have appeared in trade magazines and lower tier publications, and have generally been devoid of data or hypothesis testing. These pieces have recited instead a repetitive catechism of postulates and presumptions, grounded principally in seemingly gratuitous self-citation and "show and tell" anecdotes venerating the debriefing experience (cf. Everly, 1995; Mitchell, 1983, et seq.). A number of the "studies" put forward by Mitchell and Everly (1997) exceed this only by mere microns, relying principally on "perceptions" of helpfulness or similar subjective responses (e.g., Burns & Harm, 1993; Robinson & Mitchell, 1993). The latter approach can be specifically and, at times, dangerously misleading.

We have compared this before (Gist & Woodall, 1996) to the customer service surveys one finds at the neighborhood doughnut shop: One can determine very precisely that people (especially people who choose to come to such shops) tend to like doughnuts—that tells us, however, absolutely nothing about their nutritional worth. Many people like and even crave doughnuts for precisely those properties that render them nutritionally undesirable. We certainly wouldn't accept an argument that preferences of the palate translate into dietary superiority.

Those studies appearing in the primary scientific literature rely instead on objective, standardized measures of outcome, administered under controlled conditions to test well-defined and specified hypotheses. Findings reported in these venues give us yet another cause to take serious pause: Perceptions of benefit from those debriefed are generally found, even where objective measures show neutral or negative outcomes. Perhaps even more significantly, some recent studies report that those who perceived the greatest benefit were not necessarily any better in their emotional adaptation (e.g., Lee et al., 1996), and may in fact have been those who showed the more negative objectively measured impacts (Bisson et al., 1996; Hobbs et al., 1996). Taken in this light, many of the findings on which debriefing proponents have relied may demand some very serious reconsideration.

Tracing citations to their source

A search of the references cited by Mitchell and Everly (1997) as constituting "the scientific evidence" for their rubric lends very little in the way of support from any of the generally accepted venues of scientific psychology. The sources they offer for support range from unpublished accounts bearing incomplete citations to their own newsletter (*LifeNet*), popular press articles, and vanity press books (i.e., their own paperback books from their own Chevron Publishing). It is telling, perhaps, to note that those few entries they list from the principal literature of the psychological disciplines either have nothing to say about CISD *per se* (e.g., Bordow & Porritt, 1979; Helzer, Robins, & McElvoy, 1987; Seligman, 1995), criticize the concept directly (e.g., Kenardy et al., 1996; McFarlane, 1988), or commit what Mitchell and Everly contend to be a fatal flaw by not directly following their precise model in their prescribed context (e.g., Flannery, Fulton, & Trausch, 1991)—a rather peculiar standard that would effectively negate any scientific generalizations whatever, from animal studies of pharmaceuticals to the controlled manipulations characteristic of laboratory science, whether physical, chemical, biological, or psychological.

The largest contingent amongst the references cited is composed of unpublished conference presentations, dissertations, theses, and such—worth considering carefully, perhaps, but also very cautiously because none of the checks, balances, or quality controls inherent in the refereed scientific press necessarily appertain. Studies in mainstream scientific venues have generally been subjected to critical blind review before being allowed to seek stature as theorematic assertions in the evolution of a topic or question—theses and dissertations in particular serve quite another function and must be treated rather differently.

The general purpose of a thesis is to have a student demonstrate to a committee of his or her graduate faculty a set of research and writing skills sufficient to warrant a passing grade. Although journal reviewers are carefully chosen for their specific expertise regarding the topic under review and are conventionally kept blind as to authorship of the manuscripts evaluated, thesis committees are most often recruited by the student, are intimately involved in the generation of the paper itself, and are frequently less sophisticated in the specifics of a topical area than might be expected of a journal reviewer. Moreover, not all theses in any given program are of comparable merit, not all programs within any given university are equally rigorous, and certainly not all schools are comparable in curriculum or standards—whether for admission, retention, or graduation.

Data from theses and dissertations often appear later as articles in the refereed literature of their disciplines, but most have generally been rewritten, refined, and reworked to meet the more specific and more rigorous standards of the academic press before formal publication. Some argue that thesis data should hold no credence unless and until they have withstood such scrutiny—at the very least, however, responsible assessment of thesis and dissertation data demands that one retrieve the actual document and review it in critical detail before accepting any second-hand proclamation regarding its findings or their implications.

This is not always a simple chore. Mitchell and Everly (1997), in their review, rendered it nearly impossible through uncommonly poor citation form. The purpose of any citation is to permit the reader to readily locate the source from which a construct was derived, particularly the original repository of those data on which conclusions were based. Few of the citations given for theses, and dissertations in the Mitchell and Everly piece contained the basic information needed to successfully complete that process.

We had earlier, for example, sought the Bohl dissertation given prominent play by Mitchell and Everly (1997, p. 89) after its author, presenting her report as derived of her doctoral dissertation in clinical psychology, published similar contentions in a fire service trade magazine (Bohl, 1995). A written request for full citation information was mailed, including a prepaid business reply envelope; no response was ever received. Meanwhile, attempts to locate the dissertation through alternative means led to the rather astonishing findings that the author was not, in fact, licensed as a psychologist or otherwise entitled to that moniker; that the school from which the degree was received was not, in fact, an accredited clinical psychology program; and that the dissertation was not, in fact, readily available through the international system of archiving used for such documents. Those data have accordingly remained unavailable for proper scrutiny.

Yet another dissertation (Lanning, 1987) given prominent play in the Mitchell and Everly (1997) piece was retrieved from the School of Family and Consumer Studies at Texas Woman's University and reviewed to determine the extent to which the data presented would support its purported conclusions. The dissertation, in fact, provided no meaningful assessment of intervention efficacy nor any contrast of treatment conditions—it measured endorsements of a collection of qualitative statements by occupational and demographic groups, but it lent no empirical support for any conclusions about the effects of either treatment or its absence.

Nowhere in the refereed literature do the data from these dissertations appear; never have they stood to independent scrutiny in actual venues of the discipline (both arose from ancillary and remote sources well outside the ordinary boundaries of academic psychology). Contrast this with the dissertation findings of Redburn (1992), generated within the confines of an APA-designated community psychology program and later reported in Gist, Lubin, and Redburn (1998; see also this volume). Here, direct comparisons were made on standardized measurements of symptoms and reactions between defined and partitioned groups subjected to a singular, well-defined set of stimuli (a prototypical "critical incident"); no effects were found traceable to the event, no benefit was derived of debriefing, and some negative impact was suggested. The difference is much more than cosmetic—it entails a chillingly basic distinction that permeates many of the popularized "New Age" modalities.

Do you know who your friends are?

Dawes (1994) quoted Lee Sechrest, then president of the Clinical Psychology Division (Division 12) of the APA, as expressing this concern about the future of the discipline as more and more programs, many outside traditional university departments and settings, keep producing ever-swelling legions of practitioners holding doctoral certification: "One of the fundamental problems is that I don't think we are graduating thousands of psychologists. We are graduating thousands and thousands of practitioners who are peripherally acquainted with the discipline of psychology" (pp. 16–17). Nowhere, perhaps, has this been more brazenly evident than in the wildly proliferating arena of traumatic stress and disaster response. A burgeoning number of practitioners has been attracted to this bandwagon in recent years (see Gist et al., 1998, for an historical perspective), the majority of whom seem to hail from those strata of the helping professions less schooled in and socialized regarding the critical scientist-practitioner ethos of psychology itself. Even among those ostensibly practicing psychology, those from less traditional programs and preparation would seem disproportionately represented.

We would not for a moment argue that providers outside the fraternity of university-educated, doctorally prepared scientist-practitioners have no valid or legitimate role in treatment, prevention, or programming; our colleagues in many disciplines and at many levels of preparation have very significant roles to play, indeed. But where the issues become explicitly matters of academic or applied research, theoretical development, empirical validation, and such, it is certainly reasonable to expect that those electing to espouse viewpoints said to reflect the rigor and precision of the scientific academy should, at the very least, be among its legitimate members. Moreover, it is always important to be clear and declarative about who we are and who we are not in our professional enterprises and credentials—for actual psychologists, in fact, it is an explicit ethical imperative (APA, 1992, Section 3.03). Should our standing, our preparation, or our work be misrepresented through the statements of others, it is our affirmative responsibility to attempt correction (APA, 1992, Section 3.02).

The problem is, unfortunately, not a matter of isolated individuals and incidents, nor is it limited to any one of the "alphabet interventions" popularized among trauma counselors. CISD's Mitchell, for example, has been often presented as a psychologist but holds no academic or professional claim to the title[2]; though these misattributions have been observed

[2] U.S. laws regarding the designation "psychologist" are very explicit, and limit use of the term to those licensed by a state authority to practice independently. Exceptions are generally made in both statute and convention for academic psychologists engaged in teaching or research in psychological programs of accredited colleges and universities, for those employed under that title in certain government facilities (e.g., community mental health centers), and for certain specialties (e.g., social psychology) when the individual is a graduate of an accredited program under that designation, engages specifically in its application, and notes the specialization in all applications of the protected term. Neither Mitchell's doctoral preparation in Human Development Education (a successor to Home Economics) nor his part-time academic appointment as an instructor in a paramedic education program qualify for such exception.

to have been made in Mitchell's personal presence as well as in print and press, no correction arising from Mitchell himself has been read or heard by these authors or by any others queried. EMDR™'s Shapiro is a graduate of an unaccredited, now defunct, "free-standing" California school; another of her chief spokespersons traces his academic training to a similarly unaccredited alma mater. The "founder" and chief marketer of EFT™, a derivative of Callahan's TFT™, freely admits that he holds no professional education or certification whatever, other than his training in the Callahan Techniques™.

Gary Craig, the founder and advocate of the EFT™ meridian-tapping technique, has argued freely in the trauma lists of the Internet that neither his lack of education in psychological matters (he is, he has said, an engineer) nor his lack of training in the very fundamentals of psychological science should inhibit his promotion of an ostensibly therapeutic intervention. In response to an academic psychologist's post to him outlining approaches one might responsibly take to validation of a proposed intervention, he responded in part (Craig, personal communication, Oct. 5, 1997):

> Another reason I'm not going to do this myself is that I haven't the foggiest idea how to do it. To you it is so simple and it is so easy for you to say, "Why don't you just do it, Gary?" You apparently spend a fair amount of time in these pursuits and they are commonplace for you. But please understand, I don't even know what $N = 1$ means. Also, I have never heard of:
>
>   The PTSD Interview (Watson)
>   The PSS (self-rating; Foa)
>   The IES (Haeres)
>   The Mississippi Scale (Keane)
>   The Symptom Checklist -90-R (Derogatis)
>   The Beck Depression Inventory (Beck)
>   The Spielberger State-Trait Anxiety Inventory (Spielberger)
>
> and I'm not about to drop what I'm doing to learn them just so I can satisfy someone else's need to prove what is so obvious to me and the growing number of therapists who are using EFT (including many PhDs and MDs).

He concluded by boldly stating, "In the future I will make whatever claims about EFT that I feel are justified," and by accusing his correspondent, in essence, of casting ad hominem arguments.

Postmodernism, ad hominem, and the Internet

The accusation of ad hominem has become a seemingly standard deflection for any questioning of competence or credentials. Oddly enough, however, such questions are explicitly recognized as ad rem when the argument at issue hinges on testimony rather than data (Kahane, 1995).

When asked to base judgment on the competence, character, or qualification of the source as the principal vehicle of persuasion, just who that source may be, what that source might know, or where and how well that source may have learned a trade or body of information all become critical to evaluation of the assertions proffered. When a source offers simply, "whatever claims that (he or she) may feel are justified," it is left up to each consumer of information to evaluate whether such justification rises to the standard of acceptance—the merit of the claim becomes, in effect, but an extension of the credibility of the source.

The postmodern psychological landscape has become, to many reared in the academic traditions and expectations born of the scientist-practitioner heritage, a rather chilling portrait painted in the school of social and intellectual surrealism. Information no longer begins in the laboratory or research center, working its way past the careful and critical scrutiny of the refereed literature before it may lay any claim to the mantle of science and the credence it holds before the lay public; no longer is it readily clear from the title accompanying a purveyor's name just what sort of background he or she might bring to bear on the issue at hand. Treatments and advice pop directly from the mind of whomever may conjure a notion into the self-help press, the proprietary seminar circuit, and the late-night infomercial. Afternoon talk shows are overrun with "instant experts" offering their opinions on whatever dysfunction parades across the set. Acronyms, monikers, and ersatz certifications flow like alphabet soup spilled across the kitchen floor, giving the unwitting consumer an impression of education with no guarantee of its substance, while even the legally protected and time honored title "psychologist" can no longer reliably distinguish the scientist-practitioner schooled at the most rigorous university from bearers of those "life experience" degrees hawked in the classified advertisements of frequent flyer magazines.

Add to this disheartening equation the awesome capacity of the Internet to circumvent what little may remain in our field of the social pragmatics of science, and the consequences for both public and practitioner turn worrisome indeed. The vehicle created to allow the rapid and effective exchange of information between researchers and academics has now turned in many quarters to subvert both the moral and the epistemological fabric from which science itself was woven. List-serves, user groups, bulletin boards, and such allow any group with like prejudices to fold itself efficiently into an insular cyber-klavern in which "groupthink" can prosper unfettered by the mitigating forces of empirical counterargument and academic debate. Websites and FAQ lists abound like the spores of the most prolific fungus, spawning a world in which the ramblings of a paranoid or the biases of a bigot hold equal billing with the empirical and the erudite. Challenge or argument can simply be dismissed, disregarded, shouted down, or altogether avoided while those of like predilection bask in the warm comfort of their common illusions.

Science is not an egalitarian marketplace of ideas. Unlike religious belief, where personal commitment is given great deference and peaceful co-existence of differing systems is the ideal, science is an enterprise in which ideas are cast into the arena to purposefully compete for ascendance; most are quickly consumed by the lions with little fanfare or mercy. Those who confuse their ideas with their identities find little comfort in its exercises; those who have strong needs for unconditional acceptance are unlikely to find its practice rewarding. Where the postmodern practitioner might prefer an afternoon of lawn tennis or croquet accompanied by the reading of Tarot cards, science is an odd mixture of rugby and chess followed by spirited public house debate.

SHAMANS, SHOWMEN, AND SCIENCE

The saddest part of this sorry tale may be that the capacity to command public trust in the professional stature and integrity of our discipline has been reduced, in effect, to another application of caveat emptor: "Let the buyer beware." Like any profession, we are judged by our lowest common denominator and our most visible emissaries. These were once august scientist-practitioners who set a high standard for knowledge, integrity, and discipline; current exemplars are found on afternoon talk shows, in the self-help sections of franchised book stores, and on the dog-and-pony show circuits of seminars and medicine shows. In this peculiar postmodern marketplace, we peddle what our grandmothers always knew as if some potent patent remedy and we sell, in the process, the integrity of our profession, if not our very souls.

These insidious phenomena cannot be discounted as if only the tragic comedy of postmodern foolishness. They have led to a nearly ubiquitous collection of nested presumptions that sometimes so obscure our objectivity that even the best of scientists can be led to look right past gaping holes in the fabric of theory and data that might otherwise have been chillingly obvious. Consider an elaborate epidemiological study from the Centers for Disease Control, published in the prestigious *New England Journal of Medicine* (Krug, Krenow et al. 1998). A number of explicit conclusions were entered that seemed to derive from strong statistical findings regarding suicides increasing following various sorts of natural disasters, reported in terms of aggregated percentages across counties affected by various types of catastrophe. The authors offered a particularly strong summary conclusion that these data "confirm(s) the need for mental health support after severe disasters" (p. 373). Spurred by publicists and press releases, these findings were widely and aggressively disseminated throughout popular media and professional digests alike.

The study, however, made no attempt to examine the presumed mechanisms for these calculated increases; it made no foray into risk factors, vectors, mechanisms, or methods. It explored no avenues of surveillance that might shed light on such critical factors, nor were any data whatever developed regarding the efficacy, absolute or relative, of *any* approach to intervention. These issues alone would be sufficient to render suspect so bold a conclusion regarding the need for structured and orchestrated intervention.

But the larger issue, despite the seeming mathematical sophistication of the piece, was essentially one of "innumeracy" (Paulos, 1989). When reduced to the level of its principal data unit (individual counties), the net increase in suicides was about one per county—from about six to about seven, on average—in the wake of a Presidentially declared disaster. Where seemingly alarming increases were found—say, for example, in the first year following earthquakes—these became a different matter altogether as critical scrutiny of the data revealed that only four very large and quite atypical counties experienced such events during the period of analysis. But the more salient implication may have been this: What justification have we to say that any intervention we might rush to mount would successfully find that one extra case in 52,000 folk (the average population of a county in this study), and what legitimate assurance can we give that broad-brush efforts to do so would do no harm, much less do any good?

Sadly, this story took yet another couple of tragic twists in the months following its much promoted original appearance. Shoaf (1998) made gentle reference to exactly those shortcomings raised above in a brief letter to the editor of the journal shortly after the original report appeared; she aptly noted that the data as reported indicated that severe impacts such as suicide were, in fact, remarkably rare and that those data spoke much more eloquently to resilience than to risk. Krug, Powell, and Dahlberg (1998), in their rejoinder, argued again that the increases were real, significant, and a symptom of a much larger mental health problem that demanded concerted address.

Before a year had passed, however, Krug et al. (1999) were compelled to print a nearly complete retraction of their data and results. An error in their processing of data led one year—exclusively a postdisaster year for their rubric—to be counted twice. When this error was corrected, essentially all of the statistically significant findings so touted a few months earlier evaporated into astoundingly trivial differences. Indeed, the alarming increase of nearly two-thirds following earthquakes reduced to a slight *decrease* in the corrected analysis, and the only value even approaching statistical significance was an 8.7% *decrease* in suicides in the years following severe storms. Even then, though, the authors rejected the resilience hypothesis and its concomitant suggestion that the focus return to more instrumental forms of postdisaster assistance in favor of a renewed, now principally rhetorical argument to maintain the original conclusion—never directly explored in their study or supported in their data —that mental health services are vitally needed.

We have said elsewhere (Gist, 1996; Gist et al., 1997; Gist et al., 1998) that the most important lessons to guide helping efforts in times of turmoil came from Grandma rather than from grad school: People are resilient; friends are important; conversation helps; time is a great healer; look out for others while you look out for yourself. Attempts to translate such simple wisdom into proclamations of pathology and peril do no one any particular favor, and render to some particular harm.

Science is, as noted before, a humble and a humbling enterprise. Shamans and showmen have built fortunes and followings for generation after generation by selling repackaged aphorism as an antidote to universal and inescapable angst. The scientist's role remains, as it has always been, to fan away the fog and return the focus to those fundamental principles that underlie our basic enterprises; even when functioning as practitioners, we are first and foremost defenders of science and its principles as the foundation of our practice and the standard for its success.

Science is hard-nosed and hard-headed, but that should never be construed as hard-hearted. Too often, it has been noted (Myers, personal communication, March 23, 1998), the kind-hearted tend also to be soft-headed—but soft-headed pseudoremedies are, at the end of the day, anything but kind-hearted in their effect. The most often-repeated lament in our enterprise, one must suspect, may be something along the lines of "It seemed like a good idea at the time"—hardly a compelling rationalization when applied to such significant matters as drug abuse education (Stuart, 1974), driver safety programs (Robertson, 1980a, 1980b, 1981), suicide prevention (Gist & Welch, 1989), or other life safety interventions where programs intended to promote safety have been found instead to have jeopardized those they were intended to protect.

"Fact" has never been some plural derivative of "anecdote"; repetition does not establish validity, nor is persuasion a suitable substitute for precision. Science demands something much more from its disciples than faith or fervor—science demands instead an absolute readiness to discard self-affirming beliefs in the face of disconfirming data. Myrmidons and sycophants may shoot at messengers and defend to the death their misplaced faith, but facts have a life all their own. The message of science is as simple as it is clear: *Trust all who seek truth; doubt all who claim to hold it.*

REFERENCES

American Psychological Association. (1992). *Ethical principles of psychologists and code of conduct.* Washington, DC: Author.

Anderson, C. A., Lepper, M. R., & Ross, L. (1980). Perseverance of social theories: The role of explanation in the persistence of discredited information. *Journal of Personality and Social Psychology, 39,* 1037–1049.

Beers, C. W. (1907). *A mind that found itself.* Pittsburgh, PA: University of Pittsburgh Press.

Bisson, J. I., & Deahl, M. P. (1994). Psychological debriefing and prevention of post traumatic stress: More research is needed. *British Journal of Psychiatry, 165,* 717–720.

Bisson, I. J., Jenkins, P. L., Alexander, J., & Bannister, C. (1997). A randomised controlled trial of psychological debriefing for victims of acute harm. *British Journal of Psychiatry, 171,* 78–81.

Bohl, N. (1995). Measuring the effectiveness of CISD: A study. *Fire Engineering, 148*(8), 125–126.

Bordow, S., & Porritt, D. (1979). An experimental evaluation of crisis intervention. *Social Science and Medicine, 13a,* 251–256.

Brown, A. (1996). Letter to the editor. *Journal of Emergency Medical Services, 21*(11), 10–12.

Burns, C., & Harm, N. J. (1993). Emergency nurses' perceptions of critical incidents and stress debriefing. *Journal of Emergency Nursing, 19,* 431–436.

Dawes, R. M. (1994). *House of cards: Psychology and psychotherapy built on myth.* New York: Free Press.

Deahl, M. P., & Bisson, J. I. (1995). Dealing with disasters: Does psychological debriefing work? *Journal of Accident and Emergency Medicine, 12,* 255–258.

Deahl, M. P., Gillham, A. B., Thomas, J., Dearle, M. M., & Strinivasan, M. (1994). Psychological sequelae following the Gulf war: Factors associated with subsequent morbidity and the effectiveness of psychological debriefing. *British Journal of Psychiatry, 165,* 60–65.

Dickson, D. H., & Kelly, I. W. (1985). The "Barnum effect" in personality assessment: A review of the literature. *Psychological Reports, 57,* 367–382.

Dineen, T. (1996). *Manufacturing victims: What the psychology industry is doing to people.* Montreal, Canada: Robert Davies Multimedia Publishing.

Echterling, L., & Wylie, M. L. (1981). Crisis centers: A social movement perspective. *Journal of Community Psychology, 9,* 342–346.

Everly, G. S., Jr. (1995). The role of the CISD process in disaster counseling. *Journal of Mental Health Counseling, 17,* 278–290.

Flannery, R. B., Fulton, P., & Trausch, J. (1991). A program to help staff cope with psychological sequelae of assaults by patients. *Hospital and Community Psychiatry, 42,* 935–938.

Foa, E. B., & Meadows, E. A. (1997). Psychosocial treatments for posttraumatic stress disorder: A critical review. *Annual Review of Psychology, 48,* 935–938.

Gist, R., Lohr, J. M., Kenardy, J. A., Bergmann, L., Meldrum, L., Redburn, B. G., Paton, D., Bisson, J. I., Woodall, S. J., & Rosen, G. M. (1997). Researchers speak on CISM. *Journal of Emergency Medical Services, 22*(5), 27–28.

Gist, R., Lubin, B., & Redburn, B. G. (1998). Psychosocial, ecological, and community perspectives on disaster response. *Journal of Personal & Interpersonal Loss, 3,* 25–51.

Gist, R., & Welch, Q. B. (1989). Certification change versus actual behavior change in teenage suicide rates, 1955–1979. *Suicide & Life Threatening Behavior, 19,* 277–288.

Gist, R., & Woodall, S. J. (1995). Occupational stress in contemporary fire service. *Occupational Medicine: State of the Art Reviews, 10,* 763–787.

Gist, R., & Woodall, S. J. (1996, November). And then you do the Hokey-Pokey. In D. Brom (Chair), *Treating PTSD: The controversy between pathology and functionality.* Symposium conducted at the 12th annual meeting of the International Society for Traumatic Stress Studies, San Francisco, CA.

Helzer, J., Robins, L., & McEvoy, L. (1987). Post-traumatic stress disorder in the general population. *New England Journal of Medicine, 317,* 1630–1634.

Herbert, J. D., Lilienfeld, S. O., Lohr, J. M., Montgomery, R. W., O'Donohue, W. T., Rosen, G. M., & Tolin, D. F. (in press). Science and pseudoscience in the development of Eye

Movement Desensitization and reprocessing: Implications for clinical psychology. *Clinical Psychology Review*.

Hobbs, M., Mayou, R., Harrison, B., & Worlock, P. (1996). A randomised controlled trial of psychological debriefing for victims of road traffic accidents. *British Medical Journal, 313*, 1438–1439.

Hoffer, E. (1951). *The true believer.* New York: Harper & Row.

Hopper, L. (1988, November). Stress recovery: An interview with Jeffrey Mitchell, Ph.D. *PM (Public Management)*, 5–8.

Hytten, K., & Hasle, A. (1989). Firefighters: A study of stress and coping. *Acta Psychiatrica Scandinavia, 355*(supp.), 50–55.

International Critical Incident Stress Foundation. (1998). *Course brochure and outline.* Ellicott City, MD: Author.

Janis, I. (1972). *Victims of groupthink: A psychological study of foreign policy decisions and fiascoes.* Boston: Houghton Mifflin.

Kahane, , H. (1995). *Logic and contemporary rhetoric* (7th ed.). Belmont, CA: Wadsworth.

Kaminer, W. (1992). *I'm dysfunctional, you're dysfunctional: The recovery movement and other self-help fashions.* Reading, MA: Addison-Wesley.

Kenardy, J. A., & Carr, V. (1996). Imbalance in the debriefing debate: What we don't know far outweighs what we do. *Bulletin of the Australian Psychological Society, 18*(2), 4–6.

Kenardy, J. A., Webster, R. A., Lewin, T. J., Carr, V. J., Hazell, P. L., & Carter, G. L. (1996). Stress debriefing and patterns of recovery following a natural disaster. *Journal of Traumatic Stress, 9*, 37–49.

Krug, E. G., Kresnow, M., Peddicord, J. P., Dahlberg, L. L., Powell, K. E., Crosby, A. E., & Annest, J. L. (1998). Suicide after natural disasters. *New England Journal of Medicine, 338*, 373–378.

Krug, E. G., Kresnow, M., Peddicord, J. P., Dahlberg, L. L., Powell, K. E., Crosby, A. E., & Annest, J. L. (1999). Retraction: Suicide after natural disasters. *New England Journal of Medicine, 340*, 148–149.

Krug, E. G., Powell, K. E., & Dahlberg, L. L. (1998). The authors reply (to Shoaf, 1998). Letter to the editor. *New England Journal of Medicine, 338*, 1852.

Kunhart, P. B., Jr., Kunhart, P. B., III, & Kunhart, P. W. (1995). *P. T. Barnum: America's greatest showman.* New York: Alfred A. Knopf.

Lanning, J. K. S. (1987). Posttrauma recovery of public safety workers for the Delta 191 crash: Debriefing, personal characteristics and social systems. Unpublished dostoral dissertation, School of Family and Consumer Studies, Texas Woman's University.

Lee, C., Slade, P., & Lygo, V. (1996). The influence of psychological debriefing on emotional adaptation in women following early miscarriage: A preliminary study. *British Journal of Medical Psychology, 69*, 47–58.

Lohr, J. M., Tolin, D. F., & Lilienfeld, S. O. (1998). Efficacy of Eye Movement Desensitization and Reprocessing: Implications for behavior therapy. *Behavior Therapy, 29*, 123–156.

Lohr, J. M., Lilienfeld, S. O., Tolin, D. F., & Herbert, J. D. (in press). Eye Movement Desensitization and Reprocessing: An analysis of specific versus nonspecific factors. *Journal of Anxiety Disorders*.

Marx, M. H., & Hillix, W. A. (1987). *Systems and theories in psychology.* New York: McGraw-Hill.

McFarlane, A. C. (1988). The longitudinal course of posttraumatic morbidity: The range of outcomes and their predictors. *Journal of Nervous and Mental Disease, 176*, 30–39.

McNally, R. J. (In press). EMDR and Mesmerism: A comparative historical analysis. *Journal of Anxiety Disorders*.

Meichenbaum, D. (1994). *A clinical handbook/practical therapist manual for assessing and treating adults with posttraumatic stress disorder.* Waterloo, Ontario, Canada: Institute Press.

Mitchell, J. T. (1983). When disaster strikes...the critical incident stress debriefing process. *Journal of Emergency Medical Services, 8*(1), 36–39.

Mitchell, J. T. (1986). Living dangerously: Why some firefighters take risks on the job. *Firehouse, 11*(8), 50–51, 63.

Mitchell, J. T. (1992). Protecting your people from critical incident stress. *Fire Chief, 36*(5), 61–67.

Mitchell, J. T., & Everly, G. S., Jr. (1997). The scientific evidence for critical incident stress management. *Journal of Emergency Medical Services, 22*(1), 86–93.

Ostrow, L. S. (1996). Critical incident stress management: Is it worth it? *Journal of Emergency Medical Services, 21*(8), 28–36.

Paulos, J. A. (1989). Innumeracy: Mathematical illiteracy and its consequences. New York: Hill and Wang.

Raphael, B., Meldrum, L., & McFarlane, A. C. (1995). Does debriefing after psychological trauma work? Time for randomised controlled trials. *British Journal of Psychiatry, 310*, 1479–1480.

Redburn, B. G. (1992). Disaster and rescue: Worker effects and coping strategies. Doctoral dissertation (community psychology), University of Missouri-Kansas City [University Microfilms No. AAD93–12267; *Dissertation Abstracts International, 54*(01-B), 447].

Robertson, L. S. (1980a). Crash involvement of teenaged drivers when driver education is eliminated from high school. *American Journal of Public Health, 70*, 599–603.

Robertson, L. S. (1980b). Fact and fancy in the formation of public policy. *American Journal of Public Health, 70*, 627.

Robertson, L. S. (1981). Patterns of teenaged driver involvement in fatal motor vehicle crashes: Implications for policy choice. *Journal of Health Politics, Policy, and Law, 6*, 303–314.

Robinson, R. C., & Mitchell, J. T. (1993). Evaluation of psychological debriefings. *Journal of Traumatic Stress, 6*, 367–382.

Rose, S., & Bisson, J. (1999). Brief early psychological interventions following trauma: A systematic review of the literature. *Journal of Traumatic Stress, 11*, 679–710.

Shoaf, K. I. (1998). RE: Suicides after natural disasters. Letter to the editor. *New England Journal of Medicine, 338*, 1851–1852.

Seligman, M. E. P. (1995). The effectiveness of psychotherapy. *American Psychologist, 29*, 965–974.

Sorell, T. (1991). *Scientism: Philosophy and the infatuation with science*. London: Routledge & Kegan Paul.

Stephens, C. (1997). Debriefing, social support, and PTSD in the New Zealand police: Testing a multidimensional model of organizational traumatic stress. *Australasian Journal of Disaster and Trauma Studies, 1*. Electronic journal accessible at http://massey.ac.nz/~trauma/issues/1997–1/cvs.htm

Stuart, R. B. (1974). Teaching facts about drugs: Pushing or preventing? *Journal of Educational Psychology, 66*, 189–201.

Szasz, T. S. (1970). *The manufacture of madness: A comparative study of the inquisition and the mental health movement*. New York: Harper & Row.

Szasz, T. S. (1974). *The myth of mental illness: Foundations of a theory of personal conduct*. New York: Harper & Row.

Wessley, S., Rose, S., & Bisson, J. I. (1998) Brief psychological interventions ("debriefing") for treating immediate trauma-related symptoms and preventing post-traumatic stress disorder (Cochrane Review). *The Cochrane Library, 1*. Oxford, UK: Update Software.

Wright, R. M. (1993, May). Any fool can face a crisis: A look at the daily issues that make an incident critical. In R. Gist (Moderator), *New information, new approaches, new ideas.* Overland Park, KS: Johnson County Community College, Center for Continuing Professional Education.

Chapter 12

Pseudoscience and the Commercial Promotion of Trauma Treatments

Jeffrey M. Lohr, Robert W. Montgomery, Scott O. Lilienfeld, and David F. Tolin

INTRODUCTION

The last decade has witnessed a rapid expansion in interest surrounding the nature of trauma, its psychological repercussions, and the psychological amelioration of those repercussions. Most specifically, there has been an increased interest in the effects of trauma on intense and/or long-lasting psychological phenomena and on psychopathology. As naturally occurs, an increased interest in acquired psychopathology is followed by an increased interest in the therapy of that pathology. As some intense and repetitive traumata (e.g., combat experience) can have long-lasting effects and pervasive effects in some people, there is good reason to search for treatments that can prevent or limit trauma sequela. Difficulty, however, arises in proportion to the over-extension of the pathology model, and in the over-extension of therapy to psychological distress.

Although the overextension of the pathology model is a substantial problem, it is not assessment and "diagnosis" of human misery that catches the attention of the consumer or the general service provider. It is the issue of "treatment" that captures the imagination of both the afflicted and the healer. It is in this domain that treatments and the "theories" of their putative effects find their most eager audience. There has recently developed a large number of treatment procedures designed to eliminate or reduce the negative effects of trauma experienced at the hands of others or in the context of natural disaster.

There are, in addition, a large number of treatments that have been applied not only to trauma-related distress, but also to more long-standing difficulties such as phobic and other disorders of anxiety. Behavioral treatments such as systematic desensitization, exposure, response prevention, and social skills training are treatments of choice across a wide range of anxiety disorders (Barlow, 1993; Chambless, 1995). Treatment procedures arising outside of traditional scientific scrutiny have recently been widely discussed in professional education "workshops" and special interest networks on the Internet (Callahan, 1995; Figley, personal communication, July 31, 1995; Figley & Carbonell, 1995; Gallo, 1995). In addition to eye movement desensitization and reprocessing (EMDR), these include thought field therapy (TFT; Callahan, 1985, 1987), traumatic incident reduction (Gerbode, 1995), and visual/kinesthetic dissociation (Bandler & Grinder, 1979). These treatments have been referred to (not facetiously) as power therapies (Gallo, 1995). Although they are analogous to validated treatments in their structured, prescriptive, and time-limited nature, none is supported by published validational research. Nonetheless, all have generated considerable interest among mental health practitioners for whom research findings (or lack thereof) mean little. Although several of these fringe treatments are vying for the attention of traumatologists, the two most visible are EMDR and TFT.

TFT (Callahan, 1995), previously known as "the Callahan Techniques" (Callahan, 1985, 1987), has been advertised as a cure for phobia and has been applied to a variety of other disorders involving anxiety, emotional memories, or both. The treatment follows scripted formulae (called "algorithms") that include somatic stimulation (tapping) by the therapist, along with focused attention to fear symptoms, positive self-talk, humming a happy tune, counting, and the rolling of eyes (Callahan, 1995; Figley, personal communication, July 31, 1995). Treatment effectiveness is judged by changes in subjective units of discomfort (SUD) that have been used in other procedures, such as systematic desensitization (Wolpe, 1958). The technique has been aggressively disseminated in trade magazines, the popular press, television, professional meetings, and Internet lists.

The dissemination of the clinical procedure of EMDR (Shapiro, 1995a) has been accomplished in much the same way. EMDR Institute, Inc. (1997) boasts of 19,000 licensed clinicians having been trained since the initial published account of its application (Shapiro, 1989). The dissemination of the technique is rivaled only by the number of different clinical conditions to which it has been applied in clinical and research contexts. EMDR Institute, Inc. distributes promotional literature that alleges application to myriad conditions ranging from post-traumatic stress disorder (PTSD) to "self-esteem issues" (EMDR Institute, 1996).

THEORETICAL ANALYSIS OF ALLEGED TREATMENT EFFECTS OF EYE MOVEMENT DESENSITIZATION AND REPROCESSING

Since the original publication alleging beneficial effects of EMDR (Shapiro, 1989), little in the way of theoretical analysis has been published. Speculation has centered around the possible effects of eye movements on relaxation and anxiety (Hedstrom, 1991), more traditional learning processes (Dyck, 1993), and the orienting response (Armstrong & Vaughan, 1996). This has been understandable, as it was serendipitously discovered through Shapiro's phenomonological experience—the now famous "walk in the woods" (Rosen, 1995). With the publication of the first book on the subject (Shapiro, 1995a), we have the opportunity to examine the substance of the conceptual analysis as well as the details of procedure.

Shapiro's (1995a) model of psychopathology is seriously flawed in several ways. The most obvious flaw is a basic lack of understanding of the concepts Shapiro attempted to explain and use. The conceptual framework is based on physiological concepts closely related to neurological processes. The analysis, however, is no more than a series of elaborated metaphors that Shapiro called a "working hypothesis." The language used in the analysis is little more than jargon and results in an embarrassing form of cognitive-neuro-pseudo-science. This limitation is most obvious when attempting to apply the loosely organized information-processing metaphor to the analysis of the psychopathology of fear, anxiety, and trauma. The model ignores the work of such scholars as Keane, MacLeod, Mathews, Barlow, Hollon, and M. Eysenck (see Martin, 1991), who have applied the concepts of cognitive neuroscience to clinical problems. Instead, Shapiro appealed to "neuro networks" that, as memory structures, are presented as the locus of cognitive pathology. In both the conceptual and graphic form, they are simplistic and naive. In particular, Peter Lang's (1985) bioinformational analysis of affective imagery, with its use of propositional networks, is mentioned only in passing. There are similar conceptual contrivances, including "state-specific" and "frozen" memories, and "process" phobia.

The model as presented shows a profound lack of understanding of the psychopathology of cognition and emotion. These limitations extend directly to the mechanisms of therapeutic change. There is no consideration of substantial learning processes, such as habituation and extinction. Instead, accelerated information processing is invented. We are told (Shapiro, 1995a) that "The key to psychological change is the ability to facilitate the appropriate information processing. This means making connections between healthier associations" (p. 48). The astute reader, however, will quickly recognize that the making of connections *is* the process of association. A substantive and non-tautological analysis would tell us what phenomena are connected, how the "illness" of such associations is to be judged, and what change leads to better health. Instead, we are presented with a metaphorical process that is akin to a psychic immune system (p. 31). "Healing" occurs after eye movements and other features of the clinical protocol unlock the pathological condition. This analysis does not represent a meaningful understanding of psychoneuroimmunology and cannot be taken seriously.

Shapiro's analysis of the psychological function and therapeutic necessity of eye movements is badly muddled. There are a number of terminological confusions regarding movements of the eye including rapid eye movement (REM), nystagmus, and "saccades" in other of her writings. She also used terms in a confused and erroneous manner, as all eye movements are considered in the same breath. Although all are conjugate eye movements, induced (tracking) movements are smooth pursuit movements; they are involuntary in that a moving object must be present for them to occur. Saccadic movements are ballistic in nature and occur as the point of fixation changes; these are very short (20 to 50 ms) and have a small arc (10 to 20 degrees). Optokinetic nystagmus is involved in motion detection, and are quick movements followed by a rapid return to the point of fixation. These are produced either by inducing motion with reference to the environment or by moving the environment. Vestibular nystagmus results from stimulation of vestibular organs and is involved in orientation and posture. These last three have nothing to do with smooth pursuit movements and none has anything to do with REM during sleep. Nonetheless, Shapiro related these terms to alleged common pathological and therapeutic processes, as when she discussed dream sleep (p. 39). In a similar discussion of nystagmus (p. 24), she failed to appreciate that nystagmus is not consciously detectable and serves a totally different perceptual function than the one she is addressing.

The general function of the analysis is to convince the reader that eye movements are the essence of the therapeutic process. We are also informed, however, that eye movements can be supplanted with other lateralized stimulation, such as finger taps (Shapiro, 1995a, p. 31). Although this assertion is presented as fact, it is merely a statement of opinion. Nonetheless, we are asked to conclude that the changes in verbal reports of distress without eye movements can still be considered the effects of treatment, rather than a non-specific artifact. As the research has shown, however, eye movements (or other lateralized stimulation) are not necessary for the change in verbal reports of symptoms (see below).

At first glance, EMDR appears to be an instance in which an inductively derived clinical procedure gives rise to a theory of pathology and therapeutic change. The "theory," however, is a systematic confusion based on simple-minded metaphors. It is an analysis based on an analogy that is devoid of significant explanatory value, either at a conceptual or empirical level. Nonetheless, it is a conceptual scheme that functions very well as a marketing tool for a ready-made readership; the 19,000 "licensed clinicians" who have completed EMDR training (EMDR Institute, 1997). Unfortunately, a large proportion of these individuals may not have sufficient grounding in psychology and research methodology to identify its limitations.

TFT

A comparable explication of TFT theory has not been made (Callahan, 1995). Instead, the mechanisms of action must be inferred from more informal descriptions of the procedure and rationale (Callahan, 1995). The locations of somatic stimulation (tapping) are similar to those used in acupuncture treatments (acupoints). Promoters of TFT (Callahan, personal communication, December 19, 1996; Gallo, 1995) suggest that tactile stimulation of acupoints transduces mechanical energy into "bioenergy" and modifies the "bioenergetic system." Pathology involves a disturbance (perturbation) or blockage in the bioenergetic system, which results in symptomatic negative emotions. Tapping and other specific procedures provide physical energy that is transformed into energy of the "meridian system" that removes or transforms perturbations and blockages. There are a number of ancillary processes ("psychological reversal") that are incorporated into the conceptual analysis and treatment procedures. The content and the sequence of the algorithms are specifically designed for specific psychological difficulties. It is these procedural techniques that are marketed and taught at TFT workshops. A detailed critique of TFT can be found in Hooke (1998).

EMPIRICAL VALIDATION RESEARCH

In evaluating the "treatment approach" to trauma experience, we will review the published research addressing the effectiveness of EMDR and TFT to evaluate the theoretical analysis that is presented to explain the procedures and justify their application. The empirical data on outcome and process will then be related to theoretical constructs. Subsequently, we will attempt to account for the popularity of these procedures through pseudoscientific promotion, pseudoscientific communication, and the demands of the clinical market place.

EMDR

One can reasonably surmise that the popularity of EMDR among mental health clinicians is due primarily to the remarkable claims of its proponents, including rapidity, permanence, and generality of its effects. Such claims are often made on the basis of clinician testimony (workshop training and word-of-mouth) and published case studies. Nevertheless, as philosopher David Hume noted, extraordinary claims require extraordinary evidence. Although testimony and clinical claims have abounded, systematic evidence has been more difficult to come by.

Critical evaluations of EMDR were published soon after the initial experimental outcome study and a large number of descriptive case studies (Herbert & Mueser, 1992; Lohr et al., 1992). These reviews attempted to alert researchers to the methodological issues involved in valid measurement of the clinical conditions, valid application of the clinical procedure, and the control for procedural confounds and non-specific effects of treatment. Following the publication of a number of subsequent experimental investigations, Lohr, Kleinknecht, Tolin, & Barrett (1995) concluded that (a) the protocol frequently reduces verbal report and independent observer ratings of distress, (b) psychophysiologic indices show little effect of treatment, (c) there is little evidence to indicate an effect of treatment on behavioral indices, and (d) eye movements do not appear to be an essential component of treatment. Similar conclusions were arrived at independently (Acierno et al., 1994).

Since these reviews, the empirical literature has expanded rapidly and experimental rigor has improved greatly. Moreover, the improved methodologies have been applied across a range of clinical problems. Despite the improved controls, however, the evidence in support of the effectiveness of the procedure is no greater now than before. As indicated in Lohr et al. (1995), the major procedural limitations have been in the control for the non-specific effects of treatment per se, rather than the specific effects of eye movements and other supposed "active ingredients" of EMDR.

A number of strategies and tactics have been used to control for non-specific effects (Borkovec, Kaloupek, & Slama, 1975; Mahoney, 1978; O'Leary & Borkovec, 1978). One tactic is the use of additive or subtractive experimental manipulations to identify the functional significance of treatment procedures (Rehm et al., 1982; Nezu, 1986; Nezu & Perri, 1989). Subsequent studies have adopted this tactic in evaluating the effect of EMDR on public speaking fear (Foley & Spates, 1995), test anxiety (Gosselin & Matthews, 1995), spider phobia (Muris & Merckelbach, in press), panic disorder (Feske & Goldstein, 1995), and PTSD (Boudewyns & Hyer, 1996; Devilly, Spence, & Rapee, 1998).

Examination of the current published and professionally presented research reveals evidence that is far from remarkable and does not contradict our earlier conclusions (Lohr, Lilienfeld, & Tolin, 1999; Lohr, Tolin, & Lilienfeld, 1998). The findings of the relative effects of different experimental control conditions used in these studies are summarized in Table 1. As in our earlier review, the recent research clearly shows that application of the EMDR procedure is consistently followed by changes in verbal reports of distress and standardized self-report measures, and that no treatment or delayed treatment control conditions show little change (Bates, McGlynn, Montgomery, & Mattke, 1996; Boudewyns, Stwertka, Hyer, Albrecht, & Sperr, 1993; Boudewyns & Hyer, 1996; Devilly, Spence, & Rapee, 1998; Feske & Goldstein, 1995; Foley & Spates, 1995; Shapiro, 1989; Wilson, Becker, & Tinker, 1995). The treatment effect, however, is not universal (Bates et al., 1996; Jensen, 1994), and Devilly et al. (1998) have found that the effects are not stable over a period of 6 months. Moreover, the findings show that no-movement imagery or lateral stimulation analogs also show reliable changes in the same measures (Boudewyns & Hyer, 1996; Boudewyns et al., 1993; Devilly et al., 1998; Dunn, Schwartz, Hatfield, & Weigele, 1996; Feske & Goldstein, 1995; Foley & Spates, 1995; Gosselin & Matthews, 1995; Hazlett-Stevens, Lytle, & Borkovec, 1996; Pitman et al., 1996; Sanderson & Carpenter, 1992). Three studies show that a lateral stimulation analog results in positive change (Bauman & Melnyk, 1994; Foley & Spates, 1995; Pitman et al., 1996), and one study shows no change (Wilson, Silver, Covi, & Foster, 1996). These findings, however, are not remarkable, as they can be attributed to measurement artifact and incidental effects of the treatment procedure.

Some studies comparing EMDR with no treatment, no additional treatment, or wait-list controls show greater effects of EMDR on self-report measures (Bates et al., 1996; Boudewyns & Hyer, 1996; Foley & Spates, 1995; Rothbaum, 1995; Wilson et al., 1996), though some studies show no immediate difference (Bates et al., 1996; Devilly et al., 1998; Jensen, 1994). These results are not extraordinary, however, in that they can be attributed to any number of incidental effects including differential credibility, expectation for improvement, experimental demand, and therapist–experimenter allegiance effects (Bootzin, 1995; Evans, 1985; Gaffan, Tsaousis, & Kemp-Wheeler, 1994; Grunbaum, 1985).

Grunbaum (1985), in an analysis of "placebo" effects, has argued convincingly that the empirical test of characteristic features of a treatment (e.g., eye movements) and incidental features of the treatment can best be conducted in relation to the theory that justifies the treatment. If the theory of treatment considers eye movements to be the most characteristic feature of the treatment, then control conditions manipulating eye movements are necessary. Determination of the functional significance of

Table 1 Results of comparisons between EMDR and control conditions

Clinical problem	Authors	Trained in EMDR?	Comparison condition(S)	SUD	VoC	Standardized measures	Psycho-physiologic data	Behavioral assessment
PTSD	Rothbaum (1995)	Trained	No treatment	—	—	Yes	—	—
	Boudewyns & Hyer (1996)	Trained	Closed eyes	No	No	No	No	—
	Devilly et al. (1998)	Trained	No additional treatment	Yes	Yes	Yes	Yes	—
			Flashing light	No	—	No	No	—
	Pitman et al. (1996)	Trained	No additional treatment	—	—	No	—	—
			Finger tapping	No	—	No	No	—
Traumatic memories	Hazlett-Stevens et al. (1996)	Trained	Stationary eyes	No	No	No	—	No
	Wilson et al. (1995)	Trained	Non-direction	Yes	No	No	—	No
			No treatment	Yes	—	Yes	—	—
Various anxiety disorders	Wilson et al. (1996)	Trained	Stationary eyes	Yes	Yes	—	Possible	—
Panic disorder	Feske & Goldstein (1995)	Trained	Finger tapping	Yes	Yes	—	Possible	—
			Stationary eyes	—	—	Possible (2 OF 5)	—	—
			No treatment	—	—	Yes	—	—

	Study	Training	Comparison					
Public speaking anxiety	Foley & Spates (1995)	Trained	Bilateral auditory stimulation	No	No	No	—	—
			Stationary eyes	No	Yes	No	—	—
			No treatment	No	Yes	Yes	—	—
Test anxiety	Gosselin & Mathews (1995)	Trained	Stationary eyes	No	No	No	—	—
Spider phobia	Muris & Merckelbach (1997)	Trained	Imaginal exposure	No	—	—	No	No
	Bates et al. (1996)	Not trained	In vivo exposure	Yes	—	No	—	No
			No treatment	—	Yes	—	No	No

Note. SUD = Subjective units of distress; VoC = Validity of cognitions scale
No = EMDR not superior to control condition;
Yes = EMDR superior to control condition;
Possible = EMDR appears superior but critical statistical comparisons not made;
— = Not Obtained.

incidental features (e.g., imagery re-exposure, re-attribution) requires control of these elements and comparison with the effects of the characteristic component(s). The vast majority of studies comparing EMDR with a no-movement imagery analog control show no difference in immediate effectiveness (Boudewyns & Hyer, 1996; Boudewyns et al., 1993; Devilly et al., 1998; Dunn et al., 1996; Foley & Spates, 1995; Gosselin & Matthews, 1995; Hazlett-Stevens, Lytle, & Borkovec, 1996; Muris & Merckelbach, 1997; Sanderson & Carpenter, 1992) or long-term effectiveness (Devilly et al., 1998). Feske and Goldstein (1995) have shown short-term, but not long term, differences in favor of EMDR. When a no-movement imagery analog procedure is compared with a lateral stimulation analog procedure, there is no significant difference (Foley & Spates, 1995; Wilson et al., 1996). When EMDR is compared with a lateral stimulation analog, three studies show no significant difference (Bauman & Melnyk, 1994; Foley & Spates, 1995; Pitman et al., 1996). These latter findings should not necessarily be interpreted as evidence for the effectiveness of eye movement and other lateral stimulation. The change following these procedures is more parsimoniously interpreted as a function of imagery re-exposure that is common to both, and which is suggested by the findings of Muris and Merckelbach (1997).

The specific (characteristic) effects of EMDR on psychophysiologic indices and behavioral indices of fear and anxiety are even more meager. The only controlled studies using avoidance (behavioral) measures show no significant difference between EMDR and no treatment (Bates et al., 1996), a no-movement imagery analog (Dunn et al., 1996; Hazlett-Stevens et al., 1996), imaginal exposure (Muris & Merckelbach, 1997), in-vivo exposure (Muris & Merckelbach, 1997), and non-directive treatment (Hazlett-Stevens et al., 1996). Most studies using psychophysiologic measures show no effect of EMDR compared with a no-treatment control (Bates et al., 1996) and a no-movement imagery analog (Boudewyns & Hyer, 1996; Devilly et al., 1998; Pitman et al., 1996). If there is a characteristic effect of the EMDR protocol, it does not seem to be disorder-specific (see Table 1).

Only one study (Wilson et al., 1996) reported the superiority of EMDR over a no-eye movement analog and an alternative lateral stimulation analog condition. This study, however, is fatally flawed not only in its data analysis, but also in the assessment of several psychophysiologic measures. Moreover, the reported effects, even if replicable, must be interpreted against possible therapist–experimenter allegiance effects (Gaffan et al., 1994). These researchers have long been recognized as ardent supporters and promoters of the treatment that they presume to objectively evaluate. The same caution should be exercised in the interpretation of other studies that are often cited as demonstrations of EMDR's effectiveness (Shapiro, 1989; Silver, Brooks, & Obenchain, 1995; Wilson et al., 1995). It should also be noted from Table 1 that all but one study used therapists that were trained under the auspices of EMDR Institute, Inc. The issue of training will be elaborated when we discuss the relationship between ratings of treatment fidelity and treatment outcome (see below).

THE EFFECT OF EMDR ON PTSD

A more detailed examination of several studies will illustrate the limitations of EMDR in the treatment of PTSD.

Rothbaum (1995) reported that EMDR reduced rape-related PTSD symptoms more than a wait-list, measurement-only condition, but there were no other procedural controls. In the absence of such controls, the change in reported symptoms is no more convincing than that reported in similar studies (Boudewyns et al., 1993; Shapiro, 1989; Wilson et al., 1995).

Boudewyns and Hyer (1996) compared EMDR with a no-movement imagery analog (EC) and a no-imagery control (C) procedure in the treatment of combat-related PTSD. All participants received 8 sessions of the standard inpatient or outpatient PTSD treatment program at the Augusta Veterans Administration hospital. Participants in the EMDR group received between five and eight sessions of EMDR. Participants in the EC group received the same number of sessions. The EC participants did not engage in eye movements during individual treatment, but kept their eyes closed and engaged in imaginal exposure for the same period of time. Participants in the no-imagery control (C) condition received only the standard group treatment. Outcome measures included the Clinician Administered PTSD Scale (CAPS), the Impact of Events Scale (IOE), Profile of Mood States–Anxiety (POMS), Subjective Units of Discomfort (SUD), and heart rate (HR) in response to a tape-recorded script of the participant's most disturbing memory. All measures were obtained before and after treatment by a clinician blind to experimental condition. Mixed-model 3×2 analyses of variance (ANOVAs) were conducted on the CAPS, IOE, and POMS. Analysis of covariance (ANCOVA) using pre-treatment HR as a covariate was applied to post-treatment HR data. The analyses revealed that the EMDR and the EC conditions showed greater change than the control condition on SUDS, POMS–Anxiety, and HR, but they did not differ from one another. In addition, the analyses indicated that the three groups showed equal change on the CAPS and all groups showed no significant change on the IOE. Thus, it appears that neither eye movements nor lateral stimulation are necessary for measured change, and that imagery exposure may be sufficient for change on some indices of PTSD (HR, SUDS, POMS–Anxiety) but not for others (CAPS). These null effects for EMDR per se are consistent with those of Jensen (1994) and Boudewyns et al. (1993).

Devilly et al. (1998) also reported a study using combat-related PTSD patients. In a fashion similar to Renfrey and Spates (1994), EMDR was compared with a no-movement imagery analog condition presented to participants as "reactive eye dilation desensitization and reprocessing," which involved the same EMDR protocol except that a flashing light was substituted for lateral eye movements. Both treatments were compared with a no-extra treatment control condition that included the same assessment battery as in the treatment conditions. All participants had received or were receiving psychological services from community or governmental agencies. Treatment effectiveness measures included standardized anxiety, depression, and PTSD scales, as well as HR and blood pressure. The results showed that both treatment groups improved by post-treatment, but that there was no difference between the two treatment conditions. Participants in the two treatment conditions did not differ on standardized measures from the control condition, but they did improve more than the control condition when the reliability change index on the Mississippi–PTSD scale was used as a measure of clinical improvement. Nevertheless, there was no statistical or clinical difference in symptomatology from pre-treatment data to 6-month follow up. The authors concluded that eye movements are not the mechanism of change and that other non-specific (e.g., placebo) effects are responsible for the high levels of efficacy reported in previous research conducted without adequate procedural controls.

Pitman et al. (1996) used a cross-over design in which combat-related PTSD patients were randomly assigned to one of two treatment sequences using EMDR or no-movement imagery analog (fixed-eye) treatment. The analog control procedure consisted of all the EMDR components including movement of the therapist's hand. The participant, however, maintained eye fixation and tapped one finger to correspond with therapist hand movement. Each treatment was applied to a separate traumatic memory, and each was applied for a maximum of six sessions once per week. All therapists obtained complete EMDR training, and both treatments were observed by an EMDR expert and rated for treatment integrity. Treatment process variables included SUD ratings and four psychophysiologic indices: HR, skin conductance, and two electromyographic measures. Treatment outcome measures included IOE Intrusion and Avoidance scores on the two images, Mississippi–PTSD scores, SCL-90–R scores, Clinician-Administered PTSD Scale (CAPS), and a cued intrusive thought log. Paired t-test comparisons showed that SUD scores significantly decreased (habituated) in both treatment conditions within and across treatment. Analyses showed that psychophysiologic indices were significantly reduced in 9 of 16 comparisons (56%). In the movement condition, psychophysiologic indices were significantly reduced in 62.5% of the comparisons; in the fixed condition, they were significantly reduced in 50% of the comparisons. ANOVAs between treatment conditions showed no statistical differences between treatment conditions on any process variable. Paired t-test comparisons showed that both the EMDR and the control procedure resulted in the reduction of 3 of 8 process variables. A comparison of the treatment conditions showed that the control procedure was superior to the EMDR procedure on IOE–Avoidance scores.

The authors concluded that there was "partial emotional processing" during the treatment sequence on SUD ratings and some psychophysiological measures. The results, however, showed that on outcome variables, there was limited change (only 3 of 8 measures) within each of the procedures. Moreover, the analyses indicate little difference between the two procedures except for the possible superiority of the control procedure on IOE scores. The overall findings of this study show that only SUD ratings decreased following either procedure. The use of the control procedure indicates that eye movements confer no clear advantage over other forms of stimulation. This finding is consistent with those of other studies providing procedural controls (Boudewyns & Hyer, 1996; Devilly et al., 1998; Dunn et al., 1996; Feske & Goldstein, 1995; Foley & Spates, 1995; Gosselin & Matthews, 1995).

The findings of Pitman et al. (1996) also speak to the issues of EMDR training and treatment integrity. All therapists were fully trained under the auspices of EMDR Institute, Inc., and approximately 25% of the treatment sessions were rated for treatment integrity on a scale from 0 to 6 by an acknowledged EMDR expert. The mean rating for the EMDR condition was 3.1 (*moderately acceptable*) and 2.4 (*low acceptable*) for the fixed-eye condition. Analysis of ratings showed no differences between conditions on any outcome measure. In both treatment conditions, there were 2 of 6 significant positive correlations between treatment integrity ratings and outcome measures (Pitman, personal communication, October 21, 1996). The mean correlation between expert ratings of integrity and treatment outcome measures in the EMDR condition was $r = .23$ ($r^2 = .05$). The mean correlation between ratings and outcome measures in the fixed-eye condition was $r = .42$ ($r^2 = .18$). These low correlations suggest that there is little association between the "correct" application of EMDR and measured treatment outcome.

The irrelevance of eye movements was suggested in early controlled research on EMDR (Renfrey & Spates, 1994; Sanderson & Carpenter, 1992), and these findings have been since replicated a number of times (see Table 1). Because these findings will not go away, Shapiro (personal communication, January 16, 1996) has resorted to what some might call a theoretical sleight of hand in order to accommodate the obvious. We are now told that the eye movements are not necessary:

> EMDR is not simply eye movement. Eye movement, or other stimulation is merely one component of a complex method that combines aspects of many of

the major modalities. That is why behaviorists, congnitivists, psychodynamic [sic], etc.... are able to find EMDR useful. Remove the eye movement and there is still a very powerful method.

Shapiro (1996c) also stated:

EMDR is an eight-phase methodology that catalyzes and accelerates the healing process. Observations from thousands of treatment sessions indicate that an innate processing system is physiologically geared to take disturbance to mental health (Shapiro, 1996b, p. 14).

Such statements and others (Shapiro, 1995a, p. 31) represent a serious obfuscation of the empirical and theoretical issues. If eye movements are not necessary, then it is incumbent on Shapiro to specify the essential (characteristic) features of the treatment to permit independent controlled experiments assessing the relative effects of procedural artifacts and the substantive clinical procedure (Grunbaum, 1985).

But consider, for a moment, the conclusions of Pitman et al. (1996):

Scientific theories are meaningless if they are not falsifiable. The finding that eye movements may be deleted from the EMDR procedure without loss of emotional processing (and therapeutic benefit) necessarily falsifies neurologic (including REM) theories of eye movements in EMDR's mechanism of action. (p. 426)

Beyond meaninglessness, we believe there are even more serious implications of the obfuscation. Without a clear specification of the specific (characteristic) features of treatment, any number of convenient auxiliary hypotheses (Meehl, 1990) may be advanced in the face of disconfirmatory evidence. Under such conditions, the theory is untestable. This is the pseudoscientific "babble" of which O'Donohue and Thorp (1995) have spoken in their review of Shapiro (1995a). More important, such theoretical hocus-pocus threatens to turn legitimate inquiry into pseudoscientific twaddle.

In the overall summary of the empirical findings, there is little reason to alter the earlier conclusions of Lohr et al. (1995) and Lohr et al. (1998), except to conclude that eye movements or other lateralized stimulation are superfluous. It is now clear that there is little ordinary evidence (and no extraordinary evidence) to support the extraordinary claims of the promoters of EMDR or those mental health practitioners who believe in its unique efficacy. Indeed, the supporting evidence is so meager that one wonders if these enthusiastic practitioners have approached these issues with the scientific skepticism that empirically trained clinicians should exercise. Of course, there are many mental health practitioners who are not trained in the empirical tradition, and there are many others who have abandoned it. Thus, the enthusiasm may not be all that surprising.

TFT

In comparison with EMDR, outcome and process research on TFT is non-existent. There are no published randomized, pre-post, no-treatment (or wait-list control) experiments. In fact, there are no published reports of any kind. Callahan (1987) has described a successive case report of phobia treatment in a proprietary archive, but repeated attempts to obtain an original copy of the manuscript have gone unanswered (Tolin, personal communication, September 6, 1996, September 19, 1996). A study alleged to be a replication of Callahan (1987) has been described in a promotional announcement (Leonoff, 1995). An unpublished doctoral dissertation supervised by Callahan (Wade, 1990) reported on the effects of phobia treatment on self-concept. A report in an electronic publication described the effect of TFT, EMDR, visual dissociation therapy, and trauma incident reduction (Figley & Carbonell, 1995) in a non-randomized, uncontrolled outcome study. The report in the electronic medium, however, does not provide sufficient detail to evaluate methodological issues of assessment and the incidental effects of intervention; again, repeated attempts to obtain more specific details have gone unanswered (Lohr, 1996, personal communication, September 1, 1996, October 1, 1996). The remainder of the communications regarding treatment effectiveness consist of clinician testimonials on Internet postings. Serious tests of this treatment could be conducted easily by comparing a "correct algorithm" with control procedures reversing the algorithm procedures, randomization of the procedures, or the use of an algorithm for a different treatment. In any case, it is incumbent on Callahan to specify what would be a strong test of validity of his procedure.

IMPLICATIONS FOR INTERVENTION ON THE TRAUMA EXPERIENCE

The EMDR research investigating the functional significance of eye movement (Boudewyns & Hyer, 1996; Feske & Goldstein, 1995; Foley & Spates, 1995; Gosselin & Matthews, 1995; Renfrey & Spates, 1994) has rendered "orienting response and accelerated information processing models" into explanations in search of a phenomenon. It is peculiar that such speculation has occurred with little appreciation for the quality of experimental methods and the limitations of the data. It is almost as if there were presumptive validity of the procedure, followed by attempts to understand it. Yet such speculation and promotion of the procedure proceeds undeterred.

The proponents of EMDR have found two different but related venues for the promotion and expansion of the treatment procedure. One is cognitive-behavioral therapy, which has gained ascendance in validated treatment because of its emphasis on experimental analysis of treatment outcome and process. Moreover, these treatments predominate the inventory of treatments for anxiety and mood disorders (Chambless, 1995) and are the same disorders to which EMDR is most frequently applied.

The relation between the development of EMDR and behavior therapy is not coincidental. The use of the term *desensitization* is not a semantic accident, as Wolpe (1990) has argued that the process developed by Shapiro may be variant of more established behavioral change mechanisms. Clinicians treating fear-related conditions are now faced with clinical procedures that are alleged to be more efficient and long-lasting than behavioral exposure treatments. In the vacuum of substantive positive data, there has occurred the promotion of a technique that, in terms of quantity and quality, can best be described as "commercial." The same can be said of TFT.

The burgeoning specialty of "traumatology" has provided the other venue for the promotion of EMDR and TFT. In recent years there has been an expansion of the signs and symptoms attributed to post-stress clinical conditions, so much so that the diagnostic criteria for PTSD have become more general and a new stress-related diagnosis (acute stress disorder) has been added (American Psychiatric Association, 1994). In addition, the context for trauma effects has been expanded beyond natural and man-made disasters (e.g., combat, torture) to include negative life events occurring in the contexts of child rearing, family dynamics, and marital conflict. This expanding context has led to an expansion of "mental health clinicians" providing services for those alleging clinical consequences of negative life events, including psychologists and social workers, but also massage therapists and marriage and family counselors. Although some learned societies (such as the International Society for Traumatic Stress Studies) are essential in identifying the nature and process of acquired stress symptoms, there are many other less meaningful assemblages of people who identify themselves as traumatologists.

One means by which this group identification is established and validated is the Internet, on which various newsgroups exchange information. Two of the most prominent and active are the Traumatic Stress list (traumatic-stress@freud.apa.org) and the EMDR list (emdr@stjuvm. stjohns.edu). This vehicle has supplanted more traditional means of communication (e.g., scholarly journals) regarding the empirical validation of such procedures as EMDR and TFT for the treatment of trauma. Other means include the formal and informal communication that occurs in the training of these various techniques.

TFT theory is an amalgam of pseudoscientific allusions to "bioenergetic" phenomena. EMDR theory is cloaked in the jargon of computer technology, which serves as a facile means explaining its alleged effects. Part of the commercial popularity of EMDR can be attributed to its use of the information-processing metaphor and to the fact that the procedure has been subjected to empirical scrutiny. In this way, EMDR appears to be both scientific and scientifically validated. We argue that both of these techniques are little more than pseudoscience, but their pseudoscientific basis can serve as an effective means by which it can be marketed to mental health clinicians with minimal training in the scientific evaluation of theory, research procedures, and data.

EMDR, TFT, AND PSEUDOSCIENTIFIC EXPLANATION

Definition of pseudoscience

Although philosophers of science have yet to reach complete consensus on the definition of pseudoscience, most definitions share a common core of features. Logical positivists (Blitz, 1991; Carnap, 1967) regard pseudoscientific concepts as those incapable of logical definition and not reducible to physical and measurable entities. The traditional demarcation between science and pseudoscience hinges on the concept of falsifiability. A theory is scientific if, and only if, proponents can specify a priori findings that would definitively refute it (Popper, 1965). Pseudoscientific theories are often underdetermined, in that they contain fewer parameters than the unknowns that are to be explained (Loehlin, 1992). As a result, underdetermined models are untestable because they can achieve good fit with any set of data. The theoretical and empirical necessity of eye movements will serve as one means to examine the pseudoscientific nature of EMDR. Similarly, the necessity of the tapping, humming, counting, and eye-rolling of TFT will serve as another means to examine its pseudoscientific nature.

Scientific theories are almost always tested in conjunction with one or more auxiliary hypotheses, that is, hypotheses not directly relevant to, but nonetheless needed to test, the substantive theory of interest (Lakatos, 1970, 1978; Meehl, 1978, 1993). According to Lakatos, scientific theories are characterized by two crucial components: a "hard core" of fundamental presuppositions and a "protective belt" of auxiliary hypotheses required to test the theory in question. When the results of a test fail to corroborate a theory, the theory is virtually never immediately abandoned. Instead, its advocates typically perform a strategic retreat to the "protective belt" to modify or tinker with its embedded auxiliary hypotheses (e.g., "perhaps our measure of anxiety was not sufficiently sensitive; perhaps our intervention was not delivered properly").

Lakatos (1970) distinguished between "progressive" and "degenerating" theories on the basis of the temporal relation between theory and data. In progressive research programs, the theory tends to precede data; that is, theoretical predictions successfully anticipate new data. In a degenerating research program, data tend to precede theory. Unexpected and/or disconfirmatory findings repeatedly send its proponents scrambling back to their protective belt to "explain-away" the anomalies. Pseudoscientific theories are those that have degenerated to the point of being incapable of producing corroborated hypotheses. Their advocates spend most of their time attempting to account for unpredicted findings by means of strategic retreats. With EMDR, null results are repeatedly interpreted as a consequence of inadequate training, invalid application of the "protocol" by the researcher, or both (Jensen, 1994; Sanderson & Carpenter, 1992; Shapiro, 1995a). When comparable effects are found for control procedures intended to manipulate the effect of eye movement, we are told that the control procedure actually is a form of treatment (Boudewyns & Hyer, 1996a; Renfrey & Spates, 1994; Shapiro, 1995a). This is pseudoscience at work.

Bunge (1967, 1991) described four key features shared by most or all pseudosciences, such as astrology and parapsychology. First, pseudosciences typically do not "ground (their) doctrines . . . in our scientific heritage" (Bunge, 1967, p. 36). In other words, pseudosciences tend not to draw or build on existing scientific concepts but instead purport to create entirely novel paradigms. In the case of EMDR's modification of fear and anxiety, we hear nothing of habituation or extinction and a great deal about "neuro networks" (Shapiro, 1995a). From Callahan (1995), we hear of "bioenergies." Second, pseudosciences characteristically refuse to subject their theories to the risk of falsification and interpret potentially disconfirming data as either confirming or irrelevant. Thus, we hear that researchers who report null results were not trained (or trained well enough) in EMDR to obtain clinical effects. In the case of TFT, randomized, controlled outcome studies have been assiduously avoided. Third, pseudosciences are not self-correcting: A pseudoscientific research program interprets every failure as confirmation and every criticism as an attack (Bunge, 1967, p. 37). Thus, we hear of the advances of EMDR at yearly conferences assembled specifically to promote EMDR, and we hear of the narrow provincialism of EMDR and TFT critics (Callahan, 1995, personal communication, December 19, 1996; EMDR Institute, Inc., 1996). In the end, the principal goal of pseudoscience is persuasion (promotion) rather than truth seeking through the creative skepticism of the scientific enterprise.

COMMON PRACTICES IN PSEUDOSCIENCE

Unlike science, which seeks empirical refutations, pseudoscience seeks verification through uncontrolled but vivid demonstration. In other words, proponents of pseudoscience tend to search for and attend to confirming findings (proof), and to avoid and neglect potentially disconfirming findings (disproof). Bunge (1967) has observed that "the pseudoscientist, like the fisherman, exaggerates his catch and neglects his failures or excuses them" (p. 36).

Shapiro (1995a, personal communication, June 6, 1995, November 6, 1995, 1996a) provided just such an analysis in her review of the research findings that she used to justify the application of EMDR to a wide range of clinical problems. Published accounts that cast doubt on the effect of treatment are ignored or discounted for insubstantial reasons. For example, Shapiro (1995) alleged that the null findings researchers who have not had EMDR, Inc.-sanctioned training (Jensen, 1994; Montgomery & Ayllon, 1994a, 1994b) are due to invalid treatment application, when in fact no data exist to support this assumption. Unpublished and in-group reports (e.g., EMDR conference papers) are afforded the same credence as peer-reviewed publications, the result of which is the magnification of treatment effectiveness. As an example of a positive treatment outcome study, Shapiro (1995) cited an unpublished opinion survey of therapist satisfaction (p. 332) and then includes it in the text as an appendix. All of this stands in stark contrast to independent reviews (Acierno, Hersen, Van Hasselt, Tremont, & Mueser, 1994; Herbert & Mueser, 1992; Lohr et al., 1995; Lohr et al., 1998) that reveal that treatment effects are limited to verbal reports of distress and that note inadequate controls for procedural artifacts (e.g., non-specific effects) or comparisons with other treatments.

Dissimulation is another common practice of pseudoscience. Van Rillaer (1991) outlined two techniques of dissimulation used in pseudoscience. The first is the use of obscurantist language to compensate for an absence of content and to discourage would-be skeptics. Shapiro (1995a) has used this tactic in the development of her "accelerated information processing" model of pathology and treatment: "With each set of eye movements, we move the disturbing information—at an accelerated rate —further along the appropriate neuro-physiological pathways until it is adaptively resolved" (p. 30). In a similar fashion, Callahan (1995) has ascribed the effects of treatment to changes in "bioenergetic" processes:

> The procedure may be described as a body energy, bioenergy (meridian or the inappropriate "acupuncture") procedure. An integration of clinical psychology with body energy is developed with the diagnostic procedures which require the "tuning of the thought field" (thinking about the problem) (p. 2).

Second, many pseudoscientists liberally and loosely borrow concepts from allied disciplines. In pseudoscientific research, concepts are typically adapted not to buttress or foster integration with legitimate scientific concepts but to adorn the discipline with the superficial trappings of science. This appears to be yet another function of Shapiro's variant of cognitive science and Callahan's expropriation of acupuncture and chiropractic.

THE SALE OF PSEUDOSCIENCE

Sales tactics

Pratkanis has described the commercialization of persuasion in general (Pratkanis & Aronson, 1991) and the sale of pseudoscience (Pratkanis, 1995) as related social influence processes. The sale of pseudoscience involves a number of principles, some derived from social psychological research, that have been successfully used by those who sell pseudoscientific materials, ideas, or treatments to the public. These same principles of persuasion can help to explain how mental health practitioners (presumably inoculated by education) can be convinced of the efficacy of ineffective and bogus treatment techniques like facilitated communication in the treatment of autistic disorders (Delmolino & Romanczyck, 1995; Jacobson, Mulick, & Schwartz, 1995). We believe that the same principles can help to explain the popularity of EMDR and TFT. Many mental health providers, consumers, and health care agents have overestimated the efficacy of EMDR through common, age-old fallacies of judgment. We suggest that those who are involved in the promotion of EMDR, being human, are subject to the same fallacies described by Pratkanis. The promotion of pseudoscience includes promotional tactics and the operation of ubiquitous social psychological processes. The promotional tactics include the creation and use of phantom goals, the construction of vivid appeals, the use of pre-persuasion, the use of the rationalization trap, and the establishment of a professional granfalloon.

Phantom goals

Pratkanis (1995) suggested that pseudosciences are first directed toward the attainment of highly desired but distant goals. The initial step in the promotion of a pseudoscience is the creation of a "phantom" and the development of a means to attain it (p. 20). Phantom alternatives, according to Pratkanis and Farquhar (1992), are desirable goals that appear credible but are currently unavailable to the individual seeking change. In the original published account (Shapiro, 1989), EMDR was touted as a powerful (single-session) treatment for PTSD symptoms. Likewise, Callahan advertises TFT as a "cure" for phobia and related disorders in the American Psychological Associations's *APA Monitor* (1996) and numerous popular press magazines. The phantom is thus a quick "cure" for a refractory condition (Solomon, Gerrity, & Muff, 1992).

Vivid appeals

A related process in the promotion of pseudoscience is the construction of vivid appeals to persuade potential consumers. Vividly presented case studies can be far more convincing than scientific data; as a result, isolated "hits" receive greater weight than null results in the laboratory. Uncontrolled case reports (e.g., Marquis, 1991; McCann, 1992) have made extraordinary claims, suggesting that EMDR can not only eradicate the symptoms of PTSD but can bring about tremendous life changes in catastrophically traumatized individuals. For example, McCann (1992) reported that he not only cured a case of refractory PTSD using brief EMDR treatment, but also brought about dramatic life changes. Marquis (1991) used case studies to claim that EMDR was effective not only for PTSD but also for depression, eating disorders, and learning disabilities. Other case reports proclaim that EMDR is an effective treatment for sexual dysfunction (Wernik, 1993), alcoholism (Shapiro, Vogelmann-Sine, & Sine, 1994), and dissociative disorders (Lazrove, 1994). Callahan has taken this process one step further, demonstrating TFT in the fashion of stage hypnotist on numerous television talk shows. Thus, clinicians and the lay public may be initially attracted to EMDR and TFT in the hopes of finding a "miracle cure" for very difficult, and often debilitating, forms of pathology.

Some individuals may well improve after experiencing EMDR or TFT, but it is not terribly difficult to find individuals who respond positively to most any intervention. Moreover, such case studies can serve to undermine the persuasive power of adequately controlled experiments that yield null results. The vivid individual case is often more compelling than substantive but dry experimental procedure. It is to the vivid and compelling case study that many mental health clinicians are exclusively drawn. Indeed, Callahan has stated publicly that stage presentations are more convincing and trustworthy than empirical investigations carried out in "the hidden and highly safe secrecy of the ... laboratory" (Callahan, personal communication, December 19, 1996).

Pre-persuasion

The use of pre-persuasion is a third means of promulgating pseudoscience. Pre-persuasion consists of defining the situation or setting the stage in one's favor. One way in which this is accomplished is by interpreting results in support of prior expectations. This form of reasoning has been called "affirming the consequent," or as Pratkanis (1995) called it, the "illusory placebo effect" (p. 23).

In the case of EMDR, ambiguous or null results are interpreted in favor of EMDR. For example, Renfrey and Spates (1994) found no differences in outcome between EMDR and a control condition in which participants tapped their fingers rather than moved their eyes. The appropriate interpretation of this null result is that EMDR is no better than placebo treatment. Nevertheless, Renfrey and Spates (1994) interpreted their null results to mean that both EMDR and finger-tapping are viable treatments. In a review of Renfrey and Spates's study, the EMDR Institute, Inc. (1996) described the placebo condition as "EMDR using fixed visual attention" (p. 3); in other words, eye movement treatment without eye movements. Thus, even null results are interpreted as supporting claims of efficacy. Critical evaluation of these null results, however, requires the rejection of neurological "explanations" of alleged clinical effects (Pitman et al., 1996). It also requires us to interpret these circumlocutions as manifestations of pseudoscience.

This process capitalizes on what Popper (1965, 1983) and Meehl (1978, 1990) called "auxiliary hypotheses" in explaining contrary or undesirable results. Sometimes such hypotheses are legitimate alternative explanations that help to generate further predictions. In the case of pseudoscience, however, auxiliary hypotheses are simply invoked *post hoc* to explain away results that would otherwise place the original hypothesis in doubt. The process of pre-persuasion thus provides a means by which empirical falsification can be conveniently avoided. It is but a short step to the sacrifice of disconfirmability. In the case of TFT, the avoidance of any meaningful test of the treatment completely obviates the need for pre-persuasion. Instead, persuasion is the only means by which the procedure is promoted and sold.

Rationalization trap

A fourth process in the selling of pseudoscience involves the use of a "rationalization trap." The rationalization trap is based on the principle that quick commitment on the part of the consumers changes their perspective. Consumers who might initially have been skeptical are now compelled to rationalize the commitment they have made and will alter their beliefs accordingly.

During the past few years, the rationalization trap has been achieved by requiring all EMDR trainees to initially make a small, but psychologically important, commitment. Trainees have been required to sign two consent forms: The first states that because EMDR is a powerful procedure that could be dangerous in the wrong hands, the trainee will not teach others how to perform the technique. The second consent form states that because of its potential power, EMDR could be dangerous to trainees suffering from certain psychological disorders and that the trainee assumes full responsibility for any negative effects they might experience during the practice sessions. Shapiro (personal communication, June 6, 1995) has asserted that these forms are necessary for client protection and for the assurance of treatment fidelity in empirical research. These claims may be true; however, they have the added psychological effect of persuading the trainees (even before the training has taken place) that (a) EMDR is a powerful, quasi-mystical procedure and (b) training by "official" EMDR Inc. representatives is crucial. Notice also that it asks the trainee to affirm the conclusion (the logical error) that is at issue, namely the question of EMDR's efficacy. Bearing this in mind, it is little wonder that Lipke (1994) reported that 77% of the most highly trained EMDR participants, surveyed after completion of training, agreed that extensive training by Dr. Shapiro was a vital step in using the technique. Callahan's sale of various levels of treatment at exponentially increasing costs represents a rationalization "pit."

The Professional "granfalloon"

The fifth process facilitating the sale of pseudoscience is the establishment of what Vonnegut (1976) called a "granfalloon": a proud and meaningless association of human beings. Granfalloons are easy to create, and they establish a sense of social identity among the consumers of the persuasive message. Once such a group has been established, individuals become reluctant to express beliefs that are inconsistent with those of the group.

To some extent, this phenomenon is seen broadly in the field of disaster and trauma by practitioners who refer to themselves as "traumatologists," a label that indicates not only a select service and client population, but also a shared set of beliefs and assumptions about the nature of trauma. In the case of EMDR, the granfalloon is easily observable. At EMDR training, as already described, trainees have to sign a vow not to train "others" (i.e., those not in the granfalloon), after which they observe Dr. Shapiro in the company of her "facilitators," a specially identified group of clinicians who have particular responsibilities at training sessions and whose special status is recognized (Leeds, personal communication, July 3, 1996). The initial training workshop is followed by "Level 2" training at which distinctive treatment protocols and special clinical applications are discussed.

This process continues when the trainee is invited to become a member of the EMDR Network, an assemblage that provides special privileges, such as a newsletter, research summaries, and patient referrals. This is followed by membership in the Eye Movement Desensitization and Reprocessing International Association (EMDRIA). The most recent granfalloon is an EMDR Internet newsgroup (emdr@sjuvm.stjohns.edu), which requires one to identify one's "level of training" and which imposes sanctions on commentary critical of EMDR proponents and procedures (Leeds, personal communication, July 3, 1996).

The group identity of EMDR trainees is further solidified through a number of means, such as technical jargon and specialized information. The EMDR training process is characterized by specialized terminology

(Shapiro, 1995a) that is unique to those who are members of the granfalloon. Anxiety-eliciting thoughts and memories are referred to as "hot spots." Certain fears are known as "process phobias." Eye movements are performed in "saccade sets." The therapeutic modeling of adaptive self-statements is called "cognition installation." The linking of one idea to another is called "cognitive interweave" (e.g., Shapiro, 1995a). Such terms represent the "obscurantist language" of pseudoscience described by van Rillaer (1991) and discussed earlier.

The granfalloon also functions as a means of acquiring specialized information. Collective compliance with the "no-training" contract creates a sense of group identity among trainees. EMDR trainees are said to possess special knowledge; those who are skeptical of EMDR and who are not privy to this knowledge are frequently criticized. As Shapiro (1994) has stated, "unless they were trained [by us], we have no way of knowing [what was done]." Despite the fact that Shapiro (1995a) described her technique thoroughly in her book, and despite the fact that she has stated privately that she no longer requires a vow of non-disclosure from her trainees, she continues to defend her right to do so (Shapiro, personal communication, June 6, 1995). Thus, there remains an aura of exclusivity surrounding authorized training. So extreme is this position that Shapiro has threatened legal action against those who have published research on the effects of EMDR but who do not belong to the training granfalloon (Shapiro, personal communication, September 12, 1996).

Mechanisms in the sale of pseudoscience

The sale of pseudoscience is not composed merely of marketing tactics and procedures, it is also based on substantive social psychological processes. Pratkanis (1995) described the use of heuristics and commonplaces in the promotion of pseudoscience. *Heuristics* are defined as simple "if–then" rules or norms that are widely accepted; for example, if something is expensive, then it is of high quality. *Commonplaces* are widely accepted beliefs that form the basis for an appeal; for example, arguments from researchers are invalid because scientists do not fully understand therapeutic issues (assuming that mistrust of science is a widely accepted belief among some practitioners). Heuristics and commonplaces are powerful tools because they are widely accepted and rarely questioned.

In the scarcity heuristic, things that are rare or difficult to obtain are, ipso facto, valuable. One cannot obtain EMDR training just anywhere; complete training (Levels 1 and 2) must be obtained through the EMDR Institute at a price of over $600. Callahan's promotion of "voice technology" ranges from $10,000 to $100,000. The bandwagon heuristic suggests that if everyone agrees, then the message is probably true. EMDR promotional materials are replete with personal testimonials, as well as the claim that over 19,000 mental health clinicians have been trained in EMDR (EMDR Institute, 1997).

The message-length heuristic may be summarized by the statement "if the message is long, it is strong." The EMDR Institute (1996) provides an extensive list of references that appear to demonstrate the efficacy of EMDR. The reader who does not bother to examine the original articles is left with the impression that EMDR has been convincingly shown to be superior to patent treatments. Closer examination, however, shows that many of the studies included on the list are unpublished paper presentations at professional meetings. As most published experiments on EMDR treatments contain lethal methodological flaws (Lohr et al., 1995; Lohr et al., 1998), conference papers may also contain such flaws. In an extreme manifestation of insularity, some EMDR proponents have argued that the peer-review system of scholarly journals damages the process of empirical inquiry, and that informal communications represent a more valid form of scientific communication (Lipke, 1996; Silver, personal communication, November 2, 1995). In the same way, TFT is routinely described in lengthy advertisements in the *APA Monitor* and other trade magazines. As noted earlier, Callahan (personal communication, December 19, 1996) has suggested that the demonstration of TFT on the television stage is more substantial than scholarly, academic research.

In the representative heuristic, things that resemble each other on some salient dimension are treated as similar or as the same thing. This error is seen in the rapid spread of the application of EMDR to disorders other than PTSD. Clinical problems that even remotely resemble PTSD, the logic goes, must act like PTSD. Thus, EMDR has been offered as a "cure" not only for PTSD, but also for most other anxiety disorders, multiple personality disorder, children of alcoholics issues, low self-esteem, and substance abuse (EMDR Institute, 1996). The same is true of the promotion of TFT. The prescription of different "algorithms" for different problems gives the impression of treatment generality and reifies the underlying "bioenergetic" explanation of treatment effectiveness.

There are a number of commonplaces that foster the belief in a pseudoscience. The science commonplace, according to Pratkanis, is a paradoxical form of logic. On the one hand, science is seen as all-powerful and references to science bolster the credibility of the pseudoscientist. As is stated on the EMDR Internet site and in promotional materials, "More controlled studies of EMDR exist than for any other treatment of PTSD." The accuracy of this statement depends on the definition of experimental control, but the facile nature of such an assertion lends credibility to EMDR without any actual disclosure of the data. On the other hand, the science commonplace suggests that science is limited and cannot replace personal experience as a source of evidence. In the case of EMDR and TFT, uncontrolled case studies are the medium of choice. Critics of these procedures are frequently dismissed because of their lack of personal experience with EMDR (Shapiro, 1995a).

Finally, pseudoscience flourishes when skepticism and skeptics are effectively devalued. Pratkanis has argued that skeptics are often attacked through innuendo and character assassination rather than through reasoned argumentation. By attacking one's opponents in this fashion, the debate is quickly removed from the theoretical and empirical issues at hand (e.g., does a given treatment work?) and instead moves to the personal arena of ad hominem assault (e.g., is this critic someone we should listen to?). This process, unfortunately, has become so common that one might consider it a "signature" of the proponents of power therapies. Critics are attacked with questions about their professional training (e.g., Jensen, 1994; EMDR Institute, 1996; Shapiro, personal communication, September 12, 1996) and their motives (e.g., Lohr et al., 1995; Shapiro, personal communication, January 16, 1996).

Scientific skepticism does not characterize EMDR or TFT publicity. Instead, dissemination of information emphasizes personal anecdote, clinical observation, and personal experience of "training" that increases belief in the communicator and the message being presented. We are left with more of the process of belief promotion and with less of the progress of science. It is this context that has led a number of commentators to characterize EMDR as pseudoscience in both the contemporary (Herbert, Lilienfeld, Lohr, Montgomery, O'Donohue, Rosen, & Tolin, in press; Lohr, 1996; O'Donohue & Thorp, 1996) and historical perspectives (McNally, 1996).

The Professional Communication of Pseudoscience

Having reviewed the current empirical and theoretical status of EMDR, one is reminded of Valenstein (1986). In his book, he developed the argument that the rapid adoption of and support for psychosurgery, in the absence of methodologically sound research support, was in part due to the "impractical" nature of traditional psychotherapy that required many sessions of one-to-one contact. Valenstein (1986) pointed out that not only did the medical profession rapidly adopt and promote psychosurgery, but that "Lobotomy was promoted by the popular press.... [who] popularized each new 'miracle cure' with uncritical enthusiasm" (p. 5). We can see parallels today in the rapid adoption and uncritical dissemination (ABC News, 1994; Elias, 1994) of treatments for long-standing psychiatric disorders such as PTSD that are relatively resistant to traditional treatments.

Tactics of dissemination and promotion

The status of the research is crucial in evaluating the promotion of EMDR and TFT, and the manner in which this research is portrayed has important implications for their promotion. Attempts have been made (Acierno et al., 1994; Herbert & Mueser, 1992; Lohr et al., 1992; Lohr et al., 1995; Lohr et al., 1998; Tolin et al., 1996) to evaluate this research in academic journals, but the major source of information for mental health practitioners has been through the workshop training itself. More recently, Shapiro's (1995a) book describing the technique and the rationale has attempted to present the research in a light favorable for commercial promotion. Another means by which the research is used as a promotional device is the use of the electronic media, such as specialty networks, (e.g., Traumatic-Stress list, EMDR Institute Discussion list, and the EMDR Institute, Inc. web site). The accuracy of the representations on these networks is difficult to determine, given the informal and transient nature of the electronic medium. Nevertheless, examination of Shapiro's (1995a) analysis of EMDR provides some indication of the function that electronic dissemination is meant to serve.

Published accounts that cast doubt on the effect of treatment are ignored or discounted for insubstantial reasons, and positive findings are consistently over-interpreted. Unpublished and in-group reports are afforded the same credence as peer-reviewed publications, the result of which is the further magnification of treatment effects. Similar material is available from the EMDR Institute. In addition to homepage information, the list-servers provide a means to exchange information about EMDR and TFT. Frequently, individuals (including Shapiro and Callahan) who identify themselves variously as EMDR "trainers" or "facilitators" make pronouncements on such list-servers regarding the status of theory, application, and the literature as it relates to the treatment. It is here that the information transfer engine of the Internet is being used to its maximum potential.

Although promotional errors are predominantly excesses, errors of omission are also a regular occurrence. Promotional materials typically omit articles published in peer-reviewed journals that have not supported the effectiveness of EMDR (e.g., Herbert & Mueser, 1992; Lohr et al., 1992; Montgomery & Ayllon, 1994a, 1994b). Selective deletion of negative findings is but one means of managing the flow of information to clinical consumers. Other promotional errors are more basic to the scientific enterprise. Others researchers (e.g., Foa, Rothbaum, & Molnar, 1995; Herbert & Mueser, 1992; Lilienfeld, 1996; O'Donohue & Thorp, 1995) have pointed out the lack of rigorous attempts to provide for the means of obtaining disconfirming evidence. O'Donohue and Thorp (1995) observed that "little intellectual honesty prevailed" (p. 18) in the development of strong or risky tests of the treatment procedure.

Misdirection occurs in a variety of ways in the presentation of EMDR. Promotional materials repeatedly appeal to the fact that thousands of clinicians world-wide have been trained in EMDR. The number of people trained in a technique or adhering to a theory is not germane to the validity of a treatment's therapeutic effect and, as a result, the appeal to popularity is a specious argument. If the number of "believers" were relevant to arguments regarding scientific knowledge, then phrenology would still be a dominant factor in the analysis of personality and the prediction of behavior.

ACCEPTANCE OF EMDR BY MENTAL HEALTH CLINICIANS

In the sale of any commodity, a transaction takes place between two parties; the seller and the purchaser. Although we have emphasized the selling of EMDR and TFT, it is also necessary to examine important aspects of its purchase. In an ideal scientific world, the decision to purchase and use clinical procedures would be determined solely by the content of academic and professional training (knowledge) of the purchaser and by the empirical validation of those procedures (commodity). The clinical armamentarium would consist of effective and validated assessments and treatments. We do not live in an ideal world, however, and clinicians purchase procedures outside the context of formal training and research. Indeed, the split between the scientist and the practitioner appears to be ever-widening, and it is important to identify the processes by which the incorporation of unvalidated procedures occurs.

One process is that of clinical and financial expediency. New, unique, or intractable cases may require the application of experimental procedures, and they should be identified as such. Nevertheless, there appears to be a much more subtle and substantive dissociation of the practitioner from the body of empirical science.

This dissociation appears to be based partly on the professionalization of psychology and the development of an alternative model of clinical knowledge (Tsoi-Hoshmand & Polkinghorne, 1992). This alternative model is based on postmodern knowledge and epistemology (Kvale, 1992). The increasing influence of postmodern attitudes in academic circles, as well as the reasons underlying this trend, have recently been documented by Gross and Levitt (1994). Postmodern thinking may no longer be limited, however, to the halls of the academy.

Although postmodernism is difficult to define, its central tenets include the propositions that (a) all knowledge that is contextual is therefore relative, and (b) science represents only one "mode of discourse" among many, and that scientific claims to knowledge are no more privileged than alternative claims (e.g., assertions based on intuition or personal experience). Most post-modernists therefore believe that the concept of "truth" is a dangerous and misleading illusion. Because all "facts" are situated in a specific cultural and historical context, such "facts" can never attain the status of universal knowledge claims.

Postmodern modes of thinking lend themselves in many cases to a willingness to accept claims on the basis of subjective convictions. According to most post-modernists, such convictions are not inherently inferior to beliefs derived from systematic scientific research. As Englebretsen (1995) noted,

> Premoderns and moderns based their willingness to accept or reject a speaker's claim on their judgment of how well it seemed to fit the facts of the case and to what extent it was logically consistent with the speaker's other claims or assumptions. By contrast, postmoderns "play the believing game," accepting the speaker's claim according to the degree of sincerity the speaker exhibits. Truth and coherence are no longer allowed to bully us in our communicative efforts. Expertise and authority are no longer the possession of only an elite few. (p. 52)

Some postmodern thinkers in psychology have further suggested that psychotherapeutic procedures should be based as much on "validation through practice" (Kvale, 1992), that is, on a tacit learning of what works by means of experience, as on research findings derived from controlled outcome studies (see also Schon, 1983). Tsoi-Hoshmand and Polkinghorne (1992) have similarly argued that clinical reflection and intuition (i.e., "practicing knowledge") should be placed on a par with scientific knowledge in the formal training of psychotherapists. They noted that "in relating theory to practice, research traditionally served as gatekeeper for entry into a discipline's body of knowledge" (p. 62) and that "in practicing knowledge, however, the test for admission is carried out through the use of reflective thought" (p. 62; see also Polkinghorne, 1992). Remarkably, such discussions contain virtually no mention of the factors (e.g., absence of immediate and consistent feedback) that often prevent psychotherapists from learning from experience, or of the social cognitive errors (e.g., selective recall, availability biases, self-fulfilling prophecies) that tend to create an illusion of such learning in its absence (Dawes, 1994; Dawes, Faust, & Meehl, 1989).

Are we stretching matters too far to suggest an analogy between postmodern thinking and the premature and uncritical acceptance of EMDR and TFT by many practitioners? Regrettably, we do not think so. The disturbingly rapid embrace of EMDR and TFT by thousands of clinicians prior to the publication of adequately controlled research suggests a willingness to place personal experience over scientific evidence, to value anecdote and clinical surmise over experimentation. Meehl (1993) has recently warned of this ominous trend in much of modern clinical psychology. His comments serve as a needed reminder to those who might be inclined to dismiss EMDR and TFT as isolated infections in an otherwise healthy discipline:

> My teachers at Minnesota (including Hathaway, Paterson, Skinner, and Feigl) ... shared what Bertrand Russell called the dominant passion of the true

scientist—the passion not to be fooled and not to fool anybody else. Only Feigl was a positivist, but all of them asked the two searching questions of positivism: "What do you mean? How do you know?" If we clinicians lose that passion and forget those questions, we are little more than be-doctored, well-paid soothsayers. I see disturbing signs that this is happening and I predict that, if we do not clean up our clinical act and provide our students with role models of scientific thinking, outsiders will do it for us. (pp. 728–729)

IMPLICATIONS FOR TRAUMA TREATMENT

If EMDR and TFT were the only treatments being commercially promoted, the task of empirical evaluation would be large but not insurmountable. It would take time and professional resources to rectify the commercial excesses, but the effort would be worth the outcome. For example, several years elapsed following the introduction of facilitated communication for the treatment of severe autistic and developmental disorders, but its empirical debunking has been convincing if not complete (Delmolino & Romanczyck, 1995; Jacobson, Mulick, & Schwartz, 1995).

There are, however, a large number of fringe therapies being actively marketed to those providing "traumatology" services, including critical incident stress debriefing (CISD; Mitchell, 1988), trauma incident reduction (Gerbode, 1995), and visual kinesthetic disassociation (Bandler & Grinder, 1979). Indeed, these represent an entire cottage industry of treatments that have either not been investigated with controlled studies, or that have been found to be no more effective than control procedures. Were that not sufficiently problematic, two of these procedures, EMDR and CISD, are now being integrated in the "treatment" of emergency service personnel (Solomon, 1996). Thus we have the promotion and marketing of clinical service that combines a procedure for which there is no controlled data with another procedure for which the controlled data show that it is no more effective than existing procedures.

The conservation of scarce financial and personnel resources is not guaranteed by facile but convincing marketing techniques. Resources are best preserved by cautious cost-benefit judgments that incorporate conservative evaluations of empirical research into the nature of psychological problems and the means of treating them. Simplistic theories of trauma pathology based on clumsy analogy may provide the appearance of an "explanation" of what is wrong and how to correct it. Inadequate understanding of research methodology by those promoting the service may provide the rationale and justification for adopting those services. It is the independent and skeptical evaluation of those theories and therapies that is the essence of the long and sometimes dry scientific enterprise.

Nonetheless, the appreciation and application of that enterprise will maximize the use of limited resources in the face of human trauma and its psychological consequences. There is no silver bullet for the treatment of trauma in the foreseeable future. We believe that this set of circumstances gives new meaning to the phrase *Caveat Emptor*: "Let the buyer beware."

REFERENCES

ABC News. (1994, July 29). *When all else fails.* "20/20" transcript.

Acierno, R., Hersen, M., Van Hasselt, V. B., Tremont, G., & Mueser, K. T. (1994). Review of the validation and dissemination of eye-movement desensitization and reprocessing: A scientific and ethical dilemma. *Clinical Psychology Review, 14,* 287–299.

American Psychiatric Association. (1994). *Diagnostic and statistical manual of mental disorders* (4th ed.). Washington, DC: Author.

American Psychological Association. (1996). Paid advertisement; "There is a cure." *APA Monitor, 27,* 14.

Armstrong, M. S., & Vaughan, K. (1996). An orienting response model of eye movement desensitization. *Journal of Behavior Therapy and Experimental Psychiatry, 27,* 21–32.

Bandler, R., & Grinder, J. (1979). *Frogs into princes: Neuro-linguistic programming.* Moab, UT: Real People Press.

Barlow, D. (1993). *Clinical handbook of psychological disorders.* New York: Guilford Press.

Bates, L. W., McGlynn, F. D., Montgomery, R. W., & Mattke, T. (1996). Effects of eye movement desensitization versus no treatment on reported measures of fear of spiders. *Journal of Anxiety Disorders, 10,* 555–569.

Bauman, W., & Melnyk, W. T. (1994). A controlled comparison of eye movements and finger tapping in the treatment of test anxiety. *Journal of Behavior Therapy and Experimental Psychiatry, 25,* 29–33.

Blitz, D. (1991). The line of demarcation between science and nonscience; The case of psychoanalysis and parapsychology. *New Ideas in Psychology, 9,* 163–170.

Bootzin, R. R. (1985). The role of expectancy in behavior change. In L. White, B. Tursky, & G. E. Schwartz (Eds.), *Placebo: Theory, research and mechanisms* (pp. 196–210). New York: Guilford Press.

Borkovec, T. D., Kaloupek, D. G., Slama, K. M. (1975). The facilitative effect of muscle tension-release in the relaxation treatment of sleep disturbance. *Behavior Therapy, 21,* 301–309.

Boudewyns, P. A., Stwertka, S. A., Hyer, L. A., Albrecht, J. W., & Sperr, E. V. (1993). Eye movement desensitization for PTSD of combat: A treatment outcome pilot study. *The Behavior Therapist, 16,* 29–33.

Boudewyns, P. A., & Hyer, L. A. (1996). Eye Movement Desensitization and Reprocessing (EMDR) as treatment for Post Traumatic Stress Disorder. *Clinical Psychology and Psychotherapy, 3,* 185–195.

Bunge, M. (1967). *Scientific research.* New York: Springer.

Bunge, M. (1991). What is science? Does it matter to distinguish it from pseudoscience? A reply to my commentators. *New Ideas in Psychology, 9,* 245–283.

Callahan, R. (1985). *Five minute phobia cure.* Wilmington, DE: Enterprise.

Callahan, R. (1987). Successful psychotherapy by telephone and radio. *Collected papers of the International Society of Applied Kinesiology.* Proprietary Archive. .

Callahan, R. (1995, August). *A Thought field therapy (TFT) algorithm for trauma: A reproducible experiment in psychotherapy.* Paper presented at the 105th Annual Convention of the American Psychological Association. New York.

Carnap, R. (1967). *The logical structure of the world and pseudoproblems in philosophy.* (R. A. George, Trans.) Berkeley: University of California Press. (Original published 1928).

Chambless, D. (1995). Training in and dissemination of empirically validated psychological treatments: Report and recommendations. *The Clinical Psychologist, 48,* 3–23.

Dawes, R. M., (1994). *House of cards: Psychology and psychotherapy built on myth.* New York: Free Press.

Dawes, R. M., Faust, D., & Meehl, P. E. (1989, March 31). Clinical versus actuarial judgment. *Science, 243,* 1668–1674.

Delmolino, L. M., & Romanczyck, R. G. (1995). Facilitated Communication: A critical review. *The Behavior Therapist, 18,* 27–30.

Devilly, G. J., Spence, S., & Rapee, R. (1998). Statistical and reliable change with Eye Movement Desensitization and Reprocessing: Treating trauma within a veteran population. *Behavior Therapy, 26,* 435–455.

Dunn, T. M., Schwartz, M., Hatfield, R. W., & Weigele, M. (1996). Measuring effectiveness of eye movement desensitization and reprocessing (EMDR) in non-clinical anxiety: A multi-subject, yoked control design. *Journal of Behavior Therapy and Experimental Psychiatry, 27,* 231–239.

Dyck, M. J. (1993). A proposal for a conditioning model of eye movement desensitization treatment for post traumatic stress disorder. *Journal of Behavior Therapy and Experimental Psychiatry, 24,* 201–210.

Englebretsen, G. (1995, May–June). Postmodernism and New Age unreason. *Skeptical Inquirer, 19,* 52–53.

Elias, M. (1994, November 29). Cover story: Eyeing new treatment for trauma. *USA Today,* D1, D2.

EMDR Institute, Inc. (1996). *Efficacy of EMDR: Research and publications.* Pacific Grove, CA: Author.

EMDR Institute, Inc. (1997). Promotional advertisement. *APA Monitor, 28,* 49.

Evans, F. J. (1985). Expectancy, therapeutic instructions, and the placebo response. In L. White, B. Tursky, & G. E. Schwartz (Eds.), *Placebo: Theory, research and mechanisms* (pp. 213–228). New York: Guilford Press.

Feske, U., & Goldstein, A. J. (1995, November). *Eye movement desensitization and reprocessing (EMDR) treatment for panic disorder: A controlled treatment outcome and partial dismantling study.* Paper presented at the 29th Annual Convention of the Association for the Advancement of Behavior Therapy, Washington, DC.

Figley, C. R., & Carbonnell, J. (1995, March 23). A systematic clinical demonstration methodology: A collaboration between practitioners and clinical researchers. *Electronic Journal of Traumatology* [On-line serial]. Available E-mail: Majordomo@freud.apa.org

Foa, E., Rothbaum, B. O., & Molnar, C. (1995). Cognitive-behavioral therapy of Post-traumatic stress disorder. In M. J. Friedman, D. S. Charney, & A. Y. Deutch (Eds.), *Neurobiological and clinical consequences of stress: From normal adaptation to PTSD* (pp. 483–493). Philadelphia: Lippincott-Raven Publishers.

Foley, T., & Spates, C. R. (1995). Eye movement desensitization of public-speaking anxiety: A partial dismantling study. *Journal of Behavior Therapy and Experimental Psychiatry, 26,* 321–329.

Gaffan, E. A., Tsaousis, I., & Kemp-Wheeler, S. M. (1994). Researcher allegiance and meta-analysis: The case of cognitive therapy for depression. *Journal of Consulting and Clinical Psychology, 63,* 966–980.

Gallo, F. P. (1995, March 23). Reflections on active ingredients in efficient treatments of PTSD, Part 1. *Electronic Journal of Traumatology* [On-line serial]. Available E-mail: Majordomo@freud.apa.org.

Gerbode, F. (1995, May). *Presentation on traumatic incident reduction.* Paper presented at the Active Ingredients in Efficient Treatments of PTSD Conference, Florida State University, Tallahassee.

Gosselin, P., & Matthews, W. J. (1995). Eye movement desensitization and reprocessing in the treatment of test anxiety: A study of the effects of expectancy and eye movement. *Journal of Behavior Therapy and Experimental Psychiatry, 26,* 331–337.

Gross, P. R., & Levitt, N. (1994). *Higher superstition: The academic left and its quarrels with science.* Baltimore: The Johns Hopkins University Press.

Grünbaum, A. (1985) Explication and implications of the placebo concept. In L. White, B. Tursky, & G. E. Schwartz (Eds.), *Placebo: Theory, research and mechanisms* (pp. 9–36). New York: Guilford Press.

Hazlett-Stevens, H., Lytle, R. A., & Borkovec, T. D. (1996, November). *Efficacy of eye-movement desensitization in the treatment of cognitive intrusions related to memories of a past stressful event.* Paper presented at the 30th Annual Convention of the Association for the Advancement of Behavior Therapy, New York.

Hedstrom, J. (1991). A note on eye movements and relaxation. *Journal of Behavior Therapy and Experimental Psychiatry, 22,* 37–38.

Herbert, J. D., Lilienfeld, S. O., Lohr, J. M., Montgomery, R. W., O'Donohue, W. T., Rosen, G. M., & Tolin, D. F. (in press). Science and pseudoscience in the development of Eye Movement Desensitization and Reprocessing: Implications for clinical psychology.

Herbert, J. D., & Mueser, K. T. (1992). Eye movement desensitization: A critique of the evidence. *Journal of Behavior Therapy and Experimental Psychiatry, 23,* 169–174.

Hooke, W. (1998). A review of Thought Field Therapy. *Electronic Journal of Traumatology* [*online*], *3.* Available at http://rdz.stjohns.edu/trauma/contr3:2.html

Jacobson, J. W., Mulick, J. A., & Schwartz, A. A. (1995). A history of facilitated communication: Science, pseudoscience, and antiscience. *American Psychologist, 50,* 75–765.

Jensen, J. A. (1994). An investigation of eye movement desensitization and reprocessing (EMD/R) as a treatment of posttraumatic stress disorder (PTSD) symptoms of Vietnam combat veterans. *Behavior Therapy, 25,* 311–325.

Kvale, S. (1992). Postmodern psychology: A contradiction in terms? In S. Kvale (Ed.), *Psychology and postmodernism* (pp. 31–57). London: Sage.

Lakatos, I. (1970). Falsification and the methodology of scientific research programmes. In I. Lakatos & A. Musgrave (Eds.), *Criticism and the growth of knowledge* (pp. 91–195). Cambridge, England: Cambridge University Press.

Lakatos, I. (1978). Introduction: Science and pseudoscience. In J. Worrall & G. Currie (Eds.), *The methodology of scientific research programmes: Philosophical papers* (Vol. 1, pp. 1–7). Cambridge, England: Cambridge University Press.

Lang, P. J. (1985). The cognitive psychophysiology of emotion: Fear and anxiety. In A. H. Tuma & J. D. Maser (Eds.), *Anxiety and the anxiety disorders* (pp. 131–170). Hillsdale, NJ: Erlbaum.

Lazrove, S. (1994, November). *Integration of fragmented dissociated traumatic memories using EMDR.* Paper presented to the Annual Convention of the International Society for Traumatic Stress Studies, Chicago, IL.

Leonoff, G. (1995). The successful treatment of phobias and anxiety by telephone and radio: A replication of Callahan's 1987 study. *Thought Field Therapy Newsletter, 1,* (pp. 1, 6)

Lilienfeld, S. O. (1996). EMDR treatment: Less than meets the eye? *Skeptical Inquirer, 20,* 25–31.

Lipke, H. (1994, August). *Survey of practitioners trained in eye movement desensitization and reprocessing.* Paper presented to the Annual Meeting of the American Psychological Association, Los Angeles, CA.

Lipke, H. J. (1996, January). Letter to the editor. *APA Monitor,* p. 3.

Loehlin, J. C. (1992). *Latent variable models* (2nd ed.). Hillsdale, NJ: Erlbaum.

Lohr, J. M. (1996). Analysis by analogy for the mental health clinician: A review of Shapiro (1995). *Contemporary Psychology, 41,* 879–880.

Lohr, J. M., Kleinknecht, R. A., Conley, A. T., Dal Cerro, S., Schmidt, J., & Sonntag, M. E. (1992). A methodological critique of the current status of the eye movement desensitization. *Journal of Behavior Therapy and Experimental Psychiatry, 23,* 159–167.

Lohr, J. M., Kleinknecht, R. A., Tolin, D. F., & Barrett, R. H. (1995). The empirical status of the clinical application of eye movement desensitization and reprocessing. *Behavior Therapy and Experimental Psychiatry, 26,* 285–302.

Lohr, J. M., Tolin, D. F., & Lilienfeld, S. O. (1998). Efficacy of Eye Movement Desensitization and Reprocessing: Implications for behavior therapy. *Behavior Therapy, 29,* 123–156.

Lohr, J. M., Lilienfeld, S. O., & Tolin, D. F. (1999). Eye Movement Desensitization and Reprocessing: An analysis of specific versus nonspecific factors. *Journal of Anxiety Disorders, 12,* 185–207.

Mahoney, M. J. (1978). Experimental methods and outcome evaluation. *Journal of Consulting and Clinical Psychology, 46,* 660–672.

Marquis, J. N. (1991). A report on seventy-eight cases treated by eye movement desensitization. *Journal of Behavior Therapy and Experimental Psychiatry, 22,* 187–192.

Martin, P. R. (1991). *Handbook of behavior therapy and psychological science: An integrative approach.* New York: Pergamon Press.

McCann, D. L. (1992). Post-traumatic stress disorder due to devastating burns overcome by single session eye movement desensitization. *Journal of Behavior Therapy and Experimental Psychiatry, 23,* 319–323.

McNally, R. J. (1996). Review of "Eye movement desensitization and reprocessing: Basic principles, protocols, and procedures. *Anxiety, 2,* 153–155.

Meehl, P. E. (1978). Theoretical risks and tabular asterisks: Sir Karl, Sir Ronald, and the slow progress of soft psychology. *Journal of Consulting and Clinical Psychology, 46,* 806–834.

Meehl, P. E. (1990). Appraising and amending theories: The strategy of Lakatosian defense and two principles that warrant it. *Psychological Inquiry, 1,* 108–141.

Meehl, P. E. (1993). Philosophy of science: Help or hindrance? *Psychological Reports, 72,* 707–733.

Mitchell, J. T. (1988). Development and functions of a critical incident stress debriefing team. *Journal of Emergency Medical Services, 13,* 42–46.

Montgomery, R. W., & Ayllon, T. (1994a). Eye movement desensitization across images: A single case design. *Journal of Behavior Therapy and Experimental Psychiatry, 25,* 23–28.

Montgomery, R. W., & Ayllon, T. (1994b). Eye movement desensitization across subjects: Subjective and physiological measures of treatment efficacy. *Journal of Behavior Therapy and Experimental Psychiatry, 25,* 217–230.

Muris, P., & Merckelbach, H. (1997). Treating spider phobics with eye-movement desensitization and reprocessing: A controlled study. *Behavioural and Cognitive Psychotherapy, 25,* 39–50.

Nezu, A. (1986). Efficacy of a social problem-solving therapy approach to unipolar depression. *Journal of Consulting and Clinical Psychology, 54,* 1210–1244.

Nezu, A., & Perri, M. G. (1989). Social problem-solving therapy for unipolar depression: An initial dismantling investigation. *Journal of Consulting and Clinical Psychology, 57,* 408–413.

O'Donohue, W., & Thorp, S. (1996, March). EMDR as marginal science. *The Scientist Practitioner, 5,* 17–19.

O'Leary, D. K., & Borkovec, T. D. (1978). Conceptual, methodological, and ethical problems of placebo groups in psychotherapy research. *American Psychologist, 33,* 821–830.

Pitman, R. K., Orr, S. P., Altman, B., Longpre, R. E., Poire, R. E., & Macklin, M. L. (1996). Emotional reprocessing during eye movement desensitization and reprocessing (EMDR) therapy of Vietnam Veterans with post-traumatic stress disorder. *Comprehensive Psychiatry, 37,* 419–429.

Polkinghorne, D. E., (1992). Postmodern epistemology of practice. In S. Kvale (Ed.), Psychology and postmodernism (pp. 146–165). London: Sage.

Popper, K. R. (1965). *The logic of scientific discovery*. New York: Harper.

Popper, K. R. (1983). *Realism and the aim of science*. Totowa, NJ: Rowman and Littlefield.

Pratkanis, A. R. (1995). How to sell a pseudoscience. *Skeptical Inquirer, July/August, 19*, 19–25.

Pratkanis, A. R., & Aronson, E. (1991). *Age of propaganda: The everyday use and abuse of persuasion*. New York: W. H. Freeman.

Pratkanis, A. R., & Farquhar, P. H. (1992). A brief history of research on phantom alternatives: Evidence for seven empirical generalizations about phantoms. *Basic and Applied Social Psychology, 13*, 103–122.

Rehm, L. P., Kornblith, S. J., O'Hara, M. W., Lamparski, D. M., Romano, J. M., & Volkin, J. (1982). An evaluation of the major components in a self control behavior therapy treatment for depression. *Behavior Modification, 5*, 459–489.

Renfrey, G., & Spates, C. (1994). Eye movement desensitization: A partial dismantling study. *Journal of Behavior Therapy and Experimental Psychiatry, 25*, 231–239.

Rosen, G. (1995). On the origin of eye movement desensitization. *Journal of Behavior Therapy and Experimental Psychiatry, 26*, 121–122.

Rothbaum, B. O. (1995, November). *A controlled study of EMDR for PTSD*. Paper presented at the 29th Annual Convention of the Association for the Advancement of Behavior Therapy, Washington, DC.

Sanderson, A., & Carpenter, R. (1992). Eye movement desensitization versus image confrontation: A single-session crossover study of 58 phobic subjects. *Journal of Behavior Therapy and Experimental Psychiatry, 23*, 269–275.

Schon, D. (1983). *The reflexive practitioner: How professionals think in action*. New York: Basic Books.

Shapiro, F. (1989). Efficacy of the eye movement desensitization procedure in the treatment of traumatic memories. *Journal of Traumatic Stress, 2*, 199–223.

Shapiro, F. (1994, November). *Eye movement desensitization and reprocessing*. Special interest group meeting at the meeting of the Association for the Advancement of Behavior Therapy, San Diego.

Shapiro, F. (1995a). *Eye movement desensitization and reprocessing: Basic protocols, principles, and procedures*. New York: Guilford.

Shapiro, F. (1995b, November 6). *EMDR research evaluations* [on-line]. Available: traumatic-stress@netcom.com

Shapiro, F. (1996a). Errors of context and review of eye movement desensitization and reprocessing research. *Journal of Behavior Therapy and Experimental Psychiatry, 27*, 313–317.

Shapiro, F. (1996b, December 11–15) *Promotional description of a presentation at the Brief Therapy Conference*. San Francisco, CA: Milton H. Erickson Foundation.

Shapiro, F. (1996c). *psyusa@stjuvm.stjohns.edu* electronic mail posting, August 20.

Shapiro, F., Vogelmann-Sine, S., & Sine, L. (1994). Eye movement desensitization and reprocessing: Treating trauma and substance abuse. *Journal of Psychoactive Drugs, 26*, 379–391.

Silver, S. M., Brooks, A., & Obenchain, J. (1995). Treatment of Vietnam War veterans with PTSD: A comparison of Eye Movement Desensitization and Reprocessing, biofeedback, and relaxation training. *Journal of Traumatic Stress, 8*, 337–342.

Solomon, R. M. (1996). *Basic CISD program for EMDR therapists*. Ellicott City, MD: International Critical Incident Stress Foundation.

Solomon, S. D., Gerrity, E. T., & Muff, A. M. (1992). Efficacy of treatments for posttraumatic stress disorder. *Journal of the American Medical Association, 268*, 633–638.

Tolin, D. F., Montgomery, R. W., Kleinknecht, R. A., & Lohr, J. M. (1996). An evaluation of eye movement desensitization and reprocessing (EMDR). In S. Knapp., L. van de Creek, & T. L. Jackson (Eds.), *Innovations in clinical practice: A source book* (Vol. 14). (pp. 423–437). Sarasota, FL: Professional Resource Press.

Tsoi-Hoshmand. L. T., & Polkinghorne, D. E. (1992). Redefining the science-practice relationship and professional training. *American Psychologist, 47*, 55–66.

Valenstein, E. S. (1986). *Great and desperate cures: The rise and decline of psychosurgery and other radical treatments for mental illness.* New York: Basic Books.

van Rillaer, J. (1991). Strategies of dissimulation in the pseudosciences. *New Ideas in Psychology, 9*, 235–244.

Vonnegut, K. (1976). *Wampeters, foma, and granfalloons.* New York: Dell Books.

Wade, J. F. (1990). *The effects of the Callahan phobia treatment technique on self concept.* Unpublished doctoral dissertation, Professional School for Psychological Studies, San Diego, CA.

Wernik, U. (1993). The role of the traumatic component in the etiology of sexual dysfunctions and its treatment with eye movement desensitization procedure. *Journal of Sex Education and Therapy, 19*, 212–222.

Wilson, S. A., Becker, L. A., & Tinker, R. H. (1995). Eye movement desensitization and reprocessing (EMDR) treatment for psychologically traumatized individuals. *Journal of Consulting and Clinical Psychology, 63*, 928–937.

Wilson, D. L., Silver, S. M., Covi, W. G., & Foster, S. (1996). Eye movement desensitization and reprocessing: Effectiveness and autonomic correlates. *Journal of Behavior Therapy and Experimental Psychiatry, 27*, 219–229.

Wolpe, J. (1958). *Psychotherapy by reciprocal inhibition.* Stanford, CA: Stanford University Press.

Wolpe, J. (1990). *The practice of behavior therapy* (4th ed.). New York: Pergamon Press.

Chapter 13

In the Public Arena: Disaster as a Socially Constructed Problem

Lennis G. Echterling and Mary Lou Wylie

INTRODUCTION

Hurricanes, earthquakes, tornadoes, floods, volcanic eruptions, and tsunamis are only a few of the powerful natural forces that can have enormous impacts on ecosystems. When humans inhabit the affected environment, these natural forces can cause injuries and deaths of many people; destroy homes, neighborhoods, and entire communities; disrupt the economic, social, and political functioning of a society; and inflict psychological distress on their victims. In other words, what was a meteorological or geological event has now become a social problem. Although it is obvious that most people are not prepared for the physical onslaught of a disaster, it is also true that they are ill-prepared to deal with the loss of a sense of control, meaning, and security. Individuals, groups, communities, and cultures struggle to interpret this extraordinary and catastrophic event, to understand its meaning, to shape the issues surrounding it, and to take steps to address the problems that have emerged in the wake of the disaster.

How an individual copes with a disaster is a function of several preliminary steps, including the person's awareness of distress, interpretation of the problem and consideration of coping alternatives (see Chapter 6). Even at this level of analysis, a personal problem is not a private matter that involves only the individual. Providing a conceptual link between the individual and the community, Mills (1959) portrayed such "personal troubles" as individual expressions of "public issues." A public issue transcends the individual and is woven throughout the fabric of community life. Conceptualizing a disaster as a social problem can be useful in examining the response process from a community perspective. How a condition is defined as a social problem and how it should be addressed can be seen as the products of a complex, collective process (Spector & Kitsuse, 1977). In this chapter, we discuss the important elements involved in this conceptualization of disaster as a social problem: framing the issues, public discourse, and implications for action.

FRAMING THE ISSUES

The process of framing the issues of a social problem and developing solutions to these concerns takes place in public arenas (Hilgartner & Bosk, 1988). From this perspective, public attention and societal resources are limited but essential assets for addressing social problems. A community must first recognize a condition to be a problem and define its parameters before it can decide on strategies to deal with that problem. As a result, there is stiff competition among groups who wish to promote different social problems as well as to propose alternative ways of conceptualizing them.

How the issues are framed will ultimately guide the actions taken by the affected communities to ameliorate their problems. For example, most discussions of natural disasters recognize them as complex social problems involving environmental, economic, political, psychological, social, and spiritual facets. However, some groups may propose framing the disaster in such a way that one particular facet is seen as the primary concern. The competition to frame the issues of disaster recovery may involve heated debates and intense disputes (Tierney, 1989). Some may present the natural disaster as fundamentally an economic problem that requires extraordinary measures, including the discarding of environmental regulations to facilitate redevelopment. Some may frame the disaster as essentially an ecological crisis that reflects the inhabitants' neglect of the environment. Others may argue that the disaster is a spiritual crisis that reflects the sins of the people.

Once the issues have been framed in certain ways, disasters have often served as catalysts for social movements and other dramatic changes in policies, laws, customs, and even in popular culture. For example, the debates regarding the issues presented by the Johnstown Flood of 1889 emphasized the need for an early warning system and for a nationally organized response to large-scale disasters (McCullough, 1968). The consequences of this discourse not only led to the development of the American Red Cross as a national disaster volunteer work force, but also inspired the standard comic line, "Run for the hills, the dam's busted," that would amuse audiences for generations to come. The discourse concerning the Great Mississippi River Flood of 1927 led to even more dramatic changes. It accelerated the migration of African Americans to the North, affected the outcome of the 1928 presidential election, and led to legislation that was more comprehensive and expensive than any previous law in history (Barry, 1997). More recently, following the Loma Prieta earthquake, California citizens took the unusual action of voting to increase the sales tax in order to improve the capacity of highways to withstand future earthquakes (Smith, 1992).

Recently, disasters have been conceptualized as threats not only to the economic well-being, living environments, and physical health of the victims, but also to their mental health (see, e.g., Myers, 1994; Weaver, 1995). The introduction of the construct of posttraumatic stress disorder also has stimulated research focusing on the psychopathological consequences of disaster (Joseph, Williams, & Yule, 1993).

PUBLIC DISCOURSE

People frame social issues through the process of public discourse. The public discourse—the way survivors talk about their disaster concerns—may involve presenting interpretations, spreading rumors, sharing personal experiences, offering information, and discussing policies. The public arenas in which this discourse takes place include the popular media, such as television, movies, magazines, newspapers, radio and books; the journals and books published by the research communities, professional societies, and academic presses; and the materials produced by educational institutions, service agencies, private foundations, and religious organizations (Hilgartner & Bosk, 1988). The arenas may involve thousands, even millions, of people, such as those arenas that involve the mass media. However, the discourse may take place on a smaller scale, in arenas such as church congregations, volunteer organizations, coffee klatches, and support groups. Whether the arena is a local bar, editorial page, legislature, classroom, radio talk show, board room, or a court, disaster issues are considered, discussed, framed, dramatized, packaged, and presented to others.

In the following section, we explore the framing of disaster in four contrasting public arenas: the mass media, the marketplace, religious settings, and interpersonal relations.

Mass media

The mass media are commonly seen as indispensable communication tools in dealing with disaster. They can prepare the public to meet disasters, provide warning and coping information, offer a forum for public reactions, and provide a record of the events (Wilkins, 1985). Because people are also much more likely to turn to mass media for announcements and information after a disaster, particularly if the damages are extensive (Mileti & O'Brien, 1992), interveners have used the media effectively in designing community-wide responses to disaster (Gist & Stolz, 1982).

In spite of offering vital public services before, during, and after disasters, the media's treatment of victims has often been characterized as exploitative, intrusive, and even traumatic (Butcher & Dunn, 1989). Media consumers themselves may also find their encounters with the media to be distressing. Television viewers, particularly those who identify with the participants, report higher levels of distress following exposure to a traumatic event, even when the event has no direct or indirect consequences on their lives (McGolerick & Echterling, 1995).

More relevant to the present argument is the criticism that the images and accounts of disaster reactions presented in the mass media and popular entertainment are often misleading, exaggerated, and inaccurate (Fischer, 1994). The media often portray individuals affected by disaster either as panicked, pathetic victims (Elliott, 1989) or as inspiring heroes overcoming extraordinary obstacles (Gans, 1979). In sharp contrast to these extreme portrayals in the media, the vast majority of disaster victims are neither superhuman nor completely helpless. Instead, they respond rapidly to the disaster with active coping (see Chapter 2). Immediately after a natural disaster, victims also turn to others for social comparisons in order to validate their own assessments and reactions. If their primary means of social comparison is through the media, however, their examples are most likely to be the outliers or extreme cases favored by the media. Consequently, it is difficult for victims to have a sense of sharing the same fate and reactions of others when their comparisons are with inspirational heroes and pathetic victims. These sensationalized portrayals also have influenced the beliefs of the general public regarding the degree of psychological impairment and distress of disaster victims (Yates, 1992).

In the popular media, particularly movies, there has been an almost obsessive fascination with disaster. In the 1930s, popular movies depicted such natural disasters as earthquakes ("San Francisco") and volcano eruptions ("The Last Days of Pompeii"). In the 1970s, "Earthquake," "The Towering Inferno," and "The Poseidon Adventure" were box office hits. More recently, Hollywood has produced such disaster movies as "Twister," "Dante's Peak," and "Volcano." Particularly in the contemporary movies, the portrayal of disaster has been technically masterful. The deep rumblings of THX Dolby sound and the computer-generated special effects realistically depict the physical devastation of disasters in spectacular fashion. In all these movies, however, the portraits of psychological and social reactions are stereotypical, superficial, misleading, and inaccurate. Focusing on the frantic efforts of (the many) panicked victims to flee the hazards and of (the few) bold responders to rescue those in peril, disaster movies end shortly after the disaster, with a sense of relief and a suggestion that, now that the adventure is over, people and communities will quickly return to their previous routines. The complex and challenging process of recovery is almost never treated in disaster movies.

Patterned as simplistic morality tales, disaster movies portray the multitudes as being complacent in their misguided sense of security, unheeding of the growing signs of danger, dismissive of the warnings of the lone prophet, and hesitant to take bold action until it is too late to be saved. The message of these movies seems to be that the meek shall inherit the earthquake. The movies also play on cultural stereotypes and myths by reserving particularly gruesome deaths for villains and violators of social norms. It once was a movie cliche that teenaged couples had sealed their fate once they have engaged in illicit sex. Now, lawyers, inept bureaucrats, and conniving investors are crowd-pleasing victims, encouraging audiences to blame the victims. Because exposure to popular culture influences attitudes regarding violence, gender roles, and appearance, it may also affect expectations regarding reactions to disasters. Just as heavy television viewing is associated with overestimating the extent of violence in society, reliance on television for disaster information leads to overestimating the extent of short-term psychological dysfunction and the risk of future psychopathology (see Chapter 3).

Mass media influence the framing of the disaster in other, more subtle ways. News reports focus on specific victims or heroes and offer detailed accounts of discrete events immediately following a disaster. Instead of providing the context of a long-term community response, they tend to obscure the real meaning of these events (Smith, 1992). The popular narrative form of problem, rising action, and climax dominates the mass media because reporters attempt to tell stories that are factual but also compelling and dramatic. This reliance on the narrative form attempts to personalize issues by focusing on individuals and distinct experiences that seem self-contained and isolated. In the process, media accounts too often abandon the "wide-angle lens" that a broader perspective and abstract analysis can offer. Because the mass media highlight the random dramatic events of destruction or heroism, the public is exposed to these sensational scenes, but rarely has access to a more complete, balanced account of the resiliency of communities in coping with disasters.

Besides emphasizing the dramatic and the personal, the media's short attention span leads to framing disaster issues in certain ways. The "action news" formula of many local news programs offers sound bites and fleeting images of destruction, but no coherent, organizing framework to provide meaning over time (Gamson, 1995). This fragmentation of meaning begins by emphasizing the immediate over the long-term, the unusual over the typical, and the personal over the social. As a result, the media neither present a comprehensive examination of the complex connections between different facets of disaster response nor portray the everyday, ordinary resilience that communities, in the long run, display.

Many people, even victims who directly experienced the catastrophe, rely on the extent of media coverage to confirm and certify the extraordinary nature of a disaster. Smith (1992) noted the stunning comment of one airline passenger who miraculously survived the crash landing, near Sioux City, Iowa, of United Flight 232, which killed 112 people. The survivor remarked, "We knew something was wrong. We didn't know it was that bad until we saw it on the news" (p. 1).

Marketplace and political arena

Crises, it has often been said, can also be opportunities—and there is no shortage of entrepreneurs, politicians, and activists who see disasters and other traumas as opportunities to address the needs of victims while also advancing their own financial interests and political agendas. Individuals, civic groups, volunteer organizations, professional societies, foundations, and corporations may have personal, political, and even financial interests in promoting certain social problems and in framing them in particular ways. Consequently, these individuals or groups are likely to attempt to boost public awareness and shape public attitudes regarding an issue to conform to their own agendas. These intense efforts can be pivotal in changing the shape and content of social issues.

The formulation that comes to dominate public discourse has profound implications for the future of the social problem, for the interest groups involved, and for social policy. In both the marketplace and the political arena, individuals and groups are often involved in "selling" products, programs, and policies to the public. Unfortunately, like the marketplace, the political arena too often measures success solely in terms of approval ratings or number of supporters. Vote tallies and market share, rather than program efficacy or product quality, become the bottom line.

In recent years, a number of people have entered the marketplace and political arena to offer intervention programs for trauma and disaster victims. With impressive rapidity, these individuals have commandeered these ideas into large-scale enterprises that franchise, package, and promote specific therapeutic techniques. These interventions include critical incident stress debriefing (CISD), eye movement desensitization and reprocessing (EMDR), and thought field therapy (TFT). Comprehensive reviews of the research literature have found no convincing evidence for the therapeutic efficacy of either CISD (Gist, 1996) or EMDR and TFT (see Chapter 12). These same reviews have dismissed such interventions as merely cult-like fads and examples of pseudoscience. Nevertheless, although the techniques' therapeutic effectiveness has consistently failed to be demonstrated, their promoters are clearly successful franchisers, packagers, and marketers.

Franchising   The rapidity of the growth in popularity of these techniques and their promotional tactics parallel those of social movements (Gist, 1996; Gist & Woodall, 1995). While the development of CISD, EMDR, and TFT do not meet all of the criteria of social movements, there are some similarities that are striking. Echterling and Wylie (1981) conceptualized the proliferation of telephone hotlines and crisis centers in the 1970s as a social movement with comparable generating conditions, leadership styles, organizational structures and adaptation processes. It is notable that many corporations—such as McDonald's, which promotes franchises, and other business enterprises, such as Amway, that rely on recruiting people—have beginnings that also correspond to social movements.

Social movements begin out of dissatisfaction with current conditions and a desire for dramatic change by involving others in a collective effort. Certainly, the pervasive psychological distress following the economic, environmental, and social devastation of a disaster presents conditions that can be highly conducive to the development of social movements. The promoters of CISD, for example, portray the disaster as posing the risk of psychopathology through exposure to critical incidents. Such a portrayal capitalizes on how the media reinforce disaster myths and frame disaster issues (Wenger, Dykes, Sebok, & Neff, 1975). One myth is that most disaster survivors are helpless victims who desperately require immediate intervention, relying entirely on the heroic efforts of responders. Another myth is that victims are at great risk for developing psychopathology. Like the "poster child" of a disease, the televised image of a disaster victim personalizes this issue and communicates a sense of urgency. Furthermore, the mass media's emphasis on the immediate over the long-term, the dramatic over the ordinary, and the personal over the social frames disaster issues in ways that encourage using short-term and powerful techniques with individuals and small groups perceived to be at risk.

Given this framing of the disaster, it is not surprising then to read recent reports of disruptions of services at some large-scale and highly publicized disasters because responders were beset by legions of therapists volunteering to offer immediate interventions (see Chapter 1). Practitioners with vested interests in using therapeutic techniques with survivors may be less motivated to correct inaccurate perceptions of disaster response. In fact, promoters may make use of those widely-held popular myths and perceptions to influence public attitudes to promote the use of such interventions.

The originators of social movements typically have leadership styles characterized by personal charisma, intense beliefs, and passionate commitment to the movement's ideology. Many entrepreneurs have successfully launched their financial enterprises by mimicking this evangelical zeal of social movement and religious cult leaders. A case in point can be drawn from the remarkable similarities between the emotional rhetoric, dramatic demonstrations, amazing testimonials, and sheer decibel levels of infomercials and the same attributes of TV evangelists' programs. Communicating a personal commitment to a vision is an effective recruitment and motivational tool in both the political arena and the marketplace. The developers of CISD, EMDR, and TFT also have displayed similarly forceful personalities as well as a total commitment to the ideology of their techniques. These charismatic individuals typically rely on colorful narratives, compelling testimonials, and a consistent vision in their discourses on the treatment of trauma (Callahan, 1985; Mitchell & Bray, 1990; Shapiro, 1995). Such proponents are usually less inclined to present critical analyses and skeptical inquiries.

Product development   Like other commercial products, EMDR and TFT both have registered trademarks that are prominently displayed in their promotional materials. CISD, EMDR, and TFT all involve standardized procedures that, their originators claim, must be followed exactly. New practitioners learn these procedures from the developers or their anointed disciples. At some point in the development of social movements, the charismatic leaders may develop institutes or foundations to coordinate functions and complete bureaucratic tasks involved in marketing and recruiting. These foundations also may promote their interests by lobbying policy makers, joining in coalitions with other groups, and adding a certain luster and prestige to their activities. At the present time, these enterprises have spawned the EMDR Institute, Inc., Callahan Techniques, and the International Critical Incident Stress Foundation, Inc.

Marketing   Organizations competing in the marketplace or political arena may use public relations experts, cultivate the endorsements of influential individuals and organizations, offer self-serving pronouncements, and design publicity campaigns to market their products or programs. In the case of CISD, EMDR, and TFT, marketing to practitioners or potential clients is primarily based on anecdotes, vivid personal testimonials, case studies, demonstrations, and advertisements in trade magazines.

For example, TFT displays full-page ads that are filled with hyperbole ("one of the major discoveries in psychology" and "five-minute phobia cure"), endorsements, and the liberal use of exclamation points (Callahan Techniques, 1997). Satisfied customers, identified with their institutional affiliations, offer testimonials, but there is little evidence supplied to support these claims. The "intensive" 4-day seminar covers both diagnosis and treatment "to help most psychological problems." The ads include classic sales techniques and inducements, including free material, special offers, and bonuses.

Other marketing efforts besides advertisements include dissemination of information in arenas that are easily accessible and involve frequent contacts, such as the Internet, and through word of mouth. These media for dissemination contrast with those typically used for therapeutic techniques, such peer-reviewed articles in professional journals, which are not as easily accessible.

Responding to negative information   People sometimes respond to disconfirming evidence with renewed commitment or greater strength in beliefs, a process discussed by Festinger, Riecken, and Schachter (1956). The promoter of CISD has been criticized for assuming unjustified credit for successful operations, relying on anecdotal evidence for support, ignoring the growing body of published studies that has failed to lend support, and marketing an enterprise that appears to be more concerned with the financial results than empirical support of effectiveness (Gist, 1996; also see Chapter 1). The immediate response to this initial criticism was a letter from a foundation attorney to the publication editor (Gist, personal communication, September 9, 1997). In general, the responses to criticisms of these therapeutic techniques have been to question the beliefs, training, or motives of the critic (Mitchell, 1996), or to threaten legal action (see Chapter 12). All of these are common strategies in the markplace or the political arena, though veritable anathemas in the discourse of science.

Measuring success   Success of the program is measured by popularity and satisfaction of the therapist, not by rigorous evaluation of behavior change in clients. One common strategy in the marketplace is to declare the large number of customers (as McDonald's signs proclaim, "Billions and Billions Sold"). EMDR advertisements in the trade journals (EMDR Institute, Inc., 1997) now boast that 22,000 licensed clinicians have been trained by EMDR Institute, Inc. Because the psychological symptoms of natural disaster survivors typically decrease rapidly following a disaster (Cook & Bickman, 1990), these techniques may be perceived by many, including the participants, as effective (Gist, Lubin, & Redburn, 1998; see also Chapter 1 in this book). As Gist and Woodall (1996) pointed out, "This is about scholarship rather than showmanship or salesmanship;

quality is measured through hypotheses tested and rejected, not through T-shirts sold or 'memberships' minted" (p. 16).

Religious arenas

In the 15th century, a series of natural disasters, including floods, freezes, and droughts, rocked the Aztec culture. Engineers and politicians framed the issues as technical or economic problems that required a sophisticated system of dikes or major changes in social policy. The priests of Mexico, however, were ultimately successful in promoting their interpretation that these events were signs that the gods were dissatisfied with the infrequency of human sacrifices in recent years. As a result, hundreds of victims were slaughtered in rites of placation throughout the Aztec cities. The purpose of the sacrifices was to atone for their parsimony, pacify the gods, and prevent future disasters (Brundage, 1972).

Even today, people commonly refer to a natural disaster as "an act of God," view the destruction as a form of supernatural punishment (Bushnell, 1969), attribute the event to the work of a supreme being (Pargament & Hahn, 1986), interpret it as a sign of the coming apocalypse, and perform religious ceremonies in response to a natural disaster (Ahler & Tamney, 1964). Consequently, the clergy and religious organizations can play an important and unique role in disaster intervention (Bradfield, Wylie & Echterling, 1989; Smith, 1978). When a disaster strikes a community, many people turn to their clergy for practical assistance, emotional support, rituals, and meaning.

Now, most clergy members in western societies, although emphasizing the spiritual implications of a disaster, do not present a cataclysm as evidence of a wrathful God (Bradfield et al., 1989). They instead portray the catastrophe as a time of spiritual crisis that challenges survivors to reaffirm their fundamental values, to demonstrate their religious commitments to care for fellow human beings, and to integrate this traumatic experience into the context of their theological beliefs. As disaster victims struggle with the problems of rebuilding their homes and their lives, they also grapple with deeper and more profound issues. The clergy depict these survivors as facing the same questions that have plagued theologians throughout the centuries: How could God allow such misfortunes to occur to them and their loved ones? What is the meaning of a life that can be so frail and ephemeral?

Clergy are often involved in all facets of the flood relief work: rescuing people at risk; helping in clean-up; providing food, clothing and shelter; offering emotional support; organizing relief programs; and generating and dispensing donations. Nevertheless, even in the midst of the rubble, clergy also respond to a disaster by convening their congregations as soon as possible to lead them in prayer, song, and other religious rituals in order to foster a sense of unity in vision, inspire a feeling of hopefulness, and help survivors to begin finding meaning in their suffering. As a result, the clergy offer a unique contribution of helping survivors to integrate the tragic disaster events into a meaningful theological framework (Echterling, Bradfield, & Wylie, 1992).

Many clergy members not only encourage framing the issues in ways that promote a positive meaning, they also counter the assertions of "street theologians" who voice the belief that whether a house was spared or not was a measure of the righteousness of its inhabitants (Bradfield et al., 1989). The clergy combat what they see as an example of using theology to blame the victim. However, in the massive destruction that is common in disasters, it is often easy to discover obvious exceptions to such a glib assertion. One minister noted with some amusement that these same people had great difficulty interpreting the miraculous way that flood waters skirted a local bar.

Framing the disaster as a challenge to do God's work on a large scale, many religious organizations, including Mennonite Disaster Relief, the Salvation Army, and the Interfaith Disaster Services, have formed to offer coordinated and long-term assistance to disaster survivors.

Interpersonal arena

Because a disaster is a time of heightened uncertainty, people are involved in attempting to make sense of the situation by looking to others for help in interpreting the circumstances and engaging in social comparisons with other victims (see Chapter 6). A common coping strategy is to engage in downward social comparisons—identifying others whose losses are greater in order to reduce their own distress (Taylor & Lobel, 1989). The interpersonal level of discourse includes rumors, gallows humor, and personal narratives.

Rumors are commonly observed after disasters. They reflect people's attempts to frame the issues of the disaster by proposing conspiracies, secret causes of the disaster, other potential hazards, and concerns that reflect prejudices and personal fears. For example, after the Johnstown Flood in 1889, there were numerous unsupported rumors that Hungarians were looting, dancing, cursing, and fighting amid the ruins (McCullough, 1968). In actuality, the Hungarian victims were afraid to seek any flood assistance and were often beaten. Negative rumors, in particular, are more likely to maintain their momentum and be passed along to others (Hobfoll, Briggs, & Wells, 1995).

"As long as natural and human-made disasters occur," Dundes (1987) pointed out, "jokes about these disasters are probably inevitable." (p. 80). The lore regarding humor is that it generally is a natural and effective coping strategy, but gallows humor is often seen as a sign of burnout (Weaver, 1995). Gallows humor and sick jokes, however, can also be seen as creative and defiant forms of discourse that reframe the disaster by poking fun at the threat (Thorson, 1993). It is coping by giving disaster the "raspberry." In addition to being a method that individuals use to handle their personal distress, humor also offers a means to bond with one another.

In addition to rumors and jokes, people share with others powerful accounts of their experiences and reactions after a natural disaster. Every survivor has a story to tell, and a need to give voice to the experience. Telling one's survival story is more than merely recounting the events of one's personal encounter with disaster; it is a complex, multifaceted, coping strategy that should not be discounted as unnecessary or minor in the often chaotic wake of such events. Telling one's story offers the survivor an opportunity to face, acknowledge, accept, and ventilate powerful emotions. The process can aid a survivor in beginning to recognize the enormity of what has happened and its consequences. The act of telling the story may itself help the survivor to organize the information needed to assess the disaster's impact and to think more clearly and completely about the current circumstances. Perhaps more importantly, because a disaster shatters assumptions about the world in which the victim lives (Janoff-Bulman, 1992), the process of telling one's story helps a survivor in the search to find some meaning in the event that has taken place (Meichenbaum, 1995).

Whereas children may struggle to capture their disaster experiences in pictures or play, most adolescent and adult survivors try to give voice to their ordeal and to bring coherence to what had been chaos. One man shared this story as one that had helped him through the disaster recovery process:

> We had an empty canning jar with a lid on it way back behind our basement stairs. When we were cleaning up after the flood, we found that jar unbroken and it still had its lid on it. But what was so amazing was that canning jar was now half full of flood water. We've left it there way back in the basement all these years. We decided we'd leave it for the next owners.

The story describes a ritual that expressed the survivor's acceptance of the flood experience. The storyteller cleaned up and rebuilt his home and his life, but he also kept a souvenir, a reminder that, deep down inside, the flood is still a part of his life. The healing power of this story seems to lie in its ultimate acceptance of the flood experience as one of the defining events in his life. Many survivors have used stories, rituals, philosophical reflections, and theological contemplations to find meaning in the trauma and long-term consequences of a natural disaster. Survivors who found some positive meaning in the traumatic event (Thompson, 1985) or identified positive outcomes of the disaster experience (Tobin & Ollenburger, 1996) were able to cope better and evidenced less post-disaster stress.

Whereas psychotherapists have applied the concept of narrative to the formal treatment of personal problems (White & Epston, 1990), we conceptualize narrative as an important dynamic at the community level. Because sharing stories necessarily involves others to hear them, the process helps to reconnect survivors, who may feel alone and alienated, to one another as they form a collective identity. The sharing of narratives also helps a community to gather individual experiences together to construct a mosaic of shared meanings of the disaster. Disaster victims and interveners often develop a standard repertoire of stories that portray the catastrophe and frame the disaster issues.

These personal narratives are often variations of three fundamental themes: horror stories, war stories, and happy endings (Fine, 1995). Each of these stories invites the audience to engage in "emotional hitchhiking" (Klapp, 1991) by sharing the affective state of the survivor. Although they may welcome the stories of others during the early days of disaster recovery, many survivors ultimately grow reluctant to serve as an audience to others' narratives (see Chapter 2).

Discourse about a disaster evolves and changes over time. Although survivors discard some stories, they may retell, revise, and refine others. Many survivors pass along disaster narratives to younger generations. A few stories go on to become family legends. In particular, many survivors find that the anniversary serves as an occasion for recollecting the traumatic experience. The memories become not only more frequent, but also more vivid and clear. "Now I can remember it like it just happened yesterday," said one survivor on the anniversary of a disaster. "I can close my eyes and see that water gushing through my window." The anniversary also spurs many to reflect on its meaning and place in their lives. "How can we ever forget the lives, homes, property, and businesses that were destroyed in the raging waters?" asked one minister on the anniversary. "One year later, we take time to pause, reflect, and remember." The anniversary encourages assessments of the disaster's impact, and prompts a review of the changes that have taken place during the past year.

Over the years, the personal narratives of survivors may become more reflective, dramatically reframing the disaster's issues and meaning. For example, in 98 interviews with flood survivors 7 years after the disaster, 64% of the survivors stated that the disaster experience had affected their thinking about how good life is. Because the flood was the single most destructive event in their lives, it seems only reasonable to assume that the disaster would affect survivors' opinions about the benevolence of life. However, surprisingly, a large majority (75%) of the subjects whose beliefs changed reported that these changes actually were for the *better*. As one woman said, "It made me stop and think of how fortunate I was." Another explained, "I'm thankful we are still here, and it's good to be alive." "I don't take anything for granted," declared one man. "I realized how lucky we are for what we have and we almost lost it all ... It put things into perspective."

Fewer (27%) of the survivors believed that the flood experience had affected their opinions about themselves. But when the subjects did report a change in opinion, it was nearly always for the better. Fully 94% described these changes in positive terms. "I'm more compassionate and understanding of others," said one survivor. "I'm older and wiser now," said another. "I wonder how I did what I did. I found out I could do some amazing things that I never imagined I could do."

Finally, 58% of the survivors reported that the flood had changed their beliefs about the meaning of life, and nearly all of them described the changes positively. One man expressed it this way, "It made me think, 'Why did this thing have to happen?' I value life much more. I take it one day at a time and value each day."

In interviews with clergy over 6 years after a disaster (Echterling et al., 1992), some acknowledged that the long-term impact continued to include distress and pain. One minister, for example, shared, "Around the anniversaries of the flood, I go into withdrawal. I pretend that it doesn't exist. To this day, I have less interest in Halloween because the rains started on Halloween." Another confided, "I left my congregation one and a half years after the flood because I felt burnt out. I'm invited back there often, but ... I feel uncomfortable going back. I avoid the memories of those times." In their struggle to face and meet the needs of their traumatized community, the clergy themselves suffered distress. As a result, the distinction between disaster helper and disaster victim becomes blurred because everyone in a community, in a very real sense, is a survivor of the event.

IMPLICATIONS

The way the issue is framed determines the action taken

One consequence of framing disasters as a mental health problem is that the interventions then involve the use of either traditional mental health services, such as formal psychotherapy, or the use of more informal psychotherapeutic techniques, such as crisis counseling and CISD. One probably misguided strategy, therefore, has been to expand the availability of clinical services, although the use of these services rarely increases following disasters (see Chapter 3). A second consequence is that the personnel available to carry out these interventions are often limited to mental health professionals. Therefore, one common activity for disaster preparedness is to identify those psychotherapists who are willing to offer pro bono counseling to disaster victims (Carll, 1996). The Disaster Services Regulations and Procedures of the American Red Cross, for example, include staffing guidelines that allow only licensed mental health professionals to participate in their training to offer disaster mental health services (American Red Cross, 1991).

Suggesting that all disaster victims need formal mental health interventions sabotages a sense of self-efficacy (see Chapter 1). The process of disaster recovery cannot depend only on professionals, who are limited in their number and available time. Besides, the vast majority of disaster victims develop into survivors without formal intervention. In most communities, a natural helping network evolves to promote the recovery process by offering practical assistance, sharing stories, giving emotional support, and performing rituals. Fundamentally and ultimately, the recovery depends on the members of the community. Instead of framing the disaster problem as one of individual psychopathology, a community can frame the issue as a measure of its resilience, coping, and competency.

Be wary of unrealistic promises

There is certainly no lack of cautionary tales of reform movements and fads that begin optimistically with unrealistic promises and end in disappointment. For example, moral treatment, mental hygiene, and community mental health have been three major reform movements in the United States over the past two centuries (Morrissey & Goldman, 1984). Specific techniques, such as facilitated communication, have also completed the cycle of promise, doubt, debunking, and discarding. Skepticism encourages us to critically assess assumptions, evidence, and conclusions from a disinterested position. If the claims for a treatment technique sound too good to be true, they probably are.

Be aware of vested interests and "safe" political decisions

For better or worse, both politicians and entrepreneurs place a high premium on public perception. It is now virtually mandatory, for example, that political leaders personally survey the damage immediately after a disaster. While this activity serves no practical purpose and may disrupt an already demanding schedule during a time of crisis, leaders nevertheless participate in this ritual to foster the perceptions of concern and support. In a similar vein, some organizations may continue to sponsor interventions, such as CISD, in spite of the lack of any empirical support regarding effectiveness. The primary motivation for doing so may be that providing such a labor-intensive and highly visible intervention communicates public concern for the welfare of victims and responders. A secondary advantage of offering such programs is that they focus on the individual changing his or her response to the conditions rather than organizing to deal more effectively with the challenges themselves, thus giving the appearance of concern about stressful events while allowing the organizations to continue unchanged (Echterling & Wylie, 1983).

A final point about vested interests is that privileged groups have much more influence in setting the agenda for the discussion and in determining the outcome. Power determines how problems are defined and what solutions are likely to be implemented (Neubeck & Neubeck, 1997). Groups have different self-interests to advance or protect, and those that cannot mobilize power (even if only to disrupt the status quo) are likely to lose out to those whose dominance is well established.

Use the media both to inform and to frame the issues

The fundamental implication of this perspective for disaster interveners is to recognize the power of the media not only to provide information, but also to create myths. Disaster interveners do not constantly have their handkerchiefs ready, expecting to hear only the tragic stories of wretchedly pitiful victims who are in desperate need of rescue. Although victims may be distressed and deal with painful losses, nearly all these people come to consider themselves survivors—not hopeless victims—and would be offended by any displays of pity or attempts to rescue them. Instead, interveners should be ready to get their hands dirty as they make themselves useful in a variety of practical ways. On the other hand, disaster interveners should not expect to always hear uplifting, inspirational, and heroic stories of people overcoming the incredible power of a natural disaster. Recovery from disaster is more complicated than either a simple tragedy or inspirational story. Disaster intervention is facilitating that recovery process of individuals and communities.

Disaster interveners should establish quickly a close relationship with the media. Immediately following the disaster, interveners can initiate a comprehensive community education program. The campaign should involve all of the public media, including local newspapers, television, and radio stations. Also, disaster counselors have found success in offering presentations to neighborhood organizations, church groups, work groups, parent–teacher associations, and other community groups. They can design brochures that provide practical, helpful information on such topics as managing stress, handling the reactions of children, and preparing for possible disasters in the future.

Consider long-term needs

Recognizing the importance of meaning for long-term coping, interveners should collaborate more closely with the clergy and others who help survivors to give coherence to these experiences. Through such collaboration, interveners could encourage community networks to offer not only emotional and material support, but also opportunities to create meaning.

Unfortunately, disaster intervention programs often have been presented as providing only formal, intensive, short-term, and immediate help. The natural disaster may be a time-limited event, but its physical, economic, ecological, social, and psychological consequences are long-term. Although many interveners have come to emphasize the traumatic stress of disasters, they often fail to recognize the chronic stresses that disaster survivors face. Survivors facing the chronic stresses of a disaster also require ongoing information, support, and counseling.

Many survivors find that the anniversary serves as an occasion for recollecting the traumatic experience and reflect on its meaning and place in their lives. Also, the emphasis on the anniversary effect as a normal, natural response to a disaster can be reassuring to many survivors. They realize that they are not alone in having this common reaction. Unfortunately, disaster intervention programs often have been limited to providing intensive, short-term, and immediate help. An aggressive outreach approach is another necessary condition for an effective anniversary program. In disaster work, it is vital that interveners actively seek out the potential users of their services because disaster survivors are not likely to contact mental health workers for treatment or consultation.

Finally, social scientists and disaster interveners can join the discourse by participating in all public arenas and exploring how different community members construct their disaster experience. The relationship between interventionists, scholars, and citizens needs to be based on collaboration. As Kaniasty and Norris (see Chapter 2) urge, "We need to do more than to speak *for* them. We must speak *with* them." It is when we engage in such a collaborative discourse that we can gather individual experiences together to construct a community mosaic of shared meaning and a reservoir of collective resilience.

REFERENCES

Ahler, J. G., & Tamney, J. B. (1964). Some functions of religious ritual in a catastrophe. *Sociological Analysis, 25*, 212–230.

American Red Cross. (1991). *Disaster mental health services: Disaster services regulations and procedures* (ARC Document No. 3050M). Alexandria, VA: Author.

Barry, J. M. (1997). *Rising tide: The Great Mississippi Flood of 1927 and how it changed America*. New York: Simon & Schuster.

Bradfield, C., Wylie, M. L., & Echterling, L. G. (1989). After the flood: The response of ministers to a natural disaster. *Sociological Analysis, 49*, 397–407.

Brundage, B. C. (1972). *A rain of darts: The Mexica Aztecs*. Austin: University of Texas Press.

Bushnell, J. H. (1969). Hupa reaction to the Trinity River floods: Post-hoc recourse to aboriginal belief. *Anthropological Quarterly, 42*, 316–324.

Butcher, J. N., & Dunn, L. A. (1989). Human responses and treatment needs in airline disasters. In R. Gist & B. Lubin (Eds.), *Psychosocial aspects of disaster*, (pp. 86–119). New York: John Wiley & Sons.

Callahan, R. (1985). *Five minute phobia cure*. Wilmington, DE: Enterprise.

Callahan Techniques. (1997, September/October). Promotional advertisement. *Family Therapy Networker*. 114.

Carll, E. K. (1996). *Developing a comprehensive disaster and crisis response program for mental health: Guidelines and procedures*. Albany: New York State Psychological Association.

Cook, J. D., & Bickman, L. (1990). Social support and psychological symptomatology following a natural disaster. *Journal of Traumatic Stress, 3*, 541–556.

Dundes, A. (1987). At ease, disease—AIDS jokes as sick humor. *American Behavioral Scientist, 30*, 72–81.

Echterling, L. G., & Wylie, M. L. (1981). Crisis centers: A social movement perspective. *Journal of Community Psychology, 9*, 342–346.

Echterling, L. G., & Wylie, M. L. (1983, August). *Political conservatism and stress management: Emotional stability and social immobility*. Paper presented at the meeting of the Society for the Study of Social Problems, Detroit, MI.

Echterling, L. G., Bradfield, C., & Wylie, M. L. (1992, August). *Six years after the flood: Clergy's long-term response to disaster*. Poster session presented at the 100th annual meeting of the American Psychological Association, Washington, DC.

Elliott, D. (1989). Tales from the darkside: Ethical implications of disaster coverage. In L. M. Walters, L. Wilkins, & T. Walters (Eds.), *Bad tidings: Communication and catastrophe* (pp. 161–170). Hillsdale, NJ: Erlbaum.

EMDR Institute, Inc. (1997, September/October). Promotional advertisement. *Family Therapy Networker*, 73.

Festinger, L., Riecken, H. W., & Schachter, S. (1956). *When prophecy fails*. New York: Harper & Row.

Fine, G. A. (1995). Public narration and group culture: Discerning discourse in social movements. In H. Johnston & B. Klandermans (Eds.), *Social movements and culture* (pp. 127–143). Minneapolis: University of Minnesota Press.

Fischer, H. W. (1994). *Response to disaster: Fact versus fiction and its perpetuation: The sociology of disaster*. Lanham, MD: University Press of America.

Gamson, W. A. (1995). Constructing social protest. In H. Hohnston & B. Klandermans (Eds.), *Social movements and culture*. Minneapolis: University of Minnesota Press.

Gans, H. J. (1979). *Deciding what's news*. New York: Random House.

Gist, R. (1996). Is CISD built on a foundation of sand? *Fire Chief, 40*(11), 38–42.

Gist, R., Lubin, B., & Redburn, B. G. (1998). Psychosocial, ecological, and community perspectives on disaster response. *Journal of Personal and Interpersonal Loss, 3*, 25–51.

Gist, R., & Stolz, S. B. (1982). Mental health promotion and the media: Community response to the Kansas City Hotel disasters. *American Psychologist, 37*, 1136–1139.

Gist, R., & Woodall, S. J. (1995). Occupational stress in contemporary fire service. *Occupational Medicine: State of the Art Reviews, 10*, 763–787.

Gist, R., & Woodall, S. J. (1996, November). *And then you do the hokey-pokey, and you turn yourself around…* Symposium paper presented at The 12th Annual Meeting of the International Society for Traumatic Stress Studies, San Francisco, CA.

Hilgartner, S., and Bosk, C. L. (1988). The rise and fall of social problems: A public arenas model. *American Journal of Sociology, 94*(1), 53–78.

Hobfoll, S. E., Briggs, S., & Wells, J. (1995). Community stress and resources: Actions and reactions. In S. E. Hobfoll & M. W. de Vries (Eds.), *Extreme stress and communities: Impact and intervention* (pp. 137–158). Boston: Kluwer Academic Publishers.

Janoff-Bulman, R. (1992). *Shattered assumptions: Towards a new psychology of trauma.* New York: The Free Press.

Joseph, S., Williams, R., & Yule, W. (1993). Changes in outlook following disaster: The preliminary development of a measure to assess positive and negative responses. *Journal of Traumatic Stress, 6*, 271–279.

Klapp, O. (1991). *Inflation of symbols.* New Brunswick, NJ: Transaction.

McCullough, D. (1968). *The Johnstown Flood.* New York: Simon & Schuster.

McGolerick, R., & Echterling, L. G. (1995, August). *Vicarious impact of a public trauma.* Poster session presented at the annual meeting of the American Psychological Association Annual Convention, New York, NY.

Meichenbaum, D. (1995). Disasters, stress and cognition. In S. E. Hobfoll & M. W. de Vries (Eds.), *Extreme stress and communities: Impact and intervention.* Boston: Kluwer Academic Publishers.

Mileti, D. S., & O'Brien, P. W. (1992). Warnings during disaster: Normalizing communicated risk. *Social Problems, 39*, 40–57.

Mills, C. W. (1959). The sociological imagination. New York: Oxford University Press.

Mitchell, D. J. (1996, November). Standing up for CISD. *Fire Chief, 40*(11), 19.

Mitchell, J., & Bray, G. (1990). *Emergency services stress.* Englewood Cliffs, NJ: Brady.

Morrissey, J. P. & Goldman, H. H. (1984). Cycles of reform in the care of the chronically mentally ill. *Hospital and Community Psychiatry, 35*, 785–793.

Myers, D. (1994). *Disaster response and recovery: A handbook for mental health professionals.* Washington, DC: U.S. Department of Health and Human Services.

Neubeck, K. J., & Neubeck, M. A. (1997). *Social problems: A critical approach* (4th ed.). New York: McGraw Hill.

Pargament, K. I., & Hahn, J. (1986). God and the just world: Causal and coping attributions to God in health situations. *Journal for the Scientific Study of Religion, 25*, 193–207.

Shapiro, F. (1995). *Eye movement desensitization and reprocessing: Basic protocols, principles, and procedures.* New York: Guilford.

Smith, C. (1992). *Media and apocalypse: News coverage of the Yellowstone forest fires, Exxon Valdez oil spill, and Loma Prieta Earthquake.* Westport, CT: Greenwood Press.

Smith, M. H. (1978). American religious organizations in disaster: A study of congregational response to disaster. *Mass Emergencies, 3*, 133–142.

Spector, M., & Kitsuse, J. I. (1977). *Constructing social problems.* Menlo Park, CA: Cummings.

Taylor, S. E., & Lobel, M. (1989). Social comparison activity under threat: Downward evaluation and upward contacts. *Psychological Review, 96*, 569–575.

Thompson, S. C. (1985). Finding positive meaning in a stressful event and coping. *Basic and Applied Social Psychology, 6*, 279–295.

Thorson, J. A. (1993). Did you ever see a hearse go by? Some thoughts on gallows humor. *Journal of American Culture, 16*(2), 17–24.

Tierney, K. J. (1989). The social and community contexts of disaster. In R. Gist & B. Lubin (Eds.), *Psychosocial aspects of disaster.* (pp. 11–39). New York: John Wiley & Sons.

Tobin, G. A., & Ollenburger, J. C. (1996). Predicting levels of postdisaster stress in adults following the 1993 floods in the Upper Midwest. *Environment and Behavior, 28*, 340–357.

Weaver, J. D. (1995). *Disasters: Mental health interventions.* Sarasota, FL: Professional Resource Press.

Wenger, D. E., Dykes, J. D., Sebok, T. D., & Neff, J. L. (1975). It's a matter of myths: An empirical examination of individual insight into disaster responses. *Mass Emergencies, 1,* 33–46.

White, M., & Epston, D. (1990). *Narrative means to therapeutic ends.* New York: W. W. Norton.

Wilkins, L. (1985). Television and newspaper coverage of a blizzard: Is the message helplessness? *Newspaper Research Journal, 6*(4), 51–65.

Yates, S. (1992). Lay attributions about distress after a natural disaster. *Personality and Social Psychology Bulletin, 18*(2), 211–222.

Epilogue

Slightly more than a year before the uncanny timing of TWA Flight 800's fiery crash into the waters off Long Island so vividly riveted our attention on the profound shifts in mental health response to disasters in the 15 years since the collapse of Kansas City's Hyatt Regency skywalks had first thrust us into that arena (see the *Preface*, this volume), the bombing of the Alfred P. Murrah Federal Building in Oklahoma City had given us serious pause for similar reflections. Officers from several fire service agencies with whom we had worked in various projects were called to that event within hours; indeed, the senior editor had been in Oklahoma as part of a research and training project involving personnel from a number of regional fire and emergency medical authorities scarcely a month before. We quite specifically did not, however, join the astounding convergence of mental health providers that descended on the community in the days and weeks that followed—it was abundantly clear from the very beginning that help would be more than plentiful.

Where we had "beat the bushes" in 1981 to muster fewer than three dozen mental health providers to facilitate community support groups, the Sunday *Oklahoman* listed more than 40 agencies ready to see clients and take calls only 4 days after the Wednesday morning explosion. Inside pages bore stories of other mobilizations, ranging from Red Cross family assistance efforts to corporate contracts for quasi-clinical "SWAT" teams to debrief employees. Search and rescue personnel brought back stories of what some came to call "the gauntlet"—the line of well-intentioned would-be helpers that they had to negotiate to get from their assignments to their beds. What was initially a symbol of help and concern for their emotional needs became, for a number of visiting rescuers, a progressively irritating and repetitive barrier to meeting their even more primary instrumental needs.

That point of perturbation at which help can turn toward hindrance is neither abrupt nor is it easily identified, especially by those too close to the enterprise to visualize its broader implications. Where rendering presumptive aid becomes an identity even more than an activity, the objectivity so essential to constructive analysis can be quickly added to the casualty list. Loss of that objectivity is typically a fatal flaw in the epistemology of science; those emotionally enmeshed in the conduct, context, and content of these very consuming efforts are quite often and quite naturally strongly skewed in their views of their necessity, desirability, and nobility—as a very natural correlate and consequence, they are also strongly and emotionally convinced of their efficacy.

As Paul Simon so aptly observed in one of his earlier compositions, "A man hears what he wants to hear and disregards the rest." It should not be surprising that most persons subjected to intense instrumental and emotional stress are appreciative of those who express concern; it is also no evidence of meaningful contribution beyond that offered by any other concerned persons. A counselor with a chainsaw is a lot of help after a tornado strike, but so also is a trucker with a chainsaw, a baker with a chainsaw, or any other neighbor with a useful tool and the willingness to apply it. We can very easily look right past the basic things that help the most—the best remedy for the stress of homelessness after a hurricane is to help rebuild the home; the most helpful people in resolving that stress bring wheelbarrows, shovels, hammers, and saws. More importantly, they stay to help rebuild, rather than swooping through at the crux of the crisis and packing up just as the real work is only starting.

The serious observer and commentator must constantly apply measure after measure to ensure that he or she listens with an ear finely attuned to the actual happenings beneath the hyperbole. That skeptical, quizzical, critical ear is our best and only hope to hear the muffled murmurs of Nature amidst the clamor and confusion of our own apprehensions, needs, and beliefs. Although the verve exhibited by those who have invested their identity and effort in "disaster mental health" is viewed by proponents as fierce and admirable commitment, those whose roles demand that they function more stoically at the empirical foundations of the enterprise often see that same verve as a blinding and disturbing bias. Both are usually correct.

Our initial vision of assistance in disasters very explicitly saw the psychologist as one who would support existing sources of instrumental assistance and social support, certainly not as one whose efforts would in any way supersede or supplant any element of those natural systems. The basis to effective disaster recovery is found in commonwealth, community, and social integration—these are not principally or even primarily clinical matters. Such matters demand very hard work at a very practical, very pragmatic level; that work involves dirty fingernails, sore muscles, much time, and its own brand of intense and persistent commitment. It's tiring as Hell and anything but sexy...in the end, however, it's what seems to matter most.

In Oklahoma City, as in many communities, many persons found that foundation to be intimately linked to their religious beliefs, and much of the most significant work in the recovery effort fell, one way or another, to the clergy. The essence of what we have learned in our decades of intermingling research and practice is captured in remarks prepared for a clergy retreat a few weeks after the bombing (Gist, 1995):

> Every life, at some points, must be tested by adversity. We must face losses we can neither prevent nor reverse, confront threats we can never fully neutralize, and master challenges both sought and assumed. With adversity come sorrow and distress, but from its mastery come strength, character, and resolve.
>
> When adversity strikes us as individuals, our resolution is influenced most by the capacity of our social networks and referent groups to provide a protective fabric of support and reassurance that can help restore a disrupted view of the predicability of life, reassert some sense of control over the course of its events, re-equilibrate the perspectives that mediate our values and sentiments, and assist in the evolution of strategies through which such mastery can begin to emerge.
>
> The most significant sources for that support are those primary social affiliations that define the daily conduct of our lives and provide the foundation for our beliefs about our world and our interactions within it. It is here that we look for our bedrock when all else is shaken; it is in this atmosphere of community and camaraderie that we can safely react, adjust, and adapt.
>
> Perhaps no social institution is so crucial for so many people in times of crisis or transition as is their religion. The elements that mediate adaptation and promote resolution are, in the end, intangibles—faith, courage, hope, resolve. What each of us must ultimately seek distills to a singular, simple, but nearly subliminal notion: We must seek to face our adversities with dignity and grace. It is that which makes the human spirit truly transcendent.
>
> Several weeks ago, Kansas City's fire chief and I sat among your citizens and parishioners as our community's representatives to your Governor's prayer service at the State Fairgrounds. I have thought many times since of the third stanza of a hymn we sang that afternoon, one often sung by persons weathering crises of great magnitude, and of the power of those particular lyrics:
>
> > Through many dangers, trials, and snares,
> > I have already come;
> > 'Twas grace hath brought me safe thus far
> > And grace will lead me home.
>
> Too often, it seems, my colleagues in clinical and counseling endeavors and those of the media seek to draw our attention toward presumed pitfalls in the processes of adjustment rather than toward the models of resilience and resolution that quietly abound; far too commonly we begin to label the widely ranging concomitants of our efforts to grapple with cognitive and emotional disequilibrium with such potentially iatrogenic monikers as "symptoms" and "traumata." Our problem, we might rightly suggest, lies no longer in the

acceptance and recognition of the pathognomonic...it has now quite paradoxically become acceptance and mastery of the very normal but at times profoundly distressing experience of confronting injury, injustice, and inequity, and the resolution of our faith in the fair and the just despite glaring evidence of its frailty.

This is not a new challenge at all. It is the same essential challenge that has marked the heritage of our species and defined the human spirit throughout our recorded history; it is the same essential challenge that has transcended culture and epoch, and which has left for each future generation an ever constant legacy of triumph over despair. Nearly two decades of serious research and practical experience have brought me full circle in my own understanding of crisis and catastrophe, and have taught me very important lessons in faith and humility...none, however, has been more significant than the realization that the human spirit is indomitable, and that my best efforts must lie in helping those who guard its most precious metaphors to keep the faith alive. We have developed in our research and practice a substantive body of theory and information which can perhaps help you to define your tasks and objectives, anticipate their timing, refine your strategies, and prepare your processes and material—we can help you with the packaging and delivery, but the contents lie within that domain which has always been yours.

Perhaps we should be less inclined to insert ourselves visibly and directly into those intimate and essential processes of community, but should rather turn our attention again toward quiet, barely visible efforts to marshal, empower, and support those resources in the most nonintrusive ways we can craft. There is little of consequence to be gained from rushing toward each successive tragedy as if another opportunity to "strut one's stuff" or show one's wares—there are, in our experience, far too many such chances in any community on any day, and each is sorrowful enough without inserting ourselves where we may objectively hold no truly necessary role. Our grandparents distilled in their descendants a set of values seemingly quite different from those that appear to drive at least the most vociferous among the emerging legions of "trauma tourists" we now encounter at every turn—we were led, perhaps, to seek the simpler and more intrinsic rewards captured in the most classic of all American hymns:

'Tis a gift to be simple,
'tis a gift to be free;
'tis a gift to come down
where you ought to be...

Our efforts for a number of years now have turned from attempts to place psychologists and mental health workers into these contexts, and have centered instead on working within those systems, both formal and informal, that daily support the efforts of communities to support the lives and maintain the contributions of their citizens. Ultimately, we've decided, disaster response is governed by a peculiar parallel to the physical principles of thermodynamics: to wit, that which fills a small space will readily and naturally expand to fill the largest vessels; that which fills the larger vessel, though, cannot be compressed into small spaces without extraordinary expenditure of energy and notable loss of efficiency. Those efforts we make to help those who address the daily crises of individuals do so with purpose, design, and impact are ultimately our strongest contribution toward ensuring that massive and monumental community catastrophes will be met by resilience and mastered in recovery.

The senior editor, called by a participant on an Internet "trauma list" to justify this position, penned this impromptu response regarding his daily work, later quoted as the closing to a professional symposium where several academic scientists-practitioners had joined to raise our growing concerns (Gist & Woodall, 1995):

I am a scientist and scholar; that is the calling I chose. I am a practitioner at times by happenstance and necessity, applying what I know and can figure out *in situ* to very real issues in very real situations. This week alone I have had to evacuate and then repatriate an entire working class neighborhood where a 28 inch gas main ruptured and ignited, creating fire and noise of a magnitude hard to imagine in an area where another natural gas explosion recently killed a small child; I have had to hold the hand of an aging wife while we watched her husband die before us; I have had to help the few remaining parishioners of an historic African-American church sort through the rubble of their history for what little a fire might have left for them; I have had to visit three children hospitalized with varying extents of serious burns and continue to support their parents—one of whom received full thickness (third degree) burns to her torso carrying her flaming infant, burned well past life or recognition, from her home.

These are not "troubled souls" and wounded people, however—these are very real people in very real trouble with very real challenges that I can only hope I would find the strength and grace to face as now they must. I try to do what my Grandma told me to do, backed by the very best I can think through and understand from the most critical approaches to information I can muster. The profundity of their circumstances is such that they deserve the most critical, focused work we can possibly create regarding what will truly aid them —to offer instead any self-serving blither about how any ministration that lets *me* (emphasis on the self-centered "I" of the messianic therapist) emerge as helper by tossing some dab of moisture into the desiccation, no matter how trivial its true effect, unconscionably diminishes the true focus these people deserve.

It is that research that forms my contribution—as a helper, I'm just a poor adjunct to a fireman, an unworthy companion to a priest, and a meager substitute for my Irish grandmother. I help those folk to do better what they've done for generations, and I keep myself as invisible as possible so as not to interfere. I would never grow so impertinent as to insinuate that my quiet intervention was in any way at all, however tiny, the substance of their salvation.

Some might say that we have become dinosaurs in the very movement we helped to create; most certainly, we have shifted with age and academic rank from its avant garde to its "old guard" in what seems no more than the batting of an eyelash. Yet we feel today as passionate and as alive in our assertion that solid empirical study and critical scientific analysis must form the foundation of any rational enterprise in our realm as we did it those heady years of our early careers and schooling. We believe even more fervently that the products and principles evolved of nearly two decades of synergistic interplay between the scientist and the practitioner in us and in the colleagues who joined us to create this text have brought us to a fuller realization of the challenges community crisis presents and the processes by which communities react, both in recoil and in resilience. We are convinced, too, that our understanding remains primitive and very rudimentary, and that it will continue to evolve in direct proportion to our allegiance to the scientist-practitioner symbiosis that fundamentally defines the work of the community psychologist even more, perhaps, than that of our various clinical cousins.

Disaster, after all, is a phenomenon inherently defined by its relationship to community—a cataclysm qualifies as a disaster only to the extent that it overwhelms the capacity of a community to contain and control its consequences. It is not at all, then, a collection of individual experiences, though these certainly merit address; it is, in many ways, the quintessential socially defined and socially constructed collective experience, wherein the definitions we assign and expectations we create regarding everything from attributions of cause to subjective elements of reaction become reified through the elements of social comparison and mutual exchange accelerated by the impact of novel and threatening experience.

The unique capability of the community psychologist to build an understanding from such a range of ordinarily insular realms of both theoretical and applied psychology, and to translate that information into practical and useful strategies for the array of community agents with whom recovery will reside, is both our challenge and our calling in response to disaster. Our contribution can be significant if we hold fast to our foundation.

REFERENCES

Gist, R. (1995, June 1). Remarks prepared for Indian Nations Presbytery.

Gist, R., & Woodall, S. J. (1996, November). And then you do the Hokey-Pokey. In D. Brom (Chair), *Treating PTSD: The controversy between pathology and functionality.* Symposium conducted at the 12th Annual Meeting of the International Society for Traumatic Stress Studies, San Francisco, CA.

Index

CPSIA information can be obtained at www.ICGtesting.com
Printed in the USA
LVOW10s0802240116

471502LV00009B/75/P